The *LIGHT* and the *GLORY*

The LIGHT and the GLORY

Peter Marshall
David Manuel

Fleming H. Revell Company
Old Tappan, New Jersey

Unless otherwise identified, Scripture quotations in this volume are from the Revised Standard Version of the Bible, copyrighted 1946, 1952, © 1971 and 1973.

Scripture quotations identified KJV are from the King James Version of the Bible.

The Scripture quotation identified AMPLIFIED is from The Amplified New Testament © The Lockman Foundation 1954, 1958, and is used by permission.

Library of Congress Cataloging in Publication Data

Marshall, Peter, 1940-
    The light and the glory.

    Bibliography: p.
    Includes index.
    1. United States—History—Colonial period, ca. 1600-1775. 2. United States—History—Revolution, 1775-1783. 3. United States—Church history—Colonial period, ca. 1600-1775. 4. History (Theology) 5. Providence and government of God. I. Manuel, David, joint author. II. Title.
E189.M36   209'.73   77-23352
ISBN 0-8007-0886-5

TO

the memory of all the nameless early Americans
who chose the Covenant Way

WE GRATEFULLY ACKNOWLEDGE . . .

On a project of this size, it is impossible to thank all of those who have been so generous with their help and their prayers. But we would like to specifically mention: Cay Andersen and Judy Sorensen, the directors of the Community of Jesus, for their initial encouragement and continuing support; Professor Peter Gomes of Harvard, for his historical perspective; Pastor Ron Minor and the people of the First United Presbyterian Church of Cambridge, and John Harrison and his staff at Yale, for tracking down hard-to-find volumes; all the members of the East Dennis Community Church who helped us preview our research material; Bill Andersen and Sister Suzan of the Community, for helping us to keep to our schedule, and the other members of the Community, for their sustained prayer support; Fred Hills, for his editorial advice; Catherine Marshall and Len LeSourd, for their close-in suggestions; Ev Sahrbeck, for his work on the jacket; the East Dennis people who helped with the typing and proofreading, especially Joyce Campbell and Margaret Guyer; and our patient wives, Edith Marshall and Barbara Manuel, for all the disruptions they cheerfully put up with.

Above all, we would like to acknowledge the continuing grace and inspiration of our heavenly Father, without which this book could never have been written.

PETER MARSHALL
DAVID MANUEL
Cape Cod, Massachusetts

Contents

"I am well aware of the toil and blood and treasure that it will cost us to maintain this Declaration, and support and defend these States. Yet through all the gloom I can see rays of ravishing light and glory. I can see that the end is worth more than all the means."

—*John Adams to Abigail Adams,*
on the passing of
the Declaration
of Independence, July 2, 1776

The Search

America, America—until about fifteen years ago, the name by it-self would evoke a feeling of warmth. Whether it was pride or gratitude or hope, the response of the majority of people on earth was deeply positive. America's moral and fiscal currency was the soundest in the world; you could bank on it, and most of the world did. Abroad, we were the free world's policeman; an encouraging older brother to those young nations struggling to achieve democ-racy; and the hope of all peoples still in bondage. In general, we were the most steadying influence on an uneasy globe. And at home, we were supremely confident that we were indeed making the world a better place to live in. We believed that technologically and diplomatically, it was only a matter of time before this assign-ment would be satisfactorily completed.

America itself already *was* a better place to live. Despite the setbacks, there had been a gradual, sustained improvement that most men could trace in their own lifetimes, and there was every indication that this would continue. Technologically, we were on the brink of so many breakthroughs that it was difficult for science-fiction writers to keep ahead of what was happening in the laboratories. Intellectually, we were developing radical, new "sen-sitive" approaches to education, which were going to revolutionize the learning process and bring the next generation into an earlier, fuller, and more creative maturity. Medically, we were on the verge of conquering every disease in sight, while psychiatry would take care of the occasional aberrant personality which had trouble adjusting to it all. In a word, *optimism* summed up America. The American Dream was about to come true.

And then, with a suddenness that is still bewildering, everything went out of balance. Our military ventures ceased to go according to the script. And our young President, the personification of The Dream, was assassinated. Our young people began to revolt on a scale that no generation ever had before—indiscriminately lashing out at all authority or escaping into the mindless self-destruction of drug abuse. The emerging nations, to whom we had given so freely,

13

were almost unanimous in their hatred of us. Our foreign policy devolved into one of *re*action, rather than action; in effect, we *had* no foreign policy.

Domestically, our economy waxed increasingly erratic; economists could no longer predict its gyrations, let alone do anything to stabilize it. Our children's mathematics and English aptitudes were plummeting; by college-entrance standards they were two years behind the averages of a decade before. Our technologists, to whom we had gratefully turned with all our problems, seemed to create new and totally unforeseen dilemmas for each one which they were able to solve. And psychiatry could not begin to cope with the tidal wave of mental and emotional disorders which seemed to break upon the land, claiming one hospital bed in three. Our optimism was rapidly turning to despair.

But perhaps the most mystifying indicator of all was the loss of moral soundness. To be sure, there had always been pockets of dissolution, but we had thought of them as isolated situations— surface cavities which needed to be drilled and filled. Now we were finding that what was actually needed was root-canal work, if it was not already too late.

And yet, the sexual promiscuity, which we scrambled to accommodate through legalized abortion, permissive sex education, and ever more effective birth preventatives, was not in itself the most telling sign of the depth of the moral decay. Nor was it the dis-integration of the family unit, the common thread which was all that was keeping the fabric of America from coming apart at the seams. And indeed, the American family seemed to be unraveling: a divorce rate that was approaching one marriage in two, when two generations ago divorce had been almost unheard of; the sudden prevalence of child abuse which had been even rarer; the wholesale abdication of parents from their traditional roles of leadership; and the determination of each member of the family to achieve independence—as much and as soon as possible.

The most significant index of the extent of our moral decay was our very indifference to it. Pornography had insinuated itself into practically every level of our daily life, including our language. Corrupt personal and business practices which once would have erupted into major scandals, today seemed scarcely scandalous. But where once we would have been up in arms, speaking out, writing letters, and voting, now we just shook our heads and counted it as another sign of the times.

If any one event could be isolated as that which marked the

moment when our despair had begun to harden into indifference, it was when our President was caught lying to the people, and then manipulating our trust in the office in his attempt to cover up the lies.

As a nation, we were shocked and sickened that the decay had gone that far. To us, the Presidency was a symbol of all that was right and decent in America. We had chosen to believe that the men who assumed that office grew in stature to fulfill our image of it (which was really our image of ourselves). And thus we ignored the rumors about certain Presidents' personal lives, though with each seamy disclosure it was becoming increasingly difficult to do so. Our belief in the sanctity of the office was becoming more and more an article of blind faith, clung to tenaciously in the face of mounting facts to the contrary.

This explains why, when the events of Watergate tore down the idol of our "civil religion," it was such a shattering experience for so many. It also tells us why, after our initial rage at the man (not so much for what he had actually done, as for what he had destroyed), we tended to put him completely out of our minds. For as much as we would have liked to affix all the blame to this one man, we sensed in our hearts that his fall was merely a reflection of what had happened to the American Dream.

What *had* happened to The Dream? Less than two decades earlier, when we were still confident of finding the answer and getting things straightened out, the Communists were the first to be blamed. The capitalists blamed the Communists, who blamed the imperialists, who blamed the doves, who blamed the hawks. The young people blamed everyone over thirty; the blacks blamed everyone who was not black; and then everyone blamed the technologists, who said that it was not their fault—all *they* were doing was trying to give people what they wanted. And the same excuse was echoed by the politicians when it came their turn. So, as it finally became apparent that there were not going to be any scapegoats, that our best thinkers could not come up with any conclusive answers, many Americans gave up asking what had happened.

And yet, this book has an answer. To many, the answer will be incredible, even preposterous, although two hundred years ago, the majority of Americans would have accepted it readily enough. And a hundred and fifty years before that, for the first settlers who found their way to these shores, it would have been the *only* answer.

Night had fallen on the small New England harbor, and the fishing boats rocked gently at anchor. Inside the nearby chapel, a gathering of some two hundred people was illuminated by electric candles which glowed softly against the wood paneling. The speaker came quickly to the heart of his message: "This nation was founded by God with a special calling. The people who first came here knew that they were being led here by the Lord Jesus Christ, to found a nation where men, women, and children were to live in obedience to Him . . . This was truly to be *one nation under God."*

The speaker paused. "The reason, I believe, that we Americans are in such trouble today is that we have forgotten this. We've rejected it. In fact, we've become quite cynical about it. We, as a people, have thrown away our Christian heritage."

That was a strong statement; would he be able to back it up? One of the listeners in the audience wondered what exactly our Christian heritage *was*—and had wondered it before: four years before, to be exact. The listener was David Manuel, who, while an editor at a major New York publishing house, had discovered to his dumbfoundment that God was real. And not only was God real, but He loved him beyond all human comprehension and had been waiting all of David's life for him to realize it. The discovery turned David's world upside down. And not long after, he felt that God would have him use whatever writing or editing ability he might have in the service of His Kingdom. He had several book projects in mind, one of which would trace the spiritual legacy of our Founding Fathers. But that idea had lain very dormant—until the speaker seemed to be reopening the file.

The speaker was Peter Marshall, who had grown up in rebellion against the spiritual legacy of two famous Christian parents: the late Chaplain of the Senate, also named Peter, and his author-wife Catherine. He had given up this rebellion in 1961, when he, too, entered into a personal relationship with God, and before long had committed his life to serving a living, risen Saviour. This service took him into the ministry and eventually to Cape Cod, where he became pastor of the East Dennis Community Church, and a wide-ranging national speaker.

That night, on the eve of the first National Day of Repentance to have been called in modern memory, Peter was speaking in the chapel of the Community of Jesus, also on the Cape, where David and his family were members.

What made the nation's need even more compelling, he said, was the realization of how much God's hand had played a part not only in America's founding, but, indeed, in its very discovery.

"I want to read to you what Christopher Columbus himself said about why he came here." Peter began to quote to the audience a few translated excerpts from an obscure volume [1] of Columbus's which had never previously appeared in English.

It was the Lord who put into my mind (I could feel his hand upon me) the fact that it would be possible to sail from here to the Indies. All who heard of my project rejected it with laughter, ridiculing me. There is no question that the inspiration was from the Holy Spirit, because He comforted me with rays of marvelous inspiration from the Holy Scriptures . . . .

I am a most unworthy sinner, but I have cried out to the Lord for grace and mercy, and they have covered me completely. I have found the sweetest consolation since I made it my whole purpose to enjoy His marvelous presence. For the execution of the journey to the Indies, I did not make use of intelligence, mathematics or maps. It is simply the fulfillment of what Isaiah had prophesied . . . .

No one should fear to undertake any task in the name of our Saviour, if it is just and if the intention is purely for His holy service. The working out of all things has been assigned to each person by our Lord, but it all happens according to His sovereign will, even though He gives advice. He lacks nothing that it is in the power of men to give Him. Oh, what a gracious Lord, who desires that people should perform for Him those things for which He holds Himself responsible! Day and night, moment by moment, everyone should express their most devoted gratitude to Him.

Stunned amazement swept the chapel audience. Did Columbus really think that way? All we had ever read or been taught had indicated that Columbus discovered the New World by accident, while seeking a trade route to the Indies. No mention had ever been made of his faith, let alone that he felt he had been given his life's mission directly by God. Nor had we suspected that he felt called to bear the Light of Christ to undiscovered lands in fulfillment of biblical prophecy, or that he had been guided by the Holy Spirit every league of the way—and knew it.

Moreover, this was not the wishful thinking of some overly enthusiastic fundamentalist; *these were Columbus's own words*— words that few Americans had ever read before they had appeared in the article Peter had quoted. To David, seated in the audience, the impact of this revelation was staggering. For the thought sud-

---

[1] For acknowledgments and sources, see notes at the back of the book.

denly occurred to him: *What if God had conceived a special plan for America?*

What if Columbus's discovery had not been accidental at all? What if it were merely the opening curtain of an extraordinary drama . . . ? Hadn't Peter just referred to the first settlers as having been called by God to found a Christian nation?

Did God have a plan for America? Like all those who have discovered the reality of the living Christ, we knew that God had a plan for each individual's life—a plan which could, with spiritual effort, be discerned and followed. *What if He dealt with whole nations in the same way?*

The Bible said He did, of course; that the Jews were His chosen people, and that, if they would obey His commandments, He would bless them *as a nation*. The Book of Deuteronomy was quite explicit about that:

> For you are a people holy to the Lord your God; the Lord your God has chosen you to be a people for his own possession, out of all the peoples that are on the face of the earth. It was not because you were more in number than any other people that the Lord set his love upon you and chose you, for you were the fewest of all peoples; but it is because the Lord loves you, and is keeping the oath which he swore to your fathers, that the Lord has brought you out with a mighty hand, and redeemed you from the house of bondage, from the hand of Pharaoh king of Egypt. Know therefore that the Lord your God is God, the faithful God who keeps covenant and steadfast love with those who love him and keep his commandments, to a thousand generations . . . (Deuteronomy 7:6–9).

Throughout their history, as long as the Israelites kept their end of the covenant, God blessed them. Yet scarcely did He begin to do so, than they would turn away from Him, often in less than a generation. They would grow so hard of heart that they would stone the prophets He sent to persuade them to humble themselves, seek His forgiveness, and by His grace change their ways—i.e. to repent. Yet, because He did love them, He would not wash His hands of them, no matter how sorely they tried Him. All too often, however, they left Him no choice but to lift His grace and allow drought or flood or pestilence, or war or bondage or persecution, to turn His people back to Him.

Many modern Christians believe that this idea of a corporate covenant relationship ceased with the coming of Jesus Christ. They feel that, with the advent of Christianity, man's relationship to his God became an individualized and highly personal matter.

But what if God's point of view had never changed? What if, in addition to the intimate relationship with the individual through Jesus Christ the Saviour, God continued to deal with nations corporately, as He had throughout Old Testament history? What if, in particular, He had a plan for those He would bring to America, a plan which saw this continent as the stage for a new act in the drama of mankind's redemption? Could it be that we Americans, as a people, were meant to be a "light to lighten the Gentiles" (Luke 2:32)—a demonstration to the world of how God intended His children to live together under the Lordship of Christ? Was our vast divergence from this blueprint, after such a promising beginning, the reason why we now seem to be heading into a new dark age?

It all seemed pretty fantastic, but as David and Peter talked about it after the meeting that night, the whole hypothesis became more and more plausible. And so, one sunny May morning in 1975, they—we—were on our way to Boston to ascertain whether research would bear out these ideas—possibly even provide enough evidence for a book. Although Peter had majored in history, that was fifteen years ago, and neither of us had ever done any serious research after our student days. We did not even know that one had to be affiliated with Harvard to use their Widener Library. For that matter, we had only the vaguest idea of how to go about finding what we were looking for, and no idea of how to assemble it, if we did find anything. The one thing we did know was that we had prayed about the project, and we felt that God would have us proceed. If we had heard correctly, and He *was* in it, then we would have to trust Him to guide each step.

Emerging dejectedly from Widener, after having been turned away, the only course of action that came to mind was to try the Boston Public Library. But as we were walking back to the car, the idea suddenly occurred to us to stop in at the Harvard Book Store, across the street. There, on the history shelves in the basement, the first book which we came across happened to be *Redeemer Nation* by Ernest Lee Tuveson. As Peter read the jacket copy aloud, it became clear to us that here we were indeed onto something—that there had been others who had felt that God did have a specific and unique plan for America. Further browsing in the history section indicated that the first settlers consciously thought of themselves as a people called into a continuation of the covenant relationship with God and one another which Israel had entered into.

We later discovered that they even felt that passages in the Bible such as this one (which was originally addressed to Israel) applied in particular to them:

> For the Lord your God is bringing you into a good land, a land of brooks and water, of fountains and springs, flowing forth in valleys and hills . . . . a land in which you will eat bread without scarcity, in which you will lack nothing, a land whose stones are iron, and out of whose hills you can dig copper. And you shall eat and be full, and you shall bless the Lord your God for the good land he has given you (Deuteronomy 8:7, 9).

Furthermore, they saw themselves as called into their new Promised Land in order to found a new Israel, which would be a light to the whole world. "A city set upon a hill" was how John Winthrop, the first Governor of Massachusetts, put it.

Our exuberance at this discovery was attracting a few stares. More soberly we went upstairs to the checkout counter, purchased our books, and beat a hasty retreat. But once in the privacy of our car and headed for the Boston Public Library, we were like Forty-niners on their way to the gold fields.

The spirit of adventure stayed with us that afternoon as David went through the card files and tracked down titles on the shelves, while Peter pored through the armloads of books which he had brought to him. A dozen musty volumes might yield one of interest. Then, by "coincidence," a title near the book which we were looking for would happen to catch our eye, and we would discover a nugget like *Remarkable Providences,* edited by John Demos. This, among other things, contained diary and letter accounts of God's "wonder-working providences" in the lives of settlers in Jamestown, Plymouth, and the Massachusetts Bay Colony.

But it was piecemeal work, and we still had no way of knowing what we might be inadvertently overlooking. And then Peter remembered that he had Nelson Burr's critical bibliography of books on religion in America. Now we could be selective about what we had to get, but the quantity was overwhelming: nearly two hundred volumes! And most of them so old and/or rare that there was almost no chance that the Boston Public Library would have them. But by "coincidence," a Christian friend of David's, John Harrison, had just been made director of public services for Yale's vast (600-man staff) Sterling Memorial Library. And so, two weeks later, we were making an unexpected trip back to our alma mater, the first for both of us since graduating.

It was strange to be back, as if we were walking around the set of a movie we had seen and forgotten long ago. And entering the huge Gothic pile of Sterling Library, where we had often come as undergraduates, was like being caught in a time-warp. But going into

Beinecke, the new rare-book library with the translucent marble walls, was the eeriest experience of all. There was a reverent, almost holy atmosphere in the place, and the hushed whispers in which we instinctively spoke were not from customary library courtesy, but from real awe of our surroundings. It was as if we were standing on holy ground. And then it struck us: in a sense, we *were*. There, before us, in thousands of ancient volumes in a six-story-high, climate-controlled glass cube, was the sum and pride of man's intellect, enshrined in matchless splendor. We shuddered and went downstairs to the call desk.

Yet that afternoon, in the basement reading room of Beinecke Library, we made the discovery which would prove to be the most exciting of the entire project. In Columbus's journal, he described an incident which took place on his fourth and final voyage, after he had been made "Governor of *Española* (Hispaniola)" and had then been relieved of that command for mismanagement. Sick with a fever and in the depths of despair, he had a half-waking dream in which he heard a stern voice strongly rebuke him for self-pity. The voice (quoted in chapter 2) reminded him that the Almighty had singled out him, of all the men in his age, for the honor of bearing the Light of Christ to a new world, had given him all that he had asked for, and was recording in heaven every event of his life!

John Harrison and his staff proved invaluable in tracking down hard-to-find documents and books, and soon several cartons of material were on their way from New Haven to the Cape. And by still another "coincidence," Ron Minor, a friend of ours who was pastor of the First United Presbyterian Church in Cambridge, told his people about the project. When they heard of it, several members who were graduate students at Harvard, offered their services, and soon there were more cartons arriving. But this now presented us with our biggest problem of all: if we both did nothing else but read, it would take us more than a year to get through it all!

Again, God had mercy on us, this time in the form of Peter's congregation, of whom many were keen to help in any way possible. These volunteers were pressed into service as research assistants, responsible for reading through each book, article, sermon, and letter, and making a preliminary assessment of its potential usefulness. In this fashion, we were left with a distillation which could be assimilated in a few months.

In the meantime, by a series of "coincidences" so improbable that we stopped using the word, we met Peter Gomes, minister of the Memorial Church in Harvard Yard and Professor of Christian Morals in the history department of Harvard University. His field just happened to be Puritan New England! In the office study of this gracious professional, with books piled everywhere, we came into contact with a keen historical mind, and a heart that was full of encouragement for what we were attempting. We left his office more aware than ever of how unqualified we were to undertake the project, and how totally we would have to rely on God.

In truth, this book is not intended to be a history textbook, but rather a search for the hand of God in the different periods of our nation's beginnings. We feel, due to the extreme gravity of America's present spiritual and moral condition, that it is imperative that we Americans rediscover our spiritual moorings. Thus, as we sought to discern what might have been God's perspective on American history, we found ourselves so personally caught up in the search that we felt we should occasionally share with the reader the issues and struggles which we faced. For the most part, these comments take the form of brief chapter preludes, and will be set off by this symbol:

Wherever possible, we have let the players speak for themselves, bringing only their imaginative spelling and nonchalant punctuation into some conformance with modern usage. Occasionally we would have a key episode for which there was no eyewitness account, and here we have reconstructed such an episode from the details available and the underlying attitudes of the principals.

Our basic presupposition—that God had a definite and extremely demanding plan for America—was confirmed, albeit in a number of surprising ways. Men like Columbus turned out to be far more dedicated to God's service than we had imagined. Others, like Thomas Jefferson, whom we had assumed to be reasonably devout, turned out to be quite the opposite.

Once it had become clear that God did have a plan for America, our search for evidence of this plan became akin to tracking a rich vein of gold through a mountain. The vein of gold had four main characteristics.

First, God had put a specific "call" on this country and the people who were to inhabit it. In the virgin wilderness of America, God was making His most significant attempt since ancient Israel to create a new Israel of people living in obedience to the laws of God, through faith in Jesus Christ.

At first glance, anyone actually believing that would appear to be guilty of supreme arrogance. In fact, so radical is such a concept that it has to be either the height of spiritual self-righteousness—or the truth.

Certainly, there was no question in the minds of the Puritans themselves. Trained to view history Christologically and typologically, they saw the shadow of Christ extending over the Old Testament as well as the New. In the Exodus of the Israelites from Egypt they found a prefiguring of their own circumstances. "Let Israel be . . . our glass to view our faces in," wrote Samuel Fisher in his *Testimony in Truth* in 1679.[2] A generation later, John Higginson would sum up their thinking in his preface to Cotton Mather's history of New England: "It hath been deservedly esteemed one of the great and wonderful works of God in this last age, that the Lord stirred up the spirits of so many thousands of His servants . . . to transport themselves . . . into a desert land in America . . . in the way of seeking first the kingdom of God . . ." for the purpose of "a fuller and better reformation of the Church of God, than it hath yet appeared in the world." [3] As such, the Puritans understood New England to be "a type and emblem of New Jerusalem." [4] And prior to both of these definitions, the president of Harvard, Urian Oakes, gave this simile in 1673: "If we . . . lay all things together, this our Commonwealth seems to exhibit to us a specimen, or a little model of the Kingdom of Christ upon Earth . . . wherein it is generally acknowledged and expected." [5]

A new Jerusalem, a model of the Kingdom of Christ upon earth—we Americans were intended to be living proof to the rest of the world that it *was* possible to live a life together which reflected the Two Great Commandments and put God and others ahead of self.

Second, this call was to be worked out in terms of the settlers' covenant with God, and with each other. Both elements of this covenant—the vertical relationship with God, and the horizontal relationship with their fellowmen—were of the utmost importance to the early comers (as the first Christian settlers called themselves). Concerning the vertical aspect of the covenant, they saw no delineation between the two Testaments, believing that an unchanging God had written them both. They saw themselves as being called into a direct continuation of the covenant relationship between God and Abraham: "Now the Lord said to Abram, 'Go from your country and your kindred and your father's house to the land that I will show you. And I will make of you a great nation, and I will bless you, and make your name great, so that you will be a blessing' " (Genesis 12:1, 2).

" 'And I will establish my covenant between me and you and your descendants after you. And I will give to you, and to your descendants after you . . . the land of your sojournings, all the land of Canaan, for an everlasting possession; and I will be their God' " (Genesis 17:7, 8).

And the early comers knew that Jesus had shown them the only way that it would or could work: ". . . If any man would come after me, let him deny himself and take up his cross daily and follow me" (Luke 9:23). This meant a daily commitment to the crossing out of self-love and self-will, in order to obey God and love one another. For the more selfless they became, the more they could truly love their neighbors. This was crucial to God's plan: it was His clear intent that, as they lived the Christian life, they would grow into such unity that they would become, in effect, a *body* of believers—His body, until His return. How unified God intends the Body of Christ to be was summed up by the apostle Paul, in his letters to the first Christians: "So we, though many, are one body in Christ, and individually members one of another" (Romans 12:5). "If one member suffers, all suffer together; if one member is honored, all rejoice together" (1 Corinthians 12:26). This was the way the early comers covenanted together, as each group formed its church.

And as each church-community grew and became, in effect, a town, these covenants provided the pattern for the first successful civil governments in the western hemisphere. Historians and sociologists alike have long regarded the early New England town meetings as the purest and most successful form that democracy has ever taken. But few, if any, have acknowledged what lay at the core of *how* and *why* they worked so well. There would be many modifications, but American democracy owes its inception to the covenants of the first churches on her shores.

God did keep His end of the bargain (which is the third major theme), and He did so on both an individual and a corporate basis. It is a sobering experience to look closely at our history and see just how highly God regarded what can only be called "a right heart attitude." One finds long droughts broken by a settlement's deliberately fasting and humbling itself, turning back to the God whom they once trusted and had imperceptibly begun to take for granted. One also finds instances of one settlement being spared from Indian attack, while another is decimated, when the only apparent difference seemed to be in their heart attitude towards God and one another.

Whenever we began to wonder if we might not be "shoehorning" history to fit our presuppositions, we had the recorded beliefs of the settlers themselves as a guide. And in page after page of private diary or public proclamation, the immediate response to any disaster, human or natural, was "Where do we need to repent?" In fact, there seemed to be a continuing, almost predictable cycle: in great need and humility a small body of Christians would put themselves into the hands of their Lord and commit their lives to one another. They would do their best to live together as He had called them to live. And He, in turn, would begin to pour out His blessing on them with health, peace, and bounteous harvests. As they grew affluent, they would also become proud or complacent or self-righteous.

Nonetheless, the blessing would continue unabated, sometimes for generations, as God continued to honor the obedience of their fathers and grandfathers (Deuteronomy 7:9). But inevitably, because He loved them (and because even God's patience has an end), He would be forced to lift the grace which lay upon their land, just enough to cause them to turn back to Him. A drought, or an epidemic of smallpox, or an Indian uprising would come, and the wisest among them would remember . . . . Like the prophets of old, they would call the people to repentance. And if there was a true and lasting change in their heart attitudes, God would forgive their sins, and His grace would be returned.

That a drought could be broken, or an Indian attack averted, by corporate repentance is an idea which sounds alien to many Christians today. Yet it was central to the faith which built this country, and is one of the most prominent, recurring themes in the Bible. One of the most familiar examples is, "If my people who are called by my name humble themselves, and pray and seek my face, and turn from their wicked ways, then I will hear from heaven, and will forgive their sin and heal their land" (2 Chronicles 7:14).

The key, of course, was that His people—three thousand years ago, three hundred years ago, or today—had to first see that they were sinners. Without accepting that truth, there could be no repentance, for they would not see any need for humbling themselves. This was the linchpin to God's plan for America: that we see ourselves individually and corporately, in a state of continuing need of God's forgiveness, mercy, and support. And this was the secret of the horizontal aspect of the covenant as well: for only at the foot of the Cross can we be truly united in Christ. Only starting from that position of each of us having to see our own sin, can we be truly one in the Spirit.

And incidentally, from *this* position, it is impossible to enter into nationalistic pride. Inherent in God's call upon our forefathers to found a Christian nation was the necessity to live in a state of constant need and dependency upon His grace and forgiveness. Anyone tempted today to take an elitist attitude regarding our nation's call need only look at how badly we have failed—and continue to fail—to live up to God's expectations for us.

Yet in the early days of our history, it is astonishing to see how few people it took to begin a cycle of repentance, followed by the return of God's grace. And so, this was the final major theme we found: that when a group of people, no matter how small or ordinary, was willing to die out to their selfish desires, *the life which came out of that death was immeasurable, and continued to affect lives far into the future.* This was especially true of the leaders God raised up for these early settlers. Men like Bradford, Winthrop, and Washington, instead of aspiring to greatness (which is so often the goal today), truly wanted nothing more than to serve God's people. And because these servant-leaders were living out the example of Jesus Christ, who said, "I am among you as one who serves," God was able to use them mightily to show the way in the building of His new Promised Land.

In 1775, as the U.S. Marine Corps was founded, their recruiting slogan stated that they "were looking for a few good men." That is essentially what God said to Gideon in ancient Israel, when He reduced His army from thirty-two thousand men to three hundred. And it was what He seemed to be saying three and a half centuries ago, as He began to gather those who were willing to give up everything for His sake to dwell in His New Jerusalem. How many of the incredible blessings which have been poured out upon this land—how much of the grace which continues to cover this country today—were a direct result of their obedience and willingness to die out to self, only God knows for certain.

That grace seems to be lifting now, but as we look at our nation's history from His point of view, we begin to have an idea of how much we owe a very few—and of how much is still at stake. Because the call of God on America has never been revoked.

America, America, God shed His grace on thee . . . .

1

Christ-bearer

Columbus . . . . We were familiar enough with the schoolbook hero, and our research had given us a new appreciation for his seamanship and navigational abilities. But he was still an enigma, a bronze figure on horseback, his arm outstretched, pointing westward. Would this figure become real for us? What was the man really like, who had written so passionately in his journal of his desire to serve Christ and carry His Light to heathen lands? Only God knew what had been locked in the secret places of his heart; only God could open them to us through revelation.

By the grace of God, as we finished our research on Columbus, scenes from his life began to come alive. We could feel the lift of the *Santa Maria*'s afterdeck beneath our feet, hear the groaning of the masts and yards far above, taste the salt spray on our lips. Next to us stood a tall, lean man, deeply tanned, with squint lines etched at the corners of clear blue eyes. The once-red hair was shot through with gray, but the hand on the taffrail was steady. The voice, passing commands, had the timbre of authority.

Sometimes we would see this man in his moments of supreme triumph and watch with him during the long nights of despair and bitterness. For in Columbus's heart, he was a sinner like the rest of us. That was our point of entry into understanding him. To know Columbus was to know one's own desire for the rewards of this world: fame and power and all manner of ego gratification. So we came to have compassion for him, and to wonder whether, had we been tried and tempted as Columbus was, we would have fared half as well.

As the pages flowed through David's typewriter, it seemed that, rather than creating scenes, we were merely describing what we were seeing. This had begun one afternoon, a few months earlier, in the darkened stacks of the Yale Library. There, in the midst of that mysterious, labyrinthine maze of tiered volumes, only the occasional echo of a distant footfall broke the silence. Peter stood in a lonely pool of light beneath an old metallic lampshade. Open in his hand was a translation of Columbus's journal of his first voyage . . . .

Tuesday, October 9—he sailed southwestward; he made five leagues. The wind changed, and he ran to the west, quarter northwest, and went four leagues. Afterwards, in all, he made 11 leagues in the day and 20½ leagues in the night; he reckoned 17 leagues for the men. All night they heard the birds passing.[1]

Something else happened on that October 9, Anno Domini 1492, which Columbus chose to leave out of his personal journal: an emergency conference at sea between himself and the captains of the *Pinta* and the *Niña*.[2] The previous evening at sunset, a calm sea permitting, the three ships had hove to into the wind, with the smaller caravels maneuvering into position on either side of the *Santa Maria*, to enable their captains, Martin Pinzón and his brother Vicente, to come aboard. But none of the men topside or aloft exchanged greetings, as the ships came together, and the Pinzón brothers strode grimly across the *Santa Maria*'s deck.

Columbus alone seemed cheerful as he welcomed them, but in the privacy of his cabin, Columbus's smile vanished, as he noted their expressions. The Pinzóns came right to the point: they had requested the meeting—no, *demanded* it, when Columbus, ever impatient at the least delay, had attempted to put them off. Martin and Vicente Pinzón were convinced that if they continued one day further on their present course, they would have mutiny on their hands. After thirty-one straight days of heading almost due west from the Canaries, the mood of their crews was ugly, and no amount of cajoling, or promising rewards for the first sighting, or display of confidence was going to make a difference. Worse, the Pinzón brothers could no longer be certain of their officers, if, God forbid, it came to mutiny. Their pilots and masters knew enough about dead reckoning (the art of estimating one's position solely by compass and a guess at one's speed through the water) to begin to suspect that Columbus was deliberately shortening the daily estimates passed from the flagship.

When they told him this, Columbus must have reacted in great frustration and anger. They were not just asking him to cancel the voyage, but to give up everything he had lived for—all his dreams, all his plans. Every *maravedi* he owned or could borrow had been invested in this venture, and he had suffered through eight long years of humiliation, being rejected by one royal court after another. Even Ferdinand and Isabella had been strongly advised against having anything to do with his wild scheme. If he turned back now, he—and they—would be the laughingstock of all Europe. Which meant that there would not be another chance—ever.

And yet, Columbus knew that the Pinzóns were not exaggerating the gravity of the situation. He himself had to admit that all week long the men on his own ship had been grumbling. Once he had even heard one jokingly suggest that they throw their captain overboard and go back with the story that he had lost his balance while taking a sight on the polestar. Columbus knew that it was only a matter of time before it would cease to be a joke. In anguish, he turned away from the Pinzóns. Striding to the aft window, he gazed at the dying rays of the sun on the endless expanse of sea behind them. All his dreams . . . .

There was an even deeper reason for his despair, one which he had never divulged to anyone. He had long been convinced that God had given him a special, almost mystical mission: to carry the Light of Christ into the darkness of undiscovered heathen lands, and to bring the inhabitants of those lands to the holy faith of Christianity. His own name, Christopher, which literally meant *Christ-bearer,* was to him a clear indication that God had called him to do this. Indeed, he found confirmation of his call almost everywhere he looked. He would quote in his journal such lines of Scripture as those in Isaiah which meant so much to him: "Listen to me, O coastlands, and hearken, you peoples from afar. The Lord called me from the womb, from the body of my mother he named my name . . . . I will give you as a light to the nations, that my salvation may reach to the end of the earth" (Isaiah 49:1, 6).

It was hard to say when his sense of mission had crystallized; it may have been while he was still a teenage boy in Genoa, carding wool in the family wool shop, as his father and grandfather had before him, and going to sea at every opportunity. Or it could have come later, in Lisbon, the sea-faring capital of the world, where the year 1484 found him and his brother Bartolomeo employed in the exclusive profession of mapmaking. He would have been just thirty-three then—the year Italians call *Anno de Cristo,* the Year of the Christ, which, according to folk tradition, is a year especially reserved for revelation, being Christ's age at His death.

As a mapmaker, Columbus was privy, not only to the geographic knowledge of the ancients, but to the latest information being brought back from the ever-expanding limits of the known world. He would have studied the global projections of Eratosthenes, the Greek geographer who, two thousand years before, had calculated the circumference of the earth to within 10 percent of its actual dimension.

In Columbus's own time, the newest world map was that of Toscanelli of Florence. Based on Marco Polo's eye-witness account of Cathay, Chiambra (India), and the fabulous islands of Cipangu (Japan), it placed the latter only 4,700 miles west from Lisbon. But it was not until Columbus's own navigational skills had become perfected—on voyages as far north as Thule and as far south as Guinea on the coast of Africa—that the dream finally came within reach. He made his own calculations and arrived at the conclusion that, traversing the 28th parallel, the distance from the Canary Islands to Cipangu was only 750 leagues, or approximately 2,760 miles. (No matter that Columbus had compounded the errors inherent in the accepted cosmography of his day with one or two of his own; God knew that there *was* something waiting out there— barely 150 leagues beyond Columbus's estimate!) [3]

Now, it was not a question of *if,* but *when,* and Columbus's sense of urgency was whetted by the Danish expedition which just eight years before had rediscovered the barren Norse "islands" of Helluland or Markland (Labrador) far to the north. There were other tantalizing elements: pieces of carved driftwood found west of the Azores, and the two bodies of Chinese-looking men that had washed up on Flores in the Azores. And on Corvo, the westernmost island, there was a natural rock formation of a horseman pointing west across the Ocean.[4] All that remained was to convince King John II of Portugal to send him.

For Columbus's only hope was to interest a reigning monarch; he had worked out the cost of outfitting three of the fast, light ships called *caravels,* which were ideal for exploring, stocking them with provisions for a year, and providing wages for the ninety men required to man them. The total came to around two million maravedis (or about a third of a million 1977 dollars)—an amount which very few private individuals could lay hands on in those days.

In 1484, he presented his plan to John II. The King turned his proposal over to a royal commission of scholars for their study and recommendation. After long deliberation, they found his scheme to be utterly fantastic, and the man himself to be arrogant and overbearing. Undaunted, Columbus dispatched his brother Bartolomeo to Henry VII of England, to see if he would be interested. After brief consideration, the opinion of the English court was that Bartolomeo was a fool and his ideas madness.[5]

Columbus now became convinced that God had reserved for Ferdinand and Isabella of Spain, the honor of sending forth the expedition that would bring the Gospel to undiscovered lands. Were they not renowned throughout Christendom for their devotion to the Saviour? To Columbus, this explained why he had been turned down in Portugal and England, and at first he was not dismayed that he was having no success in gaining an audience with the Sovereigns of Castile. They were at Granada, preoccupied with directing the current holy war against the Turkish Moslems, who had invaded southern Spain more than seven centuries earlier and had held it ever since.

But the weeks became months. Finally, through the intercession of the Count of Medina Celi, his suit was brought to the attention of Their Catholic Majesties in May, 1486. They were sufficiently interested to turn it over to their own royal commission, which took another four and a half years to reach the same conclusions their Portuguese counterparts had: Columbus's scheme "rested on weak foundations," such that its success seemed "uncertain and impossible to any educated person." [6]

Ferdinand and Isabella did not close the door entirely, inviting him to resubmit his proposal when the Moors were finally vanquished. But for Columbus, this was the end of hope. He had no alternative now but to go to the King of France. Yet his heart was not in it. He had been so sure that God had intended it to be Ferdinand and Isabella . . . . Could it be that he was also wrong about other things? For the first time since he had conceived of his venture—God's venture—dark shadows of doubt crept into the corners of his mind, while all his pride and self-esteem drained away. As he walked along the cold, deserted road that led to *La Rábida,* the Franciscan monastery on the Rio Tinto where he had left his young son Diego, he had probably never felt so alone or so empty.

The prior of the monastery was Juan Perez, a man of unusual spiritual wisdom, who had served as the Queen's confessor. He was now responsible for the spiritual well-being of the monks and missionaries whose life would one day make La Rábida famous the world over. One can imagine what transpired that evening as he and Columbus talked far into the night. Columbus was profoundly depressed, yet he was respectful of his host, and was so drawn to the Order of St. Francis that some time before he had taken lay orders himself. Finding an intelligent and compassionate listener who heard his dream with an open heart, Columbus unburdened himself of all the hurts, the snubs, the disappointments that had hardened into a rock of bitterness in his chest. How many times at court had he heard words like: "Ah, here comes our vagabond wool carder again, with his pathetic prattling about spheres and parallels. Tell us, Cristoforo, does the world appear any rounder to you today?"

But in the cool stone cloister of the monastery, we can almost hear Father Perez as he might have reminded Christopher that all of the things which had tormented him—the elusive recognition, wealth and position which he wanted so desperately and which always seemed just out of reach—these were the world's inducements, not the things that concerned the Lord Jesus. Did Christopher not see that as long as he persisted in trying to achieve his own goals in his own strength, God could not possibly bless him or use him? How long had it been since he had knelt at the foot of his Saviour's Cross and asked forgiveness for going his own way in so many things? How long had it been since he had been willing to accept with a trusting and grateful heart whatever his heavenly Father saw fit to bestow upon Him?

Slowly and patiently, this Shepherd of shepherds would have led the lost sheep back to the fold, for Columbus's heart belonged to God and always had. Thus would he have come into repentance, his eyes brimming with sorrow, not for his own plight but for how he had wounded the heart of his beloved Saviour. He would have made his confession then, received absolution, and partaken of the Body and the Blood. Once again he would have come into that peace which does indeed pass all understanding.

Whatever did transpire that night at La Rábida, it marked the turning point of God's plan to use Columbus to raise the curtain on His new Promised Land.

On the following morning, Father Perez dispatched a messenger to the Queen, stating that he was convinced that God's hand rested upon Christopher Columbus, and urging Her Majesty to reconsider his proposal. And Columbus tarried at La Rábida and awaited a reply, convinced that, after his own arm of flesh had been exhausted and all his hope abandoned, God in His infinite mercy had intervened. Not only had He altered circumstances, but far more important, in Columbus He had exchanged a heart of stone for a heart of flesh.

The Queen's answer came soon enough: Columbus was to return immediately to *Santa Fé*, the City of the Holy Faith, which the besieging Christian forces had raised up outside the massive walls of Granada, and from which they determined to conclude what everyone hoped would be the *last* crusade. What was more, in a singularly thoughtful gesture, the monarchs included a draft for funds with the letter. This meant that Columbus would be able to replace his worn attire and tattered cloak, and purchase a mount on which to return. Once again God was bestowing His favor on His son Christopher.

When Columbus arrived at Santa Fé, at the end of 1491, there was tremendous excitement throughout the city: the Moors were about to surrender! Armor was being burnished, battle standards were being set up, women were stringing pennants and bunting from the tops of tents and houses. Finally, as the afternoon sun fired the walls of the Alhambra, the citadel at the heart of the city, the Moorish banner came down, and the huge gates of Granada slowly swung open. Out came the Moorish King at the head of a column of noblemen, while lining his path on either side were mounted Crusaders in full armor, their white surplices with the red crosses blazing in the sun. They stood perfectly still, their lances upright. Not a sound was heard, save the footfalls of the Moorish horses.

At the end of the way, under a pavilion waited Ferdinand and Isabella. The Moorish King dismounted, walked up to them, knelt, and kissed their hands. And the mightiest cheer ever heard in Andalusia erupted. The war was over! The last Moorish foothold in Europe had been dislodged, and Christ reigned supreme in Castile! Pandemonium broke out—as war-weary Christian soldiers wept and cried and gave thanks to God.

Full of joy himself, Columbus was nonetheless impatient to see the King and Queen. He may have been the only Christian in Granada that night not completely given over to the exhilaration of the moment. He was not kept waiting long. Exhausted as they were, Their Catholic Majesties listened attentively to Columbus. And as it turned out, there had never been a time when they could have been any more receptive to his proposals. God had granted them a tremendous victory, and they had not yet thought of how they might show the heavenly Father their gratitude—build a cathedral, make a pilgrimage, erect shelters for the poor . . . . And now a far more modest possibility presented itself. Here, back again, was the Genoese visionary, with his proposal for his own Crusade: to discover new lands for the glory of God and His Church, and to spread the Gospel of the Holy Saviour to the ends of the earth.

What if he *were* God's man, as Perez seemed to think that he was? Could this be how God would have them show their gratitude?

Thinking it over, it seemed very much so to them. Promptly they summoned Columbus to tell him that they agreed to his plan. In that instant of victory, Columbus reverted to his old proud, untrusting, ambitious self. In return for his services, he loftily stipulated the following demands: one tenth of all the riches that might be found in any of the lands he might discover, the unprecedented rank of Admiral of the Ocean Sea, and the positions of both Viceroy and Governor of all discovered lands.

The King and Queen were stunned at his peremptory response; they dismissed him summarily. And were it not for the intervention of Luis de Santángel, that would have been the end of it. But this skilled diplomat, who had long been one of Columbus's few supporters at court, now spoke with such clarity that the Queen was persuaded to change her mind. She even offered to pledge her personal jewelry as collateral to help finance the expedition, but Santángel, who was also the royal treasurer, assured his Queen that this would not be necessary. They would raise the money through loans from regional governments. Thereupon, a messenger was sent at the gallop to bring Columbus back.

The next eight months were to prove among the happiest of Columbus's life. As a result of his typically meticulous care in the fitting out of his ships, his expedition would be better equipped than many which would cross the Atlantic two centuries later. In Martin and Vicente Pinzón, he had two experienced mariners who shared his vision, and were then as anxious to realize it as he was. They were also natives of the port of Palos, a few miles up the Rio Tinto from La Rábida, and thus they were able to raise first-class crews. On his own, Columbus would have had to rely largely on convict labor.

Best of all, Martin Pinzón owned two caravels that were ideally suited for the expedition—at a time when good ships were extremely hard to come by, because wealthy Jews were frantically buying up practically everything that was seaworthy. With the end of the Holy War, the Spanish Inquisition, originally commissioned to seek out hidden heresy, now focused its attention increasingly on *merranos*—Jews who had "converted" to Christianity, perhaps to escape mounting persecution or to avoid having to leave their native soil. The Inquisition set out to test the faith of these converts, for now that the Moors had been banished, only the Jews remained to defile Spain's "purity."

It is ironic that Spain contained the very best of fifteenth-century Christianity, and its very worst. In monasteries like La Rábida, a life of true humility, service, and sacrifice was being lived. And some of the most revered missionaries in the history of the Christian faith—men who taught the life of Jesus not so much with words but by their own example—would come forth from these ancient walls. Similarly, Spain's convents would produce saints like Teresa of Avila, whose inspiration would change thousands of lives through the ages.

The Inquisition, on the other hand, was spiritual pride and self-righteousness taken to its unholy nadir. It too would have its echo in a future century—in Nazi Germany. The Inquisition and the monastic orders were in diametric opposition, but the former held more temporal power, and for the moment, evil triumphed. *Their* final solution to the "Jewish problem" was disseminated by a royal decree issued in the spring of 1492: All Jews were given three months to get out of the country.

So Columbus had to settle for a heavier, slower flagship than he would have desired. But then came news that cheered him immensely. His royal benefactors had acceded to yet a further request: he himself would be permitted to invest in the expedition to the extent of one-eighth of its total funding, and to receive that percentage of any profits. His friends, presumably including the Duke of Medina Celi and Santángel, loaned him the funds to invest. Thus, on the morning of August 3, 1492, as Columbus knelt on the dock in the predawn half-light to receive Holy Communion, his heart must have been soaring. His dream was about to come true.

As the tide began to turn, he was rowed out to the ship where his men waited, and assumed his first command crisply and confidently. In moments, and "in the name of Jesus," the *Santa Maria* had weighed anchor, set sail, and was gliding down the river with the ebbing tide. As they reached the place where the Tinto joined the Saltés, just before emptying into the Ocean, a last shipload of Jews was also waiting for the tide. They too were leaving now, bound for the Mediterranean and lands of Islam. It is doubtful they thought of one another beyond a routine log entry. And even if they had, none of that forlorn shipload of Jewish exiles could have dreamed that the three other ships on the river were leading the way to a land which would one day provide the first welcome haven to their people.

Columbus's journal also mentions that as they passed by La Rábida close aboard, they could hear the monks chanting the ancient verses for the first service of the day, with its haunting refrain that ends *Et nunc et in perpetuum*—"Now and forever." [7] As the sails began to fill with the sea breeze, the great red crusaders' crosses on them were thrust forward, as if going on before. The great orb of the sun came up behind the ships, seeming to ignite the surface of the water and turn it, for a moment, into a river of molten gold.

The first days of the voyage could not have gone more smoothly. Columbus steered southwest by south, making for the Canaries. His pilots may have wondered why he did not head due west from the Azores. But not doing so was the hidden key to the puzzle, the inspiration that would give him success where others had already tried and failed. Word had already reached him that John II had sent one of his own mariners due west from the Azores—only to see the man give up, after days of battling incessant headwinds.

In all of the extensive north and south voyages he had made in the past, Columbus had noted that while westerlies prevailed in the northern Ocean, once one dropped below the Tropic of Cancer, the winds became northeasterly. Hence, it should be possible to have following winds out, and then on the way home go north and ride the westerlies. It was that simple, but no one had ever thought of it before. Columbus regarded it as a revelation, and he knew Whom to thank.

They reached Grand Canary Island on August 9, reprovisioned and made repairs, and finally launched out into the unknown September 8.

These were beautiful days—a following sea under azure skies, fresh winds billowing the white sails, flying fish and petrels skimming the waves. As the three small vessels sailed on, the succession of days settled into a familiar rhythm, with each new dawn being greeted by one of the ship's boys singing:

> Blessed be the light of day
> and the Holy Cross, we say;
> and the Lord of Veritie,
> and the Holy Trinity.
> Blessed be th' immortal soul,
> and the Lord who keeps it whole,
> Blessed be the light of day,
> and He who sends the night away. [8]

And yet, with the light of each new day, they sailed farther and farther out into waters where no man had ever ventured before. And gradually, suspicion and fear began to dog their wake. None of them had ever been farther than three hundred miles offshore; now they were well over three thousand, and still going . . . .

Reluctantly, Columbus turned from the window to face the Pinzón brothers—and reality. He consented to turn back. He had no choice, really. But he extracted one more promise from them: three additional days. If they had not sighted land by the twelfth, they would come about and head home. Not at all sure they had three days of goodwill remaining, the Pinzón brothers left.

We can imagine Columbus sitting alone in his cabin, after their departure, staring at the last entry in his journal, the quill pen motionless in his hand. Outside, the masts groaned—*she was pulling well,* he thought. Not that it mattered any more. It was all over. The specter of defeat seemed to stand by his side, resting a bony hand on his shoulder. Columbus shuddered. Glancing down, he noticed that he had absently written his name, Christopher—*Christo-ferens.* Christ-bearer.

He might have recalled the legend then, of the giant pagan named Christopher who sought to know Christ. To please Him, he lived as a hermit by a swift river, at a place where there was no bridge or boat to carry wayfarers across. Instead, he would carry them on his shoulders, with the help of a large staff. One night, asleep in his hut, he was awakened by the voice of a small boy, asking to be carried across. Christopher shouldered his charge easily enough, but as he went farther and farther into the current, the burden grew progressively heavier, until it seemed like he was carrying the whole world on his back. It was all he could do to keep from going under. When he finally reached the far bank, he fell exhausted on the ground, gasping for breath, and wondering to himself what had happened. "Marvel not, Christopher," said his small passenger then, "for indeed you have borne the world on your back, and Him who created it. I am the Christ, whom thou servest by doing good. As proof, plant your staff by your hut, and in the morning it will be covered with blossoms and fruit." And it was.

Columbus rubbed his eyes. The weight of his own burden had become more than he could bear; the difference was, he couldn't see the other side. Three more days . . . .

But three days were still three days! And God was still God! He was the God who had answered his prayers so often in the past, sometimes at the last moment, when all hope was gone and *only* a miracle could save the situation. Columbus must have prayed then as he had never prayed before.

The next morning, his journal records that during the previous twenty-four hours they had made an incredible fifty-nine leagues, more than they had covered on all but one day of the whole voyage! In fact, so fast were they now sailing that the men on the *Santa Maria* grew more alarmed than ever at how rapidly they were widening the distance from their homeland. For the first time the crew openly challenged their commander. According to the historian Las Casas, who personally knew Columbus: "The Admiral reassured them as best he could, holding out to them bright hopes of the gains which they would make, and adding that it was useless to complain, since he was going to the Indies and must pursue his course until, with the help of the Lord, he found them." [9]

This could hardly have been reassuring. Their mood must have been blacker than ever. An even greater miracle was needed.

On the morning of the eleventh, as they continued to fly along, aboard the *Pinta* a great shout went up: a reed was sighted and a small piece of wood that had unmistakably been shaped by a man. And over on the *Niña*, this news was answered with the sighting of a small twig with roses on it. These sure signs of land instantly transformed the mood of the three ships into the happiest they had been in weeks!

The prize for the first person to sight land was an annuity of ten thousand maravedis, and now the men were clamoring to take turns aloft as lookouts. The ships seemed to be racing one another, with first one and then another forging into the lead. As night fell, instead of taking in sail, they elected to plunge on into the darkness at an almost reckless pace, luminescent foam curling up from their bows. At 10:00 P.M., Columbus and one of the sailors simultaneously sighted a tiny light, far ahead of them.

As Las Casas retells it from Columbus's journal, "It was like a small wax candle being raised and lowered. Few thought that this was an indication of land, but the Admiral was certain that they were near land." Whatever the light was, Columbus took it as a strong encouragement from the Lord to press on as fast as possible.

At 2:00 A.M, with less than four hours remaining before the dawn of the third and final day, aboard the *Pinta* the electrifying cry at last rang out, *"Tierra! Tierra!"* The lookout had spied what appeared to be a low white cliff shining in the moonlight, and Martin Pinzón confirmed the sighting by firing a cannon as a signal. *Land!*

Immediately they took in sail and turned south, staying well offshore, to avoid piling up on the barrier reefs. The remaining hours until daybreak they felt their way along cautiously. One can imagine Columbus's prayers now, as full of passion as before, but overflowing with gratitude.

They reached the southern tip of the island, just as the sun rose above the blue horizon on their larboard beam. A new day was dawning, a new era for mankind. The fears and aches of weeks at sea seemed like nothing at all now. In every heart was dawning an awareness of the enormity of what they had accomplished—and the awe of it was overwhelming! Whereas, at the time of the first sighting, there had been laughing and dancing, now they were silent, as every eye followed the coastline slowly unfolding before them, glowing in the morning sun.

Rounding the southern end of the island and making their way up the lee side, they were speechless at the lushness of the foliage, the blueness and clarity of the waters they were gliding over. It was noon before they came to a break in the reefs wide enough to permit them entrance. Columbus donned the scarlet doublet he had been saving for the occasion, and the officers put on their best attire. Boats were lowered and the landing party rowed ashore— not all the way ashore, for the tide was out, and they would have to wade the last part of the way. Joyful now as they splashed through the sun-dazzled water in full armor, they called their commander for the first time by his awarded title: Admiral of the Ocean Sea.

Columbus was the first to set foot on dry land, carrying the royal standard, with the brothers Pinzón directly behind him, bearing a huge white banner with a green cross and the crowned initials of Ferdinand and Isabella on either side of it. The men kissed the white coral beach, which was almost too bright to look at in the noonday sun. Then their eyes filled with tears, as they knelt and bowed their heads. Columbus christened the island *San Salvador*—"Holy Saviour"—and prayed: "O Lord, Almighty and everlasting God, by Thy holy Word Thou hast created the heaven, and the earth, and the sea; blessed and glorified be Thy Name, and praised be Thy Majesty, which hath deigned to use us, Thy humble servants, that Thy holy Name may be proclaimed in this second part of the earth."

Eyes peered out through the screen of heavy foliage, well hidden from the view of the shining figures on the beach. (The inhabitants of the island could not bring themselves to refer to them as men, for they had skins of gleaming metal and appeared to have descended from heaven in huge canoes pulled by white clouds.)

But they seemed to be friendly gods, not angry, and they were obviously happy—one could hear them laughing. One at a time, the timid inhabitants stepped forward and let themselves be seen. At first, the white gods seemed frightened, but then they beckoned to them to come closer. And so they did.

Columbus was impressed at what a handsome race they were, tall and well proportioned, "with no large bellies on them," but no clothes either, and as innocent as babes when it came to the tools of war: ". . . for I showed them swords, and they took them by the blade and cut themselves through ignorance."

The Admiral further records: "So that they might be well-disposed towards us, for I knew that they were a people to be delivered and converted to our holy faith rather by love than by force, I gave to some red caps and to others glass beads, which they hung around their necks, and many other things . . . At this they were greatly pleased and became so entirely our friends that it was a wonder to see . . . I believe that they would easily be made Christians, for it seemed to me that they had no religion of their own. Our Lord willing, when I depart, I shall bring back six of them to your Highnesses, that they may learn to talk our language."

Columbus had already foreseen the necessity of having interpreters, but was it the Lord's will? By automatically assuming superiority and taking these men forcibly from their own native soil, he was establishing a precedent that would have tragic repercussions.

The second unfortunate precedent followed soon thereafter. Columbus noted that some of the natives, whom he called Indians (having no reason to believe that he had not reached the Indies), wore tiny gold ornaments in their noses. Through sign language, he began to inquire where the gold had come from. "From signs, I was able to understand that in the south there was a king who had large vessels of gold and possessed much of it. I endeavored to make them take me there, but later I saw that they had no desire to make the journey . . . So I resolved to go southwest, to search for gold and jewels."

Gold—one can see the hand of the Devil here. Unable to overcome the faith of the Christ-bearer by sowing fear and dissension in the hearts of his men or by paralyzing him with despair, Satan had failed to keep the Light of Christ from establishing a beachhead in practically the only part of the world in which he still reigned unchallenged. So he now moved to destroy the army of holy invaders from *within* their ranks. And he chose the one instrument which almost never failed: the love of money.

And so the seed was planted. It would take time for it to germinate, to put down its taproot. In the meantime, Columbus and his men were enjoying the fruit of this bountiful Eden, to which a merciful Creator had led them. They ate of food that no white man had ever tasted before—sweet, juice-giving fruit, and corn, and a pulpy bread made from cassavas—and they drank water purer than any they had ever known.

But Columbus was anxious to go discovering—to locate Cipangu, which must be nearby, or possibly to strike out for the mainland of Cathay, which he was convinced lay only a few days further west. He was eager to locate the source of the gold. And the natives, seeing how animated he became whenever he questioned them about it, told him of vast quantities of it—for they had become fond of him and wanted to please him.

Eventually, Columbus came to understand that there was an island to the south, so large that it took twenty days to get around it in a canoe. The natives called it Cuba, but it had to be Cipangu. Without further delay, the three ships departed for it, and on October 26, they hoisted flags and pennants in celebration of its sighting.

But where were the fabulous cities that Marco Polo had described? Where were the temples and palaces covered with gold? As far as they could see in either direction, there was nothing—nothing but a couple of rude, deserted huts on the beach. The natives had run away at the sight of them. They were met by a lone dog, which was wandering along the beach and did not even bother to look up at them as they came ashore.

Never mind—the scents of the rain forest were intoxicating, and large birds with plumage of bright reds and yellows and greens filled the air with strange songs. Columbus recorded that it was so wonderful that he never wanted to leave. As he proceeded northwest along the coast, his opinion of what he had found changed. He now became convinced that they were tracing the eastern coast of Cathay. But before long, fierce headwinds caused him to turn back. (Apparently, it was not God's time to reveal the true mainland—Florida lay only ninety miles away, in the direction they had been steering.)

On every island at which they stopped, Columbus had his men erect a large wooden cross "as a token of Jesus Christ our Lord, and in honor of the Christian faith." Almost always, they found the inhabitants peaceful, innocent, and trusting, and the Admiral gave strict orders that they were not to be molested or maltreated in any way. He had determined that their own reputation, which was obviously preceding them through the islands, would be as favorable as possible. But nowhere did they find the quantities of gold, either in its natural state or in artifacts, that the Indians had so obligingly promised.

Aboard the *Santa Maria,* the native captives (or "interpreters," as Columbus referred to them) were beginning to enjoy their roles as resident experts and the prestige their position gave them over the other Indians with whom they came in contact. They now told Columbus and the others of an island called Babeque, where the inhabitants collected nuggets of gold on the beaches by firelight and hammered them into bars. At this news, gold fever ran through the little fleet. Some of the captive natives were aboard the *Pinta,* and on November 18, that ship simply sailed away from the other two. Columbus was convinced that greed had overcome Martin Pinzón, and that he had gone in search of Babeque, and in his journal the Admiral recorded that there were many other unspoken things between him and Pinzón. The gold was beginning to do its work.

On December 5, Columbus made his own try for Babeque, but bad weather forced them back, and they were blown to another large island. The natives called it *Bohio,* but they named it *Es-pañola,* because of its almost dreamlike similarity to the sere plains and distant purple mountains of Andalusia. As they felt their way east along its northern coast, Columbus ran out of superlatives to describe it; not even Castile could compare with it.

And then, a little before dawn, on Christmas morning, the dream received a jolt. Becalmed in a cove, all those aboard the *Santa Maria* had gone to sleep, save a young ship's boy who had been left to mind the tiller. But an unnoticed swell developed which gently wafted the ship ever closer to shore. Suddenly the rudder struck bottom, the boy cried out, and Columbus hurried topside to take command of the situation. He ordered the longboat lowered, to carry the anchor astern, that they might quickly winch themselves off the reef, before the tide went further out. But the men in the longboat panicked and rowed frantically for the *Niña,* despite the shouted commands and threats of the Admiral.

Vicente Pinzón, seeing what was happening, sent his own boat to be of assistance, but it was too late: the *Santa Maria* was soundly beached. Worse, as the tide left and she keeled over, the sharp coral tore open her seams, water poured in, and in a moment she was finished.

But what appeared to Columbus to be utter disaster turned out to be one of the greatest blessings of the entire voyage. For the people ashore were kind beyond belief. And here at last was the gold Columbus had been so ardently searching for—masks of gold and bracelets and necklaces and rings! The natives helped the seamen off-load the *Santa Maria,* stored their goods for them in their own houses, and posted guards to make sure that no one touched anything.

So far beyond anything they had yet experienced was the treatment they received, that Columbus gave thanks to the Lord for allowing the shipwreck to happen and depositing them there. What was more, it was obvious to him that God intended them to establish a settlement there. He named the place *La Navidad,* for the Nativity, and they set about laying the groundwork for a fort, complete with moat and tower.

Thirty-nine men gladly volunteered to remain behind, and Columbus was confident that, upon his return in a year's time, through diligent trading with the Indians, they would have gained a whole barrelful of gold. Moreover, he counted on them discovering the mine which was supplying the gold, so that within three years the Sovereigns would have the finances to equip the greatest expedition of all: the Crusade that would finally free the Holy Land from the grip of the Moors. "For I maintained to your Highnesses that all profits from this enterprise should be devoted to the conquest of Jerusalem, and your Highnesses smiled and said that such was your will, and that even without these gains, you had the same earnest desire."

But that was for the still-distant future. Columbus, and the thirty-eight men remaining with him, boarded the *Niña* and headed northeast, to catch the prevailing westerlies and a free ride home. Three days out, and working their way through the islands, whom should they come across but the *Pinta!* When the two captains met, there was an angry clash. Martín Pinzón had his excuses, which Columbus finally decided to accept, though he did not believe them. Las Casas wrote: "The Admiral does not know the reasons for his [Pinzón's] shameless and disloyal conduct, but the Admiral was ready to forget it, so that he should not help Satan in his evil design to do all he could to hinder the voyage, as indeed he had done up to that time."

For three-quarters of the voyage home, they could not have asked for better conditions—calm seas, sunny skies, and a steady, following wind—for which they repeatedly thanked God, as the pumps were barely able to keep ahead of the leaks. Then, on the night of February 12, began the worst storm that any of them had ever experienced. The waves were huge and sharp, crossing one another. This meant that at intervals cold green sea water came crashing down on them from both sides at the same time, threatening to swamp them. They had no choice but to abandon their course and run before the storm, letting it take them where it would.

Extra lights were hung on both ships, to help them keep track of one another, but as the wind built up even higher, the *Pinta* fell farther and farther behind. Finally, her lights disappeared entirely, and when morning came, there was no sign of her anywhere.

The storm was wearing them down now, and they were running on nerves and instinct. The shrieking of the wind must have seemed to Columbus like the baying of the hounds of hell. Unable to thwart the Christ-bearer's mission or keep him from invading his domain, Satan seemed to be making an all-out effort to sink the ships and stop the word from getting back to Europe. If he could succeed, the settlers at La Navidad, with no one left who knew of their whereabouts, would perish soon enough.

Always in the past, turning to God in great need and concerted prayer had been enough to break the power of the Evil One. But this time prayer seemed to bring no results, and an angry, bitter Columbus may have been tempted, like Job, to raise his fist at God. Was He now indifferent to the very mission He had called into being? And ironically, the story of Job, with which Columbus was familiar, contained the answer:

> If you return to the Almighty and humble yourself, if you remove unrighteousness far from your tents, if you lay gold in the dust . . . and if the Almighty is your gold, and your precious silver; then you will delight yourself in the Almighty, and lift up your face to God. You will make your prayer to him, and he will hear you; and you will pay your vows. You will decide on a matter, and it will be established for you, and light will shine on your ways. For God abases the proud, but he saves the lowly (Job 22:23–29).

God might have had two reasons for permitting the storm to rage on unabated. First, because He loved His son Christopher and was deeply concerned for the present state of his soul; He could have been doing all in His power to get him to see how proud and vain he had become with the success of his mission. For already the ravenous ego which was determined to have all that was coming to it, all that had been denied it for so many years, was enjoying fantasies of fame. And if this were the heart attitude of the Admiral of the Ocean Sea now, the actual rewards themselves would be pure poison to him—and could well destroy any further effectiveness Columbus might have in God's service.

And God may have had another concern: that His grand design

for the New World get off on the right foot. He had withheld it from man's knowledge this long, in almost virginal purity. He had stocked it with an abundance of game and fertile soil, natural resources and beauty—all that a people would ever need—as a fitting abode for the followers of His Son. And He had chosen Christopher to raise the curtain. It was important that this same Christopher proceed in the spirit of Christ and not in self. Therefore God may have permitted the winds to roar and the seas to heave, hoping that Christopher would look into his heart, see himself through God's eyes, and humble himself.

But if this *was* God's message to Columbus in the storm, i.e., his paramount need to come home in an attitude of humility, then Columbus failed to grasp it. His journal records that he knew God had a reason for allowing the violence of the storm, but in his mounting frustration, rather than repenting, Columbus tried to maneuver his way out of disaster.

Calling the crew together, he suggested that they should appease God with a sacrificial offering in the form of a solemn vow, jointly undertaken. If God would deliver them, one of their number would make a pilgrimage to Santa Maria de Guadalupe in Estremadura. The men quickly agreed. So Columbus took thirty-nine dried beans, cut a cross on one of them, and put them into a hat, shaking them together. The Admiral himself drew the marked bean. Everyone marveled at this, and took it as a sign that God's hand was upon him. So did Columbus—with a good deal of pride. It never occurred to him that, like Jonah, *he* was the problem, and that through the drawing of lots the Holy Spirit might be trying to show him that he, of all the men, was at that time the most spiritually needy.

When it became obvious that the storm was not dying down, Columbus proposed another pilgrimage, and a second drawing. This time the lot fell to another, and there was still no change in the weather. They agreed upon yet a third pilgrimage, and miraculously Columbus drew the marked bean for the second time—and took quiet pride in the fact that God was requiring more of him than of any of the others. And on struggled the little *Niña*, looking as if she would never rise to meet the next wave.

Finally, in desperation, the whole crew got down on their knees and cried out for mercy, loud enough to be heard above the storm, promising the Blessed Virgin that if she would only pray for them now, they would, as soon as they reached land, go barefoot and in shirtsleeves to the nearest chapel dedicated to her and there say a solemn Mass. But the storm seemed not to hear.

All that day and the next, the weather continued to explode

about them, till they reached such a state of numbness that it seemed they were dreaming it all. And then, towards evening, for no apparent reason, the storm gradually subsided. Not only that, but a sliver of land appeared on the northeast horizon. Some thought it was the island of Madeira, off the coast of northern Africa: others were sure it was the coast of Portugal. But their captain correctly identified it as one of Portugal's Azores.

The pounding and slamming, the groaning of the masts and timbers, the shrieking and wailing of the wind, the constant drenching—it was all over now, as if it had never been. Blessed silence—*it was over*. But they were too exhausted to care.

2

"If Gold Be Your Almighty"

Pennants streaming to leeward, the gold and crimson standard of Spain unfurled atop her mainmast, the *Niña* turned gracefully into the wind and dropped anchor in the Azorian harbor of Santa Maria Island. She made an impressive sight for such a small ship, but the dash of her colors and the bright heraldic shields hung over her bows in no way reflected the mood of her crew. It was Tuesday, February 19, 1493, and they had slept hardly at all since the storm had hit the previous Wednesday.

And Columbus least of all. He had remained topside in the full fury of the storm, conning the ship from the sterncastle, though his eyes were red-rimmed and his legs could barely support him. Like his men, he was grateful, but too bone-weary to do more than send a landing party ashore to make contact with the Portuguese and seek a suitable chapel for the fulfilling of their vow. Rest and peace were all they wanted, but rest and peace were not to be their portion on this island.

In the morning, Columbus and his crew prepared to disembark, to celebrate the barefoot, shirt-sleeved Mass which they had promised. However, at the last minute something made Columbus decide to send his men in two groups. It was a providential decision, for the commander of the island had taken prisoner all those who had first gone ashore.

In a delicate gambit of threat, bluff, and counterthreat, Columbus finally outmaneuvered his adversary and regained his full crew intact. It was then that he learned that the commander of the island was acting under direct orders from King John in Lisbon. The King had sent word to Madeira, the Cape Verde Islands, and all other Portuguese possessions, if Columbus put in at any of them on his way back to Spain from a successful voyage, he and all his men were to be detained incommunicado, while Portugal readied its own expedition. Columbus took delight in imagining the consternation of John II, when he would learn that the Admiral of the Ocean Sea had slipped his net!

But scarcely had they cleared the Azores and set their course at last for home than *another* monstrous winter storm struck them. This one sprang up so suddenly that it tore off all their sails, and left them totally at the mercy of the howling gale—and God. For five straight days they were driven northeast under bare masts, their pumps slowly losing ground.

Once again they prayed, vowing another pilgrimage, and drawing lots. For the third time Columbus picked the bean with the cross carved on it. (Coincidence? The odds against it were 60,880 to 1! Surely now he would get the message. But he did not.) Every man on board knew that it was God, though none of them—and saddest of all, not even Columbus—knew why.

Their vow apparently had no effect; if anything, the storm increased in its fury. On the sixth day, they sighted land. This time, it *was* the coast of Portugal, and again Columbus alone correctly placed them just above the River of Lisbon. This river, less than a day's journey from the court of John II, was the last place in the world Columbus would have chosen to seek refuge from the storm.

All morning long a growing crowd on the shore watched the progress of the little vessel, as it was blown ever closer to its doom. The storm peaked in its intensity. In minutes they would be dashed to pieces on the rocky coast. With huge waves breaking on the shore, there was no way any of them would survive. One slim chance remained, if they could make it to the river's mouth. But that would mean they would have to take the wind almost broadside—dangerous enough under the best of conditions, suicidal without sails. The crew prayed with the knowledge that only God could save them now.

It is easy to imagine the scene on the afterdeck of the *Niña*. With a practiced eye, the Admiral gauged their drift, and ordered the helm over accordingly—as much as he dared, before she would broach to. Noting their speed through the water and the action of the waves at the river's mouth, he called out constant corrections to the helmsman at the tiller, as he compensated for the ship's yaw. Though he had to shout to make himself heard above the din of the storm, he was at once calm and exhilarated—for he was being challenged to the limit of his God-given abilities by a worthy opponent.

He wiped the rain from his burning eyes and peered ahead. Everything was happening much faster now; already he could hear the crashing of the breakers on the shore. In fact, it seemed as if the coast were rushing out to meet them. It would all be decided in the next minute. One mistake now, one error of judgment, and things would compound so quickly that there could be no time for correcting. "Lean her to starboard! More! That's it—hold her there—now steady, steady as she goes—*Now! Hard a-larboard! Hold her, hold her!*"

The whole ship groaned and heeled over so far that the sea began to comb over her gunwales. The men screamed; it looked as if she were about to go all the way over. But she held, and then slowly straightened, and a giant wave lifted her and fairly hurled her into the river's mouth.

The roar of thundering waves and flying foam was stupendous, but above it, Columbus heard something else—it sounded like cheering. Clearing his eyes again, he could see the men waving and dancing and yelling themselves hoarse. They had made it!

He had brought them through.

Without stopping, the *Niña* rode the tide on up to the major port of Rastelo, where they finally lowered anchor. There they learned that some of the ships in the harbor had been pinned there for four months by the worst storms in Rastelo's history. Columbus recorded in his journal that twenty-five ships had gone down that winter off the coast of Flanders alone!

News of the battered caravel's triumphant return from the Indies spread rapidly. Columbus, mindful of their experience in the Azores, took immediate steps to insure the safety of himself and his crew. Making use of several highly placed and trusted friends from his days in Lisbon, he sent abbreviated reports of his voyage to Ferdinand and Isabella by different routes, to make sure word got through.

That done, they could breathe more easily, and begin to enjoy their growing fame. Since the continuing storm precluded their sailing for Palos, Columbus felt that he could accept the invitation that had just arrived—bearing the seal of the King of Portugal.

John II was all smiles and silken words, as he greeted Columbus—and subsequently sought to glean morsels of useful information from Columbus's glowing generalities. Though the Admiral seemed relaxed and expansive, underneath he was on guard, for this was the man who had very nearly stolen the Indies from him—twice. What happened next is best described in Las Casas's words, from his *Historia de las Indias:*

While the King was speaking with the Admiral, he commanded that a bowl of beans should be placed on a table beside them, and then indicated by signs that one of the Indians who was there should arrange the beans in such a way as to show the many islands in that kingdom which Columbus claimed to have discovered. The Indian immediately showed him Española, Cuba, the Lucayos Islands, and others. The King watched this sullenly, and a short while later brushed the beans away, as if by accident. He then told another Indian to replace the beans, and this one arranged them as quickly, and as readily, as the first Indian had done, and went on to lay out more countries and islands, explaining all the reasons in his own language, which, of course, nobody could understand. And when the King fully realized the extent of the new discoveries, and the wealth they contained, he could not conceal his sorrow at the loss of such invaluable treasures, but beat his breast and cried out in passion: "Oh, man of little understanding! Why did you let such an enterprise fall from your hands?" [1]

For Columbus, this was a moment of supreme vindication. Yet where in the past he had been able to forgive, as in the case of Martin Pinzón, now the temptation to drink of the cup of retribution proved too much for him. According to Columbus's most recent biographer Landström, "The Portuguese chroniclers write that the Admiral was so boastful and supercilious, saying that it was the King's fault for having rejected his proposals in the first place, that the courtiers, when they saw the Admiral so insolent and the King so unhappy, offered to kill Columbus and prevent his taking the news to Castile. But the King would not agree to that."

Columbus may have gloated that night, but it is doubtful that God shared his delight. God and Columbus had entered into a covenant. Because Christopher had dedicated his life to serving Christ, God had given him an assignment that would test him to the limit, and indeed, much of the hardest testing had come before he set sail for the Indies. For the sake of Christ, Columbus had been willing to be taken for a fool—not once or twice, but over and over again, for eight long years. And then, as the days at sea became weeks, and pressure mounted on him to turn back, he had remained obedient to his call and pressed on into the dim unknown, when perhaps not another ship captain on earth would have done so.

Despite all his shortcomings, Columbus had time and again remained faithful to the point of death. He had poured himself out totally, holding nothing back. He had won the victory. And God intended to honor his obedience.

Before the voyage had begun, Columbus had been a beggar before God, all his hopes hanging on Ferdinand and Isabella's approval. But the moment they had agreed to back him, his innate arrogance reasserted itself. And in the critical area of reward for his service, he decided that he could not be sure that God's will would be done through others—that he could not, in fact, trust anyone but himself. So he dictated to those in authority over him what his rewards were to be.

Columbus chose the three things the world prizes most: money (his percentages), position (the titles of Viceroy and Admiral of the Ocean Sea), and power (the governorship of all he discovered)— the very things God would least likely have rewarded him with. For Columbus was totally unsuited to govern anybody. Vain, impractical, and emotionally immature, he was quick to judge others, yet incapable of accepting correction himself. He demanded absolute submission from his subordinates, yet refused to come under any authority save the Sovereigns themselves (and not even them in his heart).

When things went wrong, he would go into anger and self-pity, or unreality, rather than assume any responsibility himself. In fact, he was only able to command his ships as well as he did through the gifts and extraordinary guidance with which God blessed him. Even there, he would not delegate any decision-making authority; so weakened that he could not stand, he would order a shelter rigged on the sterncastle, that he might continue to con the ship from his bed. He had to be in total control—of his ship, and of his life.

But Columbus in control meant there was really no leaning on God at all. And so, because God really loved Christopher, He may have endeavored to jolt him out of his control and into humility, through two terrible storms. One wonders what might have happened if Columbus had, at the height of those crises, made a different vow: to trust God with every detail of his life, rescinding his demands and leaving his future up to Him.

By gifts and temperament, Columbus was ideally suited for exploration. He was at his best when in command of a ship, facing the challenge of uncharted waters and the mysteries of undiscovered lands. At such times he was also the most anxious to share the Light of Christ—which was his original call. Is it unreasonable to speculate that God might have used him further in just this fashion?

One can envision him, equipped with fast vessels and hand-picked crews (possibly including some friars from La Rábida), coasting the shores of North and South America. Perhaps God might have climaxed his career by leading him through the very straits which would within a generation bear the name of another devout Christian, Ferdinand Magellan, and as He did with Magellan, guide him on across the Pacific to Cipangu and Cathay. Had he done so, no name in the annals of exploration would have won half his acclaim.

But Columbus trusted Columbus. His will was set, and he would not let even God Himself dissuade him.

On March 15, 1493, if the Franciscan brothers in the fields at La Rábida rested for a moment, leaning on their hoes and looking over the river, they would have seen a weatherbeaten little ship with spanking new sails and long pennants flying making her way up-river to Palos. The *Niña* was coming home!

Palos erupted with joy. Families were being reunited and stories told, and while some were disappointed that their husbands or fathers had elected to stay on Española, the overall mood was jubilant—for word had also reached them that the *Pinta* was not lost as had been supposed. Blown nearly to Africa, she had finally reached the southern coast of Spain and was on her way home even now. As much as Columbus might have liked to tarry, he had vows to fulfill, and now set about his pilgrimages.

Soon after Columbus completed them, a letter reached him, addressed to: DON CRISTÓBAL COLÓN, OUR ADMIRAL OF THE OCEAN SEA, VICEROY AND GOVERNOR OF THE ISLAND HE HAS DISCOVERED IN THE INDIES. He was directed to commence immediately preparations for a return expedition, and then to come to Their Majesties' winter court in Barcelona as soon as possible. By return messenger, he sent his detailed plans for colonization which he had drawn up on the long voyage home. Having purchased a suitable wardrobe for court, he set out for Barcelona, bringing with him several of his officers, six Indian interpreters, and numerous artifacts and curiosities.

A grateful Ferdinand and Isabella had Barcelona decorated as if for a festival. What a splendid entrance Columbus must have made! We can see him riding at the head of a small column, tall and erect in the saddle, one hand holding the reins, the other resting proudly on his hip. The morning sun had not yet burned away the low-lying mists, and as he emerged from the fog—first a silhouette and then a reality—the sun behind him surrounded his broad-brimmed hat and flowing cape with a corona of gold.

Word spread ahead of him, and courtiers and a mounted escort were sent forth from the Alcazar, Their Majesties' winter palace, to accompany him. Soon he was flanked by Spanish nobility and preceded by a color guard, the sun dancing on their burnished helmets.

His dream was coming to pass, and more richly than he had ever dared hope! How he must have loved every element of it, down to the *chinking* of the spurs and silver-adorned saddles—which soon could no longer be heard above the cheering of the people lining the streets. All the way to the Alcazar, the crowds grew larger. From upper balconies draped with colorful capes, dark-eyed señoritas showered the procession with rose petals. As he reached the entrance of the palace, a tremendous roar of acclamation went up, and he could not help raising his hand to acknowledge it.

It was a moment too vivid ever to be forgotten. Yet what transpired that evening surpassed it. As Columbus made his entrance into the grand throne room, with its marble columns softly glowing in the light of a thousand candles, the court chroniclers record that his deeply tanned complexion, gray hair, long nose, and noble bearing reminded them of a Roman senator.

Respectfully he approached the throne of his beloved Sovereigns. As he did so, they did something no one had ever seen them do before: they rose to meet him. And when he knelt to kiss their hands, they raised him up and ordered a chair brought for him—another unprecedented honor.

At their invitation he began to tell his spellbinding story. Time and space seemed to drop away as he unfolded before them visions of dense, green rain forests with sweet exotic perfumes and parrots of startling colors, and even more startling cries. He told of unbelievably blue waters, so clear that you could see schools of fish swimming at a depth of several fathoms—strange fish of bizarre shapes and colors. He told of naked natives, so shy and innocent, and of an island more beautiful than the plains and hills of Castile. And he told of the loss of the *Santa Maria*, and how, largely through the friendly reception of the natives, it turned out to be such a tremendous gain.

And with that, he summoned the Indian interpreters, clothed in little more than their native attire—carrying parrots, live jungle rats two feet in length, dogs that could not bark, and strange salted fish. The courtiers were astonished.

He then had valuable trade goods brought in—aloes, cotton and spices. But he had saved the best for last. In his narrative, he had told them in passing that these naive Indians had gold ornaments, which they were delighted to exchange for hawk's bells and other worthless trinkets. Now he had a large, oaken chest brought in, which he dramatically threw open. An exclamation of amazement greeted the sight; there, gleaming in the candlelight, were crowns of gold, strange masks covered with beaten gold, necklaces and bracelets of gold, and raw nuggets of gold. The last jaded skeptics were won over—the Indies were indeed as fabulous as he had said!

As the excitement and whispering died away, a silence fell upon the court. Then, without warning, the Sovereigns fell on their knees, and all others did the same. Lifting their faces heavenward, Ferdinand and Isabella thanked God for all His bountiful mercy, and the *Te Deum* was sung. At the last line, the Sovereigns were in tears and so was Columbus: "O Lord, in thee have I trusted, let me never be confounded." [2]

From that time forth, whenever the King went out in his carriage, there was Columbus seated beside him, an honor hitherto accorded only to royalty. But gradually, imperceptibly, the Admiral began to think of it as, after all, no more than his due. After that, there was no reaching Columbus, not by circumstances, not by Father Perez, not even by God Himself.

On the surface, however, things could not have been going better. Even the Pope sent his congratulations to Their Catholic Majesties:

We heard indeed that . . . you had some time ago designed in your minds to send for and discover some islands and mainlands, remote and unknown, and hitherto undiscovered by others, in order to induce the natives and inhabitants thereof to worship our Redeemer . . . you appointed our beloved son Christopher Columbus . . . Who, at length, by divine aid, having used diligence, discovered while navigating in the Ocean, certain very remote islands and also mainland which had hitherto not been found by others; herein dwell multitudes of people living peaceably and . . . imbued with good morals; and the hope is entertained that if they were instructed, the name of our Lord and Saviour Jesus Christ might easily be introduced to the aforesaid lands and islands . . . .

ALEXANDER VI
to Ferdinand and Isabella, May 4, 1493 [3]

The preoccupation with gold, which had subtly insinuated itself into the fabric of Columbus's first explorations in the New World, was now on its way to becoming an obsession. On May 18, he was given an outright gift of 335,000 *maravedis*—for no reason other than as an expression of appreciation from a grateful country. Yet not content with the gift, on that same day Columbus claimed the 10,000 maravedis which were to be paid annually to the first person to sight land, despite the fact that in his own journal he had recorded that someone else, aboard the *Pinta*, had made the sighting. Columbus was fast losing sight of the original purpose of his mission—and his life. The verse in Job said, "If the Almighty be your gold . . ."; for Columbus, it had become reversed.

Soon he was outfitting a fleet of seventeen vessels and raising a company of twelve hundred men. This time he had no trouble getting men to sign on. Indeed, two hundred were "gentlemen volunteers," who were paying their own way and were along for gold and adventure. Here at last was a command worthy of the Admiral of the Ocean Sea! The dream continued; he was on his way to colonize his Indies.

They departed the port of Cádiz and sailed down to the Canaries, there heading west again in perfect weather and sighting land in a remarkable twenty-two days! Even more incredible was Columbus's landfall at *Dominica*—the navigating target which mariners would recommend for the next four centuries. To aim north meant possibly missing the strong trade winds; to aim south was to risk hitting dangerous reefs.[4] No wonder the sailors of his age considered Columbus to be the best dead-reckoning navigator of them all. By the grace of God, he was.

But the dream turned to a nightmare when finally they reached La Navidad. Every one of the thirty-nine colonists had been killed—some by each other, most of them by tribes of Indians other than those they had befriended.

When they found Indians who were not too frightened to talk to their interpreters, the story finally came out. No sooner had the *Niña* departed the year before, than the men had started indulging their lust with Indian women. Nor were they satisfied with one each but took as many as they could get.

No longer did they barter for gold. They simply seized it, doing violence to any Indians who protested. Quarrelling among themselves and killing one another, they had split into factions, and were thus easily ambushed and overrun.

There was no doubting the truth of the tale that they were able to piece together. From then on, Columbus's men detested the Indians, whom they regarded as lying and devious, and against whom they constantly sought opportunities for revenge. It was only with threats of capital punishment that Columbus was able to prevent a bloodbath.

The Admiral's own authority had been seriously undermined. His men were increasingly rebellious, having lost all respect for this grandiose, mercurial Italian, who had lied so blatantly about the gentleness of the Indians and the abundance of gold.

Columbus chose not to see many of the things that were going on. He turned his back on their taking native women for their pleasure—anything to appease, to avoid open confrontation. (But this unbridled lust and rape was to receive its own uniquely fitting punishment. For many of the women were carriers of a strange and deadly disease which would become known as syphilis, and the men thus infected were sentenced to a lingering, excruciatingly painful insanity and death. The sailors returning from this voyage introduced this new plague to Spain, whence it was shared with the rest of the civilized world.)

Columbus then tried to use the hunt for gold to unite his expedition, dividing the force into several discovery parties, assigned to establish outposts at various strategic places on the island. But from the beginning everything went wrong. The food supplies deteriorated in the heat; the mosquitoes were a deadly torment; several of the men contracted terrible fevers. It was soon apparent that there was no fountainhead of gold on the island. Finally, the inevitable happened, and the Governor of the Indies had open rebellion on his hands.

At sea, Columbus knew what to do when faced with a raging storm: get on his knees and seek God's deliverance. Now, faced with a storm on land, and long out of touch with God, in panic he tried to work things out himself. The result was a fiasco that was rapidly compounding itself into a catastrophe of major proportions. Totally out of control, Columbus was driven almost to distraction—but not back to his Saviour.

Meanwhile, word of the massacre at La Navidad, of the absence of gold, and of his gross mismanagement of the island expedition went back to Spain with the first ships to return for more supplies. Columbus was now all the more anxious to wrest some kind of victory from the dream-turned-nightmare. He had caught the fever himself, and for months was desperately sick. His two brothers, Diego and Bartolomeo arrived, and without the authority to do so, he immediately installed them as his lieutenants. Gradually, under the care of Bartolomeo, his health improved, but other conditions did not.

The gold was the bitterest disappointment of all. To bring in more, he commanded that each Indian must pay an annual tribute of gold or be punished. But there were no mines or fields on Española, which meant that the Indians had to pan for whatever gold they could find. Most were unable to meet their quota, even after it was eventually reduced by half. As a result, they were savagely punished by Spanish tax collectors whose own percentage depended on how much they collected. Many Indians ran away to escape them. At the same time, because the Indians were finally turning hostile, more forts were being constructed all over the island. The Indians themselves were forced to do this work and all other physical labor—having become virtually slaves on their own land. Las Casas writes:

Since violence, provocation and injustice from the Christians never ceased, some fled to the mountains, and others began to slay Christians, in return for all the wrongs and the torture they had suffered. When that happened, vengeance was immediately taken; the Christians called it punishment, yet not the guilty alone, but all who lived in a village or a district, were sentenced to execution or torture.[5]

In two years, 100 thousand of the approximate native population of 300 thousand on Española had died or been killed! According to a count made eight years later, that figure had more than doubled, and four years after that there were only twenty thousand left alive. The nightmare holocaust went on; there was no waking up from it.

For Columbus, the memory of what Española had been like when he first came must have been too painful to recall. Finally, after the putting down of a major Indian uprising, a Spaniard could now walk anywhere on the island without fear.

There was now no putting off his return home. Leaving his brothers in charge, Columbus sailed north to catch the prevailing westerlies, which this time proved anything but prevailing. The crossing seemed to take forever; their food and water ran out, and they were tortured by hunger and thirst. But eventually they arrived, and the Admiral was summoned immediately to court.

To his surprise, his Sovereigns chose to believe much of his version of why everything went wrong, and were not nearly so disturbed about the lack of gold as he. On the other hand, they were far more concerned than he about the welfare of the Indians, whom they now considered to be their subjects, and for whose safety and protection they held themselves personally responsible before God. They remonstrated with Columbus for the way he had permitted them to be treated. Yet while it was obvious that they had grave reservations about his ability to govern such a volatile situation, they felt morally bound by their original agreement to permit him to continue.

Therefore, they shored up his authority as best they could, instituting drastic reforms in the treatment of the Indians. And because the Portuguese were preparing a major expedition of their own to the New World, they sent him back as soon as a small fleet could be readied.

Once again, nothing went right. Three-quarters of the way across, they were suddenly becalmed for eight days. Such was the heat that none of them could bear to go below decks. The wheat was scorched, the salted meat went rotten, and Columbus and his men listened to the sound of their water and wine casks bursting. After much prayer, and what seemed like an eternity of this hell, a breath of wind stirred the pennants in the rigging. Soon there was a freshening breeze, and they were on their way again. The Lord had mercifully sent the trade winds to them, something which never happens at that time of year in the doldrums.[6] They finally sighted an island with three mountain peaks close together, and Columbus named it *Trinidad*, for the Holy Trinity.

Eventually, they worked their way up through the Antilles to Española—where chaos reigned. Columbus had been away for a year and a half, during which time word had reached the island that he was out of favor with Their Majesties. This so undercut the authority of his brothers, that rebellion had broken out again, and it had now reached the point that there were two armed camps on the island. Columbus handled the situation by giving in to every demand of the rebels, reinstating them with full pardons and full rights, and making their leader a mayor!

Not surprisingly, the same rebellion broke out again within six months, and with even more serious ramifications. More alarming reports were sent back to Spain. Finally the Sovereigns, for all their fondness of Columbus, felt that they no longer had any choice but to intervene for the best interests of all their subjects on Española—Spanish and Indian. They sent an old and trusted officer, Francisco de Bobadilla, to straighten out the mess, and empowered him with whatever authority he needed. Bobadilla carried with him the following letter to Columbus:

Don Cristobal Colón, our Admiral of the Ocean Sea: we have sent the Commendador, Francisco de Bobadilla, the bearer of this letter, to say certain things to you on our behalf. We desire you to place your full trust in him and pay him all respect, and to act accordingly.[7]

The first thing that Bobadilla saw when he landed on Española was the sight of seven Spaniards' bodies dangling from nooses! Then, he learned that five more Spaniards were to be executed on the following morning. Without further delay, Bobadilla read the proclamation which installed him as acting governor. When Columbus refused to acknowledge his authority, stating that the King and Queen had no right to depose him as Governor(!), Bobadilla had him and his brothers put in irons and sent them home to stand trial.

A compassionate captain offered to remove the fetters as soon as Columbus was on board, but the Admiral tearfully refused, saying that he would not permit it until the Sovereigns themselves so ordered, and that he would wear them as a token of how he was rewarded for his services.

The Sovereigns were shocked to see him in irons when he reported to them, that December of 1500. They ordered them removed, and they restored his house and all other properties on Española that had been confiscated. Then they listened with great understanding and compassion to his woeful tale. Yet they said nothing of his being reinstated as Governor.

Columbus went home, expecting momentarily to be ordered to ready another expedition. But the months went by, and no further word was heard from the court. At length, he turned his attention to preparing a Book of Prophecies, gathered from the Scriptures and the writings of the early Church prophets. Through them, he intended to prove that God had predestined Spain to be the nation which would free the Holy Land from the infidel, and that none other than himself was the man to lead the Crusade.

But such a Crusade would take much gold to finance it. Therefore he needed to make one more westward voyage of discovery. After more than a year's entreaties, and possibly just to get him out of Spain (where he was becoming an increasing embarrassment to them—he was being mocked as "the Admiral of the Mosquitoes" behind his back), Ferdinand and Isabella gave him four ships and their permission to go exploring. They made only one stipulation: he was expressly forbidden to return to Española, as they feared that his presence there might spark yet another rebellion.

Pleading ship trouble, Columbus sailed directly for Española, only to be refused entrance at the harbor. He then sailed to Cuba and struck southeast for the mainland (Honduras, in Central America). Despite unbelievable headwinds, despite being sick and feverish (he had his bed brought topside so that he could command the ship lying down), despite the fact that God Himself seemed to be blocking him every inch of the way, such was Columbus's willfulness that he finally reached the mainland which he declared to be the easternmost shore of the province of *Chiambra* (India). It had taken him thirty-eight days to cover what would normally have taken no more than three or four days, but it never occurred to Columbus to even consider that he might be out of God's will.

Columbus decided that they would follow the coast to the south, expecting it to turn toward the west at any moment. And so they proceeded down the coast of what is now Honduras, Nicaragua, and Costa Rica—where he finally found the source of gold that had been eluding him for so many years. (Which may explain why God's hand seemed to be set against his reaching this part of the mainland.)

Here the natives had such heavy artifacts of gold that a major source had to be nearby. The Indians took his men to gold fields, where the mineral was right on the surface, and in a very short space of time they were able to dig out more than a thousand maravedis' worth—with their bare fingers! That discovery raised a curtain on a drama far different from that which God had in mind for America. This drama, which would shortly begin in earnest, was to feature such stars as Cortez, Pizarro, and a supporting cast of thousands of Conquistadors, in the bloodiest rape of a country the world has ever known—and all for the love of gold. For although they undoubtedly would have colonized Mexico and Central America eventually, it was the gold that whetted the steel of their blades.

True, that the gold was there and would have been found by whomever came—but this was not the curtain that God had wanted His son Christopher to raise.

Columbus had found his gold; the last desire of his heart had been fulfilled. But at what a price! His health was ruined, his sanity nearly gone; two of his four ships would soon be too worm-eaten to go on, and he and his men would be stranded for months in the other two.

In the meantime, he carried on with his exploration, enduring in the month of December, 1502, the worst battle against the elements of all his voyages. He wrote:

> The tempest arose and wearied me so that I knew not where to turn; my old wound opened up, and for nine days I was as lost without hope of life; eyes never beheld the sea so high, angry and covered with foam. The wind not only prevented our progress, but offered no opportunity to run behind any headland for shelter; hence we were forced to keep out in this bloody ocean, seething like a pot on a hot fire. Never did the sky look more terrible; for one whole day and night it blazed like a furnace, and the lightning broke forth with such violence that each time I wondered if it had carried off my spars and sails; the flashes came with such fury and frightfulness that we all thought the ships would be blasted. All this time the water never ceased to fall from the sky; I don't say it rained, because it was like another deluge. The people were so worn out that they longed for death to end their dreadful sufferings.[8]

In addition to all these horrors, his son, Ferdinand, tells us that on Tuesday, December 13, a waterspout passed between the ships; "the which had they not dissolved by reciting the Gospel according to Saint John, it would have swamped whatever it struck without a doubt; for, it draws the water up to the clouds in a column thicker than a water-butt, twisting it about like a whirlwind." Columbus's biographer Samuel Eliot Morison continues: "It was the Admiral who exorcised the waterspout. From his Bible he read an account of that famous tempest off Capernaum, concluding, 'Fear not, it is I!' Then, clasping the Bible in his left hand, with drawn sword he traced a cross in the sky and a circle around his whole fleet."

Yet except for shipboard crises where he automatically turned heavenward for help, nothing seemed to induce him to turn back to God in repentance, not even what would soon prove to be the greatest moment of need in his life. Starting to build a settlement near the gold fields, under the supervision of his brother Bartolomeo, Columbus's men learned through their interpreters that the local tribe of Indians was planning an attack. So they launched a preemptive strike themselves, taking a number of hostages, including the chief, and as it happened, more than 100 thousand maravedis' worth of golden ornaments.

After this adventure, they were up a nearby river, getting water and provisions, when Columbus, who had been left almost alone with the ships at the mouth of the river, heard shouts and shooting. Then there was silence, and towards evening, when the tide changed, down the river floated the bodies of several of his men. Here, in his own words, is what happened next:

I toiled up to the highest point of the ship, calling in a trembling voice, with fast-falling tears, to the war captains of your highnesses, at every point of the compass, for succour, but never did they answer me. Exhausted, I fell asleep, groaning. I heard a very compassionate voice, saying: "O fool and slow to believe and to serve thy God, the God of all! What more did He for Moses or for His servant David? Since thou wast born, ever has He had thee in His most watchful care. When He saw thee arrive at an age with which He was content, He caused thy name to sound marvelously in the land. The Indies, which are so rich in a part of the world, He gave thee for thine own; thou hast divided them as it pleased thee, and He enabled thee to do this. Of the barriers of the Ocean Sea, which were closed with such mighty chains, He gave thee the keys; and thou wast obeyed in many lands and among the Christians thou hast gained honorable fame. What did He more for the people of Israel when He brought them out of Egypt? Or for David, whom from a shepherd He made to be king in Judea? Turn thyself to Him, and acknowledge thine error; His mercy is infinite; thine old age shall not prevent thee from achieving great things; He has many heritages very great. Abraham had passed a hundred years when he begat Isaac and was Sarah young? Thou criest for uncertain help. Answer: who has afflicted thee so greatly and so often? God or the world? The rewards and promises which He gives, He does not bring to nothing, nor does He say, after He has received service, that His intention was not such and that it is to be differently regarded, nor does He inflict suffering in order to display His power. His deeds agree with His words; all that He promises, He performs with interest; is this the manner of men? I have said that which thy Creator has done for thee and does for all men. Now in part He shows thee the reward for the anguish and danger which thou hast endured in the service of others."

I heard all this as if I were in a trance, but I had no answer to give to words so true, but could only weep for my errors. He, whoever he was who spoke to me, ended saying: "Fear not; have trust; all these tribulations are written upon marble and are not without cause." [9]

In his infinite mercy, God stopped at nothing to reach his beloved Christopher. *Have trust* . . . and Columbus had wept for his errors.

Yet only a few entries further on, he writes:

I declare that I am at the fountainhead [of the gold in the New World]. Genoese, Venetians, and all who have pearls, precious stones and other things of value, all carry them to the end of the world to exchange them, to turn them into gold. Gold is most excellent. Gold constitutes treasure, and he who possesses it may do what he will in the world, and may so attain as to bring souls to Paradise.

It is doubtful that he who does what he will in the world is going to be used to bring many souls to Paradise. This particular narrative goes on to reveal just how far off-center Columbus's thinking had wandered. For by the same sort of weird, convoluted reasoning that earmarks Gnosticism and so much of occult metaphysics, Columbus arrived at a monumental conclusion: he was convinced that he had found King Solomon's mines!

Columbus may have turned away from God, but God did not turn away from Columbus. By sheer grace, He brought him and what remained of his men safely home to Spain. But this time there was no royal summons inviting him to court. Queen Isabella was dying. It was the end of an era—for Castile, and for Columbus. Far older than his fifty-three years, too infirm to put to sea again, Columbus spent the next two years fretting about not receiving his proper share of the Indies gold, which had finally begun to arrive in some quantity.

In the spring of 1506, what remained of his health began to fail quickly. The tall, proud old captain could no longer walk down to the harbor to see the bright sails in the morning sun or hear the latest news from the most recent landings, or mutter that "even tailors" were going a-discovering these days.

But we can imagine him lying in his bed and reliving with great vividness his first glimpse of the moonlit cliffs of San Salvador, and the joy of his men as they yelled with glee and danced on the decks . . . the awe of the following morning, as they watched the dawning sun illuminate a new world unfolding before their eyes and realized what they had done . . . the sun gleaming on the helmets of his escort as he rode in triumph into Barcelona, the greatest hero Spain had ever known . . . and that night, as he knelt with the King and Queen, and sang the *Te Deum* before their God, tears streaming down their faces . . . .

The old man brushed away the tears at the corners of his eyes, and perhaps he spoke to God again then, for the first time in a long while.

"Father, it is over now, isn't it?"

Yes, son, he might have heard in his heart.

"Father, I'm afraid I have not done well in carrying the Light of

Your Son to the West. I'm sorry. I pray that others will carry the light further.''

They will. You are forgiven.

"It's time now, isn't it?"

Yes.

On Ascension Day, 1506, after receiving the Sacraments of the Church, Christopher Columbus said these words: "Father, into Thy hands I commend my spirit," and went to be forever with the Saviour whose name he bore.

3

Blessed Be the Martyrs

Others did carry the Light of Christ further, but so tiny were the pinpricks of illumination on the advancing tide of darkness that we almost missed them entirely. In fact, the Columbus era soon deteriorated into such a debacle of rape, murder, and plunder throughout Central America, that we could not conceive what possible connection it might have with any divine plan for the establishment of a new Christian commonwealth.

Here we were faced with one of our first real dilemmas. If God had truly been working His purpose out for America to be what the first Puritans would call the New Israel, then how could He have let everything in the New World go to seed so badly for a whole century? This was not the Master Economist that we knew. Unless we could find some discernible continuity to His work . . . . Once again, we spelled out our doubts to the Lord in prayer. If we were going to navigate through the rocks and shoals that lay ahead, He would have to put His hand on the helm, and fast.

He did. On our next trip to the Boston Public Library, we acted out a scene that would become increasingly familiar. David, perpetually optimistic, would return to the reading table with his arms laden with books, confident that he had unearthed new treasures of information. But Peter steadfastly maintained professional skepticism, scowling his way through the new ore samples, looking for the occasional nugget. Twin columns of rejects would mount at his right elbow, while there might be four or five "keepers" at his left.

The afternoon shadows were lengthening, and it was getting close to closing time, when David came up to the table with one last volume, a tall, thin book. "Thought you might get a kick out of it, just for the pictures," he said.

Peter flipped the book open to the title page, *The Pageant of America*,[1] and noted the publication date: 1928. As he riffled the pages, he shook his head; it was a picture book, and a pretty naive-looking one, at that. But the pictures toward the front of the volume caught our eye; they were largely old etchings of long-robed priests in the wilderness, accompanied by (or in some cases being tortured by) Indians. Something made us pause then, and begin to read. And thus did the Lord bring to our attention what was, in many ways, the most crucial phase in the introduction of Christ's Light into America. This was a chapter whose glory would occasionally be matched, but never surpassed.

The dawn of the sixteenth century saw more and more vessels approaching the New World, hull-down on the horizon, their square sails silhouetted against the rising sun. On they came, some Portuguese, but mostly Spanish, bound for conquest, colonization, and gold. The Aztecs greeted Cortez in 1519, believing him to be the reincarnation of their white god Quetzalcoatl, and ushering him with great ceremony into their capital (now Mexico City). Upon arrival, he promptly took their ruler Montezuma captive, and thus gained control over the native population in one efficient maneuver.

Pizarro did almost the same thing in Peru, twelve years later. Taking the Inca chief Atahualpa captive by trickery, Pizarro then demanded an impossible ransom: a large room to be filled to the ceiling with gold and silver. To the Spaniards' amazement, the Incas were able to meet the ransom, whereupon Pizarro had his hostage garroted on trumped-up charges.

This pattern continued in the Caribbean islands (now called the West Indies, to distinguish them from those of East Asia) and on the mainland, where the natives were forced to continually work the gold fields. In Mexico, where silver was abundant, the Indian farmers were forcibly taken from their fields and set to mining, with no thought for the crops on which the population was entirely dependent. Widespread famine was the result, and that, plus their total lack of immunity to the white man's diseases, amounted to genocide of mind-numbing proportions.[2]

At first glance, it would appear that God's plan for America was doomed almost before it could be set in motion. And indeed, how Satan must have gloated over the way things were turning out! The Spanish Conquistadors, in their wanton slaughter of the Indians

were proving just as cruel as the Indians themselves—those in the
Caribbean who practiced cannibalism, and the "more advanced"
civilizations on the mainland which derived such satisfaction from
ritual murder and blood sacrifice. The murderers were now themselves being murdered, and Satan's kingdom in the New World
remained intact.

Or so, at first glance, it would appear. But there was a weakness
in the fortifications, a small and unnoticed breach in the outer wall.
The Conquistadors had brought monks with them, possibly to
salve their consciences, or to boost the morale of the men who
were so far from home. But these Franciscan and Dominican friars
were not straw men; they loved God—deeply and totally. They
were as committed to serving Him, as their military masters were
to serving themselves.

It took a particular kind of Christian to enter these orders, and to
thereby relinquish the right to own, to choose, or to marry—in
short, sacrificing all for a life of service and obedience. And in
sixteenth-century Europe, while there were more than a few Christians, highborn and low, who had counted the cost of discipleship,
and were prepared to pay it, there were almost no opportunities to
fulfill such a call. In fact, with the singular exception of its monasteries and convents, the Church had lapsed into a sorry state of
complacency and hypocrisy. It was instituting Inquisitions on the
one hand, and on the other preying on the gullibility of the common
people—hawking relics and selling indulgences which supposedly
insured swifter entry into heaven. (By 1519, things had reached the
point where a devout young German monk named Martin Luther
nailed his ninety-five theses for reformation of the Church to the
door of All Saints Church in Wittenberg—and took the first step
towards what would become known as the Protestant Reformation.)

So, to a young Spaniard, who wanted to serve the Lord Jesus
Christ more than anything else in life, there was really only one
way: the taking of holy orders. And thus, some of the most gifted
young men in Spain, many from the ranks of nobility, found themselves in the plain robes of the Dominicans or the Franciscans, side
by side with sons of the simplest peasant farmers. Interestingly
enough, many of those who had once lived lives of privilege and
self-indulgence proved to be the most willing to endure great hardship and deprivation in the service of Jesus Christ.

When *God* begins a new work, He does not require a vast or-
ganization of high-powered fund-raisers and image-projectors. All
He needs are a few men who want to live totally and solely for

Him. And it has always been this way—from the Old Testament prophets, to the handful of Christ's apostles, and to the present day.

In the opening of the New World, these few were the Franciscan and Dominican friars, who had already begun to die themselves— to self-will, self-expression, self-reliance, all manner of *self*ishness. For them, the process of dying to self had begun even before they took their vows, and would continue for the rest of their lives, which might indeed end in the ultimate sacrifice: death by martyrdom. And thus, because even death itself held no fear for them, Satan found it almost impossible to neutralize their effectiveness by fear or lust, pride or jealousy, despair or self-pity. Consequently, these few men turned out to be a greater threat to his dominion on this continent than a veritable legion of do-gooders and yea-sayers.

Such was the pattern for living that God set down, as He began His work in this country; and it is as valid today as it was then. For He does not go back on His word, nor has He changed His intent.

Those first friars—the Franciscans with perhaps slightly more emphasis on simplicity, the Dominicans with slightly more emphasis on study—may have been tiny pinpricks of light, but the pins grew sharper and the light grew brighter wherever they were posted. Orphanages came into being, along with schools for the Indians and refuges for the destitute. And through the loving service of these missionaries, dozens, then hundreds, and then thousands of Indians came to realize that they had a living, risen Saviour who could renew their lives, as if they had been born all over again. What had first attracted them and awakened a deep yearning that the world could never satisfy, was the living example of these selfless men.

One of the many things that these first missionaries shared in common was a gift that God seemed to have given almost every one of them: an intense love of this strange new land to which He had brought them. Stunned at the grandeur and the majesty of it, far surpassing anything they had ever seen, they were acutely aware of the hand of the Creator in its formation. More than that, they sensed that the reason He had created such breathtaking beauty was for the express purpose of delighting those who would one day call Him *Father*.

Imagine the sensation of being the first Christian to stand looking at the thundering falls of Niagara, or to arrive at the rim of the Grand Canyon, or gaze down on the shining rocks of the Big Sur coastline, or to be suddenly confronted with the Grand Tetons, shooting up out of the plain like a cathedral pointing to heaven? Is it so surprising that these missionaries' hearts were filled with the desire to see and to journey? Or that so many of these same men would become known to modern American school children as the great explorers who first mapped our rivers and lakes and mountain passes?

The first white man to explore territory in what is now the United States of America, was the Franciscan friar Marcos de Niza. His journey into New Mexico in 1539 led to Francisco de Coronado's famous expedition in search of the Seven Cities of Cibola, whose streets were said to be paved with gold. Once again did Satan seek to use man's lust for gold to thwart this latest thrust of Christ's Light into his darkness.

The men responsible for determining Spain's policy in the New World soon realized that when it came to pacifying the Indians and extending the frontier, one friar could accomplish peaceably what it might take a thousand soldiers to do forcibly. So they made it a policy to encourage these missionary efforts.

But their main method of colonization remained the *encomienda* system, whereby a Spanish overlord was allotted so many hundreds of acres—and whatever Indians happened to be living on them. Officially, they were in his custody for the purpose of their salvation and "religious instruction." But in actuality they were little more than slaves, and the overlords tended to run their encomiendas like medieval serfdoms.

There was one priest, however, whom the policymakers must have regretted ever encouraging—a priest who went to Cuba not long after taking his vows. There he was assigned an encomienda of his own. As the labor of his Indians began to make him rich, he awoke to the insidious evil of the system. He hated what it was doing to him, and especially how it was affecting his attitude towards the Indians. Renouncing all connection with the system, he dedicated the rest of his life to combatting it and exposing the plight of the Indians.

We have met this man before: he is Bartolomé de Las Casas, who was with Columbus on his third voyage, and who recorded the Admiral's journal for posterity. Such was his dedication, that Las Casas was eventually able to persuade Charles V to pass laws alleviating the conditions of the Indians, and ultimately revoking the encomienda system. In 1552, his history of the Indies was published, and this widely read account of what had really happened there made Spain a byword for cruelty throughout Europe.

For example, here is how he described the end of the Indian uprising on Española:

When they saw every day how they perished from the inhuman cruelty of the Spaniards, how their people were ridden down by horses, cut to pieces by swords, eaten and torn asunder by dogs, burned alive, and subjected to all kinds of exquisite torture, those of certain provinces . . . decided to resign themselves to their fate and give themselves over into the hands of their enemies without a struggle.[3]

Historia de las Indias became justly famous, but it also secured the author's alienation by practically everyone in Spain, save for his Christian brothers in the cause. Yet, this one man's willingness to be vilified and all but physically martyred for the sake of his beloved Indians—his willingness to follow in Jesus' footsteps along the Way of the Cross—bought new life for much of the remaining Indian population.

The pockets of light grew larger and brighter. More friars were outposted in New Mexico and Lower California (the Baja). Several met death at the hands of hostile Indians, but others took their place, and the light went further to the north and the east. By 1630, Alonso de Benavides, the friar responsible for the New Mexico missions, was able to record that eighty thousand Indians had been baptized, and friars based in twenty-five missions were serving ninety Indian communities.

In 1687, Father Eusebio Kino, a Jesuit (for by this time, they too were involved), refused a professorship in mathematics in his native Austria to serve the Indians in America. He founded a mission in the Sonora region of northern Mexico, and soon came to love the vast solitude of the desert, with its shifting colors and awesome stillness. From his mission base, he was to make more than fifty journeys of exploration, traveling on horseback across hundreds of miles of arid wasteland, and ranging as far north as the Gila River and as far west as the muddy Colorado. In 1700, he founded San Xavier del Bac (near the present site of Tucson), the first mission in Arizona.

As the Lord's work progressed, the Franciscans carried the Light to California, while the Dominicans served in the Baja. Fray Junípero Serra, the hero of the settlement of California, was a Spanish professor of philosophy when he felt called to the mission field at the age of fifty-five. Among the missions he founded were San Diego, San Carlos (Carmel), and San Francisco. Just before his death, he picked the site of Santa Barbara. "Love God" was his greeting for everyone he met. He was universally loved by the

Indians, his fellow friars, and even the soldiers of the Spanish garrisons.

Bit by bit, the Light progressed up the West Coast of America and began to reach inland. The pace was slow—no gold was discovered to fire men's greed, and so the only men interested in going there (aside from the missionaries) were a few pioneer ranchers and farmers. "God-forsaken" was what most civilized Spaniards might have called that land.

But was it? Or did God purposely withhold knowledge of the presence of gold in California for two centuries, in order to ensure the kind of settlement He intended in His new Promised Land? For life in the mission towns was simple, peaceful, and centered around the churches. There, both Spaniards and Indians, guided by the example of the selfless lives of the missionaries, learned to put their trust in Him.

But on the East Coast of America, a different history was unfolding. In 1513, Ponce de León, seeking the "Fountain of Youth," whose waters were said to possess magical curative powers, sighted Florida. Through the years, a number of Spanish attempts to colonize Florida failed, due to climate, disease, and the ferocity of the Indians. Then finally, in 1562, a group of French Huguenots (Protestants), seeking a haven from religious persecution, touched at what would soon be named Saint Augustine and settled at what is now Beaufort, South Carolina. Two years later, another group of Huguenots settled at the mouth of the Saint Johns River in Florida, only to be massacred by a Spanish expedition.

The Spanish themselves then attempted to settle Saint Augustine and other sites along Florida's east coast, but their efforts were plagued by an unbroken chain of misfortunes—a French reprisal, unending sickness, and frequent Indian raids.

Perhaps because of the blood of the innocent Huguenots; perhaps because the underlying motive for colonization was greed; or possibly simply because it was not God's time or place, and these were not the people He had chosen—the jealous, bickering, avaricious Spanish settlers in Florida were destined not to thrive or come into the mainstream of what God had planned for America.

Next upon the stage of North America were the French, and with them, a new breed of missionaries: the fabled Jesuits. If there was one word to describe the Jesuits, it would be *zeal*—in the very best sense of that maligned word. In 1540, Ignatius of Loyola, a former knight and soldier, founded the Society of Jesus—a band of brilliant young scholars and disciples, who had covenanted together to live in poverty and chastity under absolute obedience to the Pope. The essence of the "Jesuits" (a derogatory nickname which they came to accept as their own) was such a soldierlike unity and companionship in the service of Christ that they all but invented the phrase *esprit de corps*. Their personal aims were: (1) purification of the soul from disordered affections and worldly standards; (2) discovery of the Divine Will before making one's choice of an area of commitment within the order; (3) consecration of the individual's mind and will to the service of the Creator under the leadership of Jesus Christ.

From the beginning, the Jesuits had a deep commitment to the mission field, in the tradition of Francis Xavier, who with Ignatius was one of the founders of the society, and who became famous for his missionary work in India and Japan. From the earliest days of the order, the mission field attracted many of the finest intellects the Church could boast. By dint of the intensive discipline required of them, these men turned out to be surprisingly well prepared for the physical hardships that awaited them. In fact, as a strong man rejoices to run a race, these Christian soldiers, superbly trained and strong in the faith yet conditioned to prize humility, looked forward to the tests of the savage wilderness.

Like the Franciscan and Dominican orders in Spain, the very totality of the commitment the Jesuits required was appealing to gifted young Frenchmen who *had* experienced deep conversions to Christ, and wanted nothing more than to serve Him totally and unreservedly. And so, as the Light of the Spanish missionaries began to illuminate the southwest of America, now Light began to break across the northeast corner as well. The French missionaries moved ever deeper into the uncharted wilderness, their canoes gliding silently through the early morning mists, their snowshoes leaving lonely trails through glistening pine forests. In 1534, Jacques Cartier, discoverer of the Saint Lawrence River, erected a cross thirty feet high on the western shore of its gulf. Wherever he encountered large bands of Indians, he read to them the opening verses of the Gospel of John, and also of Christ's suffering and crucifixion.

But it was Samuel de Champlain, known as the "father of New France," who undertook the most effective measures of bringing the Light to the Indians. They were living, he said, ". . . like brute beasts, without faith, without law, without religion, without God." [4] He brought from France four gray-clad friars of the Recollets, a branch of the Franciscan order. One of these, Joseph Le Caron, pushed westward with an escort of Hurons, until he reached their towns on Lake Huron's Georgian Bay, where he built a chapel and introduced the Indians to Christian worship.

Meanwhile, the Jesuits, singly or in twos, went forth in an attitude of lowliness, meeting the Indians as equals and respecting their customs, yet sharing with them the Gospel of Jesus Christ. Year by year, the Light they imparted spread a little farther— among the Hurons around Georgian Bay, to the Algonquins north of Ottawa, to the Abenakis in Maine and Acadia (Nova Scotia), to the Iroquois south of the Saint Lawrence, and to the Chippewas, Ojibwas, Illinois and other tribes of the upper Great Lakes and Mississippi Valley. The pace was slow, as it was on the West Coast, but it was also sure.

By way of discipline, these Jesuit missionaries were required to keep a written journal of all the significant events of the year. They then submitted their journals to their Superior, who compiled them into narratives called *Relations*, which captured the essence of what God was doing in New France. The *Relations* were then published in France and subsequently created a great stir of interest in missionary work.

Among those who were profoundly inspired by the *Relations*, was a lad of seventeen, from a very wealthy family. So anxious was he to become a Jesuit missionary in America that he joined the Society with the full knowledge that it would take twelve arduous years of study and preparation before he could be ordained. His aptitude as a linguist (and much prayer) won him an assignment to New France, first to Sault Sainte Marie, and then to the southwest corner of Lake Superior. Traveling with Indians and *voyageurs* in their birchbark canoes, he adapted himself to deep-woods living and learned how to survive on just what the land (and God) provided. So adept did he become, and such was his enthusiasm, that he carried the Light of Christ deeper and deeper into the wilderness, just as he had once dreamed of doing as a youth, reading the Jesuits' *Relations*. Indeed, he was to become one of the most famous of all American explorers—Father Jacques Marquette.

Called to serve the Illinois Indians, of them he would write in his own contribution to the *Relations:* "One must not hope that he can avoid crosses in any of our missions, and the best way to live there contentedly is not to fear them . . . The Illinois . . . are lost sheep that must be sought for among the thickets and woods."

The seeking sometimes took him far afield, for he had the same joyous enthusiasm for finding undiscovered vistas of God's creation as did his fellow missionaries in the far west. In 1672, he was ordered by his Superior to "seek toward the South Sea [the Gulf of Mexico] new nations that are unknown to us, to teach them to know our great God, of Whom they have hitherto been ignorant." The following May, he and Louis Joliet began their descent of the mighty Mississippi. Daily awed by the increasing size of the vast river that swept them along, they descended as far as the mouth of the Arkansas River.

Father Marquette promised the Illinois Indians at Kaskaskia that he would come back to them to found a mission. This he did, despite health that had been broken during the long and rigorous voyage. Death took him early at the age of thirty-eight, and as a tribute, the Illinois brought his remains back to Jesuit headquarters in a procession of thirty canoes.

One of the most outstanding of the first Jesuit missionaries was Jean de Brébeuf. Tall, powerfully built and possessing a commanding presence, Father Brébeuf worked for nineteen years with the Hurons, enlarging the influence of Christ, and battling the Devil for the souls of men. And it *was* a battle, for among other things, he had to overcome the lies of jealous medicine men, who said of the Body of Christ in the Eucharist that the missionaries had concealed a corpse in their houses that was infecting the country.

In 1640, Father Brébeuf saw a vision in the sky of a great cross slowly approaching over the wilderness forests, towards the land of the Iroquois. When asked by his companions how large it was, he replied, "Large enough to crucify us all."

The martyrdom for which he had thus mercifully been prepared, and which he had always known could be the final sacrifice of his call, came nine years later, at the hands of the Iroquois. Captured with Father Gabriel Lalemant when a war party fell upon the Huron towns in which they were serving, he was subjected to every Satanic torture which his captives could devise. And there could be little doubt of the source of their inspiration, when one considers the nature of the tortures or the intensity of pleasure the Iroquois derived from leisurely inflicting them. For the myth of the noble savage was just that: a myth, created a century later by romantic English poets and artists, who had never crossed the ocean themselves, let alone witnessed the horrors of tribal warfare and custom. The lives of these Indians were an unending tableau of fear and hatred of other tribes, and a dawn-to-dusk struggle for survival.

The first Iroquois torture was to pour boiling water over Father Brébeuf's naked body, in mockery of the Sacrament of Baptism. When, by the grace of God, he denied them the pleasure of hearing him cry out in agony—for the pain of their victims was intoxicating to them—they tied a collar of metal hatchets, heated red-hot, around his neck. Again, Father Brébeuf disappointed them, and so they fastened a belt of birchbark, filled with pitch and resin, around his waist and set it afire. And still he remained dumb before his tormentors, his face set like flint.

Now Father Brébeuf did speak, but not in anguish. He called out encouragement to his fellow captives. Enraged, the Indians cut off his lips and tongue and rammed a hot iron down his throat. Then they cut strips of flesh from his arms and legs and devoured them before his eyes. But as he was dying, Father Brébeuf was gaining the victory, just as had his Saviour on the Cross before him, and the Indians sensed it. In the end, they cut his heart out and ate it, and drank of his blood, in the hope that they could thus gain the spirit power that had given him more courage than any man they had ever seen.

One of Father Brébeuf's companions for six years during his work with the Hurons was another Jesuit, Isaac Jogues. In 1642, while returning from a journey to Quebec to secure supplies, Father Jogues and his party were ambushed by Iroquois. He managed to escape, but when he saw that several of his companions had been taken prisoner, he surrendered himself and joined them. "Could I indeed abandon them without giving them the help which the Church of my God has entrusted to me? Flight seemed horrible to me. If it must be, I said in my heart, that my body suffer the fire of earth, in order to deliver these poor souls from the flames of hell, it is but a transient death, in order to procure for them an eternal life."

The Indians tore out their captives' fingernails with their teeth, gnawed their fingers, and cut off a thumb or forefinger of each. Father Jogues was not killed outright, but kept as a slave for the purpose of their future enjoyment through torturing him—torture so cruel that he longed for Christ to release him from life and let him be with Him in heaven.

Why are some Christians called to make the supreme sacrifice? Is it because they have the faith to do so? Is it because, through their example, the faith of the entire Body of Christ is strengthened? Or is it because a nonbeliever cannot gaze upon a cross or Indian burning-stake without asking questions that begin with *how*, or *why*, or *where?* Only God knows for sure. But this we may safely speculate: of all the men on earth, those whom Satan hates most are the Christian martyrs, because they remind him of Christ's willingness to die on the Cross, out of love for mankind.

No wonder, whenever he had one physically at his mercy, with servants who took such delight in inflicting pain, he provided them with tortures from the very pit of hell!

After more than a year's captivity, Father Jogues was able to escape the Iroquois and make his way to the Dutch colony at Fort Orange (Albany) and eventually back to France, to the Jesuit College at Rennes. But word of his ordeal had preceded him, and to his surprise and acute embarrassment, he was a national hero. The Queen kissed his mangled hands, and the Pope himself paid him honor. It was all more than he could bear, and he begged to be returned to duty: his one desire was to be sent back to New France, to continue to serve the Indians.

His wish was granted, and his first assignment was to act as France's ambassador to the Iroquois Nation, with whom they had just concluded a peace treaty. Father Jogues performed these duties well—the Iroquois were in awe of him—but he was more deeply concerned than ever for the state of their souls. For even while he was among them, they sacrificed a captive Algonquin woman in honor of Areskoui, their god of war, crying: "Areskoui, to thee we burn this victim, feast on her flesh and grant us new victories!" [5] And they proceeded to feast on her flesh themselves. Thus, when his task was completed, Father Jogues requested to be again assigned to the Iroquois, this time as priest, to found the "Mission of the Martyrs." While he awaited re-assignment, Father Jogues, well aware that his previous experience qualified him better than anyone else for the post, wrote to a friend:

My heart tells me that if I have the happiness of being employed in this mission, I will go and not return; but I shall be happy if the Lord will complete the sacrifice where He has begun it, and make the little blood I have shed in that land, the earnest of what I would give. [6]

And it came to pass.

The first pinpricks of Christ's Light had arrived in North America; in the span of a century and a half these tiny illuminations had become veritable spearheads of light, thrusting deeper and deeper into the heart of a dark and murderous continent. For darkness is powerless to do anything to light, except recoil before it. "The light shines in the darkness, and the darkness has not overcome it" (John 1:5).

And what of the martyrs? Other than the tremendous example of their selflessness and sacrifice, did their deaths play a part in God's unfolding plan for America? In terms of mass numbers of Indians being converted to Christ, the missionaries' impact on the continent as a whole may not at first seem to have been that significant. But God does not take the measure of men's lives by the sum of their accomplishments. Rather, in the case of the founding of America, He seems to have been more concerned with the quality and depth of commitment.

> Unless a grain of wheat falls into the earth and dies, it remains alone; but if it dies, it bears much fruit (John 12:24).

These French and Spanish martyrs were willing to be the grains of wheat which fell into the earth and died. In soil watered with the blood of their sacrifice, God could now plant the seeds of the nation which was to become the New Promised Land.

4

"Damn Your Souls! Make Tobacco!"

On the waterfront at Jamestown, atop a massive stone column, stands a magnificent statue of Captain John Smith. Here is the hero of the Virginia Colony, resplendent in full Elizabethan regalia—cape, sword, and swashbuckling boots—gazing belligerently out over the wide expanse of the James River.

By the time we visited the site of the first English colony in America, one warm, sunny afternoon at the end of April, 1976, we had learned enough of what had happened at Jamestown to know that it was not to the memory of Smith that we wanted to pay our respects. In our eyes, the real hero of Jamestown was a man few Americans had ever heard of—Robert Hunt. He also had a memorial, but set slightly back off the main path, and so modest that we almost overlooked it. A bronze relief set in stone showed a minister celebrating Holy Communion in a makeshift outdoor sanctuary. If only a few of the others had been like him . . . .

What we uncovered about the founding of Virginia appeared at first to be the largest nugget of all: sermon after sermon extolling the spiritual virtues of the Virginia Company for its courageous missionary outreach, and praising God for its selfless Partners. England might be coming onto the North American missionary field a century late, but she was coming on with a vengeance. Apparently, the Church of England was about to show the Church of Rome how it was done!

But the nugget turned out to be Fool's Gold. We learned not to be deceived by pious-sounding sermonology, not to believe that someone felt strongly about Christ, simply because he said he did. In short, we learned a lesson that stood us in good stead for the rest of the book: to judge the tree by its fruit, not by its leaves.

With a timing only God Himself could have directed, a friend happened to pass us a copy of a book: George F. Willison's *Behold Virginia!* If what Willison said about Jamestown were confirmed, then we had stumbled onto a venture that for sheer hypocrisy had few equals in the history of Christendom, and a subsequent cover-up that would rival Watergate.

A seemingly endless parade of fat galleons, crimson and gold pennants flying above their white sails, scudded across the blue Atlantic, their holds laden with fabulous treasure from the Spanish Main. England, France, and the other European powers looked on with envy, as Spain's coffers filled to overflowing with golden booty. Within a single generation, she had become the most powerful nation on earth.

England was especially vexed, for Henry VII had disdainfully dismissed the proposal of the Genoese visionary to sail *west* to the Indies. Now, nearly a century later, England had a new aggressive monarch in the iron-willed Elizabeth. The Spaniards may have taken Mexico and Central America, the Portuguese Brazil, and the French the far north of America, but that still left more than a thousand miles of coastline unclaimed, and there was no reason to let Spain have it all!

This was the climate in England, as Sir Walter Raleigh, a nobleman with a zest for new ventures, dispatched a small fleet of ships to the New World in 1585, to settle Roanoke Island, off the coast of what is now North Carolina. Even after one previous attempt had ended with the starving would-be settlers abandoning their effort, Raleigh had no trouble recruiting candidates for a new expedition. Through the fantastic tales brought back by fishing vessels which had stopped to take on wood and water along the American coast, every man in Europe had it "on good authority" that the Indians used chamber pots of solid gold, encrusted with rubies and diamonds! [1]

Surely here was the ideal solution for many desperate Englishmen: for the tenant farmer evicted from the land which his family had always worked and reduced to the life of a wandering beggar; for the cobbler or joiner who found himself in London with too many other cobblers or joiners; for the highwayman who chose to avail himself of the Queen's pardon to go on the expedition; for the professional soldier between wars; and for the Gentleman, a bit down on his luck and seeking a way to replenish the family coffers (and escape his creditors). Raleigh had all the candidates he wanted!

Where was God in all this? Apparently nowhere. Here was England, about to colonize the land which He had held back in order that it might one day become a Redeemer Nation, and the English had already succumbed to the same greed that had so blinded the Spaniards. Nor was there any spiritual guidance or direction from the throne. Following the middle-of-the-road course established by her father, Henry VIII, Elizabeth shared his view that, as Head of the Church of England, it was her duty to protect the Church from the new Protestant extremists. Religion was all right in its place, but that place was scarcely at the forefront of man's consciousness.

In large measure, Elizabeth reflected the attitude of her age, especially among the nobility and landed gentry. To be sure, there were still many praying people among the "common sort," but for the most part, men had "more important" things on their minds. The God of Martin Luther and Father Jogues did not appear to be much in fashion in Elizabethan England.

Nor was England at that time apparently much in favor with God. Certainly there was no grace accompanying the Roanoke expedition. Attacked by hostile Indians, their supplies diminishing at an alarming rate, they prevailed upon John White, the colony's governor, to sail back to England for emergency relief. This he did, leaving behind his daughter and newborn granddaughter, "Virginia" Dare, the first white child born in America.

But by the time White got back to England, the attention of Raleigh and others was totally absorbed in preparing to repel an invasion by Spain. Then came the Armada, and nearly two years would pass before a frantic John White was finally able to embark with provisions. When his ship approached the island, he must have been surprised that no one came to the shore to wave. It is not hard to imagine the ominous sense of foreboding that must have gripped his heart.

White was in the longboat as the oars dipped and pulled, guiding the craft toward the silent shore. No cheery greetings replied to the long *halloos*. There were no cries of children playing, nothing but the sound of the wind. Stepping ashore, he noted that the main gate was off of the palisade, the houses in a sad state of disrepair. The pale winter sun shone on a deserted field; nothing stirred, save the dune grass in the wind . . . .

As they walked silently through what was left of the "City of Raleigh," there was nothing—not even the human bones which might have indicated a massacre. It was as if everyone had been spirited away . . . . Then one of the crew called out. In a large tree, they saw four letters carved in the trunk: C R O A.

What did it mean? Had the colonists gone to join friendly Indians on Croatan Island? The mystery was never solved, and to this day no one knows the fate of those first Americans.

There was no question that the Lost Colony of Roanoke dampened the enthusiasm of the New World adventurers. A generation would pass before one of Raleigh's captains, Bartholomew Gosnold, was finally able to fan a spark of speculative interest into flame. The Virginia Company was formed, and plans for an expedition were formulated. Still, there was a serious obstacle to overcome: the memory of Roanoke had left such a bad taste that investors were exceedingly hard to find. But the manipulators of the early sixteenth century were every bit as adept as those of the late twentieth. The adventure was widely promoted as an admittedly risky opportunity to share in a great work of God, which would play a key role in the salvation of countless thousands of miserable Indians.

The clergy immediately took to the idea; in sermon after sermon they proclaimed the virtues of this noble evangelical outreach, while in their pews, the Partners of the Virginia Company would nod their heads. "Lastly and chiefly," these Partners would piously advise their first colonists, "the way to prosper and achieve good success is to make yourselves all of one mind for the good of your country and your own, and to serve and fear God, the giver of all goodness, for every plantation which our heavenly Father hath not planted shall be rooted out." [2] (This was to prove more nearly prophetic than any of the Partners dreamed!)

Even the new King, James I, seemed to have been taken in by the propaganda. In his preamble to the Company's charter are the words, ". . . propagating of Christian religion to such people as yet live in darkness and miserable ignorance of the true knowledge and worship of God, and may in time bring the infidels and savages, living in these parts, to human civility and to a settled and quiet government." [3]

Of course, when it came to final negotiations with a would-be investor, while it was never openly discussed, both the Partners and their prospective client knew full well that the rumors of gold had not been *dis*proved. And if they should—mind you, just should—happen to locate the fabled Northwest Passage through the New World to the Indies . . . .

Exactly how interested they really were in evangelizing the Indians is borne out by the fact that with their first expedition of some 144 men, they sent only one minister, Robert Hunt. He was hand-picked by the one Partner who was going along, the aristocratic Edward-Maria Wingfield, because he was in no way "touched with the least suspicion of a factious schismatic." [4] Hunt was, in a word, controllable. But Wingfield was in for a surprise. The Reverend Hunt's first sermon aboard ship was directed at calling idle and condescending Gentlemen to repentance: "We are all laborers in the same vineyard. . . ."

It is interesting to note that despite the mention of the fine soil and the English crops that would be planted, there were no women or families aboard. Nor were these men heads of households, bent on preparing homesteads to which they would later bring their families. They were interested in one thing: getting their gold chamber pots and returning to England as quickly as possible! Were these, then, the men through whom God had chosen to build His new Israel? Was this now His time? The future would tell soon enough.

It began telling almost as soon as the three ships weighed anchor in early December of 1606, and dropped down the Thames. Two weeks later they were back again due to foul weather, and for a month they lay anchored off the English coast, riding out one winter storm after another—and steadily consuming the food which was supposed to sustain them until they could plant and harvest crops.

Another telltale sign of the lack of God's grace on the expedition was the squabbles that started breaking out everywhere. After six weeks of storm-tossed seasickness, without even losing sight of their homeland, this was not too surprising. Still there was no logic to these squabbles, and no settling them, either. For there was no clear-cut authority on board, other than Captain Newport's, and he was in charge only until they landed.

After a stormy crossing, Newport leisurely picked his way through the West Indies up the coast of America, and into the protected waters of the Chesapeake Bay. Finally, on May 14, after having sailed some forty miles up the James River, they landed—more than five long months since they had first left England. That night, Newport broke open the sealed box which contained the names of those who would serve on the seven-man Council: himself, Wingfield, Bartholomew Gosnold (who was also along), John Smith, John Ratcliffe, John Martin, and George Kendall. It was like dropping the flag at the start of a race: from that moment on, with the single exception of Gosnold, the members of the Council were in constant contention, each one striving to advance himself by putting down all the others.

The quarreling began as soon as they set foot on land. While the Gentlemen eagerly set about opening oysters in search of pearls, the commoners labored to unload the ships, and the Council began arguing over the site of the settlement. Gosnold was in favor of finding high ground with fresh water and good drainage—open land that would be easier to clear and, if need be, defend.

But to the others, right where they stood seemed fine to them. They were on a small peninsula, which was connected to the mainland by a narrow sandy neck. Though it was heavily wooded and had no fresh water, which meant that they would have to drink the murky, slow-moving river water, it did have the advantage of such a drop-off on the down-river side that a deep-draft vessel could tie up right at the shore.

Besides which, Jamestown in early May, with its verdant growth and warm gentle breezes, is almost idyllic. So seductive are these pleasant surroundings, that coupled with their own weariness and logical reasons for staying put, the Council chose to ignore the wise advice of Gosnold. This was to be the first of many choices for the easier way—the seemingly quick and painless solution which was to become the pattern of the colony's decision making for years thereafter.

For a while, the chill of the still-frosty nights, even though it claimed the lives of some men who had contracted tropical fever in the Bahamas, worked to the settlement's advantage in keeping down the mosquitoes. But as summer came on, and the heat and humidity grew steadily more oppressive, the true face of Jamestown began to emerge. The peninsula was a low and perpetually damp place, surrounded by marshlands which fairly exuded pestilence—swamp fever (malaria), and other ills. By midsummer the colonists were in such a woeful condition that scarcely five of their number were fit enough to man the palisade.

Privation often draws men closer together in spirit. Here, the opposite proved to be true. Fully half the settlers were Gentlemen, whose code of conduct forbade them to do any physical labor.[5] To chop or dig was for them unthinkable. Even to consider doing so was to betray the code on which they based their lives. They would rather die—and so, many did.

For another thing, they had the example of their own Council. With the exception of Gosnold, who truly seemed to be more concerned for others than for himself, they became so engrossed in "garboil" as John Smith so aptly dubbed it, that they had time for little else. Certainly there was not even a semblance of listening to or considering one another.

All of a sudden, after only a week, Newport left and took with him forty of the most able-bodied men to discover the Northwest Passage—thus missing the near massacre. One of the settlers had accused one of the local Perspahegh Indians of thievery, and in the ensuing altercation, the English had run for their guns. The Indians disappeared, but a few days later they ambushed the settlers outside the palisade, killing one and wounding a fifth of them, before the shipboard cannon frightened them off. And thus was established another pattern that would continue in Virginia long after other colonies had learned to live side by side with the Indians in peace.[6] As the strokes of "bad luck" mounted, it is surprising that it did not occur to any of them that God was withholding His blessing from the endeavor.

During all the garboil and confusion, the Reverend Hunt performed the duties of his chaplaincy to the best of his ability. There were mandatory services every Sunday, at first under an awning made of an old sail, with a plank nailed between two trees serving as the altar. But without the support of the Council (who did not share Hunt's conviction about the necessity of putting their total reliance on God), his efforts were largely frustrated. Particularly trying was the attitude of the Gentlemen who loftily resented Hunt's calling upon them to give up their arrogance and join with the rest of them in working at their common task. A typical Sunday morning might see these Gentlemen assuming their "rightful" seats in the front rows, coming in a trifle late just to emphasize their status, and whispering among themselves or looking about in boredom during the sermon for the same reason. As Hunt prepared to celebrate the Holy Eucharist, one wonders if any Gentleman felt a twinge of conscience at the recital of the Prayer of Humble Access: "We do not presume to come to this thy Table, O Merciful Lord, trusting in our own righteousness, but in thy manifold and great mercies . . . ."[7]

Indirectly, however, Hunt did exert considerable influence. When not involved in priestly functions, he did more than his share of the heavy physical work, hoping in vain to influence the other Gentlemen by his example. He personally took charge of the building of Jamestown's first grist mill for the grinding of corn. And since no one else was willing to assume responsibility for the sick, he did so, and this soon became a full-time occupation. He would clean them when they were too sick to clean themselves, make sure that they got their fair share of whatever meager rations were their lot, bring them water when they thirsted, and in general, fulfilled the Lord's exhortation, "Inasmuch as ye have done it unto one of the least of these my brethren, ye have done it unto me" (Matthew 25:40 KJV).

Most of all, he would hear their confessions and pray with them as the end drew near, as it almost inevitably did when someone came down with "the fever" or "the bloody flux" (which may have been typhoid, from shallow wells too close to their waste disposal area). Sometimes only great suffering and the prospect of imminent death will suffice to turn a person to the God whom he has habitually ignored. Thus, in the Virginia Colony, many who had never thought of entering into a saving relationship with Christ, found their way into eternal life during their last few moments through the compassionate ministry of Robert Hunt.

The veteran explorer Gosnold died that summer, a victim of the fever, and without his steadying influence, the Council's conflicts boiled over. Two of its remaining members were arrested by the other two (Newport had long since departed with samples of promising ore, and Smith was off exploring)—Kendall for divisiveness(!) and Wingfield, of all people, for stealing food from the common store. The two prisoners were confined aboard the remaining sloop—and nearly succeeded in stealing it and making good their escape. For this, Kendall was put up against the palisade and shot; Wingfield, because of his connections back home, was spared and held to be shipped back to England for trial.

But as bad as the situation was at Jamestown, it soon became worse. With less than two weeks' food left, Smith, who had in the meantime returned, and nine others went trading for corn. The trading soon became raiding, because Smith was short on patience and seemed to prefer drawing his sword to drawing a bargain. Several days up the Chickahominy River, one provocation too many found Smith in more Indian trouble than he had ever dreamed possible. Having killed two Indians in a skirmish, he found himself alone and trapped in a bog. His captors took him before Powhatan, the great sachem of all the tribes in that area.

It was a warm fall afternoon, with the sun filtering through the tall fir trees of the Virginia tidelands. By Smith's own description, Powhatan sat with awesome dignity upon a raised platform at the end of a long, low building made of closely woven branches. Cushioned by embroidered leather pillows and robed in a great coonskin coat, he was attended by several hundred fierce-looking braves, their faces starkly painted, with feathers in their head-bands. Powhatan sat tall and erect, his clear gray eyes belying his sixty-odd years.

Smith, on the other hand, was a cocky swaggerer, who was forever making extravagant boasts and generous promises, only to go back on them the moment it was more convenient to do so. But he also possessed a quick mind and more physical courage than was good for him, and therein lay a paradox so typical of the Virginia Colony. For without a doubt, Smith was by nature the most capable leader of them all. But such was the demand of his insatiable ego that no amount of praise or recognition would ever satisfy it. Thus, he largely employed his perception in belittling others with the most cutting remarks, and as a consequence, for all his ability, he managed to alienate practically everyone who had to work with or under him.

But now Smith had the blood of two of Powhatan's braves on his hands, and for that he was about to pay with his own. In a clearing outside waited two large boulders against which his brains would soon be dashed. But the resourceful captain had a compass in his pocket, and on this "magical" instrument—and his ability to extemporize—hung his life. A natural tale-teller who had learned the Indians' language, Smith now did some of the fastest talking he had ever done. According to his account, he told Powhatan how the "spirit" in the needle always sought the North Star. From that lead-in, he went on to explain that the world was a sphere, that it revolved around the sun, which was also round, and that the earth also turned on its own axis as it revolved around the sun, on top of which the moon revolved around the earth, and *it* was round . . . .

Powhatan must have smiled in spite of himself. But Smith hurried on, explaining that on the other side of the round world were other chiefs—great white chiefs with so many ships that they would fill the Chickahominy all the way to its mouth. One of these ships would soon be coming to find him, captained by the great white father, Newport, the chief of all the sea, who would come looking for him with mighty guns that roared and could knock down trees standing three fields away.

Powhatan, for all his discernment, must have been suitably im-pressed. Or else he decided that anyone who could lie with such imagination was worth saving! He decided to spare Smith's life, and even gave him a gift of corn to take back to his plantation. At this point in later editions of his popular narrative, Smith would here insert a paragraph which was to become famous. The gist of it was that Powhatan was apparently *not* moved to mercy. But he had a daughter who was a particular favorite of his—a twelve-year-old minx named Pocahontas (Little Wanton) who, Smith claimed, had taken quite a fancy to him. She pleaded for his life, and when all entreaties failed, she laid her own head on top of Smith's, which was poised on the bashing rocks, and thus bought his reprieve. In any event, Smith was allowed to return to Jamestown—an act of mercy that Powhatan would live to regret.

Smith's arrival back at the plantation took everyone by joyous surprise, for he had long since been given up for dead. And Powhatan's gift of corn came none too soon. Despite their treatment of the local Indians, the latter had taken pity on them and shared their corn and venison with the starving colony, until the Indians had barely enough left to get through the winter themselves. The corn Smith brought back took the edge off the colonists' hunger, but it also provided an excuse to put off planting crops.

And here was part of the plantation's problem: *nobody* was interested in planting. After their first year—where the only thing that kept them alive was the corn they could buy, beg, or steal from the Indians—one would think that in the spring they would plant as much corn as they possibly could. But they chose the easy way—to eat what was available today and let tomorrow take care of itself. Incredibly, it would be *twenty years* before the Virginia Colony would finally plant a crop large enough to sustain itself.

Newport's much-delayed arrival in February was just in time to save Smith's neck—literally. For Smith himself had returned just as the last two remaining Council members, Martin and Ratcliffe, were casting off in the pinnace (small sailing ship) to sail for England. They insisted that they were going "to fetch more supplies," though Smith doubted that either of them would ever be seen in those parts again. Fast work with a fowling piece and a culverin put a stop to their self-authorized departure, but it also caused them to sentence Smith to death by hanging for "treason against the governing authority." Smith thus joined Wingfield under arrest until Newport set them both free. But of the 144 men that Newport had originally brought over, only 38 remained alive.

Meanwhile, total unreality continued to reign at home in England. In ensuing months all the Virginia sermons waxed more inspiring than ever, like Crakenthorpe at Paul's Cross: "What Glory! What honor to our Sovereign! What comfort to those subjects who shall be the means of furthering so happy a work!" [8]

As these men of God became increasingly enraptured, the Partners of the Company continued to nod approvingly. But they

were in deep trouble. For despite all efforts to intercept or otherwise suppress private letters from Jamestown, word was beginning
to leak out about what was really going on over in Virginia. And so
began America's first great cover-up.

To counteract the increasingly ugly tales of multiple deaths, cha-
otic administration, summary executions, and Indian attacks, the
Company mounted a propaganda barrage of astonishing magnitude. In addition to publishing every flattering sermon which they
could obtain, they rushed Smith's *True Relations* into print, criti-
cisms and all, adding only a hasty preface which asserted that the
hardest part was at last accomplished. The remaining action was
purely "honorable, and the end to the high glory of God, to the
erecting of true religion among Infidels, to the overthrow of superstition and idolatry, to the winning of many thousands of wandering sheep into Christ's fold, who (until) now have strayed in unknown paths of paganism, idolatry and superstition." [9] Even
Newport, who knew the truth, nonetheless obliged the Partners by
describing the wondrous virtues of Virginia in the most glowing
terms.

And so now, to the greed which motivated the colonists was
added the lying and deceit of the Partners. Scarcely could God
bless a venture such as this. Yet backers continued to invest, and
the Company continued to send over more ships—though each
ship was greeted with mixed reactions by the settlers already there.
While they desperately needed even the most rudimentary
supplies, and were hollow-eyed with famine, each ship seemed to
disgorge a great load of sick, weakened, and helpless adventurers.
Half of these would die before they were acclimated, and all of
them would have to be fed from the common stores. For the newcomers never seemed to arrive with more than a few days' rations
of their own. That meant that each time a ship landed, the colony's
already drastically reduced rations would be cut in half again.

But if each new shipload of settlers was a severe shock to Jamestown's central nervous system, imagine what it must have been
like to stand at the rail of one of those ships as it pulled into the lee
of the peninsula. Perhaps you might not have expected a proper
town, but there was no way you could have been prepared for the
little triangular palisade with its collection of rude huts . . . . *This*
was Jamestown? Who were these gaunt, sunken-cheeked scare-
crows wearing rags and holding out bony hands, feebly calling out
for bread . . . . Dear God, they were *Englishmen!*

And so the deep knell of misfortune continued its dismal tolling
for Virginia. That winter of 1608, fire had broken out in Jamestown,

and in minutes the little settlement was reduced to ashes. Gone were all but three houses, and more than half the supplies brought by Newport, plus most of the ammunition, blankets, bedding, and clothes—and even the palisades themselves. Robert Hunt, "that honest, religious, courageous Divine," lost the only earthly possessions that mattered to him—his books, as well as, reported John Smith, "all but the clothes on his back, [but] none did ever hear him repine at his loss." [10] Hunt seemed to be the only man in Virginia willing to "suffer the loss of all things in order to gain Christ." Worst of all, since the fire had come in "the extreme frost," many more lives were lost before new shelter could be erected.

By April, Powhatan's precious gift of corn was long gone, as was the remainder of the food supplies Newport had brought. Once again, the colony at Jamestown was entirely dependent on the generosity of the Indians. As one of them said to the settlers: "We can plant anywhere . . . and we know that you cannot live [without] our harvest, and that relief we bring you." [11] The Indians had no reason or motive for helping the Englishmen, beyond simplest compassion: if they did not, the white men would die like dogs.

Here, then, was a case where God in His mercy could move even heathen hearts. Perhaps He was holding out the slenderest hope that this first sustained English thrust into the New World might yet come under His guidance. Or possibly it was simply that a great many heartfelt prayers were going up in England. Whatever His reasons, God had intervened to keep the colony from being snuffed out altogether—though none, save Hunt, seemed to recognize His hand in it.

Already it was the planting month, and they were still living hand-to-mouth on whatever the Indians could spare. The Indians themselves were planting corn and undoubtedly offered to show them how. But more ships would surely be coming, they thought, and those who might have influenced a decision to plant had enough money so that a lively black market sprang up between them and the sailors aboard Newport's ship. Presumably the sailors were selling food and goods from their own personal possessions, but there was little doubt that it was actually coming from the ship's stores. Thus, some of those on shore were eating well, while others only a few feet away were starving to death!

And besides, all of them, the fat and the thin, had something on their minds which they considered of far more importance than planting corn. The ore samples which Newport had taken back to

England had assayed out to be worthless. In order to ensure that there would be no repetition of such an embarrassing error, the Partners had sent back with him *two* refiners, *two* goldsmiths and a jeweler.

But it is amazing to see the tricks that greed can play on the mind, once the heart has opened the door! And these so-called experts would not be the first or the last to have their professional judgment clouded by the hypnotic spell of the yellow metal. Themselves in line to become immensely wealthy, the Company's experts became convinced that by the most extraordinary coincidence, Jamestown itself actually rested upon a foundation of almost pure gold! From then on, as John Smith put it, ". . . there was no talk, no hope, no work, but dig gold, wash gold, refine gold, load gold." [12] Two weeks later, with his ship's belly full of ore, Newport cast off, warmly anticipating his reception at home as the discoverer of a new El Dorado.

By the early summer of 1608, Jamestown's relationship with the Indians was showing signs of improvement. Still, waging peace required wisdom, tact and goodwill, all woefully absent in Jamestown's leadership.

John Smith was one of those men who is constantly in need of physical challenges, in order to prove that he is as brave as he believes himself to be. As a result, he seemed to delight in any fracas, and was not above stirring one up, if there were not any at hand. Inactivity or prolonged peaceableness weakened a man, he seemed to feel. He craved action and seemed to enjoy cutting down Indians, thinking nothing of killing one for a bushel of corn.

In light of Smith's attitude and conduct, it was a miracle that the settlers were able to obtain any corn at all. For, as modern historian Edmund Morgan points out, "Smith was sure that kindness was wasted on savages . . . that the Spanish had shown the way to deal with the Indians." And Smith himself later wrote that, like the Conquistadors, the Jamestown colonists should have "forced the treacherous and rebellious infidels to do all manner of drudgery work and slavery for them, themselves living like soldiers upon the fruits of their labors." [13]

Given such an attitude, it was perhaps an even greater miracle that the Indians did not simply wipe them out! For Smith, with his indiscriminate slaughter, provoked them all—the Perspahegh, the Pamunkey, the Potomacs, and the Powhatans—and gained but a fraction of what he might have won by peaceful means. Finally, fearing for their lives, the Council forbade John Smith to do any more raiding—a command which he ignored.

Now the sweltering heat of the Jamestown summer settled in. The Parable of the Sower is singularly applicable: "When the sun rose [the seed] was scorched, and since it had no root, it withered away" (Mark 4:6). In the summer of 1608, the frail shoots of life at Jamestown were being scorched, spiritually as well as physically. And since they had no real roots of faith in God, they were truly withering away. From the steaming, fetid swamps all around them emanated a variety of diseases, the river water turned brackish, and almost all the newcomers and many of those more acclimated became deathly ill.

Which raises another Virginia paradox: Why did they not move the site of the settlement, after this second summer made it even more obvious that the soaring death rate was directly related to Jamestown's dismal location? There was even more evidence in the fact that John Smith and his men returned from *their* summer expeditions in excellent health. The fact was, they did consider moving—the suggestion had come up on more than one occasion—but each time it just seemed too much trouble. It was easier to repair than rebuild, and so they stayed and suffered out the summers . . . .

And died. The death rate in Virginia that second year was— incredibly—even higher than the first: out of every ten people who embarked for the New World, nine would die! And this withering mortality rate did *not* abate with the passing of time. (It would be the experience of other colonies that the death rate would stabilize after the first year and rapidly diminish thereafter.) For example, of the 1,200 people who went out to Virginia in 1619, only 200 were left alive by 1620.[14] A year later, according to the census taken in March, 1621, there were 843 settlers in Virginia. The following March, another census revealed that their number had increased by 397. But in the meantime, 1,580 souls had embarked for Jamestown, which meant that in one year, 1,183 had died en route or in Virginia.[15] And if that were not enough, three weeks later, a third of the remaining survivors were suddenly wiped out in the bloodiest massacre ever perpetrated on any American colony, as the Indians took long-awaited revenge.

Why this horrible continuing death rate? There is no logical explanation, except one: year after year they steadfastly refused to trust God—or indeed to include Him in any of their deliberations. Ship after ship arrived, financed by investors who believed that they were participating in the most important evangelical outreach of the age. Only somehow, no one remembered to send any ministers. And the one minister the settlers did have, who was manifesting more of the Spirit of Christ than they were likely to see in their lifetimes, went largely unheeded.

In September, 1608, Newport returned—in disgrace: his load of ore had turned out to be largely the glittering iron pyrites which have given Satan and his henchmen such a laugh over the centuries—"Fool's Gold." Now the Virginia Company had commanded him "not to return without a lump of gold, a certainty of the South Sea [the Pacific], or one of the lost company of Sir Walter Raleigh!" And if the colonists were not able to provide him with some sort of valuable cargo, they concluded ominously, "they were like to remain as banished men." [16]

With that cheery news, Newport off-loaded some seventy more newcomers, thus doubling the colony's population, with no more than a week's additional food supplies. The few survivors who had managed to come through both summers must have felt "sighs too deep for uttering." They had totally relied on Newport, and he had totally let them down, bringing no victuals, no tools, no blankets, no shoes. Nothing.

By December, 1608, their food supply was once again back to its normal state—desperately critical. And once again Smith had his standard solution: the sword. Only this time his ambition was considerably larger than a surprise attack on a nearby Indian village (not that there were any left, for they had all decamped out of his reach). He was going for Powhatan himself, either to take him for ransom or else kill him and plunder the tribal seat. His justification: Powhatan was trying to starve Jamestown! As if the Indians were under any obligation to feed these white men who made no effort whatever to feed themselves, and who thought nothing of falling upon an Indian village and slaughtering men, women, and children—less than a week after swearing a pact of eternal friendship with them!

But judging from the way he handled Smith, as the latter came to him all smiles (and looking for the right opening), Powhatan may have been the wisest ruler on either side of the Atlantic. "Captain Smith," he said, "having seen the death of all my people thrice, and not anyone living of those three generations but myself, I know the difference between peace and war better than any in my country . . . . Think you I am so simple as not to know it is better to eat good meat, lie well, and sleep quietly with my women and children, laugh and be merry with you, have copper, hatchets or what I want, being your friend, than be forced to fly from all, lie cold in the woods, feed upon acorns, roots, and such trash?"

But as historian George Willison points out, all this was but "subtle discourse" to Smith. Powhatan continued: "Let this, therefore, assure you of our love, and every year our friendly trade shall furnish you with corn—and now, also, if you would come in friendly manner and not thus, with your guns and swords as if to invade your foes . . . if you intend to be friendly as you say, send hence your arms that I may believe you, for you see the love I bear you doth cause me thus nakedly to forget myself."

Smith promised that he and his bodyguard of eight would come ashore from the pinnace the next day, unarmed. In the meantime, he arranged for a secret signal, at which his main force would suddenly swarm ashore and take Powhatan. But the canny chief was on to him, and slipped away just as he attempted to spring his trap. Then it was all Smith and his men could do to extricate themselves from the midst of several hundred thoroughly aroused warriors. Quickly dropping downriver, he reverted to his old tactics of taking smaller groups by surprise.

Was it chance that guided the first settlers to Powhatan's domain on Chesapeake Bay? The East Coast was populated by some of the most hostile Indian tribes in all America. We have already seen the ferocity of the Seminoles, who kept the Spanish from any significant colonization of Florida. And inland to the north, the diabolical Iroquois precluded any thought of French or English settlement for many years. On Massachusetts Bay, the Massachusetts Indians were sufficiently warlike to discourage all but the most foolhardy, and south of them, the Narragansetts were equally fearsome. Seen from this vantage point, the entire East Coast of America seemed fairly to bristle with arrows and tomahawks. Any one of these tribes would have annihilated the little colony without any provocation whatever, let alone the outrages that Smith was routinely perpetrating.

Or was it the hand of a merciful God that had led them to perhaps the only place on the Atlantic seaboard at that particular time where there was any real possibility of their putting down roots? Powhatan may have been the only chief on the continent who would have put up with Smith's behavior, let alone shared his people's precious corn.

As we walked through the bleak and crumbled ruins of what was once the first English settlement in America, we seemed to sense the despair of those who had starved and died there without hope. There was a barren and desolate feeling to the wild grass which caused us to shiver, despite the balmy temperatures and the late afternoon sun. At the same time we were forcefully reminded that the *only* difference between us and the Jamestown colonists was, perhaps, a little more reliance on the grace of God—except for that, there go we ourselves . . . .

April, 1609—the planting month had come again. Smith, now the sole surviving member of the Council, did endeavor to get a partial crop of corn in the ground, though some 279 bushels of plundered corn were still in the common storehouse, well-casked and waiting. As it happened, they had need of it just at that time, and opened the first cask—only to find that it had gone rotten and was half-consumed by the thousands of rats that had long plagued them. Staring down at the putrid mess inside the cask, they could not at first assess the gravity of their situation. Then it sank in: *They had nothing to eat at all!*

Jamestown was immediately abandoned. Half the company went down to the oyster banks at the mouth of the river to live on shellfish. Others went up the river, to attempt to live on acorns and berries. Still others went down to Point Comfort to fish, though in six weeks they typically could not agree once on where to cast their nets—*and so never did.* A number of colonists simply ran away to Powhatan, who let them stay, as long as they worked for their food. Of those who did not desert to the Indians, many managed to stay alive by stealing from each other—implements, kettles, and the like, even guns—and trading them to the Indians for a capful of corn.

But more than half of their dwindling number died, including "good Mr. Hunt." His death meant that they were bereft of perhaps the only man of prayer among them, their one source of spiritual solace. And he was sorely missed.

The sentiments of those he left behind are now commemorated on Robert Hunt's memorial:

He was an honest, religious and courageous Divine; he preferred the service of God to every thought of ease at home. He endured every privation, yet none ever heard him repine. During his life, our factions were oft healed and our greatest extremities so comforted that they seemed easy in comparison with what we endured after his memorable death. We all received from him the Holy Communion together as a pledge of reconciliation, for we all loved him for his exceeding goodness. He planted the first Protestant church in America, and laid down his life in the foundation of Virginia.

Just when it became obvious that the eighty haggard survivors could last no more than a few days at most, a small ship arrived, well-provisioned, under the command of Samuel Argall. Once again, they were reprieved—for the moment.

Back in England, the cover-up was going badly. Too many people knew the truth, and not even sermons like the obliging Richard Crashaw's could turn back the tide: "Let us then believe no tales, regard no slanders . . . fear no shadows, care for no oppositions, respect no losses that may befall, nor be daunted with any discouragements whatsoever . . . ." [17]
The Company's problem was that anyone who had actually been to Virginia, and then heard or read words like Crashaw's, was bound to be furious. (It struck us that it would be like a survivor of Auschwitz hearing someone, who had no concept of a concentration camp, describe it as a tough but rewarding experience.) And apparently enough people got sufficiently angry to start telling the whole truth about it.
So the Company needed a scapegoat—fast. It did not have far to look: suddenly, everything that had gone wrong was John Smith's fault. Smith would have to be sacrificed for the sake of the Company's survival. And just in case he might balk at this, he was not to be informed until it was too late for him to make a countermove.
The Company's new plan called for the liquidation of the Council, to be replaced by a single Governor. Accordingly, a new and enlarged charter was acquired from the King, appointing Thomas Gates as Governor and George Somers as his Admiral and second-in-command. For once, the Partners had made two good selections: both men had demonstrated skilled leadership in fighting for the Dutch against Spain in the Netherlands War. And both were proven administrators.
They set out with their new charter in May of 1609, with Newport as Vice-Admiral, in the flagship *Sea Venture*. Their fleet numbered nine ships, woefully overcrowded with some five hundred passengers, including the first women and children. And with typical Company "luck," they sailed headlong into a hurricane in the area now known as the Bermuda Triangle. The fleet was scattered; one ship went down, one turned back. The flagship itself, after three days of incessant storm, had ten feet of sea water in her hold and her pumps were giving out. Suddenly, on the night of August 6, there was a spectacular display of St. Elmo's fire in the rigging of the foundering ship.[18] And then, out of the darkness loomed the darker silhouette of the land known as Devil's Island. ("Hell is empty, and all the devils are here!" wrote Shakespeare of the "still-vexed Bermoothes" in *The Tempest*, the play which was

inspired by this episode.) In truth, Bermuda was "supposed to be enchanted and inhabited with witches and devils," wrote Somers, "[and] so wondrous dangerous of rocks" that none could approach it without "unspeakable hazard of shipwreck." [19]

Miraculously, the *Sea Venture* was not smashed to pieces on the barrier reef, but found itself wedged between two large coral formations—with the tide going out! The ship was unloaded with comparative ease, and dismantled. Thus, under Gates and Somers, all 150 men on board were forced by an "act of God" to spend an exceedingly pleasant nine-month interlude on a lush, uninhabited island that seemed more like paradise than hell.

The standing orders of the rest of the fleet had been quite specific: in the event that they were separated by storm, all were to rendezvous at Bermuda. Had they been obedient, passengers and crew alike would have eventually gone on to Virginia strong, fit and well rested, recovered from the plaguelike disease that had ravaged two of the ships, and with cargo holds full of fresh victuals to replace those ruined by the hurricane. And this very likely was God's intent.

But, to a man, the other captains chose the easier way; instead of finding their way back to Bermuda, they continued westward and limped up or down the coast, to Jamestown.

The little colony reeled and nearly died under the impact of four hundred sick, helpless, starving passengers. Its meager life-support system was wiped out, as the ravenous newcomers swept through the new cornfields, stripping the stalks bare of the green ears that were just beginning to appear. That fall of 1609, despair would kill as many as disease.

On learning that he had been relieved of command, but that his replacement was presumed lost at sea, Smith refused to acknowledge that he was no longer in charge. Still, a wound to his leg, which required medical attention, caused him to agree to sail with one of the ships bound for England. Several men were sent along to bear charges against him, but there is no record of the Company's starting proceedings against him. They were undoubtedly afraid of what he might say or do. But by this time, John Smith was scarcely their worst problem. For with the return of these ships to England, there were now several crews at large who had seen Virginia, and who knew the truth.

Close to panic, the Company made a desperate decision: as sincerely as possible, they would publicly declare their original intent and publish their version of what had happened at the colony.

Accordingly, they hurriedly drafted *A True and Sincere Declaration,* and rushed it into print.

> [Our] principal and main ends . . . were first to preach and baptize into Christian religion, and by propagation of the Gospel, to recover out of the arms of the Devil, a number of poor and miserable souls, wrapt up unto death in almost invincible ignorance; to endeavor the fulfilling and accomplishment of the number of the elect which shall be gathered from out all corners of the earth; and to add our mite to the treasury of Heaven . . . .[20]

In light of what had actually taken place in Virginia, it is impossible to measure such hypocrisy.

But the time was soon to come, as Christ said, when that which had been whispered in darkness would be shouted from the rooftops. John Smith was not about to sit meekly by, while his reputation was pilloried for the sake of salvaging the Company's image. So, as so many would do after him, he decided to write a book that would tell what *really* happened.

In 1612, his *Description of Virginia* created a sensation: "We did admire how it was possible such wise men could so torment themselves and us with strange absurdities and impossibilities, making Religion their color, when all their aim was nothing but present profit, as most plainly appeared by sending us so many refiners, goldsmiths, jewelers, lapidaries, stone-cutters . . . so doting on mines of gold and the South Sea, that all the world could not have devised better courses to bring us to ruin than they did themselves." [21]

Within two years, the Company would be reduced to raising funds by public lottery and a direct-mail campaign to mayors of small rural towns, urging them to invest from their municipal treasuries.

As the afternoons grew shorter and colder that fall of 1609, the foragers, root-grubbers, and mussel-diggers straggled back into Jamestown. There was nowhere else to go. At least at Jamestown there was shelter. And with the first frost, the mosquitoes were no more, and the settlers were free from the deadly pestilence of the surrounding swamps. Except for the ever-present dampness and the bad water, Jamestown in the winter was not that much worse than other places. In fact, on a day when the wan sun turned the brown field grass to gold and softened the shadows of the looming swamp forest, the handful who could still remember were reminded of the bright promise of the warm spring day in May on which they first arrived, full of hope and ready to conquer the New World.

The thought must have brought tears to several eyes. For the clothes of the conquerors were in tatters; some were barefoot, and others were sick and had the look of death about them. A year ago they might take grim solace at that thought: it would mean fewer mouths to feed and more food for the rest. But it made no difference anymore, because now there was no food at all.

And worst of all, there was no Robert Hunt any more, to comfort them or bring Christian solace. Now the prayer book was read over the new graves in a most perfunctory manner—if anybody bothered at all.

Thus did the Virginia Colony enter the dark night of its soul—the time that would soon be known as "the starving time." All the livestock had been consumed—the hogs, sheep, goats, and a few horses (those that had come over on the last ships)—every bit, even the hides themselves. Next went the dogs and cats, and the rats that had once thrived on their corn, and any field mice they could find, or little snakes. But the hunger continued unabated and now became ravenous. They dug up the roots of trees and bushes and gnawed on them, and every bit of shoe leather on the plantation—every book cover, every leather hinge or strap or fitting was boiled and eaten. The colonists grew so weak that many, lacking the strength to move, froze to death in their beds. And still, the hunger raged on.

Here, the nicer histories leave off, for a number of the settlers who were still alive began digging up the fresher corpses. These they cut up into stew meat and boiled. There is only a single (recorded) instance of one person nudging another into the stew-meat stage a little more quickly. This is the case of the man who had become "unhinged" and killed his wife, salted her down, and had already begun to partake of her, when he was discovered.[22] He was summarily executed.

Deliverance finally came in early May of 1610—and was labeled as such. It came in the form of the good ship *Deliverance*, and her sister ship *Patience*, both miraculously built from local wood (and the fittings of the *Sea Venture*) on the island of Bermuda by Gates and Somers and their resourceful crew. They plied their way up the James, and were stunned to be met by sixty shambling stick figures, moaning, "We are starved! We are starved!" Was this all that was left of the four hundred newcomers and eighty settlers who had been there the previous August? Gates and Somers were so horrified that they decided to abandon Jamestown immediately and make a run for home, even though they did not have enough victuals for the voyage. They would take the chance of being able to reprovision from a fishing ship at the Grand Banks. It was a risky business in such small ships at that time of year, with only enough supplies to get them a third of the way, but anything was better than staying in Jamestown.

A ragged cheer went up at the announcement, and it was all Gates could do to keep the survivors from putting the torch to Jamestown as a parting gesture. They were just dropping down to Point Comfort to pick up a few stragglers there, when the sails of a large and very fine ship appeared. This was Lord De La Warr, who, after word had reached England that Gates and Somers had been reported lost at sea, was persuaded to become Governor. De La Warr was in charge now, and at his command everyone turned about and headed back to the abandoned settlement. As soon as he set foot on that desolate, hated piece of land, he knelt and gave thanks to God for bringing them safely there and causing them to arrive in time to save all lives. He then had his commission read aloud to all present and proceeded to the church, where he had Richard Buck, Gates's chaplain, deliver a sermon.

The extraordinary coincidence of timing was counted by the whole world as an act of Divine Providence. "If God had not sent Sir Thomas Gates from the Bermudas," exclaimed William Crashaw, "within four days they had all been famished. If God had not directed the heart of that worthy Knight to save the fort from fire . . . If they had set sail sooner . . . *Brachium Domini:* this was the arm of the Lord of Hosts!" [23]

The Company, always quick to capitalize on any opportunity, declared: "It is the arm of the Lord of Hosts, who would have his people pass the Red Sea and the wilderness, and then possess the land of Canaan." This was from their most recent tract, a *True Declaration,* published some time after *A True and Sincere Declaration* had been thoroughly discredited.[24]

Clearly, God *had* moved to save Virginia when men had abandoned her. And though more ministers were beginning to draw the analogy of a new Promised Land, none had quite the temerity to suggest that the mixed bag of convicts, down-at-the-heels Gentlemen, professional soldiers without a war, and slum orphans (for the City Fathers in London had hit upon a unique solution for doing something about the swarming bands of street urchins) were a new

Chosen People. Certainly they did not regard themselves as such—chosen for hell on earth would have been how they would put it.

De La Warr endured it for about a year before he, and the Gentlemen cronies he had brought with him, tired of the sport of "colonizing" and returned to England. His successor, a tough, hardnosed, Netherlands War captain named Sir Thomas Dale, enforced extreme martial discipline, taking the sternest possible measures: it was now a hanging offense to be heard speaking against authority, or to be absent three times without an excuse from the twice-daily worship services. For lesser(!) offenses, Dale and his sergeants-at-arms carried *bastinados,* short sticks with which they administered corporal punishment as it was needed. Gradually order began to emerge out of chaos.

Conditions improved slowly, but then a surprising and delightful sequence of events occurred which indicated that God might at last be bestowing a modicum of grace upon the misfortune-dogged Virginia Colony. These events, however, started off anything but auspiciously: Pocahontas was kidnapped and held for ransom. Powhatan paid the bushels of corn stipulated, but Dale did not release the chief's daughter. Demanding more corn (which was not paid), he finally took a war party to confront Powhatan and discuss a treaty with him in person. As the two groups (for Powhatan had well over a hundred warriors at his back) faced each other, anything but peace seemed to be in the offing.

In the meantime, Dale had taken a personal interest in the immortal soul of the flashing-eyed eighteen-year-old, who had grown into an extremely alluring Indian maiden. He believed that he had persuaded her to embrace the Christian faith. But apparently Dale was not the only one mightily concerned for her spiritual well-being. A young Gentleman named John Rolfe had become hopelessly enamored of her, to such an extent that marriage seemed the only honorable solution to his dilemma. Accordingly, he sent Dale an extraordinary letter. The letter arrived in the middle of Dale's negotiations with Powhatan, and must have brought forth a reaction of stunned amazement from Dale. For Rolfe was asking Dale's permission to marry Pocahontas!

My chiefest intent and purpose be . . . to strive with all my power of body and mind in the undertaking of so mighty a matter—in no way led (so far forth as man's weakness may permit) with the unbridled desire of carnal affection, but striving for the good of this plantation, for the honor of our country, for the glory of God and Jesus Christ of an unbelieving creature, namely Pocahontas, to whom my hearty and best thoughts are, and have for a long time been so entangled and enthralled in so delicate a labyrinth . . . But Almighty God, who never faileth His who truly invoke His Holy Name, hath opened the gate . . . .[25]

The effect of the letter was like a sunburst through an ominously clouded sky. Both Dale and Powhatan were bemused by the prospect, and what had threatened to become a showdown, now brightened like blossoming wildflowers. Here was a most engaging sort of Divine Providence at work! There was going to be a wedding, the first between a white and an Indian, and both sides seemed eminently pleased at the prospect. Powhatan declined to attend in person (he did not trust the white man *that* far), but he sent a brother to give the bride away, and a number of his braves as a sort of honor guard.

It was a glorious, feasting affair—the first time that whites and Indians had been able to relax in each other's presence for several years. And, thanks to Powhatan's generosity, it was also the first time the settlers had been truly well fed in almost as long. It boded well. Buck performed the ceremony, and soon after John Rolfe and Pocahontas, now called by her Christian name, Rebecca, went to England at the request of the Virginia Company. (The Partners were delighted at the newfound peace between settlers and Indians—and ready to exploit it at home for any favorable publicity it might have.) Rebecca was the belle of London Society; even the ruling dowagers and dames were taken with her, and found her innocence perfectly charming.

Rebecca was taken with London, too, having no desire to return to Virginia. She had to be strongly persuaded to do so "for the good of the Company," because she was the only guarantee of continuing peace with the Indians. But as it turned out, she never did return, for she contracted pneumonia and died shortly before her scheduled departure. Grief-stricken, Rolfe returned to Virginia alone, to continue his experiments with what was soon to become the first cash crop in the New World: tobacco.

It is ironic—and yet somehow typical—that in the end Virginia would be saved by the addictive weed that would one day be a problem to so many. Yet even her salvation was to be a long, laborious process; she would continue to struggle along on the brink of disaster for years to come. Certainly any real trust in God on the part of the settlers had little to do with her final emergence: by 1622, with more than twelve hundred settlers in ten widely scattered plantations, there were in Virginia exactly three ordained ministers! In fact, the contrast between the worldly and the spiritual was never more candidly spelled out than in a future exchange between James Blair, president-elect of the soon-to-be-founded College of William and Mary, and England's Attorney General Edward Seymour, to whom he had to apply for the drawing up of the charter granted by Their Majesties. Seymour thought the college was a waste of time and good money and said so in no uncertain terms, whereupon Blair pointed out that the colonists in Virginia had souls that needed to be saved.

"Souls?" replied Seymour. *"Damn your souls! Make tobacco!"* [26] And that summed up the prevailing attitude of many toward Virginia.

Tobacco may have been the means, but God was the Agent who preserved Virginia, and who, in spite of everything, gave her yet another chance. In July of 1619, it began to look as if she might finally be getting off to a better start. Every one of the non-indentured men of the colony was given at least one hundred acres of his own, which added much incentive to planting and working.

The Company itself had finally collapsed and sold out its interest to ten Adventurers. They, in turn, established a system of independent rule, whereby two representatives (Burgesses) from each of the ten major plantations would meet to make laws and discuss mutual problems. It was a good beginning. In fact, it was more than just a new beginning for Virginia; it was the first representative assembly in North America, more than a century and a half before America would go to war to secure this privilege.

But Virginia was still Virginia. Of all the places they could have chosen to meet in the middle of summer, where did they choose? Jamestown! Within a week, two of the Burgesses had died and the other eighteen were sick.

Why had so much gone so wrong in Virginia, when at least the publicly stated motives back in England had been so right? (And so convincing that the Partners themselves had begun to believe them?) The answer is, that in an age and country where practically all the leaders acknowledged God's existence and thereby considered themselves good Christian gentlemen and ladies, hardly anyone was actually living the life Christ calls us to in His Gospel. Even among the ministers, who were extolling the need for the thrust of Christianity into heathen lands, hardly any were actually prepared to go themselves.

What happened at Jamestown is a horror that we today would like to turn away from—but if we do, we will lose the whole point.

And all of the lives so tragically lost will have gone for nothing. The point is that Jamestown was *not* an isolated instance, a unique set of circumstances unlikely ever to happen again, involving people of weaker than normal character. The people who set sail with such high hopes and ambitions to settle in the New World, were exactly like us. And the world they left behind was similar to America today, a world of noble sentiments—and watered-down commitments; a society of well-intentioned "Christians"—who had never heard of surrendering their wills to Christ.

The settlement of Jamestown was undertaken without Christ. But the next settlers to cross the Atlantic knew better than to attempt it without Him. They knew that they had no choice but to put *all* their trust in Him . . . .

5

To the Promised Land

Descending into the gloomy interior of the *Mayflower II*, the replica of the Pilgrims' ship, we were shocked at the closeness of the quarters. One hundred and two Pilgrims had been crammed into a space about equal to that of a volleyball court. Compound that misery by the lack of light and fresh air (all hatches had to be battened down because of the stormy weather). Add to it a diet of dried pork, dried peas, and dried fish, and the stench of an ever-fouler bilge, and multiply it all by sixty-six days at sea . . . .

As we emerged topside, Peter shook his head. "You know, they accepted all that without complaining. It was part of what they were willing to endure to follow God's will." He paused. "Like the exile in Holland and their indenture in the New World . . . ."

Later that afternoon, as we climbed the dirt road that is the main street of the reconstruction of "Plimoth" Plantation, we were again struck by the enormous price these people had paid—*cheerfully*. It had been one thing to see the magnificence of the poured-out commitments of the missionaries. But these Jesuit, Dominican, and Franciscan martyrs seemed almost destined for sainthood from the moment of conversion. By contrast, the Pilgrims were ordinary Christian families—not unlike our own.

In comparison to them, our commitment to Christ seemed almost insignificant. We began to be convicted of this, not by what the Pilgrims preached or wrote, but by the example of the lives they lived. It was a humble example. They considered themselves only marginally successful, and had no remote awareness of the spiritual impact that their community would have—on the Puritans who came behind them—on the founding of a Christian nation—and on those in subsequent ages who would be inspired by their example.

We had been challenged by a question Peter Gomes had put to us that day in his office: If the Massachusetts Bay Colony, in and around Boston, was directly responsible for most of the constitutional and institutional foundations of this country, why do so many more Americans prefer to visit Plymouth? Why does this comparative handful of Pilgrims, who never matched the extraordinary record of their cousins a few miles to the north, and were eventually absorbed by them, move the hearts of Americans on such deep levels? Why is a visit to Plimoth Plantation more like a pilgrimage than a sightseeing tour?

As we drove away from Plymouth that afternoon, we felt we were beginning to see the answer.

On a warm, hazy July morning in 1620, three barges could be seen gliding along a Dutch canal, en route from Leyden to the seaport of Delftshaven. In the distance, across the broad, low fields, a large stone windmill basked in the early morning sun, its huge white sails barely turning. It was a morning for tarrying, for taking in the fragrance of new-mown hay, and the muted chirping of field crickets.

But there could be no tarrying for the congregation on these barges. For a third of them, it was the beginning of a much longer voyage—a voyage from which there would be no return.

One of these was William Bradford, a young, strong, enthusiastic English farmer who was counted among their "chief men." He had been with their pastor, John Robinson, from the very beginning in Yorkshire, fourteen years before. Barely sixteen then, Bradford was an orphan being reared by his uncle in the yeoman tradition of his family. If, on the barge that morning in 1620, Bradford recalled those early years, it might have been with a sense of wonder. So much had passed into history since then . . . . He would write it all down one day, many years hence . . . .

It is well-known unto the Godly and judicious, how ever since the first breaking out of the Light of the Gospel in our honorable nation of England . . . what wars and oppositions ever since, Satan hath raised, maintained and continued against the saints [i.e., the believers who were striving to yield their whole lives to Christ] . . . Sometimes by bloody death and cruel torments, otherwise imprisonments, banishments and other hard usages, as being loathe [that his] kingdom should go down, the truth prevail, and the churches of God revert to their ancient purity and recover their primitive order, liberty and beauty.[1]

The churches to which Bradford referred were those of the Church of England, presided over by the House of Bishops. The church hierarchy had grown increasingly alarmed at the growth of two movements of "fanatics." The first and much larger group claimed to be dedicated to "purifying the Church from within," which made them suspect from the start to the Bishops, who saw nothing which needed purifying. These "Puritans," as they were sarcastically dubbed (and which epithet they eventually took for their own) did, however, at least continue to acknowledge canonical authority. Thus they could easily be kept from positions of responsibility, and otherwise ignored.

There was another element, however, which the Bishops considered more dangerous. These were radicals who held that the Church of England was already corrupted beyond any possibility of purification. Moreover, they believed that the Church could only be under the headship of Jesus Christ, and hence no person, not even the Queen, could take the title "Head of the Church." They chose to separate themselves from the Church, and conduct their own worship. And, given their way, these "Separatists" would reduce worship to primitive preaching, teaching, singing, and free praying, which would do away with sixteen centuries of established liturgical tradition.

At present, there were probably less than a thousand of this sect, but clearly, if this sort of thing were tolerated, other "believers"—who spoke enthusiastically of experiencing a personal encounter with Christ—might take it in their heads to follow their lead. Before long, you would have little churches of fanatics being raised up everywhere—with no semblance of order or conformity (and totally out of the control of the Bishops!).

Elizabeth had not really given the Bishops the free hand which they wanted to suppress this contagion before it became an epidemic. She seemed to feel that a few executions for heresy were sufficient to hold the movement in check. But now that the vain, petty (and manipulable) James I was on the throne, the Bishops had their way.

Now the Separatists were hounded, bullied, forced to pay assessments to the Church of England, clapped into prison on trumped-up charges, and driven underground. They met in private homes, to which they came at staggered intervals and by different routes, because they were constantly being spied upon. In the little Midlands town of Scrooby, persecution finally reached the point where the congregation to which Bradford belonged elected to follow those other Separatists who had already sought religious asylum in Holland.

Thus they came to Leyden, where they were forged together by adversity. For, as near-penniless foreign immigrants, they qualified for only the most menial labor, and had to work terribly hard just to subsist. Bradford wrote that before coming, they had, "as the Lord's free people, joined themselves by a covenant of the Lord into a church estate, in the fellowship of the Gospel, to walk in all His ways made known . . . unto them, according to their best endeavors, whatsoever it should cost them, the Lord assisting them." [2] It cost them dearly. By 1619, after nearly a dozen years of penurious toil, they finally decided that they had to "remove."

Bradford's reasons, stated briefly: (1) Their life (though they never complained of it) was so hard that almost no others were coming from England to join them—even after the King's edict of 1618, which decreed that all Puritans not willing to conform to ecclesiastical authority *had* to leave the country. (2) Their life was aging them prematurely [everyone old enough to hold a job worked twelve to fifteen hours a day], and was so debilitating them that, should the time come when they would have to move again, they might not physically be able to do so. (3) Their children were also being worn down, and many were being drawn away by the lures of the world around them. (4) They had cherished a "great hope and inward zeal" of at least playing a part, if only as a stepping stone for others, in the carrying forth of the Light of Christ to remote parts of the world.

Increasingly, the Separatists came to believe that America was the place to which God intended them to go, despite the horrors of Virginia's "starving time," which had reached their ears, and the well-known savagery of the Indians. While they were thinking on these things, and considering that the death rate at Jamestown was *still* well over 50 percent, an insidious counterproposal was raised. Might there not be an easier way? Why not go south, to Guiana on the coast of South America, which Walter Raleigh had so warmly described, and where the English already had a foothold? It was "rich, fruitful and blessed with a perpetual spring, and flourishing greens, where vigorous nature brought forth all things in abundance and plenty without any great labour or art of man." [3]

Then, too, Raleigh had mentioned an abundance of gold mines . . . . [4]

Thus does Satan ever seek to divide and sow dissension among the Christians he so hates. But the Leydenites were mature enough

Christians to know better than to reason things out with their intellects. The crucial question in all of this was, *what was God's will?* Where did *He* want to send them? From hard experience, they had learned that as long as they were in the center of His will, it did not matter where they were physically located.

After they thus prayed and entrusted the entire undertaking into His hands, peace returned—and with it some considerations that had hitherto escaped them: Guiana was close to the Spanish Main, and the jealous Spaniards had already wiped out the French Huguenots. And if there *were* gold there, that would only lure the Spanish more quickly. Also, the tropical climate engendered diseases which had already decimated the human cargoes of dozens of ships passing through the Bahamas . . . .

It became increasingly clear that God wanted them to go to America. Bradford summed up their strengthening resolve:

> It was answered that all great and honorable actions are accompanied with great difficulties, and must be enterprised and overcome with answerable courages. It was granted that the dangers were great, but not desperate, and the difficulties were many, but not invincible . . . . and all of them, through the help of God, by fortitude and patience, might either be borne or overcome . . . [But] their condition was not ordinary. Their ends were good and honorable, their calling lawful and urgent, and therefore they might expect the blessing of God in their proceeding; yea, though they should lose their lives in this action, yet they might have comfort in the same, and their endeavors would be honorable.[5]

As the Leydenites worked out *where* they were going, their elected pastor John Robinson was praying for a deeper revelation of *why* they were going. Did God have a special purpose for them? To Robinson and Elder William Brewster and a few of the others, that purpose was beginning to come clear. As Robinson would shortly write, he perceived that God was calling them to a new Jerusalem, to build His temple anew—with themselves as its stones: "Now as the people of God in old time were called out of Babylon civil, the place of their bodily bondage, and were to come to Jerusalem, and there to build the Lord's temple, or tabernacle . . . so are the people of God now to go out of Babylon spiritual to Jerusalem . . . and to build themselves as lively stones into a spiritual house, or temple, for the Lord to dwell in . . . ."[6]

It seemed that God had indeed chosen them, and was now in the process of preparing them to become His temple in America. Be it resolved then, that they were going, that they were already being led in a path that had been walked by another Chosen People, ". . . for we are," wrote Robinson, "the sons and daughters of Abraham by faith."

But getting to America was another question. Just the cost of transporting them over would be enormous, to say nothing of the expense of sufficient food supplies to last them until they could grow and harvest a crop. And in addition to that, they would need a pinnace with which to go fishing or trading. (The French had been successful in building up a fur trade in the far north, and it occurred to the Leydenites that they might be able to do the same.) But where were they going to get that kind of money?

The Virginia Company was the main corporate enterprise in the business of backing such ventures to America. Therefore Robinson and Brewster drafted a joint letter to Edwin Sandys, the treasurer of the Company, applying for financing and outlining their reasons for confidence:

1. We verily believe and trust the Lord is with us, unto Whom and Whose service we have given ourselves in many trials, and that He will graciously prosper our endeavors according to the simplicity of our hearts therein.

2. We are well weaned from the delicate milk of our mother country, and inured to the difficulties of a strange and hard land, which yet in a great part we have by patience overcome.

3. The people are, for the body of them, [as] industrious and frugal, we think we may safely say, as any company of people in the world.

4. We are knit together as a body in a most strict and sacred bond and covenant of the Lord, of the violation whereof we make great conscience, and by virtue whereof we do hold ourselves straitly tied to all care of each others good, and of the whole by everyone and so mutually.

5. Lastly, it is not with us as with other men, whom small things can discourage, or small discontentments cause to wish themselves at home again . . . .[7]

But while Sandys was sympathetic, the hard truth was that the Virginia Company was on the brink of bankruptcy, and "now so disturbed with factions and quarrels amongst themselves, as no business could go well forward." (And so the Leydenites were providentially spared that entanglement.)

Not long after that, they were paid an unexpected visit by a London merchant named Thomas Weston. All smiles and encouragement, Weston informed them that he was an independent adventurer, representing a group who had heard of their plight and decided to help them. The Leydenites could forget the Virginia Company (though it might be useful to sail under their charter). Instead, they could put their faith in Thomas Weston, who assured them that he felt the same way about the things of God that they did, and that he would see them through, no matter what.

Englishmen who did have money to speculate on trading, exploration, and settlement were almost exclusively being attracted to the Muscovy Company or the East India Tea Company, both of whom promised a 100 percent return on one's investment in six months. And so, as it seemed to be the only door open to them, with some misgivings the Leydenites entered into an agreement with Weston.

Should they have heeded the intuitive warnings which some of them received? Should they have waited on God a little longer, to open yet another door? As future events would indicate, this was the one time where they chose the easier way.

But now there was much to be done, as the families that were going sold their houses and all their immovable possessions, in order to give Weston cash with which to purchase shares in the plantation venture.

Their agreement was that each adult, sixteen years and older, would have one share, worth ten pounds sterling (about seven hundred modern dollars), and another, if he outfitted and equipped himself. Those with extra funds could of course buy more shares. They would all continue in joint partnership for seven years (the standard period of indenture), at the end of which time, all land and profits would be divided up according to the number of shares. Personal property, such as houses, home lots and gardens, would remain wholly the property of the planters and would not be divided up. The planters were also to be given two days a week of their own. It struck them as an eminently fair agreement. So Weston went off to London, to confer with his Adventurers, and to see about hiring a ship to transport them.

The Separatists sent two of their number to London, to represent them—John Carver and Robert Cushman. Carver had a stability and maturity about him that had already proven an asset. Cushman had a quick mind and a gift for eloquence, but he was immature and had difficulty accepting correction. While Carver was out of London, gathering supplies for the coming voyage, Weston applied pressure to Cushman, and got him to agree to certain changes in their contract.

Next on the agenda was the purchase of a pinnace, and this must have been like shopping for a used car with not enough money. Eventually they settled on an old freighter named the *Speedwell*, which would pick them up at Delftshaven and take them to Southampton. There they would join a larger merchantman, the *Mayflower*, hired by the Adventurers. But only a third of their six hundred-plus congregation could go. That meant that the man who wanted to go most, John Robinson, would have to stay behind; the main body of the flock could not be without its shepherd. So it was decided that their elder, William Brewster, would be their teacher and acting pastor until such time as Robinson could come over.

The time had come to part. Robinson declared a day of fasting and prayer to prepare them spiritually for the arduous voyage to come. At the end of the day, they had a farewell dinner, celebrating with goose and pudding and wine, and singing their favorite psalms from Ainsworth's Psalm Book, in the intricate, madrigal-like harmonies that so delighted the ear. Edward Winslow, one of the chief men going, described the scene as follows: "We refreshed ourselves, after our tears, with the singing of Psalms, making joyful melody in our hearts as well as with the voice, there being many in the congregation very expert in music; and indeed it was the sweetest melody that ever mine ears have heard." [8]

The next morning, as many as could, accompanied the voyagers by barge to Delftshaven. Looking back at the red-tiled roofs of Leyden receding in the distance and the great windmill with its white sails slowly turning, Bradford may have had a pang of regret. But if he did, it was only temporary, for "they knew they were Pilgrims, and looked not much on those things, but lifted up their eyes to the heavens, their dearest country, and quieted their spirits." [9]

When they reached Delftshaven, they made straight for the harbor, and there was the *Speedwell*—a good deal smaller and older than most of them had pictured her. The rest of the afternoon and most of the evening were spent in loading food and cargo into every conceivable cranny. Dawn on July 22, 1620, was greeted with a fair wind, and now it really *was* time to say good-bye. On the dock John Robinson slowly knelt, and all the others followed his lead. As he solemnly invoked God's blessing on their undertaking, tears came to all of their eyes, and even the young men wept unabashedly. Quickly they boarded the ship and the crew cast off.

With a following wind, Southampton was soon reached, where they joined the ninety-ton *Mayflower*. On board were their agents, Carver and Cushman, joyously reunited with their families, and about eighty "strangers." Some of these shared the Leydenites' feelings regarding the Church of England, but others were there because they had believed Weston's enticements about the profits to be had in the wilderness.

Among the "strangers" were the rambunctious John Billington, his shrewish wife, and two rebellious teenage sons; the more devout bootsmith, William Mullins, his wife, two children and 138 pairs of shoes and boots; and John Alden, the cooper that each ship was required by law to carry, in order to tend the ship's casks and barrels. One who had asked to go with them, and who was turned down, was none other than the feisty, ego-driven Captain John Smith. (Here, at least, the Pilgrims' discernment regarding people was working well!)

From the Leyden group there were sixteen men, eleven women, and fourteen children—barely a third of the combined total of saints and strangers. And of these, only Bradford and William and Mary Brewster were original members of the Scrooby church. Others among the saints included the Brewsters' two sons, Love and Wrestling; John Carver and his wife, Katherine; Edward and Elizabeth Winslow; William and Dorothy Bradford (they had left their only son behind, deciding he was too young to make the initial voyage); Dr. Samuel Fuller; and Captain Miles Standish, a tough and steady veteran of the Netherlands wars, and his wife, Rose.

The captain and part owner of the *Mayflower* was an old professional, hired with his crew to take the Pilgrims just south of the mouth of the Hudson, within the northernmost boundary of the Virginia charter. He had agreed to stay with them long enough for them to get a start on settling in; any time beyond that would cost them extra, as it would be cutting into his earning time. The captain's name was Jones, and his Christian name was the same as that of another captain God had used to bear the Light of Christ westward: Christopher.

All having been accomplished and readied for departure, Thomas Weston chose this precise moment to present his revised contract for the Leydenites to sign. Surely, with all their funds committed and their good-byes said, these rude bumpkins would knuckle under. But to his astonishment, they would not.

In an absolute rage, Weston stormed off to London, refusing to settle their final debts, which came to some sixty pounds. So they had to sell off several thousand pounds of butter, which by chance happened to be their only food surplus. And then they wrote the Adventurers in London a compromise letter, stating that ". . . if large profits should not arise within seven years, we will continue together longer with you, if the Lord give a blessing." [10] Thus, in effect, they were offering to extend their indentureship almost indefinitely. Their consciences now were as clear as their credit balance, and they were free to sail.

At this point, Brewster assembled the company to read them a letter which John Robinson had prepared for them: ". . . We are daily to renew our repentance with our God, especially for our sins known, and generally for our unknown trespasses . . . [For] sin being taken away by earnest repentance and the pardon thereof from the Lord . . . great shall be [a man's] security and peace in all dangers, sweet his comforts in all distresses . . . ."

Robinson went on to warn them that their "intended course of civil community will minister continual occasion of offense, and will be as fuel for that fire, except you diligently quench it with brotherly forbearance . . . . with your common employments you [should] join common affections, truly bent upon the general good . . . ."

In closing, he enjoined them, ". . . whereas you are to become a body politic, using amongst yourselves civil government, and are not furnished with any persons of special eminency above the rest" [i.e., no Gentlemen on the passenger list], they would have to choose their leaders from among equals. "Let your wisdom and godliness appear not only in choosing such persons as do entirely love and will promote the common good, but also in yielding unto them all due honor and obedience in their lawful administrations . . . [for] the image of the Lord's power and authority, which the magistrate beareth, is honorable, in how mean persons soever . . . ."

For a number of the strangers hearing Robinson's letter, that may have been their first realization that there were no gentry among them. What a contrast to the Jamestown situation! The Pilgrims had sought God's will in almost every step of the planning, as the Jamestown people had not, so He was more able to winnow out from among them any who might be unwilling to work with the rest. There could be no spectators—all had to participate.

They set sail for the New World on August 5, 1620, but they were barely three days out on the Atlantic before it became obvious that the *Speedwell* was in trouble. The new masts with which they had fitted her in Holland were apparently causing her seams to work open under full sail. So they had no choice but to turn back for the nearby port of Dartmouth, and re-caulk her.

One week later, they again set forth, only to encounter the same problem, this time abetted by a full gale which initiated the Pilgrims into the rigors of seasickness. Once more they were forced to turn back, this time making for Plymouth, the home of some of the best shipwrights in England. There they searched the ship for a loose seam. And how they searched! Holding lighted candles up close to each seam, they crept the length of the ship looking for the slightest waver in the flame that would indicate a less than airtight joining. Surprisingly, they found nothing wrong with her hull. In spite of that, they finally made the difficult decision not to take any further chances with the *Speedwell*. They would sell her and combine her passengers and cargo with those on board the *Mayflower*.

Some historians have found hints that the captain of the *Speedwell*, anxious to get out of his contract to spend a year at the plantation, had deliberately crowded on sail to make the seams work loose. Indeed, the *Speedwell*, later re-rigged, would see coastal service for many years.

But there was another explanation: God was using the *Speedwell*'s problems to continue to separate the wheat from the chaff. As William Stoughton later put it: "God sifted a whole nation, that He might send choice grain into this wilderness." [11]

A number of them, whose hearts themselves had seams which might divide if heavily worked, now began to wonder if it truly was God's will that they make this voyage. About twenty of them willingly dropped out. "Like Gideon's army," Bradford wrote, "this small number was divided, as if the Lord, by this work of His Providence, thought these few were still too many for the great work He had to do." [12] There were some surprises among their number, like Robert Cushman, "whose heart and courage was gone from them before, as it seems, though his body was with them till now he departed." Bradford then quoted from a letter written in Dartmouth by Cushman to a friend:

"For besides the eminent dangers of this voyage, which are no less than deadly . . . . Our victuals will be half eaten up, I think, before we go from the coast of England, and if our voyage last long, we shall not have a month's victuals when come [to] the country." (Indeed, by the time they left Plymouth, they were already consuming the precious reserves that were meant to sustain them in the New World.) "Friend," concluded Cushman, "if ever we make a plantation, God works a miracle." Though he may have spoken from despair, it was the truth. God had so intended.

There was another reason for God's narrowing the company down to one ship: to make it indeed a company. It had taken many years of baptism by fire to temper the spiritual core of the Pilgrims into hardened steel, but now there were only a few weeks available in which to temper these strangers, too, and anneal them to the Pilgrims' core. For unless they were so bonded, they would soon fly apart under the pressures that awaited them on the other side of the ocean. Much could be done, but it would require tremendous heat and pressure . . . .

The heat and the pressure began soon after they got underway: 102 Pilgrims huddled in the lantern-lit darkness of the low-ceilinged 'tween-decks; women and small children allowed to have the captain's cabin (Jones had generously offered to bunk with his petty officers); no hatches open because of continuous storms; all nonessential personnel required to stay below decks; the constant crying of small children; no chance to cook any meals.

It added up to seven weeks of the hell of an ill-lighted, rolling, pitching, stinking inferno, the kind that brings up sins that had lain buried for years—anger, self-pity, bitterness, vindictiveness, jealousy, despair. All these surfaced sins had to be faced, confessed, and given up to the Lord for His cleansing. No matter how ill they felt, or how grim the daily situation, they continued to seek God together, praying *through* despair and into peace and thanksgiving.

The weary Pilgrims were forced to endure yet another ordeal— harassment from the sailors. Several of the crew had taken to mocking them unmercifully, and their self-appointed leader had taken such a dislike to the Pilgrims that he would gloat at their seasickness and delight in telling them how much he looked forward to sewing them in shrouds and feeding them to the fish. For surely some of them would soon be dying—death was a familiar shipmate among landlubbers on these long voyages—and these were the puniest assortment of "psalmsinging puke-stockings" he had ever seen.

But just at the peak of his tormenting, this same crewman suddenly took gravely ill of an unknown fever and died within a single day! No one else caught this mysterious disease, and *his* was the first shrouded body to go over side. Thereafter, there was no more mocking from the crew.

There was only one other death during the voyage: William Butten, a servant, ignored Captain Jones's and Dr. Fuller's stern admonition about drinking a daily portion of lemon juice as a preventative for scurvy. He refused to swallow the sour stuff, and his willful disobedience cost him his life.

Still another passenger nearly paid with his life for a "minor" disobedience. A dozen or so days into the storm, John Howland, the servant of John Carver, could no longer stand the stench of the crowded 'tween-decks. The captain, Elder Brewster, and his own master had each forbade any of them to go topside, but if he didn't get a breath of fresh air soon . . . . Finally, he decided that he was going to get what he wanted, and so up he climbed and out onto the sea-swept main deck. It was like a nightmare outside! The seas around him were mountainous; he'd never seen anything like it—huge, boiling, gray-green waves lifting and tossing the small ship in their midst, dark clouds roiling the horizon, and the wind shrieking through the rigging—Howland shuddered, and it was not from the icy blast of "fresh air" that hit him.

Just then, the ship seemed to literally drop out from beneath him—it was there, and then it wasn't—and the next thing he knew, he was falling . . . . He hit the water, which was so cold that it was like being smashed between two huge blocks of ice. Instantly stunned, his last conscious act was to blindly reach out—and by God's grace, the ship at that moment was heeled so far over that the lines from her spars were trailing in the water. One of these happened to snake across his wrist, and he closed on it and instinctively hung on.

According to the U.S. Navy, a man can stand immersion in the North Atlantic in November for about four minutes. There is no telling how long Howland was in the sea, how soon someone spotted him and raised the alarm. When they hauled him aboard he was blue, but he recovered, though he was sick for several days. And he never again stuck his head above deck, until he was invited to do so.

Perhaps the most frightening experience of the voyage occurred not long after the *Mayflower* passed the halfway mark. In a particularly violent storm, she was rolling so far over on her sides that the Pilgrims must have feared she might shift her cargo and go all the way over. We can imagine what it must have been like to be in that 'tween-decks space, with little children screaming, and the sole lantern swinging so far to either side that it seemed almost parallel to the overhead beams. Suddenly a tremendous *boom* resounded throughout the ship. The huge cross-beam supporting the mainmast had cracked and was sagging alarmingly. Now for the first time, the sailors' concern matched the Pilgrims'. They swarmed about it, trying to lever it back into place, but they could not budge it. The captain himself came to see. From the look on his face, it was obvious to the Pilgrims that the situation was indeed as serious as they had feared.

The Pilgrims helped in the only way they knew. They prayed, "Yet Lord, thou canst save!" Then Brewster remembered the great iron screw of his printing press. It was on board somewhere. A desperate search was begun. Finally, it was located, dug out, hauled into place, and cranked up. It met the beam and, to the accompaniment of a hideous creaking and groaning of wood, began to raise it—all the way back into its original position. For once, the sailors joined the Pilgrims in their praises of God!

Earnestly Brewster, Carver, and Bradford questioned the captain as to the *Mayflower*'s seaworthiness. He thought about it—they were now closer to America than to England, though they would have the wind with them on the return . . . . "No, she's still sound under the water, and that's the main thing! She's made many trips in weather worse than this, and I expect she'll make this one, too, without more trouble." So they would go on.

At last, on November 9, the cry "Land Ho!" rang out from the crow's nest. These were the words they had waited so long to hear! Without waiting for the Captain's permission, they rushed up to the main deck, where they caught their first glimpse of a long, sandy stretch of coastline, covered with dune grass and scrub pine. One of the pilots identified it as a place the fishermen called Cape Cod. Despite the seemingly endless storm, they had been blown fewer than a hundred miles off their course—north, as it turned out. It would take them only a day or two to round the Cape and three or four more to reach the mouth of the Hudson. And so they started south.

But there are fierce shoals and riptides off Monomoy Point at the "elbow" of the Cape. And mixed with the headwinds they now faced, the going became progressively more treacherous. Finally Captain Jones said that he would have to head back out to sea and wait a day before proceeding further south. But now Brewster, Carver, Winslow, and Bradford, and several others, began to wonder if God really *did* want them to go to the Hudson. Perhaps He had blown them here because He intended them to remain in this place. At length, after much prayer and further discussion, they instructed Captain Jones to turn about and make for the northern tip of the Cape (Provincetown). This he did, and on November 11, they dropped anchor in the natural harbor on the inside of the Cape.

But now a new question arose: if they were to settle here, they would no longer be under the jurisdiction of the Virginia Company. And since they obviously had no patent from the New England Company, they would be under . . . no one. At this thought, rebellion began to stir in the hearts of some of the strangers, and the

Pilgrim leadership realized that they had to act quickly and decisively, to forestall the very real possibility of mutiny.

Their solution was pragmatic, realistic, and expedient. And it took into consideration the basic sinfulness of human nature, with which they had become all too familiar, during the past seven weeks. They drafted a compact, very much along the lines of their first covenant back in Scrooby, which embodied the same principles of equality and government by the consent of the governed which would become the cornerstones of American Democracy. (Actually, this concept of equality could be traced directly back to the ancient Hebrew tradition of all men being equal in the sight of God.) While the Pilgrims had no idea how significant this document was to be, it marked the first time in recorded history that free and equal men had voluntarily covenanted together to create their own new civil government.

In the name of God, amen. We whose names are under-written, the loyal subjects of our dread Sovereign Lord King James by the Grace of God of Great Britain, France, Ireland, King, Defender of the Faith, etc.

Having undertaken, for the glory of God and advancement of the Christian Faith and honor of our King and country, a voyage to plant the first colony in the northern parts of Virginia, do by these presents solemnly and mutually in the presence of God and one of another, covenant and combine ourselves together into a civil body politic, for our better ordering and preservation and furtherance of the ends aforesaid, and by virtue hereof to enact, constitute and frame such just and equal laws, ordinances, acts, constitutions and offices from time to time, as shall be thought most meet and convenient for the general good of the colony. Unto which we promise all due submission and obedience. In witness whereof we have hereunder subscribed our names at Cape Cod, the 11th of November, in the year of the reign of our Sovereign King James of England . . . Anno Domini 1620.[13]

Such ringing affirmations as: "We hold these truths to be self-evident, that all men are created equal . . ." would have to wait another century and a half, but here was their introduction onto American soil.

It is Bradford who rightly brings this chapter to a close: "Being thus arrived in a good harbor and brought safe to land, they fell upon their knees and blessed the God of heaven, who had brought them over the vast and furious ocean, and delivered them from all the perils and miseries thereof, again to set their feet on the firm and stable earth, their proper element. And no marvel if they were thus joyful . . . ." [14] They had begun their long journey by kneeling on the dock at Delftshaven to ask God's blessing; they ended it on the sands of Cape Cod, kneeling to thank Him for that blessing.

Yet Bradford, always the realist, went on to marvel at "this poor people's present condition . . . no friends to welcome them, nor inns to entertain or refresh their weatherbeaten bodies, no houses, or much less towns to repair to, to seek for succour . . . ."

With winter storms howling around the tip of the Cape, "whichever way they turned their eyes (save upward to the heavens) they could have little solace or content in respect of any outward objects. For summer being done, all things stand upon them with a weatherbeaten face; and the whole country, full of woods and thickets, represented a wild and savage hue. If they looked behind them, there was the mighty ocean which they had passed, and was now as a main bar and gulf to separate them from all the civil parts of the world . . . . Let it also be considered what weak hope of supply and succour they left behind them . . . . What could now sustain them but the Spirit of God and His grace?"

6

"God Our Maker Doth Provide"

Stranger in a strange land . . . the line from Exodus seemed singularly appropriate. It *was* a strange land—bleak and windswept, with steep dunes and a gnarled, weatherbeaten covering of underbrush that clung tenaciously to the low hills, in the face of what seemed to be a perpetual northwest wind.

They stood on the deck of the *Mayflower* breathing that fresh air, too exhausted to think beyond thanking God that their three-month ordeal was over. The wind was refreshing—but it had a rawness to it that foretold an ordeal of a different kind.

Sixteen of the men went ashore in the ship's boat to find firewood and explore. Others began to reassemble the sailing shallop, needed for exploring the inner coast of the bay, in order to find the right place for settlement. The reassembling of the shallop was a big job, because it was a large boat: thirty feet long, with oars and a large sail, capable of transporting more than thirty people, if necessary. Now it was even more difficult, because so many sections had been damaged in the storms.

As the afternoon light began to fail, the ship's boat returned. All the passengers crowded onto the main deck of the *Mayflower* to hear the news. As it happened, the men ashore *had* found something—an abandoned cache of buried corn, some thirty-six ears in a large iron pot. They were deeply grateful to their unseen benefactors and characteristically determined to repay them, if and when they met them. This was the Pilgrims' first taste of Indian corn, the staple that was to save their lives, as it had saved so many at Jamestown, and would again and again all along the eastern seaboard. It was tough eating, but it obviously kept well under the right conditions. And it looked hearty enough to grow almost anywhere. Bradford and the rest were tremendously encouraged:

these men, returning with corn, were like the Israelites sent ahead into the Promised Land of Canaan, who jubilantly returned with its fruits.

It took the better part of three weeks to ready the shallop for use and trim her out. Finally on December 6, after one premature foray, ten of their chief men and some seamen set out "upon further discovery, intending to circulate [circumnavigate] that deep bay of Cape Cod. The weather was very cold, and it froze so hard as the spray of the sea lighting on their coats, they were as if they had been glazed . . . ." [1]

That afternoon they saw some Indians up ahead on the tidal flats, cutting up a large fish which had been stranded there after a storm, but the Indians ran away before they could hail them. The second night they encamped at dusk, close to the eastern corner of the bay (Eastham). A barricade of cut boughs was erected to provide shelter against the wind, as well as protection in case of attack. During the night, their sleep was interrupted by many blood-curdling cries and howls; they were glad to be up an hour before dawn, to have prayer and then breakfast.

But presently, all of the sudden, they heard a great and strange cry, which they knew to be the same voices they [had] heard in the night, though they varied their notes, and one of their company, being abroad, came running in and cried, "Indians, Indians!" and withal, arrows came flying in amongst them . . . two muskets were discharged at them, and two more [men] stood ready in the entrance of their rendezvous, but were commanded not to shoot till they could take full aim at them . . . . The cry of the Indians was dreadful . . . .

The skirmish continued, with neither side gaining any advantage, until several of the Pilgrims, wearing coats of mail, rushed forth from the barricade and discharged their muskets together. The Indians quickly scattered, "except for one brave, who stood behind a tree within half a musket-shot, and let his arrows fly at them. He was seen to shoot three arrows, which were all avoided. He stood three shots of a musket, till one, taking full aim at him, made the bark or splinters of the tree fly about his ears, after which he gave an extraordinary shriek, and away they went, all of them."

Later, in the journal which Bradford and Edward Winslow wrote together, they added: [2]

Yet by the especial providence of God, none of [their arrows] either hit or hurt us, though many came close by us and on every side of us, and some coats which were hung up in our barricado were shot through and through. So, after we had given God thanks for our deliverance . . . we went on our journey and called this place "The First Encounter" [which name it bears to this day].

They continued south along the inner shore of the lower Cape. Their pilot, Robert Coppin, who had been there once before, told them of a good harbor further along at the mouth of a creek. He was confident they could reach it before nightfall. According to historian Alexander Young, this would have had to be the harbor at Barnstable, which they would have reached around 2:00 in the afternoon. But about an hour before that, snow began to fall in such thick, wet flakes that they sailed right past Coppin's harbor and on around the bottom of the bay.

As the afternoon wore on, the wind began to pick up.

The sea became very rough, and they broke their rudder, and it was as much as two men could do to steer her with a couple of oars. But their pilot bade them be of good cheer, for he saw the harbor. But the storm increasing, and night drawing on, they bore what sail they could to get in, while they could see. But herewith they broke their mast in three pieces, and their sail fell overboard in a very grown sea, so as they had like to have been [wrecked]. Yet by God's mercy, they recovered themselves, and having the [tide] with them, struck into the harbor.

But when it came to, the pilot was deceived in the place and said, The Lord be merciful unto them, for his eyes never saw that place before, and he and the master mate would have run her ashore, in a cove full of breakers, before the wind.

But one of the seamen, named Clark, who was steering with an oar over the stern, suddenly took charge. Shouting into the wind, he cried, "If you be men, about with her or we are all cast away!" [3]

They all rowed furiously, snatching the shallop from the very edge of the breakers. Clark continued to call out the encouragement, until they were able to find shelter in the lee of a small island which seemed to loom out of nowhere in the gathering dark. They named the island after Clark and spent a wet, miserable night on it.

. . . But though this had been a day and night of much trouble and danger to them, yet God gave them a morning of comfort and refreshing (as usually He doth to His children), for the next day was a fair sunshining day, and they found themselves to be on an island secure from Indians, where they might dry their stuff, fix their pieces, and rest themselves, and give God thanks for His mercies in their manifold deliverances. And this being the last day of the week, they prepared there to keep the Sabbath . . . .[4]

Monday morning dawned crisp and clear, washed clean by the rain and fairly glistening in the morning sun. This was to be a day of discoveries, each more amazing than the one before. The first was that the little island they were on was in the middle of a perfect natural harbor, almost completely enclosed. The next was that the harbor was deep enough to take ships of twice the draft of the *Mayflower*.

They rowed the shallop across to the mainland, and their discoveries came in quick succession. The soil was rich and fertile. There was a gentle open slope that rose up from the water's edge which would afford an ideal place to settle, with excellent drainage and an open field of fire for muskets and cannon, in case they had to defend it. There were not one but *four* spring-fed creeks close at hand, with the sweetest water any of them had ever tasted—so good that they almost did not mind the fact that their supply of beer (the common beverage, due to England's untrustworthy water) had run out. On the hill a good twenty acres of ground had already been cleared and were ready to plant, though there were signs indicating that for some reason no planting had been done for several years. Happier than they had been in weeks, they made repairs and hurried back to the *Mayflower* with the news of their find.

There was news of another sort awaiting William Bradford. His wife, Dorothy, had gone over the side of the ship and was drowned. No mention of this tragedy is made in any of his writings, and it is commented on only briefly elsewhere. This has led modern historians to speculate that she took her own life. However it happened, the young widower was now faced with a choice: he could go into self-pity, becoming increasingly bitter or passive, or both; or he could apply himself with more singleness of purpose than ever to the God-given task of planting the colony. And this is what he chose. There had already been unusual maturity in this thirty-year-old chief member; after this, there was even more.

The Pilgrims named the site Plymouth—not because it happened to be called New Plymouth on John Smith's map, but because "Plymouth in Old England was the last town they left in the native country; and for that they received many kindnesses from some Christians there." [5] They asked Captain Jones to stay on as long as he could, for they desperately needed the shelter that only the *Mayflower* could provide. And the captain agreed; the lives of these humble settlers had touched him deeply. They had borne all cheerfully, even the taunts of the bosun's mate, never complaining about their conditions or the food or the weather, and they thanked God for the merest blessings. Now that December was almost over, the worst of the winter would soon be upon them. As they laid out the main street, erected a palisade, and began the common house, the building of shelter went slowly, when hands were so cold that they had difficulty keeping hold of axe or adze.

Then, too, this was the time of the "General Sickness," when bodies, weakened from three long months at sea, finally succumbed to scurvy, despite what was left of the lemon juice. Often a lingering cold, contracted after wading ashore, trudging through the snow and sleeping on the damp ground (under continuing exertion—for there was too much to be done to stop working just for a cold), flared up into consumption or pneumonia.

The Pilgrims started dying. There were six dead in December, eight in January—they were falling like casualties on a battlefield. And in a sense, that is what they were: locked in a life-or-death struggle with Satan himself. For this was the first time that the Light of Christ had landed in force on his continent, and if he did not throw them back into the sea at the beginning, there would be reinforcements.

On January 14, a Sunday, an icy wind was blowing through the cracks of the nearly completed common house, where there lay as many sick as they could crowd in. Suddenly, before anyone knew what was happening, the thatched roof above them was blazing with fire, and the place was filled with smoke. Many started to cry out in terror, as burning embers fell from the roof. Had it not been for the supernatural strength given to some of the sick to take speedy action, they might all have been blown to pieces, for there were open barrels of gunpowder and loaded muskets in the common house. These were quickly rushed outside. Fortunately the timbers in the roof did not catch fire, so the building was saved. Much precious clothing was burned up, however, further exposing the sick to the elements of the New England winter.

But, as they themselves had said, these were not like other men. The more adversity mounted against them, the harder they prayed—never giving in to despair, to murmuring, to any of the petty jealousies that split and divide. In contrast to Jamestown, as their ranks thinned, they drew ever closer together, and trusted God all the more. And still the death toll mounted. In February, they were dying at a rate of two a day, even three on some days.

The twenty-first of February claimed four lives. And at one period, in the whole company there were only five men well enough to care for the sick. One of them was Captain Standish, who tended Bradford among the others, raising his head up and cradling it in his arm, to spoon him a bit of soup.

Standish, Brewster, and three or four others chopped wood, cleaned, clothed, cooked, and tended. They even periodically showed themselves at the palisade, just in case the Indians, whom they had seen in the distance, happened to be watching them. For the same reason, they buried their dead at night, in shallow unmarked graves, so that the red men would not know how many they had lost. In February there were seventeen deaths.

The pitched battle between love and death went on. On board the *Mayflower*, the seamen, too, began to fall. One promised his companion all his possessions after his death, if only he would look after him while he was still alive. His companion "went and got a little spice and made him a mess of meat once or twice, and because he died not so soon as he expected, [his companion] went amongst his fellows and swore the rogue [had swindled] him. He would see him choked before he made him any more meat! And yet the poor fellow died before morning." [6] (Shades of Jamestown!)

But gradually, almost imperceptibly, the Light of Christ was gaining the victory. The bosun was stricken— ". . . a proud young man who would often curse and scoff at the passengers, but when he grew weak, they had compassion on him and helped him. Then he confessed that he did not deserve it at their hands; he had abused them in word and deed. 'Oh!' said he, 'you, I now see, show your love like Christians indeed to one another, but we let one another lie and die like dogs.' " March was another killing month; thirteen more died. But that was four less than the month before.

When the worst was finally over, they had lost forty-seven people, nearly half their original number. Thirteen out of eighteen wives died; only three families remained unbroken. Of all the first comers, the children fared the best: of seven daughters, none died; of thirteen sons, only three. And the colony, which was young to begin with, was even younger now. But compared with Jamestown's 80 to 90 percent mortality rate, they came through remarkably well.

And through it all, their hearts remained soft towards God. Whether they knew that they were being tested, as Bradford later suspected, the high point of their week remained Sunday worship, when the beat of a field drum would summon them to the morning and afternoon services. All on board the *Mayflower* would come ashore, and join the procession led by William Brewster (their spiritual leader until such time as God provided them with a minister), John Carver the Governor, and the red-haired Miles Standish, in charge of defense. As they made their way up the hill, their clothes were not the somber browns and blacks of the pictures that hang in schoolrooms around Thanksgiving time. Miles Standish almost certainly wore his plum-red cape, and William Brewster had an emerald green satin doublet which might have been appropriate Sunday garb. For these were Elizabethan Englishmen; it would be their Puritan cousins of a later generation who would hold that "frivolous" clothes connoted a frivolous heart attitude.

The houses that they passed were of mud daub and wattle construction, usually with two rooms around a central fireplace, and a sleeping loft atop one of the rooms. The high-peaked roofs were of thatch, and these were especially difficult to make, because the right kind of grass grew more than a mile away. There were five such houses more or less finished, in addition to the common house at the foot of the hill, where many of them had spent the winter.

The service was held in the blockhouse at the top of the hill—an imposing building with a flat roof and a trap door—so that the house could be defended from the roof. Captain Jones had parted with one of his two huge, fifteen-hundred-pound cannon called sackers, and one of his brace of twelve-hundred-pounders called minions, plus two smaller cannon called bases. From this high point, it was possible to enfilade the main street, as well as cover the distant woods.

Inside, on rough-hewn log benches, the men would sit on the left, the women on the right. William Brewster would preach, and he had a gift for teaching "both powerfully and profitably, to the great contentment of the hearers, and their comfortable edification; yea, many were brought to God by his ministry." [7] And elsewhere Bradford comments on the fact that God used Brewster's preaching as an instrument to bring sweet repentance to their hearts for the sins they might have forgotten about.

If any one event could be singled out to mark the turning point of their fortunes, it would have been what happened on a fair Friday in the middle of March. The weather had slowly been warming, and with the iron grip of winter beginning to loosen its hold on the earth, the first shoots of green would soon be appearing. The men were gathered in the common house to conclude their conference on military instruction, when the cry went up, "Indian coming!"

Indian coming? Surely he meant Indians coming! Disgusted, Captain Standish shook his head, even as he went to look out the window—to see a tall, well-built Indian, wearing nothing but a leather loincloth striding up their main street. He was headed straight for the common house, and the men inside hurried to the door, before he walked right in on them. He stopped and stood motionless looking at them, as though sculpted in marble. Only the March wind broke the silence.

"Welcome!" he suddenly boomed, in a deep, resonant voice.

The Pilgrims were too startled to speak. At length, they replied with as much gravity as they could muster: "Welcome."

Their visitor fixed them with a piercing stare. "Have you got any beer?" he asked them in flawless English. If they were surprised before, they were astounded now.

"Beer?" one of them managed.

The Indian nodded.

The Pilgrims looked at one another, then turned back to him. "Our beer is gone. Would you like . . . some brandy?"

Again the Indian nodded.

They brought him some brandy, and a biscuit with butter and cheese, and then some pudding and a piece of roast duck. To their continuing amazement, he ate with evident relish everything set before him. Where had he developed such an appetite for English food? How, in fact, had he come to speak English? For that matter, who was he, and what was he doing here?

But they would have to wait, for obviously he did not intend to talk until he had finished his repast. Finally, the time for answering questions came. His name was Samoset. He was a sagamore (or chief) of the Algonquins, from what is now Pemaquid Point in Maine. He had been visiting in these parts for the past eight months, having begged a ride down the coast with Captain Thomas Dermer, an English sea captain who was known to the Pilgrims by reputation. He had been sent out to explore the coast for the Council for New England, the company to whom they would now be applying for a patent. Apparently Samoset's sole motivation was a love of travel, and he had learned his English from various fishing captains who had put in to the Maine shore over the years.

Now they asked the crucial question: What could he tell them of the Indians hereabouts? And the story he told gave every one of them cause to thank God in their hearts. This area had always been the territory of the Patuxets, a large, hostile tribe who had barbarously murdered every white man who had landed on their shores. But four years prior to the Pilgrims' arrival, a mysterious plague had broken out among them, killing every man, woman, and child. So complete was the devastation that the neighboring tribes had shunned the area ever since, convinced that some great supernatural spirit had destroyed the Patuxets. Hence the cleared land on which they had settled literally belonged to no one! Their nearest neighbors, said Samoset, were the Wampanoags, some fifty miles to the southwest. These Indians numbered about sixty warriors. Massasoit, their sachem (or chief), had such wisdom that he also ruled over several other small tribes in the general area. And it was with Massasoit that Samoset had spent most of the past eight months.

Who were the Indians out on the Cape, who had attacked them? These were the Nausets, who numbered about a hundred warriors. The previous summer they had attacked Captain Dermer and killed three of his men. The Nausets hated the white man, because several years before one Captain Thomas Hunt had tricked seven of their braves into coming aboard his ship on the pretext of wanting to trade with them. He had taken them, along with twenty Patuxets, to Spain, where he sold them into slavery.

By the time he was done with his tale-telling, it was nightfall. Samoset announced that he would sleep with them, and return in the morning. Captain Standish put a discreet watch on him, but Samoset slept the sleep of the untroubled. And in the morning he left, bearing a knife, a bracelet, and a ring as gifts to Massasoit.

That was the last they saw of him, until the following Thursday when he returned accompanied by another Indian who also spoke English, and who was, of all things, a Patuxet! [8] The second Indian was Squanto, and he was to be, according to Bradford, "a special instrument sent of God for their good, beyond their expectation." The extraordinary chain of "coincidences" in this man's life is in its own way no less extraordinary than the saga of Joseph's being sold into slavery in Egypt. Indeed, in ensuing months, there was not a doubt in any of their hearts that Squanto, whose Indian name was Tisquantum, was a Godsend.

His story really began in 1605, when Squanto and four other Indians were taken captive by Captain George Weymouth, who was exploring the New England coast at the behest of Sir Ferdinando Gorges. The Indians were taken to England, where they were taught English, so that Gorges could question them as to what tribes populated New England, and where the most favorable places to establish colonies would be. Squanto spent the next nine years in England, where he met Captain John Smith, recently of Virginia, who promised to take him back to his people on Cape Cod, as soon as he himself could get a command bound for there. Actually, he did not have too long to wait. On Smith's 1614 voyage of mapping and exploring, Squanto was returned to the Patuxets, at the place Smith named New Plymouth.

Sailing with Smith's expedition on another ship was Captain Thomas Hunt, whom Smith ordered to stay behind to dry their catch of fish and trade it for beaver skins before coming home. But Hunt had another, more profitable cargo in mind. As soon as Smith departed, he slipped back down the coast to Plymouth, where he lured twenty Patuxets aboard, apparently to trade with them, and promptly clapped them in irons. He proceeded down to the Cape, where he scooped up seven unsuspecting Nausets. All of these he took to Málaga, a notorious slave-trading port on the coast of Spain, where he got 20 pounds for each of them (fourteen hundred dollars a head). No wonder the slave trade was such a temptation! Most of them were shipped off to North Africa, but a few were bought and rescued by local friars, who introduced them to the Christian faith. Thus did God begin Squanto's preparation for the role he would play at Plymouth.

But Squanto was too enterprising to stay long in a monastery. He attached himself to an Englishman bound for London, and there met and joined the household of a wealthy merchant, where he lived until he embarked for New England with Captain Dermer in 1619. It was on this same trip that Dermer had picked up Samoset at Monhegan, one of the more important fishing stations in Maine, and dropped them both off at Plymouth. At which time Dermer wrote to a friend (presumably on the New England Council): "I will first begin with that place from whence Squanto, or Tisquantum, was taken away, which on Captain Smith's map is called Plymouth, and I would that Plymouth [England] had the like commodities. I would that the first plantation might be here seated . . . ." [9]

When Squanto stepped ashore six months before the Pilgrims arrived, he received the most tragic blow of his life: not a man, woman, or child of his tribe was left alive! Nothing but skulls and bones and ruined dwellings remained.

Squanto wandered aimlessly through the lands he had played in as a child, the woods where he had learned to hunt, the place where he had looked forward to settling, once his career with the English was finished. Now there was nothing. In despair he wandered into Massasoit's camp, because he had nowhere else to go. And that chief, understanding his circumstances, took pity on him. But Squanto merely existed, having lost all reason for living.

That is, this was his condition until Samoset brought news of a small colony of peaceful English families who were so hard pressed to stay alive, let alone plant a colony at Patuxet. They would surely die of starvation, since they had little food and nothing to plant but English wheat and barley. A light seemed to come back to Squanto's eye, and he accompanied Samoset, when the latter came to Plymouth as Massasoit's interpreter. For the chief himself had come with all sixty of his warriors, painted in startling fashion.

Edward Winslow was elected to meet Massasoit, and make him a gift of two more knives and "a pot of strong water." What Massasoit really wanted was Winslow's armor and sword, but before he could make this clear through his interpreters, Winslow began to discourse smoothly and at length, making a long speech which said nothing, in the finest diplomatic tradition. Eventually Massasoit nodded, smiled, and went to find Governor Carver.

He was ushered into one of the partially finished houses, to a fanfare of trumpet and drum, which pleased him immensely. Next, they drank a toast to Massasoit, who lifted the pot of strong water himself and took an enormous draft, which made his eyes water and caused him to sweat profusely.

But out of the meeting came a peace treaty of mutual aid and assistance which would last for forty years and would be a model for many that would be made thereafter. Massasoit was a remarkable example of God's providential care for His Pilgrims. He was probably the only other chief on the northeast coast of America who (like Powhatan to the south) would have welcomed the white man as a friend. And the Pilgrims took great pains not to abuse his acceptance of them. On the contrary, the record of their relations with him and his people is a strong testimony to the love of Christ that was in them.

When Massasoit and his entourage finally left, Squanto stayed. He had found his reason for living. These English were like little babes, so ignorant were they of the ways of the wild. Well, he could certainly do something about that! The next day, he went out and came back with all the eels he could hold in his hands—which the Pilgrims found to be "fat and sweet" and excellent eating. How had he ever caught them? He took several young men with him and taught them how to squash the eels out of the mud with their bare feet, and then catch them with their hands.

But the next thing he showed them was by far the most important, for it would save every one of their lives. April was corn-planting month in New England, as well as Virginia. Squanto showed the Pilgrims how to plant corn the Indian way, hoeing six-foot squares in toward the center, putting down four or five kernels, and then fertilizing the corn with fish. At that, the Pilgrims just shook their heads; in four months they had caught exactly one cod. No matter, said Squanto cheerfully; in four days the creeks would be overflowing with fish.

The Pilgrims cast a baleful eye on their amazing friend, who seemed to have adopted them. But Squanto ignored them and instructed the young men in how to make the weirs they would need to catch the fish. Obediently the men did as he told them, and four days later the creeks for miles around were clogged with alewives making their spring run. The Pilgrims did not catch them; they harvested them!

So now the corn was planted. Pointing spokelike to the center of each mound were three fishes, their heads almost touching. Now, said Squanto, they would have to guard against wolves. Seeing the familiar bewildered look on his charges' faces, he added that the wolves would attempt to steal the fish. The Pilgrims would have to guard it for two weeks, until it had a chance to decompose. And so they did, and that summer, twenty full acres of corn began to flourish.

Squanto helped in a thousand similar ways, teaching them how to stalk deer, plant pumpkins among the corn, refine maple syrup from maple trees, discern which herbs were good to eat and good for medicine, and find the best berries. But after the corn, there was one other specific thing he did which was of inestimable importance to their survival. What little fishing they had done was a failure, and any plan for them to fish commercially was a certain fiasco. So Squanto introduced them to the pelt of the beaver, which was then in plentiful supply in northern New England, and in great demand throughout Europe. And not only did he get them started, but he guided them in the trading, making sure they got their full money's worth in top-quality pelts. This would prove to be their economic deliverance, just as corn would be their physical deliverance.

There were, nonetheless, moments of sadness in the midst of all these encouraging developments. In the course of planting the corn, Governor Carver was suddenly struck down with what was probably a cerebral hemorrhage. He died in three days without ever recovering consciousness. His replacement by unanimous vote: William Bradford, who would be re-elected annually for the next thirty-six years of his life, except for the five years when he explicitly requested that they choose someone else.

Immediately after Carver's death, something else happened which could have thrown the colony into despair. The time had come for Captain Jones to leave for England. Fearful for the Pilgrims' future, Jones had begged them to come back to the mother country with him. The offer was tempting, and many of them had good cause to accept it. The sickness had ravaged them: only four of the couples who had arrived on the *Mayflower* still had each other, and a number had lost children. Yet not one of the Pilgrims responded to Jones's entreaties.

Something special had been born among them in the midst of all the dying—they had shared the love of Jesus Christ in a way that only happens when people are willing to suffer together in His causes. This was what they had come to the wilderness to find, and now none of them wished to leave it.

But now, by the twenty-first of April, the captain decided he could not stay a day longer. The *Mayflower*'s own supplies had gotten so low that he had barely enough food to get back, though he would return with only half the crew with which he had left Southampton. The entire settlement would have gathered on the rocky shore to say good-bye, and one can imagine Jones shaking hands all around, ending with William Bradford. Then he was in the boat, and his men were rowing out to the *Mayflower*.

The day was overcast, gray clouds scudding before a damp chilling offshore breeze. On shore, the little gathering could hear his first mate's commands and the chant of the seamen, as they turned the anchor windlass and slowly raised the anchor. The breeze caught the *Mayflower*'s sails, and she began to move, pointing her bow toward the harbor entrance.

The echoes of the last good-byes died out, and an apprehensive silence fell over the Pilgrims. As the small ship sailed away toward the horizon, the full weight of their situation settled in on them. Gone now was their last link with England, and there might be no new ones. Given the tone of their parting with Weston, they could not count on the Adventurers sending another supply ship. They were alone.

Brewster and Bradford and others would have been sensitive to the dangers of these lurking fears gaining control of their hearts. Fear and discouragement, Brewster knew, were two of Satan's most potent weapons. These could be dealt with best by the Sword of the Spirit, the Word of God. So passages of Scripture like Isaiah 41:8–10, read aloud in the blockhouse, would have lifted their hearts:

> But you, Israel, my servant,
>   Jacob, whom I have chosen,
>   the offspring of Abraham, my friend;
> you whom I took from the ends of the earth,
>   and called from its farthest corners,
> saying to you, "You are my servant,
>   I have chosen you and not cast you off";
> fear not, for I am with you,
>   be not dismayed, for I am your God;
> I will strengthen you, I will help you,
>   I will uphold you with my victorious right hand.

In May, as the weather began to warm up and the wild flowers were coming into full blossom, the little community had an occasion for real joy: their first wedding! Edward Winslow had lost his wife in the General Sickness, and Susanna White had lost her husband. They both felt that God did not intend for them to carry on alone, in spite of the short length of time their spouses had been gone. And so Governor Bradford joined them in holy matrimony, and there was a wedding feast with much gaiety and laughter—a cleansing and healing gift from the Lord.

That summer of 1621 was beautiful. Much work went into the building of new dwellings, and ten men were sent north up the coast in the sailing shallop to conduct trade with the Indians. Squanto once again acted as their guide and interpreter. It was a successful trip, and that fall's harvest provided more than enough corn to see them through their second winter.

The Pilgrims were brimming over with gratitude—not only to Squanto and the Wampanoags who had been so friendly, but to their God. In Him they had trusted, and He had honored their obedience beyond their dreams. So, Governor Bradford declared a day of public Thanksgiving, to be held in October.[10] Massasoit was invited, and unexpectedly arrived a day early—with *ninety* Indians! Counting their numbers, the Pilgrims had to pray hard to keep from giving in to despair. To feed such a crowd would cut deeply into the food supply that was supposed to get them through the winter.

But if they had learned one thing through their travails, it was to trust God *implicitly*. As it turned out, the Indians were not arriving empty-handed. Massasoit had commanded his braves to hunt for the occasion, and they arrived with no less than five dressed deer, and more than a dozen fat wild turkeys! And they helped with the preparations, teaching the Pilgrim women how to make hoecakes and a tasty pudding out of cornmeal and maple syrup. Finally, they showed them an Indian delicacy: how to roast corn kernels in an earthen pot until they popped, fluffy and white—*popcorn!*

The Pilgrims in turn provided many vegetables from their household gardens: carrots, onions, turnips, parsnips, cucumbers, radishes, beets, and cabbages. Also, using some of their precious flour, they took summer fruits which the Indians had dried and introduced them to the likes of blueberry, apple, and cherry pie. It was all washed down with sweet wine made from the wild grapes. A joyous occasion for all!

Between meals, the Pilgrims and Indians happily competed in shooting contests with gun and bow. The Indians were especially delighted that John Alden and some of the younger men of the plantation were eager to join them in foot races and wrestling. There were even military drills staged by Captain Standish. Things went so well (and Massasoit showed no inclination to leave) that Thanksgiving Day was extended for three days.

Surely, one moment stood out in the Pilgrims' memory—William Brewster's prayer, as they began the festival. They had so much for which to thank God: for providing *all* their needs, even when their faith had not been up to believing that He would do so; for the lives of the departed and for taking them home to be with Him; for their friendship with the Indians—so extraordinary when settlers to the south of them had experienced the opposite; for all His remarkable providences in bringing them to this place and sustaining them.

In November, a full year after their arrival, the first ship from home dropped anchor in the harbor. It was the *Fortune,* on her way to Virginia, and leaving off a cargo at Plymouth: thirty-five more colonists, including William Brewster's grown son, Jonathan, two brothers of Edward Winslow, and of all people, Robert Cushman! And he had with him a charter—their own charter—granted through the New England Company!

In the air of celebration that followed, no one stopped to think that these newcomers had brought not one bit of equipment with them—no food, no clothing, no tools, no bedding. In the cold light of the following morning, a sobering appraisal by Bradford, Brewster, and Winslow was taken, and a grim decision was reached: they would all have to go on half-rations through the winter, to ensure enough food to see them into the summer season, when fish and game would be plentiful.

And they had a difficult matter to consider: Weston was still angry that they had refused to sign his revised agreement and he was even more angry that they had sent the *Mayflower* back empty. "I know your weakness was the cause of it . . . more weakness of judgment, than weakness of hands. A quarter of the time you spent in discoursing, arguing, and consulting . . . ." [11]

A measure of the Pilgrims' spiritual maturity was that they did *not* respond in kind. Bradford wrote a dispassionate and honest answer, denying that they had spent any time discoursing and arguing, and pointing out that half of their number had died. He added that they would be sending goods just as soon as they were able.

But Weston's accusations were not the heaviest burdens which were laid upon them. For the Pilgrims were soon to learn the real purpose of Cushman's visit. Toward the end of the *Fortune*'s two-week stay, Cushman preached on "The Sin and Danger of Self-Love":

[if thou] art not sad, churlish or discontent, but cheerful in thine heart, though thy will be crossed, it is a good sign. But if not, thou art sick of a self-will, and must purge it out. I rather press these things, because I see many men both wise and religious which are yet so tainted with this pestilent self-love, as that it is in them even as a dead fly to the apothecary's ointment, spoiling the efficacy of all their graces, making their lives uncomfortable to themselves and unprofitable to others, being neither fit for church nor commonwealth, but have even their very souls in hazard thereby, and therefore who can say too much against it.

It is reported that there are many men gone to Virginia, which, while they lived in England, seemed very religious, zealous and conscionable, and have now lost even the sap of grace and edge to all goodness, and are become mere worldlings. This testimony I believe to be partly true, and amongst many causes of it, this self-love is not the least . . . . [12]

It was a strong sermon: in effect, he was saying to the Pilgrims that if they did not give up their willfulness and self-love (sins which they did have, though in far less measure than any group of people we had run across in three centuries of American history), they were in danger of winding up in the same condition as the Jamestown settlers! The Pilgrims heeded it, and sought to apply it to their personal lives.

Though Cushman had preached in all sincerity, it soon became apparent what specific "willfulness" he had in mind. Scarcely was his sermon over than he began to press Carver, Brewster, Bradford, and the other principals to capitulate to Weston's revised conditions.

Here is a striking example of how a loyal Christian's judgment and covenanted commitment can be subtly compromised, when once he chooses to give less than his all. Cushman's crisis of faith had occurred back in Dartmouth, when the *Speedwell* was having its difficulties. He had lost his heart for the Pilgrims' undertaking and had declined to go with them aboard the *Mayflower*. Choosing the easier way, he had justified it by impressing upon them how much he was "needed" in London, to act as their liaison with the Adventurers.

As it happened, he was probably the last one who should have been representing them. When Robinson and Brewster had written to reprimand him for accepting Weston's alterations without first checking with them, he had written a three-page reply, correcting his superiors for their avarice and willfulness! But the Pilgrims, perhaps because they did not want to hurt his feelings or simply because there was no one else to send, chose to overlook his shortcomings.

Weston, however, knew exactly how to manipulate Cushman. More and more, Cushman came under the worldly influence of Weston and his powerful associates. Eventually, though he was probably unaware of it, Robert Cushman came to think of himself and the Adventurers in terms of "we," and "they" were a handful of simple farmers some three thousand miles away. Thus could Cushman, with utmost sincerity, call on the Pilgrims to repent, and then give them the opportunity to demonstrate their repentance by accepting the contractual conditions which they so detested.

And the Pilgrims, their own faith momentarily shaken, again could not quite bring themselves to totally trust God, despite their previous, long-standing conviction that it was His will for them to refuse. All they could see was that further refusal would close their last channel for desperately needed supplies, and (for Cushman so assured them) they would be totally cut off. So they signed the agreement—thereby entering into a bondage to the Adventurers which would see them struggle for more than twenty years to get out from under.

The Pilgrims were mercilessly taken advantage of, at times having to borrow money at interest rates of 30 and 50 percent! Some of the most unscrupulous Adventurers, seeing that their "partners" in America were determined to pay every shilling charged to them with no questions asked, began to load them with claims so bogus that other Adventurers urged the Pilgrims not to pay, or at least to resort to the courts.

But the colonists were set on responding in the spirit of their Lord; "You have heard that it was said, 'An eye for an eye, and a tooth for a tooth.' But I say to you . . . . if any one would sue you and take your coat, let him have your cloak as well" (Matthew 5:38–40). They paid every claim assessed to them, no matter how fraudulent, and were finally able, in 1645, to buy themselves clear of the Adventurers. But at a fearful cost: it took some twenty thousand pounds to retire a debt of eighteen hundred! And to do it, Bradford had to sell a large farm, Alden and Standish, three hundred acres apiece, and Winslow and Prence, their homes.

Our own first response, had we been in the Pilgrims' place, would have been to choose another verse from Matthew to follow: "Behold, I send you out as sheep in the midst of wolves; so be wise as serpents and innocent as doves" (Matthew 10:16). But on reflection, we began to see the wisdom in the harder course they so prayerfully chose: for Satan would have liked nothing better than to have drawn them into the bitter wrangling and legal disputes which were commonplace in the business dealings of that day. Nothing corrodes the soul quite so fast or effectively. Here, too, the hand of a loving Father could be seen. For while the Pilgrims may have been out of His will when they knuckled under to Weston's demands, God was still ensuring the purity of the work which He was raising up at Plymouth. What mattered most to Him was *not* what was done to the Pilgrims (He would deal with the Adventurers in His own way, and they would regret it for a long, long time—"For insomuch as ye do it unto the least of these . . ."). What mattered to God was how the Pilgrims responded to it. And He was pleased with their response: they kept their eyes, for the most part, on Him.

Thus, they did enter their own starving time that winter of 1621–22 (with all the extra people to feed and shelter), and were ultimately reduced to a daily ration of five kernels of corn a piece. (Five kernels of corn—it is almost inconceivable how life could be supported on this.) But as always, they had a choice: either to give in to bitterness and despair or to go deeper into Christ. They chose Christ. And in contrast to what happened at Jamestown, not one of them died of starvation.

Then God had mercy on them, as He had so often in the past.

Unexpectedly, a ship put into their harbor on its way back to England, from Virginia. While the captain had no extra food on board, he did have trading goods—beads, knives, trinkets, and so on, which the Pilgrims could trade for corn. His price? Beaver pelts, for which he would give them three shillings per pound. The Pilgrims well knew that he would sell the pelts at home for *six* times as much. But they had no choice, and they were able to thank God for seeing them through that winter.

And what of Thomas Weston? "Though the mills of God grind slowly, yet they grind exceeding fine" goes the old saying. Weston, not content to wait seven years, and acting independently of the other Adventurers, set up his own fishing enterprise, just a few miles up the coast from Plymouth at Wessagusset (now Weymouth). The other Adventurers got wind of what he was up to and expelled him from their consortium. About the same time, everything began to go so badly for him, that to escape his creditors he disguised himself as a fisherman and sailed for the New World himself, planning on using his fishing station as a new base of operations.

But the fishing station was no more. The bunch of roughnecks he had sent there had consumed a year's supplies in four months, had sold their equipment to the Indians for food, and were mainly interested in staying drunk from sunup to sundown. Moreover, they had so provoked the Indians that the latter were considering a general attack on the settlers. Finally, Standish and a few men had been forced to give Weston's rowdies an ultimatum: They were welcome to come to Plymouth, or they could sail for home; but they were to be gone on the next tide. They sailed within the hour, and peace returned to Massachusetts Bay.

When Weston arrived at Charlestown, he could not believe what he had been told about his fishing station, and with another man hired a shallop to see for himself. Bad seamanship caused their vessel to founder, and Weston was then relieved of all his belongings save his shirt by some local Indians. Knowing nowhere else to go, he made for Plymouth on foot. When he finally turned up on their doorstep, he presented a sorry sight indeed.

This was a far different Weston from the imperious overlord who had bent them to his will before. Sniveling and caviling, he begged them for mercy, and for more than that: the loan of a load of beaver skins, to get him back on his feet. He assured them that he would repay them in supplies, as soon as the transaction was completed, though he assured them he would never be able to repay their compassion. They "pitied his case" said Bradford, "and helped him when all the world failed him"—[13] and gave him the beaver skins. He did eventually repay them—with scorn and vicious slander, and not a penny in recompense.

It was April of 1623, time to get the year's corn planted. But as the Pilgrims went into the fields to till the ground and put in the seed, there was a listlessness about them that was more than just weakness from months of inadequate rations. They were well aware that they needed at least twice as great a yield as the first harvest and they did not want a repeat of the half-hearted effort of the second summer (when they had been too busy building houses and planting gardens to give the common cornfields the attention they needed). So the principal men of the colony decided that there would be an additional planting. But for this second planting individual lots would be parceled out, with the understanding that the corn grown on these lots would be for the planters' own private use.

Suddenly, new life seemed to infuse the Pilgrims:

. . . it made all hands very industrious, so as much more corn was planted than otherwise would have been by any means the Governor or any other could use, and saved him a great deal of trouble and gave far better content. The women now went willingly into the field and took their little ones with them to set corn, which before would allege weakness and inability, whom to have compelled would have been thought great tyranny and oppression.

Some time after the second planting, it became apparent that the dry spell which had begun between the two plantings was turning into a drought. Week followed week (it would continue for twelve weeks in all), and not even the oldest Indians could remember anything like it. Edward Winslow described the drought, and what followed:

There scarce fell any rain, so that the stalk of that [planting which] was first set, began to send forth the ear before it came to half growth, and that which was later, not like to yield any at all, both blade and stalk hanging the head and changing the color in such manner as we judged it utterly dead. Our beans also ran not up according to their wonted manner, but stood at a stay, many being parched away, as though they had been scorched before the fire. Now were our hopes overthrown, and we discouraged, our joy turned into mourning . . . because God, which hitherto had been our only shield and supporter, now seemed in His anger to arm Himself against us. And who can withstand the fierceness of His wrath?

These and the like considerations moved not only every good man privately to enter into examination with his own estate between God and his conscience, and so to humiliation before Him, but also to humble ourselves together before the Lord by fasting and prayer. To that end, a day was appointed by public authority, and set apart from all other employments.[14]

At this point we wondered what might have caused God to visit such a judgment upon His new Chosen People? At first, we were at a loss to find anything which seemed to merit such severe, across-the-board dealing. And then it came to us: if we had been Pilgrims, how would *we* have responded after enduring months of always being hungry?

We found, when we looked at the natural inclination of our own hearts, that we too would have been out there planting as many kernels as we possibly could. And not just to ensure that we would never be that hungry again; we would have dwelt much on what we were going to get in trade for the extra ears.

And God would have been nowhere in view; we would have been totally absorbed in looking out for our own interests. If the fellow next door were not able to plant his plot as well as we could, well—too bad for him. In the end, we saw that the moment greed and self began to get the upper hand, there was little difference between golden kernels and golden coins. It occurred to us that even though the Pilgrims were unquestionably more sanctified than we, they had not been exposed to the subtle pitfalls of personal greed for a very long time. And it also seemed that God was using this whole episode to show them an area of self in which they had not actually overcome as much as they might have thought. For in a way, sin is like the layers of an onion: when one layer is peeled off, there are always more layers beneath.

Whatever may have brought on the drought, the sincere and deep repentance of each and every Pilgrim had a phenomenal effect. Winslow continues:

But, O the mercy of our God, who was as ready to hear, as we were to ask! For though in the morning, when we assembled together, the heavens were as clear and the drought as like to continue as it ever was, yet (our exercise continuing some eight or nine hours) before our departure, the weather was overcast, the clouds gathered on all sides. On the next morning distilled such soft, sweet and moderate showers of rain, continuing some fourteen days[!] and mixed with such seasonable weather, as it was hard to say whether our withered corn or drooping affections were most quickened or revived, such was the bounty and goodness of our God!

Bradford says: ". . . It came, without either wind or thunder, or any violence, and by degrees in that abundance as that the earth was thoroughly wet and soaked therewith. Which did so apparently revive and quicken the decayed corn and other fruits, as was wonderful to see and made the Indians astonished to behold . . . ." [15]

It *had* to have had a profound effect on the Indians! For while their own rain dances or the incantations of their medicine men did sometimes seem to have some effect, it is interesting to note the result, as Winslow comments: ". . . and all of them admired the goodness of our God towards us, that wrought so great a change in so short a time, showing the difference between their conjuration and our invocation on the name of God for rain, theirs being mixed with such storms and tempests, as sometimes, instead of doing them good, it layeth the corn flat on the ground, to their prejudice, but ours in so gentle and seasonable a manner, as they never observed the like." [16] There are only two origins of supernatural phenomena, and as the Pilgrims might have said, "The proof of the pudding is in the eating."

The yield that year was so abundant that the Pilgrims ended up with a surplus of corn, which they were able to use in trading that winter with northern Indians, who had not had a good growing season. A second Day of Thanksgiving was planned, and this year there was even more reason to celebrate: their beloved Governor was to marry one Alice Southworth. Massasoit was again the guest of honor, and this time he brought his principal wife, three other sachems, and *120 braves!* Fortunately he again brought venison and turkey, as well.

The occasion was described by one of the Adventurers, Emmanuel Altham, in a letter to his brother:

After our arrival in New England, we found all our plantation in good health, and neither man, woman or child sick . . . in this plantation is about twenty houses, four or five of which are very pleasant, and the rest (as time will serve) shall be made better . . . the fishing that is in this country, indeed it is beyond belief . . . in one hour we got 100 cod . . . .

And now to say somewhat of the great cheer we had at the Governor's marriage. We had about twelve tasty venisons, besides others, pieces of

roasted venison and other such good cheer in such quantities that I wish
you some of our share. For here we have the best grapes that ever you
saw, and the biggest, and divers sorts of plums and nuts . . . six goats,
about fifty hogs and pigs, also divers hens . . . A better country was
never seen nor heard of, for here are a multitude of God's blessing.[17]

What Altham neglected to mention was the first course that was
served: on an empty plate in front of each person were five kernels
of corn . . . lest anyone should forget.

These Pilgrims were a mere handful of Light-bearers, on the
edge of a vast and dark continent. But the Light of Jesus Christ was
penetrating further into the heart of America. William Bradford
would write with remarkable discernment, "As one small candle
may light a thousand, so the light kindled here has shown unto
many, yea in some sort to our whole nation . . . . We have noted
these things so that you might see their worth and not negligently
lose what your fathers have obtained with so much hardship." [18]

7

Thy Kingdom Come

"The Puritans really believed it," Peter mused, breaking the heavy silence that hung over the patio.

"Believed what?" asked David, not really caring.

We were sitting in back of Peter's parents' house in Florida, where we had met for an editorial conference—and were facing the fact that our first draft of the Puritan chapters was little more than an outline of history. Gone was all enthusiasm for the material; we sensed that we had missed the point of what God had wanted us to see.

Now, in the aftermath of that confrontation with reality, we were well into despondency. The early morning sun was filtering down through the fronds of the palm trees, bathing everything in a soft, delicate haze. Not a hint of a breeze stirred the trees. But we were oblivious to the beauty around us, as we sat staring at our coffee cups.

"They actually believed," Peter answered, speaking half to himself, "what few people have, before or since: that the Kingdom of God really *could* be built on earth, in their lifetimes . . . . They knew that they were sinners. But like the Pilgrims, they were dedicated to actually living together in obedience to God's laws, under the Lordship of Jesus Christ."

"Yes, but—" and suddenly a breeze came out of nowhere and scattered several chapters' worth of manuscript across the patio. As we gathered up the pages, it occurred to David that this was the only breeze to stir a paper in the last three days. When we sat back down, he dropped the questioning. All he said was, "Go on."

Peter paused for a moment to recapture what had started coming to him. "All it needed, they felt, was the right time, the right place, and the right people," he paused again. "All hinged on that: *if* the right people were willing to commit themselves totally."

For the next hour and a half, the Holy Spirit gave us insight after insight . . . . The Puritans were the people who, more than any other, made possible America's foundation as a Christian nation. Far from merely fleeing the persecutions of King and Bishop, they determined to change their society in the only way that could make any lasting difference: by giving it a Christianity that worked. And this they set out to do, not by words but by example, in the one place where it was still possible to live the life to which Christ had called them: three thousand miles beyond the reach of the very Church they were seeking to purify.

The Spirit also reminded us that the legacy of Puritan New England to this nation, which can still be found at the core of our American way of life, may be summed up in one word: *covenant.* We were reminded that on the night of the Last Supper, to those who were closest to Him, Jesus said, "This is my blood of *the new covenant,* which is poured out for many for the forgiveness of sins . . . ."

Covenant . . . it is a word almost never heard in American life today, for it speaks of a commitment to Christ *and* to one another which is deeper and more demanding than most of us are willing to make. And as a consequence, most of us modern American Christians are of little use to God in the building of His Kingdom. For the building of that Kingdom, as the Puritans demonstrated, requires total commitment.

Sitting on the patio that morning, we were convicted that our own commitment to the church community where God had placed us did not yet measure up to that of the Puritans.

A candle had been bravely set at Plymouth, the first to confound the darkness of New England—but what of the candles still burning in Old England? What of the Puritans, the white lights of the Protestant Reformation? They were beginning to flicker—not through any faltering of zeal, but under the combined pressure of accelerated persecution and the advanced moral decay in their society.

London in the 1620s has been romanticized almost out of reality by most modern writers. "Gay, colorful, lusty, brimming with all the drama of the Elizabethan Age"—this is the stereotype to which we have been conditioned. If one were there, one would breathe in the excitement of just *being* there, and one's step would be a bit springier with the zest of it all. For who knew what adventure lurked round the next corner?

The truth of early seventeenth-century London is about as far removed from the paperback notion of it, as today's Manhattan is from "Fun City." To begin with, you wanted to breathe in as little of old London as possible; in fact, a well-perfumed handkerchief was more a piece of survival equipment than a mannered affectation! And as for your step being springier, it had better be, considering what came flying out of upper windows, to the cry of "Gardez-loo!"

No, London was not the sort of place you would want to take your child for a walk, even in the morning. For you would have to walk warily to avoid drunkards and tosspots reeling and brawling in the narrow streets. The taverns did a roaring business around the clock, being the main source of public entertainment, especially if one were not in the mood for a hanging or a play, or watching dogs bait a bear or pull a screaming ape apart.[1]

Running the taverns a close second were the trollops that hung out of windows overhead, displaying their wares and pouring out a stream of commentary on all who passed below. And as for adventure lurking around the next corner—it was worth your life to go anywhere in London on foot. Cutpurses abounded in the teeming streets. Though robbery was a hanging crime, life had become so meaningless that it was worth risking, just to steal money enough for a few days' oblivion in a grog shop. (No wonder there were 137 capital offenses on the statute books! There *had* to be, to maintain even a semblance of law and order!)

The real tragedy of London, however, was not restricted to what was happening in its streets, but included what was happening in its heart. In the City, London's financial district, life on the other side of the massive oaken doors of mercantile power was every bit as brutalizing, though it was played in Italian silks and fine brocade. For in a godless society, when it is possible to send out a ship and have it return with a cargo worth more than the ship itself, and interest rates of 50 percent are not uncommon, money becomes almost divine. The men who handle it do so with the utmost respect and obeisance, loving, honoring—and worshiping it—and accumulating as much money as possible, as quickly as possible.

If, as Paul wrote to Timothy, the love of money *is* the root of all evil, that might explain some of the other evils at London's heart. Graft and bribery had become an accepted part of daily business. Cheating, double-dealing, the betrayal of one's word—or friend—were all part of the game. The end invariably justified whatever means were necessary to obtain it.

London was an accurate spiritual barometer for the rest of the country, for England had become a nation without a soul. A beggar could die of exposure in a merchant's doorway, and the merchant, arriving to open up in the morning would be irate at having to step over the body, and would fret about how bad it might be for business until it was disposed of.

An old acquaintance might lose several ships to pirates, and find himself fleeing the country ahead of his creditors or actually in a debtors' prison. In which case, the response of his so-called friends might be: "Too bad about Forsythe, his luck giving out that way. But then, he knew the risks . . . ."

In a transatlantic airliner, as the navigator plots the plane's projected course, at a certain point he will make a neat dot, circle it, and label it PNR. Once that point is passed, for the plane to then turn and go back to its point of departure would require more fuel than remains on board. The plane has just passed the Point of No Return. America has not quite reached that point—*yet*.

Elizabethan England reached it in 1628. That was the year that William Laud, the Church of England's "enforcer," was made Bishop of London, the most important bishopric in the country. That year also marked the beginning of the Great Migration. This lasted some sixteen years, and saw more than twenty thousand Puritans embark for New England, and forty-five thousand other Englishmen head for Virginia, the West Indies, and points south. That may not seem like a significant number, but today it would be like three million Americans packing up and leaving!

Who were these Puritans, and why was migration the only solution for them? The Puritans were a growing number of people who had entered into a deep covenant relationship with God, through the person of His Son, Jesus Christ. For each, it was the most important single decision of his life, changing that life permanently and irrevocably.

When before, life had little meaning, now it took on enormous significance. Not only had God Himself created each life; He also cared so much for each person that He sent His only Son to die for each one's sins, to bridge that irreconcilable gap between them— sin-stained as they were—and a holy just God. Thus it became the redeemed person's daily response to seek the will of the Saviour and do it, obedience being all-important.

For the Puritans were never complacent about their salvation. As the English Puritan theologian Richard Baxter put it: "Man's fall was his turning from God to himself; and his regeneration consisteth in the turning of him from himself to God . . . [Hence,] self-denial and the love of God are all [one] . . . The very names of Self and Own, should sound in the watchful Christian's ears as very terrible, wakening words, that are next to the names of sin and Satan." [2]

And Thomas Hooker, the most articulate of the ministers, spoke for all the New England Puritans, when he further identified their primary adversary as not Satan but Self. "Not what Self will, but what the Lord will!" declared Hooker. Self was "the great snare" and "the false Christ," "a spider's web [spun] out of our bowels, the very figure or type of hell." To "lay down god-Self," to purge "the Devil's poison and venom or infection of Self," was "to kill the old Adam in us" and to strike a blow against "Antichrist, that is, the Self in all." [3] The Puritan need not be overly concerned with the Devil; if he directed his energies toward Christ and against Self, Satan would have little enough access to him.

Since how a Puritan was faring in his battle against sin and self was more important to him than anything else, many of them kept spiritual journals. One of the most dedicated Puritans in England was John Winthrop. Cambridge-educated, and the owner of a sizable estate in Suffolk, Winthrop was an attorney in the Court of Wards, and a Justice of the Peace. He penned these lines in 1612 at the age of twenty-four:

I desire to make it one of my chief petitions to have that grace to be poor in spirit. I will ever walk humbly before my God, and meekly, mildly, and gently towards all men . . . . I do resolve first to give myself—my life, my wits, my health, my wealth—to the service of my God and Saviour who, by giving Himself for me and to me, deserves whatsoever I am or can be, to be at His commandment and for His glory. [4]

And in 1616 he wrote:

O Lord . . . Thou assurest my heart that I am in a right course, even the narrow way that leads to heaven. Thou tellest me, and all experience tells me, that in this way there is least company, and that those who do walk openly in this way shall be despised, pointed at, hated by the world, made a byword, reviled, slandered, rebuked, made a gazing stock, called

Puritans, nice fools, hypocrites, hare-brained fellows, rash, indiscreet, vainglorious, and all that naught is. Yet . . . teach me, O Lord, to put my trust in Thee, then shall I be like Mount Sion that cannot be moved.

Life was an unending battle between Flesh and Spirit for young Winthrop, as it is for most Christians.

Before the week was gone about, I began to lose my former affections. I upheld the outward duties, but the power and life of them was in a manner gone . . . . And still, the more I prayed and meditated, the worse I grew—the more dull, unbelieving, vain in heart, etc. so as I waxed exceeding discontent and impatient, being sometimes ready to fret and storm against God, because I found not that blessing upon my prayers and other means that I did expect. But, O Lord, forgive me! Searching my heart at last, I found the world had stolen away my love from my God . . . Then I acknowledged my unfaithfulness and pride of heart, and turned again to my God, and humbled my soul before Him, and He returned and accepted me, and so I renewed my Covenant of walking with my God, and watching my heart and ways. O my God, forsake me not.

Winthrop's covenant relationship with the Lord deepened through the years. His was to be a towering commitment to Christ, reminiscent of the French and Spanish missionaries before him.

Meanwhile, the Puritan movement was gaining momentum. When this radical, life-changing experience happened to one, the natural thing was to share it with friends. God was now blessing these lives which were being lived for Him instead of primarily for self. This, in turn, made them ever more desirous of living according to His will. Since God's will was made known to them largely through His inspired Word in the Bible, they naturally wanted to get as close to a Scriptural order of worship as possible. Indeed, what they ultimately wanted was to bring the Church back to something approximating New Testament Christianity.

What they did *not* want was to tear away from the Church of England. They condemned the Separatists for this and pledged themselves to bring about the purification of the Church through their efforts *within* its framework and by their own enlightened example. The trouble was, the Bishops in charge of the Church saw no need for any purification and resented the Puritans for what they considered to be their intrusive, presumptuous, divisive, and holier-than-thou ways. The more the Puritans pushed, the more the Bishops resisted, until there was open enmity.

The Puritan dilemma was similar to that of many newly regenerate Christians of our time. They faced a difficult choice: should they leave their seemingly lifeless churches to join or start a live one, or should they stay where they were, to be used as that small candle to which William Bradford referred? Many of them felt that God had called them to walk the harder way of staying, so they stayed.

But too often the attitude of their heart was anything but submissive. And sooner or later their heart attitude was going to make itself known. Thus many newly converted Puritans must have manifested—along with their contagious enthusiasm for the Christian life—a degree of self-righteousness, impatience, and spiritual superiority. (It is astonishing how little we "Puritans" have changed in three hundred years!)

As the Puritan movement grew older in the first two decades of the seventeenth century, it matured considerably. Adherents from all social classes and walks of life began to be attracted—including Oxford and Cambridge-trained clergy, and some of the most brilliant scholars and theologians of the age.

So now they faced their first hard testing, for Jesus had warned His disciples that the world would hate anyone who truly determined to follow Him. The Puritans were despised, but not really hated as much as the Separatists were, who had given up their homes, their jobs, their country, *everything,* to live as Jesus had called them.

Here was the core difference between the emigrating Puritans and Pilgrims: God was still leading the Puritans step by step to the place where they *would* be willing to give up what the Pilgrims had already given up. For the Puritans had more than the Pilgrims—more money, more servants, more friends in high places, more education, more business experience. They had more of everything except one thing: compassion.

Compassion is not something you can learn, or put on, or even pray for. Compassion is produced through the living out of the daily sufferings and sacrifices of a life freely given to Him. For the Pilgrims, it was the fruit of undergoing a persecution so severe that they had to leave their native land or lose their lives; of twelve years of hard, penurious exile; and four months of dark, tossing, stinking, soaking torment; and four more of cold and sickly, mortal suffering. It was the fruit of coming to know the depths of one's sinful nature, and the cleansing of daily repentance and forgiveness. It was experiencing the peace and joy that comes from *know-*

ing that one could do absolutely nothing, save for the grace of God and the Lord Jesus dwelling within.

It was the greater depth of Christlike compassion and humility which marked the difference between the Puritan and the Pilgrim (with some notable Puritan exceptions). And the selflessness and caring of the Pilgrims happened, not in a remote, cloistered setting or far-removed missionary hospital, but *here*—in America's fields and woodlands. It *was* possible . . . and it is this that draws tourists to Plymouth in such great numbers, though perhaps not one in a thousand is consciously aware of it.

But God was bringing the Puritans into compassion and humility, even as He allowed the pressure of mounting persecution to come upon them. They accepted it with grace and, as persecution often does, it served to rapidly deepen and mature the movement, bonding them together in common cause and making them more determined than ever to live as God had called them.

Now, however, there was some question as to the nature of God's call on their lives. As long as James I had been King (1603–25), the persecution had been bearable, since the Archbishop of Canterbury was both moderate and sympathetic to the Puritan cause. But the situation changed under Charles I (1625–49). No sooner had he made William Laud the Bishop of London in 1628, than Laud presented the King with a list of English clergy. Behind each name was an *O* or a *P*—if Orthodox, they were in line for promotion; if Puritan, they were marked for suppression.

For a number of Puritans, this was the watershed. It appeared no longer possible to reform the Church of England from within.

Did this now mean they would have to go underground? Would they have to start worshiping in secret? If so, then they might as well face the fact that they would sooner or later have to follow the footsteps of the Separatists, and separation was against everything the Puritans believed in! Yet they were not revolutionaries; they believed in orderly reform. The trouble was, the King and the Bishops were making it impossible!

To separate or not to separate . . . . Out of this sharpening tension grew a startling alternative—one so radical that at first it was hard to contemplate it, let alone pray about it. The possibility: the Church could still be reformed from within—but from a nine-hundred-league remove. *It could be done in America.*

America—why not a settlement of Puritans there, loyal to the Crown and to the Church, but sufficiently removed to have a chance to live in true obedience to God? If only they could have that chance—a few years in which to demonstrate what could happen when a body of Christians was allowed to live wholly and totally unto God. Surely the fruits of living that way would not only stir up the Church, they would be a beacon to all Christendom!

The right place, the right time, and the right people . . . . America was obviously the right place—virginal, wild, as yet untainted by the godless corruption that had befouled the known world, and peopled with savage heathen who had never heard the Gospel and whose hearts therefore were not hardened to it. To be sure, these heathen could be used by Satan; the New World had yet to be won from him, and the Puritans were familiar with the martyrdom of those who had gone before. But if God was with them, all the powers of hell could not prevail against them. The place was America, and more specifically, the place where God would begin was New England. For the reports out of Plymouth were uniformly encouraging and reliable, unlike the wild fabrications and gruesome truths out of Virginia.

And the time was surely now: London was a veritable sink of depravity. And now that the King had dissolved Parliament and announced that he would run the country by himself (1629), it was not a question of when, but how soon.

A few far-sighted Puritans could sense God's hand in a coincidence of timing which was too extraordinary to be accidental. Had Columbus landed farther north . . . . Had the Spanish colonization of Florida been successful . . . . Had Raleigh succeeded in settling Roanoke . . . Had Jamestown been less of a catastrophe . . . . Had America's very existence not remained cloaked until the Reformation . . . . Had her northeastern coast not been reserved for the Pilgrims and Puritans . . . . To some, it must have seemed almost as if they were standing in the middle of a gigantic model of one of those new-fangled pocket watches, with the wheels and gears of "coincidence" swinging around and meshing and turning other gears, which swung and turned others . . . .

But they could see only behind them. Today we can see what lay ahead of them as well, and sense just how extraordinary was the timing of the Puritan exodus. If Laud had not come to power and abetted the King in his drive to bring the Puritans to heel . . . . If the English Puritans' Glorious Revolution had begun ten years earlier, there might not have been a Puritan exodus in sufficient numbers to seed America with spiritual liberty. For there were not nearly enough Pilgrims to do the work that was needed, let alone withstand the concerted pressure of Church and Crown. The Puritans were the right people.

When one considers the major events swinging slowly around on the biggest gears—the American Revolution, the Age of Reason, the Industrial Revolution, the rise and wane of empires, the gradual aligning of the forces of darkness and light, and the gradual dimming of the brightest light—time seems much compressed. It becomes apparent what the Bible means when it says that to God, a thousand years is as a single day. Knowing man's nature, and how few would freely choose His way, God knew what the twentieth century would hold in store. He also knew the totalitarian darknesses that would arise out of Europe and Asia, and knew that England alone would never have the spiritual power to stop them. And so He planted the seeds of light that would make the difference early in the seventeenth century.

The astonishing alignment of all the factors of time and place reminds one of what they used to call at Cape Canaveral a *launch window*—an interval of a few hours during which every predictable factor which might affect a moon shot or a Mars probe would be as favorable as it could be. Once the window had passed, it might be weeks, months, or even years before conditions would again line up as favorably.

But the launching of the Puritan exodus to America was far more awesome. To us, from our vantage point, it looked as if in all the years of Christendom, there was only one brief window, one main chance. And rather than lifting off from a stationary launch pad, it seemed as if the Puritans were a stone placed in a whirling sling and let fly just as the tiny window hove into view. Up and out they went, arcing right through it, clear to their landing place in America.

The right place, the right time, the right people . . . . It remained to be seen if the right people would be willing to give themselves totally.

As the prospect of a Bible Commonwealth in New England became a real possibility in the thinking of the most dedicated Puritans, events began to move quickly. First, the New England Company was reorganized as the Massachusetts Bay Company. A new, enlarged charter was routinely processed through Parliament and presented for His Majesty's signature. But the King failed to notice that there was no mention of where the Company's meetings were to be held. He signed it and forgot about it. The wondrous timing of God can further be seen in the fact that, less than a week later, the King dissolved Parliament and took the reins of the country entirely into his own hands, thereafter jealously scrutinizing every document to ensure that his authority was in no way diminished!

The Bay Company's partners were privately jubilant. There was now nothing binding them to England, nothing to prevent them from moving to New England themselves—and taking their charter with them. Once removed from the suspicious eyes of Church and Crown, the Company could become a self-governing commonwealth with the charter as its *carte blanche*. Only now, they would be governed by the laws of God, not merely the laws of men. Not since God had brought the first Chosen People into the first Promised Land had a nation enjoyed such an opportunity.

The Puritans' exodus conspiracy shifted into high gear. Preparations had long been made, and soon after the new charter had been secured, two ships with some two hundred people aboard sailed past Land's End. As the coast of Cornwall faded in the distance, their leader, the Reverend Francis Higginson, exclaimed to the passengers: "We will not say, as the Separatists were wont to say at their leaving of England, 'Farewell Rome!' or 'Farewell Babylon!' But we will say, 'Farewell dear England! Farewell the Church of God in England, and all the Christian friends there! We do not go to New England as Separatists from the Church of England, though we cannot but separate from the corruptions in it, but we go to practice the positive part of church reformation, and propagate the Gospel in America!' " [5]

The exodus had begun. But in order to gain the necessary momentum, it would need a Moses. The principal partners had such a man in mind—John Winthrop. But Winthrop himself was not at all sure that it was God's will that he go. On such major steps as this, he knew that God sometimes seemed to withdraw Himself, to give the individual the opportunity to move out on faith. And so he did what so many Christians have done in similar situations: he drew up a list of pros and cons—which was later published [6]—and helped thousands of Puritans to clarify their own decisions.

His reasons for undertaking the intended plantation in New England included:

[It would be] a service to the Church of great consequence to carry the Gospel into those parts of the world . . . .

All other Churches of Europe are brought to desolation . . . and who knows but that God hath provided this place to be a refuge for many whom He means to save out of the general calamity. [La Rochelle, the seaport bastion in which the French Huguenots had held out for two years, had just fallen to Cardinal Richelieu, and in Germany, Wallenstein was pulverizing the armies of the Protestants.] And seeing the Church hath no place left to fly into but the wilderness, what better work can there be, than to go and provide tabernacles and food for her against [that time when] she comes thither.

This land grows weary of her inhabitants, so as man, who is the most precious of all creatures, is here more vile and base than the earth we tread upon, and of less price among us than a horse or a sheep . . .

. . . All arts and trades are carried in that deceitful and unrighteous course, [so] it is almost impossible for a good and upright man to maintain his charge and live comfortably in any of them.

The fountains of learning and religion are so corrupted as most children are perverted [and] corrupted . . . .

Then Winthrop went on to state objections against the plantation, with his answers. For example:

Obj: The ill success of other plantations may tell us what will become of this.

Ans: None of the former sustained any great damage but Virginia, which happened through their own sloth . . . . There were great and fundamental errors in the former which are like to be avoided in this, for their main end was carnal and not religious; they used unfit instruments, a multitude of rude and misgoverned persons, the very scum of the land; and they did not establish a right form of government.

Obj: It is attended with many and great difficulties.

Ans: So is every good action . . . . The way of God's Kingdom, which is the best way in the world, is accompanied with the most difficulties.

Thus did John Winthrop come to be persuaded that it was God's will for him to go to America. But in addition, there was an intensely personal struggle that he did not mention: on the one hand, there was his old friend and advisor, Robert Ryece, saying, ". . . the Church and commonwealth here at home hath more need of your best ability in these dangerous times, than any remote plantation." On the other hand, the principal partners, who were preparing to go themselves, considered his presence so essential that they gave him an ultimatum: if he would not lead them, they would not go either, and the founding of the plantation would be doomed.[7]

It was settled then: he would go. On August 26, 1629, he met with the other principals at Cambridge, where many of them had attended university together. They put their lives where they had already put their money and their mouths (in contrast to the Virginia and Plymouth backers). "It is fully and faithfully agreed amongst us . . . we will be ready in our persons . . . to embark for the said plantation by the first of March next . . . to pass the seas (under God's protection) to inhabit and continue in New England." [8]

As historian Perry Miller would say, "Winthrop and his colleagues believed . . . that their errand was not a mere scouting expedition: it was an essential maneuver in the drama of Christendom. The Bay Company was not a battered remnant of suffering Separatists thrown up on a rocky shore; it was an organized task force of Christians, executing a flank attack on the corruptions of Christendom. These Puritans did not flee to America; they went in order to work out that complete reformation which was not yet accomplished in England and Europe." [9]

Three days after the Cambridge Agreement, the decision was approved by the general membership of the Company, and shortly after that, Winthrop was unanimously elected Governor. He was soon burdened with the enormous headache of arranging passage for more than a thousand Puritans who were waiting to emigrate. And typically of Winthrop, the ships were ready right on schedule, and he was aboard one of the first, the *Arbella*.

By now, a farewell sermon had become a tradition, and it was preached by a stalwart young Puritan minister named John Cotton, whose star was also destined to rise over New England. He preached on 2 Samuel 7:10 (KJV): "Moreover, I will appoint a place for my people Israel, and will plant them, that they may dwell in a place of their own and move no more; neither shall the children of wickedness afflict them any more, as beforetime."

"Go forth," Cotton exhorted, ". . . with a public spirit," with that "care of universal helpfulness . . . Have a tender care . . . to your children, that they do not degenerate as the Israelites did . . ."

Samuel Eliot Morison put it thus: "Cotton's sermon was of a nature to inspire these new children of Israel with the belief that they were the Lord's chosen people; destined, if they kept the covenant with Him, to people and fructify this new Canaan in the western wilderness." [10]

And Cotton concluded his sermon:

What He hath planted, He will maintain. Every plantation His right hand hath not planted shall be rooted up, but His own plantation shall prosper and flourish. When He promiseth peace and safety, what enemies shall be able to make the promise of God of none effect? Neglect not walls and bulwarks and fortifications for your own defense, but ever let the name of the Lord be your strong tower, and the word of His promise, the rock of your refuge. His word that made heaven and earth will not fail, till heaven and earth be no more.

8

A City Upon a Hill

On June 8, 1630, John Winthrop stood at the rail of the *Arbella,* and got his first sight of New England: the fir-covered hills of Maine. He stared in wonder at pines taller than any tree he had ever seen, coming right down to the boulders on the shore. The afternoon sun was shining and an iridescent haze hung over the hills so that the firs seemed to glisten . . . .

It was so much grander than he had somehow expected. Breathtakingly beautiful, but wild and savage, too. This was not a land to be cleared and settled easily. His heart welled within him, as it occurred to him that even this forbidding wildness was a blessing, for it would discourage any who came for selfish reasons. A fresh, clear breeze came out to them over the sun-dappled waters, bearing the scent of those majestic pines, "and there came a smell off the shore like the smell of a garden." [1]

During the next few days, as they made their way down the rocky coastline, they frequently tacked in close enough to pick out individual trees and catch their delightful fragrance. It had been a peaceful voyage. Carrying a year's food supply, they did not have to arrive before the spring planting season, and so could afford to wait out the worst of the winter storms before clearing Southampton. In fact, so calm was the ocean in May, that at one point Winthrop declared a fast day, in hopes of the Lord stirring up a (moderate) wind.

A peaceful passage may not seem particularly noteworthy, but in those days it was considered another manifestation of God's special grace. As Edward Johnson, an amateur historian and contemporary of Winthrop, put it in the opening words of his *Wonder-Working Providences of Sion's Saviour in New England,* "Then judge, all you (whom the Lord hath given a discerning spirit), whether these poor New England people be not forerunners of Christ's army, and the marvelous providences which you shall now hear, be not the very finger of God." And in his first example, in this highly enthusiastic compendium of instances of divine intervention, he pointed out that, at a time when so many ships were going down in storms or being taken by pirates and privateers, only one of the 198 vessels to set sail for New England in the first half of the seventeenth century was ever lost! [2]

We can imagine Winthrop on the afterdeck, wishing his wife, Margaret, were at his side, to share all of this beauty with him. But she was back at Groton, their family estate in Suffolk (county), closing out their affairs with the help of John, Jr., and waiting for him to send for them. She had wanted to come, but had accepted that it was God's will for her to wait. She had bidden him Godspeed cheerfully, but after twenty-five years of marriage, he had sensed the loneliness in her heart and had done his best to console her, writing:

My trust is that He who hath so disposed it, will supply thee with much patience . . . . The Lord is able to do this, and thou mayest expect it, for He hath promised it. Seeing He calls me to His work, He will have care of thee and all ours and our affairs in my absence; therefore, I must send thee to Him, for all thou lackest. Go boldly, sweet wife, to the throne of Grace . . . .[3]

He knew that because they each *were* in God's will for them, she would have the same inner peace which he now had. Then too, young John was with her, and at twenty-three, he was already showing remarkable maturity and judgment. No, Winthrop's only personal concern at the moment was for his second eldest, Henry, who was with him on board the *Arbella*. Henry was the opposite of John, Jr. Seemingly determined to carve out a career as a wastrel, Henry had gone so far as to deceive his parents into permitting him to marry his cousin, with whom he was convinced that he was madly in love, by telling them that he had gotten her with child. This had turned out not to be the case, and Henry's father, after paying his son's debts, had decided to put him under firm discipline for a while, counting on the rigors of the New World to straighten him out.

On the morning of June 11, they came upon a cheerful sight: a ship at anchor with half a dozen fishing shallops around her, all bobbing up and down. A little while later, the captain informed Winthrop that they had Cape Ann in sight, which meant that they would be making Salem harbor on next morning's tide. Salem at last! After seventy-two days of waiting!

But the sight which greeted them the following morning was far from cheerful. Where was Salem? Surely this pitiful collection of huts and hovels and canvas shelters—surely *this* was not the first town of the Massachusetts Bay Company? It must be just the remnants of their first camp, temporary housing which they had not bothered to dismantle. That was it; the main town must be further back in the woods.

But as the ship drew nearer, the truth sank in: this *was* Salem. And then the people came down to the shore—gaunt and ragged-looking, glad to see the new arrivals, but something was wrong. It was something more important than their thinness or the sorry condition of their clothing—something inside of them . . . . They were listless, slow of movement, apathetic. The life was gone out of their faces, their expressions.

Deeply troubled, Winthrop went ashore in the first boat, and was met by John Endecott, the brash, quick-tempered soldier who had acted as Governor for the now-defunct New England Company, and was filling in as provisional Governor for the Massachusetts Bay Company. As soon as was politic, Winthrop arranged for a private briefing with the man he would replace. From Endecott, he learned that of the sixty-six men who had come over with him in 1628, and the two hundred who had accompanied Higginson and Skelton the following year, scarcely eighty-five remained. More than eighty had died, while the rest had quit and gone back to England. And many of those who were left were intending to do the same.

It is not difficult to imagine the sort of exchange that probably followed: "But my good heavens, man, what's to become of the plantation? This is as bad as Jamestown!" Winthrop might have exclaimed, "And these people aren't fortune hunters; they're decent Puritans! You had ministers here, good ones! Is there no teaching here?"

"We have a teaching service on Thursdays," Endecott would have hotly defended himself, "and two services on Sundays!" He sighed. "But it seems to do no good. They hear the words and nod and nothing changes." And his voice trailed off in the same defeat which Winthrop had noted outside.

Winthrop spent that night aboard the *Arbella*, undoubtedly availing himself of the privacy of the captain's cabin. It began to look as if the final curtain would ring down before the play could finish the first act. He had not even had a chance to put into practice some of the insights he felt the Lord had given him on the long voyage over. Was it all for nothing? Had he not heard God, after all? Had his selfishness or pride put all their lives into jeopardy?

He may have walked over to the port then, and looked out, recalling another time he had stood at that same port . . . .

Outside, a green-white wake trailed erratically behind them on the surface of the ocean, as they yawed this way and that under a lead-gray sky. He had been thinking for a long time about the plantation, and the quality of life which they could have together. Now, in a rush of inspiration, it was all coming together in his mind. Like all men trained to work in written words, he yearned to get out his writing box, and ink and paper, but he restrained himself until the concepts were clearly formed.

The sea had moderated somewhat, when he finally went to the chart table and took out the box. Selecting a quill, he sharpened it, dipped it into the wide-bottomed ink bottle, carefully removing the excess against the rim, and looked at the white sheet of paper before him.

What he would write next would rank in importance with the compact which the Pilgrims had drawn up aboard the *Mayflower*. Indeed, he took their concept one step further. For while they had stated what they were about to do as a body politic of equal members, gathered under God, and to be governed by their mutual consent, Winthrop now spelled out *why* it would work. His definition of covenant love has seldom been equalled.

A MODEL OF CHRISTIAN CHARITY were the words that went across the top of the sheet of paper. He went straight to the heart of the matter, beginning with some thoughts on the nature of man's love for his neighbor—what it could and should be, by the grace of God.

This love among Christians is a real thing, not imaginary . . . as absolutely necessary to the [well] being of the Body of Christ, as the sinews and other ligaments of a natural body are to the [well] being of that body . . . . We are a company, professing ourselves fellow members of Christ, [and thus] we ought to account ourselves knit together by this bond of love . . . .

Then came the heart of his vision:

Thus stands the cause between God and us: we are entered into covenant with Him for this work. We have taken out a Commission; the Lord hath given us leave to draw our own articles . . . . If the Lord shall please to hear us, and bring us in peace to the place we desire, then hath He ratified this Covenant and sealed our Commission, [and] will expect a strict performance of the Articles contained in it. But if we shall neglect the observance of these Articles . . . the Lord will surely break out in wrath against us.

Now the only way to avoid this shipwreck and to provide for our posterity, is to follow the counsel of Micah, to do justly, to love mercy, to walk humbly with our God. For this end, we must be knit together in this work as one man . . . . We must hold a familiar commerce together in all meekness, gentleness, patience, and liberality. We must delight in each other, make one another's condition our own, rejoice together, mourn together, labor and suffer together, always having before our eyes our Commission and Community in this work, as members of the same body. So shall we keep the unity of the Spirit in the bond of peace . . . .

We shall find that the God of Israel is among us, when ten of us shall be able to resist a thousand of our enemies, when He shall make us a praise and glory, that men of succeeding plantations shall say, "The Lord make it like that of New England." For we must consider that we shall be as a City upon a Hill . . .[4]

Standing now at the port and looking out at the New England night, Winthrop knew that it was God who had brought that previous time to mind, as if to remind him that He would not have given him this momentous revelation, had He not intended it to be put to use.

Winthrop soon learned what had happened that winter of 1628–29. They had suffered a General Sickness of the same sort that had stricken Plymouth during its first winter. In fact, Endecott had written Governor Bradford, appealing for help. Bradford's response was to send their doctor, Samuel Fuller, who had by now had abundant experience in treating cases of scurvy and constitutions gravely weakened by long sea voyages, as well as the various fevers and illnesses accompanying a sharp, cold winter.

Fuller stayed through the winter in Endecott's house and helped substantially. Indeed, Endecott was so impressed that he named their settlement *Salem*, the Hebrew word for peace. For this Separatist whom he had been prepared to dislike had manifested more Christian love than any Puritan he knew. The two men had often talked late by the fire. And the more Endecott learned, the more respectful he became of what God was doing forty miles down the coast.

Doctor Fuller was also a deacon, and Endecott was especially interested in the structure of their church. The Plymouth church,

under the leadership of Elder Brewster, was organizationally separate from the civil authority under Governor Bradford. Yet it obviously exercised decisive moral influence over it. Separatist church
leadership was provided by a pastor, a teacher, and a ruling elder,
but these were chosen by the membership of the church (*not* imposed by a presbytery or hierarchy of Bishops). The right to
choose freely their own spiritual leadership was zealously guarded
as one of the basic tenets of their Christian faith. What was more,
the Separatist church was open to all who cared to worship there.
But to become a *member* of the church (and thus to be eligible to
vote in both civil and religious elections), one had to convince the
eldership of the church of one's personal, saving relationship with
Jesus Christ, and of the orthodoxy of one's faith.

Winthrop may have had some private doubts about the wisdom
of giving the right to vote to non-landholders (the idea of servants
having equal voting rights with their masters smacked of "democracy"), but he held his tongue. Whatever Plymouth was doing,
from all reports God was blessing them more abundantly each
successive year. And there was no question of the fact that regardless of how radical their system, Plymouth was primarily interested
in seeking and doing God's will. According to Endecott, Bradford
declared the day before their annual election to be a day of prayer:
People were not to work, but to pray for the Lord's will as to whom
He wanted them to vote into office. Under those conditions, even
democracy might work!

The more Endecott had listened to Dr. Fuller, the more convinced he had become that this was the church model which God
intended Salem to follow as well. Thus, when the Reverends Higginson and Skelton had arrived, he told them of his decision. They
insisted that they were loyal to the Church of England, but since
they themselves had not settled on any particular church structure
before coming, they were open and receptive to Endecott's proposals. (When one considers the combinations of timing and circumstance which produced the Congregational Church, one is left
in awe of God's handiwork.) So they were duly elected pastor and
teacher, though their formal installation would have to wait until
the arrival of whomever the partners elected as Governor.

Of the "gathering" of this first Puritan church in America, we
have a vivid contemporary account from the pen of the enthusiastic
reporter Edward Johnson.

Although the number of the faithful people of Christ were but few, yet
their longing desire to gather into a church was very great . . . Having

fasted and prayed with humble acknowledgement of their own unworthiness to be called of Christ to so worthy a work, they joined together in a holy Covenant with the Lord and with one another, promising by the Lord's assistance to walk together in exhorting, admonishing and rebuking one another, and to cleave to the Lord with a full purpose of heart . . . .[5]

As Endecott was relating the account of their covenanting with God and one another, Winthrop may very well have interrupted him. "Then, that is why it's not working!" he might have exclaimed.

Endecott stared at him. "I don't understand."

"Don't you see? They love God, and they've covenanted to obey Him, or they wouldn't be here. But they're not living out their covenant with one another. They don't love one another enough to exhort, admonish, and rebuke. And at Plymouth they do. *That's* the difference!"

"But," Endecott objected, "the Separatists at Plymouth—or the First Comers, as we call them—already had been a church for years before they came, and we've only just gathered here."

"All the more reason why we've got to live up to our covenant with each other!" Winthrop paused, and looked straight at Endecott. "And it must begin with the leadership. Unless you and I demonstrate our own commitment to this plantation and to these people, unless you and I are willing to put our whole lives into the work here, we can't expect them to. Well?"

Endecott met his gaze. "You can count on it," he said.

"Good. Now, first of all, I want to get settled ashore right away. This house is large enough to accommodate both of us, is it not?"

"But Mr. Winthrop, this is *your* house; it goes to whomever is Governor. I'll find lodgings elsewhere . . . ."

"If you had room for Dr. Fuller over the winter, there is room for both of us, until we newcomers can build a place of our own."

Before Endecott could reply, he went on to the next thing on his mind. "An hour before noon, have every able-bodied man and boy assembled in the center of town." He thought for a moment. "And have the women come too, those that are healthy, and are not needed to tend the sick." He glanced at the height of the sun. "In the meantime, I will see about getting my belongings ashore, and stored here."

Winthrop started out the door, then turned back. "Oh, and tell the Gentlemen—Mr. Saltonstall, Mr. Pynchon, Mr. Nowell, and the others—that this includes them, too.'' And he smiled. ''You'd better suggest that they wear old clothes.''

''Right, Mr. Winthrop,'' Endecott said, and nodded.

Promptly at one o'clock, he came to the opening in the center of the huts and shelters that was ''town.'' A number of people were already there, staring at their Governor in amazement. Dressed in worn boots and breeches and an old frayed shirt, he looked more like an indentured servant than a Gentleman.

When most of the people had gathered, he addressed them: ''The situation here is not exactly what we in England were led to expect.'' There was some cynical laughter, but mostly silence. They were waiting to hear what would come next. ''But I think it can be rectified without too much trouble, although it's going to require hard work. By the end of the summer, every one of you is going to be in a proper dwelling. Until then, more than one family will have to live together, at least for the first winter.'' There was now a noticeable current of unbelief. ''How are we going to do it?'' Winthrop asked for them. ''By God's grace, we are going to do it, and by helping one another.''

At that moment, he was interrupted by Richard Saltonstall and a friend, who were just then arriving and carrying on a conversation of their own. Saltonstall was wearing a white shirt with a ruff at the neck. Winthrop's lips compressed, then he turned back to the rest.

''First of all, who among you has had any experience fishing?'' Eight men raised their hands, and Winthrop conferred with Endecott at his side. ''All right, Packham and Kenworthy, each of you take three men, and on alternate days you will take turns using the shallop for fishing.

''Now, the women,'' he said, looking up from his lists. ''Those of you who are able, will do field work in the mornings. The rest will be under Mr. Skelton on nursing detail. Mr. Skelton, as of this moment, you are officially responsible for what you and Mr. Higginson have been unofficially doing all along: tending the sick. Only now you are going to have more help.

''Mr. Higginson,'' and here he turned to the pastor who had lowered himself to a stump because he was unable to stand any longer, ''considering your condition, sir, you can help us most with your prayers—and a strong word on Sunday about what it means to serve God and one another.''

He returned his attention to the other minister. ''Mr. Skelton, you will also be in charge of the food stores. I want an inventory taken daily, and I would appreciate your alerting me of any projected shortfalls, as far in advance as possible. Also, by the guidance of the Holy Spirit, you are to decide what the daily ration will be. And those of you who have your own stocks will be expected to forego your ration."

He folded the lists and handed them to Endecott. "The rest of you will form into two work parties, those under forty, with Mr. Endecott, those over forty with me. Are there any questions?"

"Yes." It was Richard Saltonstall. "John, you do not really expect me to—"

"Yes, Richard, I really do."

"But common labor, John! I brought nine men with me to look after that sort of thing! And you brought more than I!"

Winthrop hesitated, before replying. "Last August, at Cambridge, you put your name to an agreement which bound you as a Christian to be ready *in your person* to further this work. So did I. This work will not succeed unless every man is willing to give his all. We are all laborers in God's vineyard, and that does not mean that, just because we can afford to, we pay someone else to do our work for us."

Saltonstall shook his head, almost too angry to speak. "This is—"

"This is the way it is going to be, I'm afraid. And I will tell you something else," he looked around. "This is for all of you who were late. I want you to know that I do not consider lateness to be merely impolite; as far as I am concerned, it is a sin against God! This is His work, and He has called us to it. To steal His time is to blaspheme against what He is trying to accomplish here!

"Starting tomorrow morning, we will meet here promptly at two hours past sunrise for daily work assignments. And bring something with you to eat at the noon hour. We will work until four hours past noon, and the rest of the day is entirely your own." There was more laughter now.

"Are there any other questions?" There were none.

Without doubt, a miracle took place upon Winthrop's arrival: a nearly dead colony was resurrected. And from all reports, God's single instrument in this resurrection was John Winthrop. Cotton Mather would refer to Winthrop as *Nehemias Americanus* [6]—in reference to the Old Testament leader who had brought the Israelites back from their Babylonian exile to the Promised Land, and had directed the rebuilding of the walls of Jerusalem. But more important, Nehemiah had inspired them to resume their covenant with God.

Another seventeenth-century report, quoted by modern Yale historian Edmund Morgan in his biography of Winthrop, said: "(So soon) as Mr. Winthrop was landed, perceiving what misery was like to ensue through their idleness, he presently fell to work with his own hands, and thereby so encouraged the rest that there was not an idle person then to be found in the whole plantation. And whereas the Indians said they [the newcomers] would shortly return as fast as they came, now they admired to see in what short time they had housed themselves and planted corn sufficient for their subsistence." [7]

To be sure, they endured the same General Sickness which seemed to afflict every shipload of settlers. And a few days after their arrival, Winthrop suffered the grievous loss of his son, Henry, who was drowned in a fishing accident. But the tragedy seemed to redouble his dedication to the business of planting the colony (much as a similar tragedy had affected William Bradford before him).

It was a sustained enthusiasm. Three months after his arrival, as he was about to lead the bulk of the newcomers to their final settling place in Boston (for there were now more than a thousand, far too many for Salem to absorb), he wrote Margaret, "I thank God, I like so well to be here . . . And if I were to come again, I would not have altered my course, though I had foreseen all these afflictions. I never fared better in my life, never slept better, never had more content[edness] of mind." [8]

Not many settlers were writing as cheerful letters home, and nearly half those who came over that first year went back. But more than half stayed, and there were far fewer graves dug that winter than there might have been.

How critically important for us Christians is this business of commitment to one another—as vital for the Body of Christ today as it was three-and-a-half centuries ago! There are *two* great steps of faith in the Christian walk, and they correspond to the two Great Commandments: "You shall love the Lord your God with all your heart, and with all your soul, and with all your mind; and you shall love your neighbor as yourself."

The first step of faith is the vertical commitment: once a person has discovered the reality of God, and has experienced the miraculous gift of salvation in His Son Jesus Christ, he then must face the prospect of accepting Christ as his Lord and Master, as well as Saviour. To do this means yielding our wills to God: "Nevertheless not my will but Thy will be done." And it *is* a covenant relationship, which means there are two parties to the agreement. As long as the Christian obeys His God in humility, God will honor his obedience, often blessing him beyond all imagining.

The second step of faith is the horizontal commitment to one's neighbor, and ultimately to that specific body of Christian neighbors of whom God calls one to be a part. In a way, this second step requires even more faith, because now one has to learn to trust a perfect God operating in and through *imperfect* vessels. We must do this, armed only with the assurance that it *is* God's will, that the other vessels' hearts are also turned towards His will, and that they too are aware of their being called to serve Him together.

The vertical aspect of the Covenant has to come first, just as the First and Great Commandment does. But as strong as it is, the vertical aspect alone, without a cross-bar, is not the Cross of Christ.

This second step calls one to yield to that local part of the Body of Christ, and to dedicate oneself to that congregation and its work. Indeed, the body's effectiveness will be magnified to the extent to which its individuals mutually dedicate themselves. This dedication accounted for the soldierly *esprit de corps* of the early Jesuits, and made them the shock troops of the army of Christ. Alone, their vertical commitment to Christ was unsurpassed—but as a body, they were renowned the world over! *Esprit de corps*—the literal translation is "the spirit of the body."

This may be one of the reasons why God permits pressures to befall the Body of Christ. For wherever there is pressure of affliction, there is a corresponding increase in commitment to one another, as well as commitment to God. This, we believe, is the reason He allowed the persecution and long exile of the Pilgrims; the four wretched months in which saints and strangers shared their plight in the belly of the *Mayflower*, before being disgorged onto the new Promised Land; the four more months of General Sickness . . . . So that when they finally stood on their feet, they stood *together*, as a body. And they were thus able to pass on to the Puritans a proven model by which to build.

"A house divided against itself shall not stand," Jesus told his disciples (Matthew 12:25 KJV), and with each New England church, God was building a house, not just assembling a pile of stones. As Peter wrote to new Christians, "[Come] and as living stones be yourselves built [into] a spiritual house . . ." (1 Peter 2:5 AMPLIFIED).

In the rocky fields of New England, God was raising up a kingdom of stone houses, with each stone in each house fitted into place by Him. This kingdom would be as close as a family, a spiritual family which would be able to withstand the most implacable pressure the world could bring to bear. As we were coming to see, these stone houses were in turn to be the foundation stones, not merely of American democracy, but of the Kingdom of God in America.

9

The Puritan Way

A recent novel by a best-selling author purports to trace the lives of the Winthrop family down through three centuries. The jacket of the book shows people dressed in the garb of different eras, all of them ominously overshadowed by a brooding gray eminence which presumably is the specter of John Winthrop, Senior. A quick look inside confirms that the author has indeed accepted the modern stereotype of the Puritans. Nearly everyone today seems to believe that the Puritans were bluenosed killjoys in tall black hats, a somber group of sin-obsessed, witch-hunting bigots, "whose main occupation was to prevent each other from having any fun and whose sole virtue lay in their furniture." [1]

How could such a monstrous misrepresentation have been so widely and so quickly accepted? For the anti-Puritan phenomenon has arisen largely within the twentieth century. Almost no negative bias can be found among nineteenth-century historians; on the contrary, they gladly gave the Puritans the lion's share of the credit for setting the direction of this nation. Why then, the sudden prejudice in so many hearts?

The answer seems to lie in the fact that not in the three hundred and fifty years of our history has a spirit of rebellion gained such a tight hold on the minds and wills of the American people. What could be more of an anathema to such an attitude than the cheerful submission to authority, holy service, and corporate commitment which the Puritans personified! If there is one people in the history of the country whose example Satan hates more than any other, it is the Puritans. And since rebellion is his specialty, it is no wonder that the Puritans have received such a bad press of late!

170

Thus, as customs which have been in effect in this country for more than three hundred years are vilified and torn down, the most withering negative epithet one hears attached to them is *puritanical*, be it the work ethic, chastity before marriage, modesty in decorum and apparel, shops closed in observance of the Lord's Day, legislation against immorality . . . . The list is endless, and the traditions are crumbling under an ever more determined onslaught.

We have found these much-maligned Christians to be sinners like ourselves, but also warm and human, and possessed of remarkable spiritual wisdom and discernment.

But, we asked ourselves, what about their legendary self-righteousness and intolerance? Had they not banished Roger Williams, simply because he spoke his mind and because his doctrine did not happen to agree with theirs? The founder of Rhode Island has become the hero of outspoken anti-establishment academics.

And had they not also expelled Anne Hutchinson? She now has a river (and a parkway) named after her. The dilemma we now faced was: If such narrow-minded self-righteousness was an inevitable by-product of man's attempts to establish the Kingdom of God on earth, did that not bring the whole matter of the feasibility of a Bible Commonwealth into question? And if the Puritans *were* attempting the impossible, how much more impossible would it be today?

The scarlet letter *A* for *adulteress* which Hester Prynne, the heroine of Nathaniel Hawthorne's famous novel, was forced to wear, seared its way into the psyche of nineteenth-century America. A century later, Arthur Miller's play about the Salem witch-hunters, "The Crucible," carried the popular image of the Puritans further. And countless other modern novelists and dramatists have presented the Puritans as morbidly preoccupied with sin and guilt. Is there any truth to the picture?

There is no question that the Puritans took sin seriously—far more seriously than most American Christians today. But they had good reason: they knew that the very success or failure of God's New Israel hung on their willingness to deal strongly with sin—in themselves first, but also in those who had been called with them to build the Kingdom. Indeed, there could be no compromise where the presence of sin was concerned. For an example of the fruit of compromise, all they needed to do was to look across the Atlantic at what was happening in England. And so they did not shy away from facing up to sin or dealing with it.

There is one modern historian who has consistently exposed the popular negative stereotype of the Puritans for the patently false view that it is. He is the late Perry Miller, widely regarded as the dean of Puritan historians. Almost single-handedly, his works have been responsible for a major revision in the thinking of serious students of American history. (But unfortunately this is only a minute segment of the American public.)

Here is what Miller had to say about the Puritans' attitude towards sin:

Puritanism would make every man an expert psychologist, to detect all makeshift "rationalizations," to shatter without pity the sweet dreams of self-enhancement in which the ego takes refuge from reality. A large quantity of Puritan sermons were devoted to . . . exposing not merely the conscious duplicity of evil men, but the abysmal tricks which the subconscious can play upon the best of men. The duty of the Puritan in this world was to know himself—without sparing himself one bit, without flattering himself in the slightest, without concealing from himself a single unpleasant fact about himself.[2]

This willingness to look unblinkingly at the worst side of their own natures made them consummate realists. It also was responsible for the extraordinary compassion which became the hallmark of such exceptional leaders among them as John Winthrop, Thomas Hooker, and Cotton Mather. For once you really *knew* how corrupt your own nature was at its core, you would be much more inclined to readily forgive the sinfulness of others.

Anyone who searches the church records will find that Puritan discipline, although strict by necessity, was almost always tempered with great mercy. The reason it was strict (and enforced by civil law), was that they all felt that the entire fabric of their covenant life together depended on living in proper order and in joint obedience to the laws of God. Thus when one sinned, it affected them all. Tryal Pore, a young girl arraigned before the Middlesex County Court in 1656, confessed that "by . . . [my] sin I have not only done what I can to pull down judgment from the Lord on myself but also upon the place where I live." [3] But Tryal Pore's tearful confession convinced the magistrates of her repentance, and they were more than ready to forgive her.

". . . I have no pleasure in the death of the wicked, but that the wicked turn from his way and live . . ." (Ezekiel 33:11).

The Puritan magistrates, whose law book was the Bible, were generally far more anxious to see a sinner come to repentance than to mete out punishment.

In case after case, the mercy, forgiveness, and pastoral concern for the defendant stand out. Yet to any modern writer who has a streak of rebellion in him, the discipline is all he sees, and the mention of discipline these days is like waving the proverbial red flag. In fact, rebellion has been so romanticized in recent years that in our time church discipline is literally unheard of. Today, if anyone were threatened with dismissal from church membership, in all probability he would simply laugh, take up his coat, and leave.

But it was a different matter three centuries ago. First a church covenanted together, *then* the town formed around it. And under those circumstances, excommunication was a matter of the utmost gravity. It meant that the local body of Christ, after repeatedly trying to bring a sinner to repentance so he or she could receive God's forgiveness, would finally have no choice but to break fellowship with the individual and turn the person over to his or her sin. This meant that person would be under Satan's influence, and for those who know the reality of the Devil, this was a fearsome turn of events indeed!

That the fruit of compassion was being worked into the hearts of the Puritan elders, magistrates and pastors, is amply evidenced in the case of Ann Hibbens. Mrs. Hibbens was the wife of one of the elders of the First Church of Boston, where John Cotton was the pastor. She had accused a woodworker named Davis (also a member of the church) of overcharging her for some decorative carving which he had done at her request. He insisted that his price had been fair, and finally the church had to step in. Impartial woodworkers from another town were summoned to assess the work, and they judged that Davis's price was fair, perhaps even low. This had humbled Mrs. Hibbens for a season, and she had confessed her error with tears.

But then, like a dog worrying a bone, she started in again. Now the church strongly censured her, and she quieted down again—for a while. But she could not simply be wrong and accept her correction; she began once more to berate poor Davis, both to his face and behind his back. Finally, the church had no alternative left but to hold an excommunication hearing.

The purpose of the hearing was to give her one last opportunity to humble herself and admit her wrongness, but Mrs. Hibbens airily refused, not deigning to answer more than the first few questions put to her. At last, Pastor Cotton addressed the congregation:

It grows now very late, and we must [ascertain whether] . . . it be the mind of the church that we shall proceed to pass the sentence of excommunication upon this Sister. We shall take your silence for your consent and approbation thereto; if any of the church be of another mind, he hath liberty to express himself. [silence] We perceive by the universal silence of the church that with one consent it is your mind [that] we should proceed. And therefore let us first seek unto God for His direction and for a sanctified use of this His ordinance, [in order] that we may proceed not out of bitterness or envy but out of tender love to her soul, and that God would give her a sight of her great and many evils and break her heart by kindly repentance [so] that she may the more speedily return to God and the church again, as now she is cast out.[4]

Following the prayer, with great reluctance Mr. Cotton proceeded to pronounce the dread sentence of excommunication:

. . . for slandering . . . for raising up an evil report . . . for several lies and untruths . . . for your stopping your ears and hardening your heart against the former admonition of the church . . . for your sowing discord and jealousies . . . for these and many more foul and sinful transgressions . . . I do here, in the name of the whole church and in the name of the Lord Jesus Christ, and by virtue of that power and authority which He hath given to His church . . . cast you out and cut you off from the enjoyment of all those blessed privileges and ordinances which God hath entrusted His church withal, which you have so long abused . . . I do from this time forward pronounce you an excommunicated person from God and His people.

Ten years later, Mrs. Hibbens would be the defendant in another trial, a civil one this time. The charge: witchcraft. The sentence: the only one worse than excommunication—death by hanging. This must have brought to many minds the reminder in the First Book of Samuel (15:23 KJV): *"Rebellion is as the sin of witchcraft."*

As Pastor Cotton indicated, the purpose of excommunication was not to condemn sinners, but to let the pressure of their sin bring them to repentance. In the case of Captain John Underhill, who was excommunicated for adultery, his being expelled was the very thing which finally brought him to repentance. He begged to be reinstated, and at length was given leave to speak before the congregation. Winthrop recorded the occasion as follows:

He came in his worst clothes (being accustomed to take great pride in his bravery and neatness), and standing upon a form, he did with many sighs and abundance of tears, lay open his wicked course—his adultery, his hypocrisy, his persecution of God's people here, and especially his pride (as the root of all, which caused God to give him over to his other sinful courses) and contempt of magistrates. He (then) justified God and the church and the court in all that had been inflicted on him.

Many fearful temptations he met with beside, and in all these, his heart shut up in hardness and impenitency as the bondslave of Satan, till the Lord, after a long time and great afflictions, had broken his heart, and brought him to humble himself before Him night and day with prayers and tears . . . in the end, he earnestly and humbly besought the church to have compassion on him, and deliver him out of the hands of Satan. So accordingly he was received into the church again . . . ." [5]

The skeptical reader might be inclined to wonder how sincere Underhill's repentance was, but the facts were that he did go on to become a famous military captain and hold many positions of responsibility.

The Puritans were willing to face the reality of their own sinful natures and the harm that sin caused their covenant life. And this willingness produced not only compassion for one another, but a remarkable maturity when it came to meeting the realities of life and death.

Infant mortality was a grim specter in the seventeenth century. There was no cure for smallpox, and even measles was a dread killer in those days—of adults as well as children. Death was an ominous and ever-present possibility. And as with everything else in a Puritan's life, there were two ways to handle it: in Christ or in self.

Perhaps the most famous Puritan was Cotton Mather, whose image has been especially maligned and distorted out of any resemblance to reality. He is painted as a witch-hunting, sadistic monster, a sort of Puritan Torquemada, when nothing could be further from the truth. Mather was an ordinary sinner and the first to admit it, but his warm humanness made him one of the most popular preachers of his age.

True, he could be self-righteous, and was not above playing pulpit politics. But Mather fearlessly proclaimed God's Word, and he truly hungered after God's righteousness and holiness. He also had a pastor's heart, for which his parishioners loved him.

The son of Increase Mather, the most prominent clergyman in New England (for many years president of Harvard College, and later New England's special ambassador to the King), Cotton Mather was also the grandson of John Cotton and Richard Mather, two of the strongest ministers in the first generation of American Puritans. Such was his upbringing that when personal tragedy came to his family—and it came repeatedly—he instinctively turned to Christ.

There was shock and grieving, fasting and praying. But there was no self-pity, no long drawn-out remorse or bitterness, no hatred of God. Each time tragedy struck, a further work was done in him, increasing his capacity for mercy and compassion. So that towards the end of his life, his prayers and counsel were highly sought by those facing a recent or impending loss in their families. Despite all his writing (and he authored more than 450 books, tracts, and treatises), he made a point of always being available to anyone in need, and he instituted what was to become an American pastoral tradition: regular calls on his aged and ailing parishioners, as well as prisoners.

It is possible to follow his spiritual growth at key points, because starting in his nineteenth year (1681) he kept a diary, as was the custom among educated men of his time. (He had already received his B.A. and M.A. from Harvard, and had begun to preach.) His first entry is a long devotional passage, full of good resolutions and signed "by Cotton Mather, feeble and worthless, yet (Lord, by Thy grace) desirous to approve himself a sincere and faithful servant of Jesus Christ." [6]

Mather was to have more than a dozen children, but only two would survive him. The first to fall ill was his four-year-old daughter Mary. On October 3, 1695, as he prayed for her, "I was unaccountably assured, not only that this child shall be happy forever, but that I should never have any child, except what should be an everlasting temple to the Spirit of God; yea, that I and mine should be together in the Kingdom of God, world without end." Three days later, the Lord took her. Her epitaph: GONE BUT NOT LOST.

In 1702 he began a seven-month-long struggle in prayer for the life of his wife, whom he referred to as his beloved consort.

In the forenoon, while I was at prayer with my dying wife in her chamber, I began to feel the blessed breezes of a particular faith, blowing from Heaven upon my mind . . . . In the afternoon, when I was alone in my study, crying unto the Lord, my particular faith was again renewed, and with a flood of tears I thought I received an assurance from Heaven that she should recover. Whereupon, I begged the Lord that He would, by His good Spirit, incline me to be exemplarily wise and chaste and holy, in my whole conversation, when I should again obtain such favor of the Lord.

She did recover, only to fall ill again before her strength could be regained, and again her imminent demise called for an all-night bedside vigil.

But in this extremity, when I renew my visits unto Heaven, a strange irradiation comes from Heaven upon my spirit, that her life shall not as yet come unto an end.

But still she hovered near death, and six weeks later, Mather wrote:

I suspect I have been too unattentive unto the meaning of the Holy Spirit . . . about my consort's being restored to me. When she has been several times on or near the last agonies of death, I cry to the Lord, that He will yet spare her. He tells me that He will yet do it . . . . But it may be, after the Lord has given me admirable demonstrations of His being loathe to deny me anything that I importunately ask of Him, and therefore does delay one month after another, the thing which I fear, yet I must at last encounter.

On October 30, in the midst of concern for his wife he wrote:

On this day my little daughter Nibby began to fall sick of the small-pox. The dreadful disease, which is raging in the neighborhood, is now got to my family. God prepare me, God prepare me for what is coming upon me.

The pestilence grew worse, and towards the end of November, his small son, Increase, was stricken down.

The little creatures keep calling for me so often to pray with them that I can scarce do it less than ten or a dozen times in a day, besides what I do with my neighbors.

Two days later, his beloved wife died.

At last the black day arrives. I [have] never yet seen such a black day, in all the time of my pilgrimage. The desire of my eyes is this day to be taken from me. All the forenoon, she lies in pangs of death, sensible until the last minute or two before her final expiration. I cannot remember the discourses that passed between us, only [that] her devout soul was full of satisfaction about her going to a state of blessedness with the Lord Jesus Christ, and as far as my distress would permit me, I studied how to confirm her satisfaction and consolation . . . .
When I saw to what point of resignation I was now called of the Lord, I resolved, with His help therein, to glorify Him. So, two hours before my

lovely consort expired, I kneeled by her bedside, and I took into my two hands a dear hand, the dearest in the world. With her thus in my hands, I solemnly and sincerely gave her up to the Lord . . . When she was expired, I . . . prayed with her father and the other weeping people in the chamber, for the grace to carry it well . . . .

And he did carry it well.

When it came to their closest relationships, the Puritans were realists in life, as well as in death. They believed that their covenant relationship with God included their children, and because they loved them, they were no more tolerant of sin in their children's lives than in their own. They would deal with sinfulness in their children as strongly as the situation required, regardless of how the children might respond at the moment.

And here is the greatest difference between the Puritans and most present-day American parents. For we are not willing to risk losing the "love" in our relationship with our children by persevering with them in matters of discipline. The biggest single cause of the breakdown of the American family is that so much of what we could call *love*, the Puritans would have another name for: *idolatry*.

By God's own definition in His First Commandment ("Thou shalt have no other gods before me"), any person, any thing, any relationship which is exalted above the Lord in one's life can be said to be an idol. And taking that one step further: any love which does not emanate from God (for God *is* Love) has to be idolatrous, by definition. No matter how noble the sentiments or how seemingly sacrificial, if it does not begin with Him and have Him as its end, it is, in reality, nothing more than a very subtle extension of our limitless capacity to love ourselves, and to entice others to do likewise.

Unlike most modern parents, the Puritans *knew* that their children did not belong to them; they belonged to God. Consequently, they did not possess them; on the contrary, they considered that their children had been entrusted to their care by God. They were to protect them, raise them, and teach them, training them up in the way that He would have them go. In other words, parenthood was a sacred responsibility in Christ, and if they failed to live up to it, they would be directly accountable to God.

This did not prevent them from loving their children; they loved them very much indeed, as we have seen from the brief glimpse into Cotton Mather's heart. But they were aware that their love should originate in the heart of God. God's love abounds with tenderness and compassion and joy, but it also contains discipline. "For the Lord disciplines him whom he loves, and chastises every son whom he receives" (Hebrews 12:6). God loves His children too much to permit them to stay in a sin which could harm their development or to allow them to persist in willfulness when they need to learn how to submit their wills to His.

It was in this area of having one's will crossed that Puritan children (just like ours) had the hardest time understanding that this was God's love for them. Many did not make the connection until their teenage years, and some never did. Often the turning point came in the whole business of courtship. This area of Puritan life affords a classic example of how God's often will-crossing love can come through parents who are willing to risk their children's anger in order to be obedient to the guidance which they feel God has given them.

As in the rest of their living patterns, the Puritan courtship gradually evolved into a code of conduct which they felt was pleasing to God, and which when adhered to, resulted in stable, fulfilling marriages. Certain evenings were set aside for "calling"—and there were strict ordinances against "night-walking"—couples wandering down inviting country lanes. As a result, the premarital birthrate was negligible, and sensual temptations were deliberately kept to a minimum. Modern writers have made this constraint a point of ridicule, but when one stops to think about it, nothing clouds the wisdom and clear discernment of two people beginning to consider marriage more than the red haze of imminent sexual gratification.

Contrary to popular opinion, the Puritans did not arrange marriages between their children; they did, however, exercise their veto. If either set of parents felt that the marriage was out of the will of God, they had no compunction about withholding their permission. For they knew from hard experience that if the marriage were not in His will, and the couple went ahead and got married anyway, they could be in for a great deal of misery and suffering. Sometimes the parents simply felt that they were ahead of God's timing, in which case the betrothal might last several years—while the boy and/or girl matured to the point where they were ready to take on the responsibility of raising a family.

Puritan parents were also well aware that they could never be that sure of always hearing the Lord's will. And so, on such an important decision as whether to permit their children to marry, they were grateful for counsel from their brothers and sisters in

Christ. And because each marriage had a deep and long-lasting effect on the covenanted community as a whole, it was a matter of personal importance to every member.

Instead of resenting the counsel of their fellow Christians, the parents welcomed it, because they *were* a big family. This was as God intended and was one of the fruits of the horizontal aspect of the covenant. As hard as that is to imagine today, that was the way they chose, and they would not have wanted it any other way. In 1636, the church in Boston renewed its covenant in the following terms:

We do give up our selves unto that God whose name is Jehovah, Father, Son and Holy Spirit . . . and unto our blessed Lord Jesus Christ . . . promising (by the help of His Spirit and grace) to cleave unto [Him] . . . by faith in a way of Gospel obedience, as becometh His covenant people forever.

We do also give up our offspring unto God in Jesus Christ, avouching the Lord to be our God, and the God of our children, and our selves, with our children to be His people, humbly adoring this grace of God, that we and our offspring with us, may be looked upon as the Lord's.

We do also give up our selves one unto another in the Lord, and according to the will of God, freely covenanting and binding our selves to walk together as a right ordered congregation and church of Christ, in all ways of His worship, according to the holy rules of the Word of God, promising in brotherly love, faithfully to watch over one another's souls.[7]

Imagine the reaction most Americans today would have at the thought that their neighbors might be watching over their souls. Even among those of us in the Body of Christ, when we say, "How are you?" and smile, we are inwardly relieved when the answer is limited to the obligatory "Fine." So many of our churches are congregations of private people, surrounded by private personal spaces and wrapt up in private thought, until it is time to smile and shake the minister's hand and get into their private cars.

In fact, for many of us Americans, privacy has become our religion, with the home as the foremost place of worship. As a result of increasingly temporary and artificial friendships, frequent uprootings, growing insecurity in the world, we turn more and more for the fulfillment of our needs to our family relationships. We place ever greater demands on husband, wife, son, daughter, mother, father, sister, brother, or whomever the person or persons might be. They become the focal point for all our hopes, our dreams, our thwarted ambitions. This other person is now expected to provide the love which we are so desperate for, and we begin to draw more and more heavily on that love. And to insure no interruption in its flow, we lavish undue attention, gifts, advice, and so on, on the other persons, believing that we are really loving them. When they do not love us back to the degree or in the way that we think they should (which is humanly impossible), we feel hurt and angry—and one way or another, we let them know it.

This is what always happens with idolatry, sooner or later, because it is a spiritual law that natural love, when crossed, turns to hate. For example, when we Americans exalt our children, they start to rebel against the role into which they have been cast—as love generators and love objects. With increasing resentment they come to see that what their parents regard as love is in reality a kind of smothering, possessive control, a vicarious reliving or ego projection.

Or possibly the children do not even know *what* it is, except that they dread going home and feel like they are suffocating while they are there. We all know about the alarming number of teenagers who are running away from so-called nice homes, because their parents are so self-loving that they do not have any time for them. But what does not make the headlines is the equally large number of teenagers who are fleeing homes where they get too much of the wrong kind of attention—idolatrous attention.

Occasionally, some children are willing to play the game for the sake of their own ego gratification, even into their middle years. And for a while the "love" cycle appears to be working. But God help the future mate of such a spoiled and self-loving person, should he or she ever decide to leave home and marry! For unless that mate is willing to be enfolded and totally absorbed into that cycle, the results will be unending conflicts, divorce, and many broken hearts.

The American family does indeed seem to be unraveling, because of the almost universal ignorance of the idolatrous nature of Christless "love." In the face of this fact, it is ironic that the larger community—that thing which privacy so effectively seals out—is (*if it is Christ-centered and covenanted*) the very thing which can restore and ensure wholesome, open, and honest family relationships.

But is it not enough, some people ask, simply to be a family which is already centered in Christ, without being committed to some body of fellow Christians? In a few rare situations, as in the case of a family being called to some remote mission field, God will provide grace commensurate with the call. But it has been our experience that we often need the discernment and counsel of other Christians outside our immediate family, in order to truly live in Christ and for Christ, instead of in and for self.

This understanding of the corporate nature of their call—now almost forgotten—was built into the foundation of the new house that God had begun to build some three hundred and fifty years ago in America. As the Boston church's covenant reveals, it was at the heart of their daily life together—to the Puritan, it was so normal, such a matter of course, that no one even thought about it.

They were *glad* that they were called together, and they liked nothing better than to work together as a large family. Usually a good deal got accomplished at such get-togethers. For there were certain things a man simply could not do alone, such as raising a roof, pulling stumps, or going to a town meeting. When outdoor work was needed and the weather was decent, the womenfolk would do the cooking and make a festive occasion of it. Frequently in the evenings there would be quilting or sewing or baking bees, and for the children, spelling bees.

John Winthrop pointed out that, just as the community was a large family, so the family was a small community. And the Puritans put great stock in that community being an orderly one, with the parents in undisputed authority. "If God make a covenant to be a God to thee and thine," said John Cotton, "then it is thy part to see to it that thy children and servants be God's people." [8] This was also the tone he set in his famous catechism on the Ten Commandments which Puritan children had to memorize and recite on Saturday afternoons in preparation for the Sabbath: "Who are meant here by [Honor thy] Father and Mother?" The correct answer was: "All our superiors, whether in family, school, church or Commonwealth."

The Puritans saw very clearly that authority, whether spiritual or temporal, invariably began in the home. "Well-ordered families naturally produce a good order in society," said Cotton Mather succinctly, and James Fitch echoed him: "Such as families are, such at last the Church and Commonwealth must be." This is obviously every bit as true today, but in Puritan New England, they took care to make sure that discipline and authority in the homes was all that it should be. For in the end a lax or loose home hurt them all, being a sin against God's plan, to say nothing of a social menace. Thus, if parents ever reached the point where they were drinking heavily, or whoring, or abusing their children, the children would be taken out of their homes and put into homes where they would receive the love (including correction) which they needed.

A great deal of emphasis was put on this matter of parental responsibility. Parents of stable families were expected to take in single men and women and raise them as part of their families, with the newcomers submitting to the heads of the house as if they were their own parents. There was even a law which required that any single person who could not afford to support a home of his own in proper order, had to live with one of the town families. In almost all cases, this proved to be a great blessing, providing a warm family environment (i.e., people who cared) which the single person did not have and often had never experienced.

The Puritan way may seem foreign to our modern American family ways, but the quality of genuine Christian love and caring for one another's souls which so characterized the family lives of our forefathers, may well contain the beginnings of answers to our own family problems.

"Gather my saints together unto me; those that have made a covenant with me by sacrifice." This fifth verse of Psalm 50 was one of the Puritans' favorite texts, for it referred directly to the sacrifice required of each of them by the covenant into which they had entered.

No one was more cognizant of the need for personal sacrifice than John Winthrop—nor was anyone ready to give as generously and cheerfully. Winthrop understood clearly that to belong to Christ *was* to belong to one another, and the situation, that fall and winter of 1630, would test their covenant commitment to the utmost. Shipload after shipload of impoverished would-be settlers was landed on shore with no supplies whatever, so that what might have started off to be ample food stocks soon dwindled away to the point where only emergency rations were left.

Once again, shellfish became a saving emergency staple, as it had before in Jamestown. Cotton Mather relates that one man, "inviting his friends to a dish of clams, at the table gave thanks to Heaven, who 'had given them to suck the abundance of the seas and the treasures of the sands.' " [9] Winthrop now had two boats fishing at all times, setting up a competition between the crews, and at low tide, the women went forth to dig at the clambanks. Edward Johnson reports a conversation among them: One woman says, "My husband hath travailed so far as Plymouth . . . and hath with great toil brought a little corn home with him." A second responds, "Our last peck of meal is now in the oven at home a-baking, and many of our godly neighbors have quite spent all, and we owe one loaf of what little we have." A third says, "My husband hath ventured himself among the Indians for corn and can get none, as also our honored Governor has distributed his so far, that a day or two will put an end to his store." [10]

Winthrop had turned out to be a superb teacher, when it came to bartering for corn with the Indians of the Bay area. "His solemnity of manner was precisely the attitude to win their respect, and he took care that relations should be on his terms, not theirs." [11] But soon, the Indians had only enough corn left to get themselves through the winter, and so the Governor dispatched a pinnace to trade with the Narragansetts. It came back with a hundred bushels, yet such were their numbers that this did not last very long.

Winthrop, however, was also graced by God with an unusual gift of wisdom. As far back as September, he had foreseen that their supplies would give out long before spring. He had sent the *Lyon* home to Bristol, with their most reliable ship captain, William Pierce, and a long shopping list of vital supplies, accompanied by a letter to John, Jr., requesting that he provide the necessary funds. This kind of sacrifice was to become a pattern with Winthrop, whose personal interpretation of the horizontal aspect of the covenant meant that one committed *everything* to the cause, even the last of one's personal funds.

When disillusioned would-be settlers (who had quit and gone back to England) began to circulate negative reports around London, the Bay Colony's sources of funds began to dry up, just as Jamestown's and Plymouth's had before them. Time and again, Winthrop would dig deeper into his own coffers to pay for desperately needed supplies. During this period, he was supporting the colony almost singlehandedly, and rapidly exhausting what remained of his own wealth to do so. But never once did he make the slightest complaint, not even in his private journal.

Finally, in the middle of that winter, they declared February 6 a day of fasting and humiliation, to search their hearts for any reasons why God might be withholding His Providence, and to pray for a miracle. There was nothing else they *could* do: the corn was gone, the ground nuts had long been scavenged, the clambanks exhausted. The *Lyon* was so long overdue that they could only assume she had been shipwrecked.

But the day of fasting never came to pass. On the morning before it was scheduled, ". . . when Winthrop was distributing the last handful of meal in the barrel unto a poor man distressed by the wolf at the door," reported Mather, "at that instant they spied a ship arrived at the harbor's mouth, laden with provisions for them all." [12]

It was the *Lyon!* She had come across a dismasted ship on her way home, and towed her to port, which accounted for the long delay. Her cargo consisted of wheat, meal, peas, oatmeal, beef, pork, cheese, butter, and suet, and what was of most importance to many of the sick, casks of lemon juice. "Circumstances no longer being appropriate for a fast, the Governor and council ordered a day of Thanksgiving . . . such was the deliverance which made a profound impression on the minds of that distressed people. It was recognized as a signal providence of God. About their firesides its story was told by fathers to their children for many a day in praise of the goodness of God and His guardianship over the colony."

Winthrop's love of his neighbors is exemplary in any age, and his commitment ranks second to none in the annals of this nation's history. One of the chroniclers of his own age sums him up thus: "His justice was impartial, his wisdom excellently tempered . . . his courage made him dare to do right . . . . Accordingly, when the noble design of carrying a colony of Chosen People into an American wilderness was by some eminent persons undertaken, this eminent person was, by the consent of all, chosen for the Moses . . . ." [13] Another historian, of the early nineteenth century, ranks him second only to Washington in terms of stature among the founding fathers, and we would agree.

"Gather my saints unto me . . . ." In Puritan New England, the saints gathered on the Lord's Day in the meetinghouse, the hub of their covenant life together. They came to worship the Lord and to be taught from His Word. Such was their hunger for the Word of God and for sound teaching to assist them in their struggle against sin and self, that surprising as it may seem by today's standards, (when if the pastor goes one minute beyond the stroke of noon, the congregation starts getting restless, because the turkey will get overdone, or because the first football game comes on at one), the Puritans welcomed sermons lasting two hours or more. In top form, their own pastor could be counted on, in the course of a sermon, for at least two turns of the large hourglass that stood in plain view near the pulpit—and then another turn and a half worth of prayers! And if a visiting preacher gave out after only three-quarters of an hour or so, they spoke of him as they might of a spavined horse which had given out between the stays.

The man who turned the hourglass was the Army of Christ's sergeant-at-arms, the redoubtable tithingman. He had many responsibilities in addition to turning the glass. It was he who checked the local inns on Sunday, to make sure they stayed closed, and it was he who stopped by the houses of known truants to make certain that they were in their appointed pews. But above all, it was he who was responsible for keeping the saints alert in their pews, as Pastor went from his "Thirteenthly" to his "Fourteenthly" (or, heaven forfend, from his "Twenty-seventhly" to his "Twenty-eighthly," which had been known to happen). Drugged by a lazy summer day, with the sound of crickets mingling with the "howsomesoevers," even the most zealous Puritan had been known to nod off.

But the tithingman, ever watchful for the saint who was "only resting his eyes," was equal to his task. He had a staff to discomfort them, usually with a foxtail or pheasant feather on one end for the ladies, and a brass knob on the other for the men. It should be noted that the tithingman was not imposed upon the congregation by some ecclesiastical or civil authority; rather, he was paid by the church members themselves. For such was their desire to learn from their pastor that they did not want to miss anything due to a betrayal of their flesh. Few Americans have better understood the meaning of Jesus' words to His disciples, "The spirit is willing, but the flesh is weak."

Although they were indeed serious about the importance of their spiritual life together, they were not as the present-day image would have them: taking themselves so seriously that they were incapable of laughing at themselves. In fact, the exact opposite was the case. They had a hearty appreciation of the silly incidents our foibles can cause, and laughter was a frequent visitor in their meetinghouses.

The tithingman in Lynn had a sharp thorn on the end of his staff for those whose sleep was especially sound. We are indebted to the journal of one Obadiah Turner for the following eyewitness account of what happened in church on the first Sunday in June, 1646.

As he strutted about the meetinghouse, he did spy Mr. Tomlins sleeping with much comfort, his head kept steady by being in the corner, and his hand grasping the rail. And so spying, Allen [the tithingman] did quickly thrust his staff behind Dame Ballard and give him a grievous prick upon the hand. Whereupon Mr. Tomlins did spring up much above the floor, and with terrible force did strike his hand against the wall, and also, to the great wonder of all, did profanely exclaim, "*Curse ye, woodchuck!*" he dreaming, so it seemed, that a woodchuck had seized and bit his hand. But on coming to know where he was, and the great scandal he had committed, he seemed much abashed, but did not speak. And I think he will not soon again go to sleep in meeting.[14]

For the Puritans, Sunday was the *first* day of the week, not the last. There was the morning service, which lasted three to four hours, after which they adjourned for a light lunch and returned for the afternoon teaching which could run another three hours. Then came Sunday dinner, the heartiest meal of the week. A nap was often in order afterwards, to sleep off the effects of so much good food and preaching.

The Puritans respected their pastor, who was generally a graduate of Oxford or Cambridge and possessed the highest classical education available. (Harvard, Yale, and other New England colleges were originally founded to provide such training to American-born ministers.) They relied on him to keep them apprised of what was going on in the world. Moreover, he was expected to have spiritual insight on the news he passed along, be it of a natural disaster or a scientific discovery or a distant war. And since the pastor was almost always the best-educated man in the community, he was counted on to bring the sum of man's knowledge, as well as God's wisdom, into his preaching. Thus, he became to them something of a spiritual Walter Cronkite, and, needless to say, influenced most of them, to one degree or another, with his point of view.

But not all Puritan ministers were of national network caliber, and even those who were, occasionally found themselves confronting rebellion. Sometimes this rebellion took the form of a willful choir, as in the case of one minister who, glaring at his choir, announced with much vehemence the hymn beginning: "And are you wretches yet alive? And do you yet rebel?" [15]

But the choirs were vital to the worship service, for most New England congregations had no accompaniment and could not remember many tunes. Even the few, commonly known melodies had become so corrupted that no two individuals sang them alike, or quite together, for that matter. Hence, a congregation singing often sounded like "five hundred different tunes roared out at the same time." [16] This being the case, the main singing was from the psalms, with an elder or deacon leading with a line, and the choir dutifully repeating it.

One Puritan deacon, rising to lead an obedient choir one Sunday, found his eyesight failing him as he started to read, and apologized, "My eyes, indeed, are very blind." The choir, assuming this was the first line of a common-meter hymn, immediately sang it, whereupon the deacon exclaimed, "I cannot see at all!" This the choir also sang. Frustrated, the deacon cried out, "I really believe you are bewitched." And when the choir sang that, too, the deacon loudly added, "The mischief's in you all," and sat down in disgust.

For Christians truly committed to Jesus Christ in a covenant life which demands all, humor and laughter become two of God's most precious gifts. The struggle against sin and self is often difficult. When one is angry, or dead tired, or on the verge of self-pity in reaction to a hard word of truth, the grace and mercy of God's holy humor provide a balm of healing ointment to the soul. The Puritans appreciated God-given opportunities to relax and perhaps even be a bit foolish with one another.

One such occasion was the dedication of the Old Tunnel Meetinghouse in Lynn, in 1682, which coincided with the installation of one Mr. Shepherd as its pastor. It was a double cause for celebration, and ministers from all the churches for miles around were invited as guests of honor. The town clerk recorded the events as follows:

The dedication dinner was had in the great barn of Mr. Hood, which by reason of its goodly size was deemed the most fit place. It was greatly adorned with green bows and other hangings and made very fair to look upon, the wreaths being mostly wrought by the young folk, they meeting together both maids and young men, and having a merry time in doing the work. The rough stalls and unhewed posts being gaily begirt, and all the corners and cubbies being swept clean and well aired, it truly did appear a meet banqueting hall. The scaffolds, too, from which provender had been removed, were swept as clean as broom could make them. Some seats were put up on the scaffolds, whereon might sit such of the ancient women as would see, and the maids and children. The great floor was held for the company which was to partake of the feast of fat things, none others being admitted save them that were there to wait upon the same. The kine [cattle] that were wont to be there were forced to keep holiday in the field.

There follows a detailed account of how the fowls who were accustomed to living in the barn persisted in flying in and roosting over the table, scattering feathers and hay on the august assembly below. Finally, the new pastor's patience was at an end. Normally the soul of dignity and decorum,

Mr. Shepherd's face did turn very red, and he catched up an apple and hurled it at the birds. But he thereby made a bad matter worse, for the fruit being well aimed, it hit the legs of a fowl and brought him floundering and flopping down on the table, scattering gravy, sauce and divers things upon our garments and in our faces . . . this did not please some, yet with most it was a happening that made great merriment.

Dainty meats were on the table in great plenty, bear-steak, deer-meat, rabbit and fowl, both wild and from the barn-yard. Luscious puddings were likewise had in abundance, mostly apple and berry, but some of corn meal with small bits of suet baked therein, also pies and tarts. We had some pleasant fruits, as apples, nuts and wild grapes, and to crown all, we had plenty of good cider and the inspiring Barbados drink [rum]. Mr. Shepherd and most of the ministers were grave and prudent at the table [except, of course, when flinging apples at the chickens], discoursing much upon the great points of the dedication sermon and in silence laboring upon the food before them. But I will not risk to say on which they dwelt with most relish, the discourse or the dinner.

Most of the young members of the council would fain make a jolly time of it. Mr. Gerrish, the Wenham minister, though prudent in his meat and drinks, was yet in a right merry mood. And he did once grievously scandalize Mr. Shepherd, who on suddenly looking up from his dish did spy him, as he thought, winking in an unbecoming way to one of the pretty damsels up on the scaffold. And thereupon bidding the godly Mr. Rogers to labor with him aside for his misbehavior, it turned out that the winking was occasioned by some of the hay seeds that were blowing about, lodging in his eye. Whereat Mr. Shepherd felt greatly relieved.

The new meetinghouse was much discoursed upon at the table. And most thought it as comely a house of worship as can be found in the whole colony save only three or four. Mr. Gerrish was in such a merry mood that he kept the end of the table where he sat in right jovial humor. Some did loudly laugh and clap their hands. But in the midst of the merriment, a strange disaster did happen unto him. Not having his thoughts about him, he endeavored the dangerous performance of gaping and laughing at the same time, which he now must feel is not so easy or safe a thing. In doing this, he set his jaws open in such wise that it was beyond all his power to bring them together again.

His agony was very great, and his joyful laugh soon turned to grievous groaning. The women in the scaffolds became much distressed for him. We did our utmost to stay the anguish of Mr. Gerrish, but could make out little till Mr. Rogers, who knoweth somewhat of anatomy, did bid the sufferer to sit down on the floor, which being done Mr. Rogers . . . gave a powerful blow and then sudden press which brought the jaws into working order. But Mr. Gerrish did not gape or laugh much more on that occasion, neither did he talk much, for that matter.

No other weighty mishap occurred save that one of the Salem delegates, in boastfully essaying to crack a walnut between his teeth did crack, instead of the nut, a most useful double tooth and was thereby forced to appear at the evening with a bandaged face.

There were further interruptions by invading roosters, staved off by barrages of flying nuts and apples, and in the end a few "maudlin songs and much roistering laughter." The account concludes, "So noble and savory a banquet was never before spread in this noble town, God be praised!" [17]

So much for the modern image of the dour Puritan!

10

The Pruning of the Lord's Vineyard

The Army of Light had established its beachhead in the new Promised Land. And as reinforcements poured ashore, the Light was advancing inland up the streams and rivers of southeastern New England. Its momentum was inexorable, and the forces of Darkness were falling back in confusion and disarray. Those who had eyes to see it recognized it as a miracle of God, of a magnitude which had seldom been equalled in the previous sixteen hundred years of the Church's history.

For in spite of the many differences of background and degree of commitment, in spite of all the temptations of jealousy and strife, in spite of wave upon wave of weak, sick, and helpless newcomers, they *were* being "knit together," to become "as one body." And the most amazing part of this ongoing miracle in God's new Israel was that it involved *so many* individuals, each of whom had his own free-will choice to either be actively committed or remain passively rebellious. God was planting a new vineyard, and many chose to be rooted into it as living vines.

Jesus said to His disciples: "I am the true vine, and my Father is the vinedresser. Every branch of mine that bears no fruit, he takes away, and every branch that does bear fruit he prunes that it may bear more fruit" (John 15:1, 2). The pruning had begun the moment they had landed in this new savage wilderness. The raw New England winter and times of famine had already prompted several shiploads of fruitless branches to return to England. Those that remained were pruned severely—and bore fruit.

With each passing season, the colony became more secure. Its roots sank deeper into American soil, which was being made more and more fertile by obedience and sacrifice. But God was looking for an abundant yield from His new vine, and so the Vinedresser's careful but incisive pruning of the Massachusetts Bay Colony continued. Three prominent branches were cut off—two wild shoots and one excellent one, suitable for transplanting.

The first branch appeared in February of 1631. He was a passenger aboard the *Lyon,* a man whom John Winthrop had known back in England as a "godly minister," one of the most ardent Puritans in their movement. Though only twenty-eight, he was possessed of a keen intellect and a gift for lyrical and inspiring preaching which had few equals.

Such was the impact of Roger Williams on New England that Cotton Mather, in his great history of God's acts in America, *Magnalia Christi Americana,* chose to introduce him in terms of the following allegory:

In the year 1654, a certain windmill in the Low Countries (Holland), whirling around with extraordinary violence by reason of a violent storm then blowing, the stone at length by its rapid motion became so intensely hot as to fire the mill, from whence the flames, being dispersed by the high winds, did set a whole town on fire. But I can tell my reader that about twenty years before this, there was a whole country in America like to be set on fire by the rapid motion of a windmill in the head of one particular man.[1]

Roger Williams was that most tragic and intriguing of all zealous Christians: a purist. "Charming, sweet-tempered, winning, courageous, selfless, God-intoxicated—and stubborn,"[2] he was so obsessed with being doctrinally and ecclesiastically pure that not even the Puritans were pure enough for him. From the moment he stepped off the boat, he brought anguish to the hearts of all who came to know him. Because to know him was to like him, no matter how impossible were the tenets he insisted upon.

And they *were* impossible. Witness his response when John Winthrop invited him to become the Boston church's teacher. At the time, the invitation actually involved assuming the pulpit, since Pastor John Wilson had gone back to England to bring over his wife. But Roger Williams did not feel that he could accept. For although the Boston church had put off all the trappings of Anglicanism, and followed Plymouth's example of self-covenanted and elected congregational autonomy, Williams would not be satisfied until they publicly repented for ever having taken Holy

Communion within the framework of the Church of England! And this they saw no need to do.

Williams's insistence upon absolute purity in the Church, beyond all normal extremes, grew out of his own personal obsession with having to be right—in doctrine, in conduct, in church associations—in short, in every area of life. This need to be right colored everything he did or thought; indeed, it drove him into one untenable position after another. For the alternative—facing up to one's self-righteousness and repenting of it on a continuing basis—was more than he could bring himself to accept.

For Williams, then, Christianity became so super-spiritualized that it was removed from all contact with the sinful realities of daily living. In his view, the saints of New England belonged to a spiritual Israel, in the same way as did all Christians everywhere. But there should be no talk of any attempt on God's part to build His Kingdom on earth through imperfect human beings. For Winthrop and the others to even suggest that God might be creating a new Israel in this Promised Land of America was to ". . . pull God and Christ and Spirit out of Heaven, and subject them unto natural, sinful, inconstant men . . . ." [3]

Williams apparently did not understand that this paradox to which he objected actually described the mystery of Christ's Incarnation, His life on earth, and His death on the Cross! Further, Jesus called all of His disciples to follow His example. But Williams could not abide this tension of being called to be "in" the world but not "of" it, of himself being subject to a congregation comprised of "natural, sinful, inconstant men." Balking at this subjecting himself to the circumstances of this world which His Saviour had willingly accepted, he instead chose to withdraw even more fully into a controlled environment of his choosing.

It appears that, of all those who tried to argue and plead with him (and that included at different times Thomas Hooker, John Cotton, William Bradford, and Edward Winslow) John Winthrop came the closest to reaching his heart. In fact, Williams may well have considered the compassionate Governor his closest personal friend throughout the remainder of his life. But when it came to a matter of principle, he would never permit himself to back down.

Besides, as much as he might have been tempted by Winthrop's vision, the covenanted kingdom which Winthrop was describing cut across the principle which Williams held to be the dearest of all: *liberty of conscience* ("Nobody is going to tell me what I should do or believe.").

Liberty of conscience is indeed a vital part of Christianity—as long as it is in balance with all the other parts. But taken out of balance and pursued to its extremes (which is where Williams, ever the purist, invariably pursued everything), it becomes a license to disregard all authority with which we do not happen to agree at the time. This was the boat which Williams was rowing when he landed at Boston. Since, at its extreme, liberty of conscience stressed freedom from any commitment to corporate unity, Williams was not about to hear God through Winthrop or anyone else. (And, tragically, he never did.)

So, off he went to Plymouth, where Separatists were truly separated. Here he charmed the people and shipped his oars, seemingly content to keep his more provocative opinions to himself—for a season. But when he discovered that the Pilgrims' agents in London had attended Anglican services there, he started rowing again, demanding that they repent or be excommunicated.

Of his two years in the Old Colony, Bradford had this to say:

Mr. Roger Williams, a man godly and zealous, having many precious parts but very unsettled in judgment, came over first to Massachusetts, but upon some discontent left that place and came hither, where he was friendly entertained, according to their poor ability and exercised his gifts among them and after some time was admitted a member of the church. And his teaching [was] well approved, for the benefit thereof I still bless God, and am thankful to him even for his sharpest admonitions and reproofs, so far as they agreed with the truth. He this year [1633] began to fall into some strange opinions and from opinion to practice, which caused some controversy between the church and him, and in the end some discontent on his part, by occasion whereof he left them something abruptly . . . . [When they refused his demand that they excommunicate their agents, he had no choice but to separate himself from them, as a matter of principle.] He is to be pitied, and prayed for, and so I . . . desire the Lord to show him his errors and reduce him to the way of truth, and give him a settled judgment and constancy in the same . . . .[4]

Both Winthrop and Bradford had essentially the same reaction to Williams: personal fondness and real anguish at the tragic course that he seemed implacably determined to pursue, steadfastly refusing to consider even the possibility that he might be wrong.

Roger Williams desperately needed to come into reality and see his sin—how arrogant and judgmental and self-righteous he was. If only he had humbled himself, he had the potential to be a great general in Christ's army, who could have led the troops smashing through the very gates of hell. Williams was tremendously gifted: in intellect, preaching, personality, and leadership ability. He attracted people in large numbers. But he had one tragic flaw: he would not see his wrongness, and he was so bound up in his intellect that no one could get close to the man, because he was forever hammering home points on "the truth." Trying to relate to him on a personal level was like trying to relate to cold steel—highly polished and refined.

No sooner had he broken with Plymouth, than the church at Salem offered him their pulpit, which he readily accepted. And now, with a church behind him, Williams began to row in earnest. Immediately, he started preaching that the King had no right to issue a charter to the Bay Colony, because the Indians (not the King) originally owned the land. He also charged the King with blasphemy for referring to Europe as Christendom.

Now Winthrop had no choice but to publicly admonish him in open court, and for a while Williams actually seemed to have had a change of heart. But within six months he was back at the oars. With John Cotton, who would become one of the greatest Puritan pastor-teachers, Williams would carry on long and tedious debates in print. But in the beginning Cotton had asked the magistrates' permission to entreat privately with him on behalf of the Bay Colony, and here, as in so many cases, Williams was shown nothing but love. For the attitude of the Bay was, in essence, "Let him believe whatever he wants, just so long as he is quiet about it. In due course, time will mellow him, and God will break him, and ultimately make good use of him."

Williams, however, seemed bent on breaking up everything else in the process. Not only did he refuse to keep his strange opinions to himself, but by assertively attacking the King, he seemed bound and determined to jeopardize the Bay Colony's charter, and bring the full wrath of the Crown down on all of them. That was going too far. Now they strongly appealed to him to cease making any further attacks on the King in regard to "liberty of conscience."

But Williams replied with a treatise which he had prepared for publication, in which he denounced the King as a liar, and recommended that the Bay Colony either send the charter back to England as fraudulent—or *return to England themselves!* Unfortunately, he was now dispensing such views as the pastor of a Congregational church, and therefore could do so with impunity. In this position, the other churches could not dismiss him, no matter how much he galled them.

But if other churches were powerless to unseat him, the civil authorities were not. And ironically, Williams might at this point have regretted his vehement insistence upon the total separation of Church and State. For the State's hands were not tied, and he was again hailed before the General Court, this time for willful and persistent heresy and troublemaking. Williams now countered that since the churches had obviously given up the principle of congregational independence, and called upon the government to help suppress him, they were no longer pure churches. Therefore, he and his congregation would have no choice but to renounce all the other churches in Massachusetts.

Here was the sort of shining moment that Roger Williams lived for: the gallant captain, fearless, intrepid, about to lead a charge against insurmountable odds. With a wave of his hand, he stepped out in front of his troops and led them on the double into battle. On and on he ran, never flagging, indeed seeming actually to gain strength the closer he came to the enemy positions. Yet if he had looked back to see how the troops following him were doing, he would have received a shock: there was *nobody* following him! But Roger Williams never looked back.

Providentially(?), at the time he led this particular charge, he was sick in bed with a cold, and so was not able to appeal to his flock in person. He had to do so in writing, and without the force of his personality to put it over, the appeal fell flat. At this juncture, his congregation finally balked and drew the line. Faced with this, the dictates of his principles were clear: he had no choice but to renounce the congregation too.

Williams, to be sure, had his day in court—and reveled in it, excoriating all present, even Winthrop, and taking great pride in his subsequent sentence of banishment. In spite of this, the court was willing to postpone sentence until the following spring (1636), provided he would not go about "drawing other people to his opinions." But that was like telling a chain-smoker he ought to give up cigarettes. In the end, the civil authorities were about to arrest him, when he fled them and went to Rhode Island, where he founded a colony of his own, which he named Providence.

When God has us "between a rock and a hard place," in order to deal with us on a level of deeply rooted sin, and we try to avoid the dealing by escaping from the physical place, we are simply forcing Him to deal with us that much harder in the next place. And so now, in Providence, God began to deal with Roger Williams in earnest. He had gone to England and procured a charter for his colony (apparently no longer having any scruples against accepting charters issued by the King). Populated at first by those who had remained loyal to him at Salem, Providence now became a magnet for every crackpot, rebel, misfit, and independent on the Atlantic seaboard. And he, as president, was responsible for keeping order.

What a nightmare! A man named Verrin refused to obey any order from the government on the grounds that it interfered with his "liberty of conscience." A seductive spellbinder named Samuel Gorton, whose philosophy was so obscure that none of his adherents could even define it, and who had been unceremoniously ushered out of the Bay Colony, had then so stirred things up down at Plymouth that he and his followers were among the few people whom the Pilgrims ever invited to leave. Then, after next being thrown out of Aquidnick, he finally descended upon Providence, where he was driving Williams to distraction. As Williams would write to Winthrop, who took it upon himself to keep up a warm correspondence with him (thereby keeping the door open, should Williams ever want to return): "Master Gorton, having foully abused high and low at Aquidnick, is now bewitching and bemadding poor Providence both with his unclean and foul censures of all the ministers of this country [sic!] (for which I myself have in Christ's name withstood him), and also denying all visible and external ordinances . . . ." [5]

But Williams's greatest problem proved to be the Quakers. Here again, the popular modern image of a humble, quiet folk, close to the earth, devout and simple in their ways, who drew people to God by their own unique brand of "friendly persuasion" is accurate enough for the eighteenth and nineteenth centuries, after they had finally accepted William Penn's offer of sanctuary, and settled down. But back in their early years in the seventeenth century, the Quakers were the wildest and most fanatical believers in all Christendom. To their way of thinking, Puritanism was hopelessly compromised and polluted, an institution which needed to be brought down by violent activism.

And violent was the word. One Sunday, a Puritan minister had barely turned the hourglass for the first time, when suddenly the door of the church burst open, and in came a fire-breathing Quaker with two bottles in his hand. Everyone held his breath, including the preacher. Up the aisle strode the Quaker, and then in the hush, bellowed, "God will shatter you for your hypocrisy, just like *this!*" and hurled the bottles on the floor, smashing them to smithereens. He turned on his heel and strode out, before anyone could collect himself. But even that was relatively minor compared to the

Quaker lass who had her own way of protesting Puritan hypocrisy: in the middle of a service, she walked in without a stitch of clothing on, went up to the altar, turned around and walked silently out.

Needless to say, the Puritans were riled to the point of apoplexy by the mere mention of the word *Quaker*. And the Quakers seemed to love every minute of it. Much like some of the more extreme cults of our day, they apparently felt truly fulfilled only when and where they were the objects of persecution. In short, if things were peaceful, they were not living up to their faith. They stirred up such horrendous turmoil in Massachusetts that they were finally banished upon pain of death, if they returned. And that was all they needed! Four of them decided that they would martyr themselves and return, which they did, only to find that they were completely ignored. Whereupon they raised such an unholy ruction that the authorities finally, albeit reluctantly, obliged them.

In Providence, they took pernicious delight in bedeviling Williams by reading back to him his most famous quotations, whenever he tried to assert his authority. In short, everything that Williams had ever inflicted upon the Bay Colony was now being inflicted upon him manyfold, till he cried out in anguish. (Concerning the Quakers, in the end he outsmarted them by simply refusing to take civil action against them, which made them loathe his colony! And it was Williams's book attacking the Quakers' doctrine which the Bay Puritans adopted as the ablest statement of their point of view.[6])

In the meantime, his obsession with purity had caused him to separate himself progressively further, until the only person whom he deemed fit to take Communion with him was his wife, and one historian says that even she was finally found to be "impure." The great danger of such obsessive self-righteousness is progressive withdrawal from society and even from other Christians. It can also lead to a dangerous, other-worldly mysticism which neutralizes any further effectiveness the believer might have in forwarding the Kingdom of God.

By the incredible workings of the grace of God, when Williams had finally reached this point, he abruptly concluded that true purity was an unobtainable goal, and in frustration he reversed himself entirely and decided to embrace everyone! The breaking process had at least begun.

Throughout the remainder of his life, nevertheless, even as his spirit mellowed, it was still of paramount importance to him that he be right. Years after his principal opponents were dead, and everyone else had forgotten the issues, he would still wage phantom debates and write wearying volumes, trying to prove that, after all, his position was the only valid one. And thus, so much of what might have worked pure gold in him, where humility and inner peace were concerned, turned him to self-pity and despair. Towards the end of his life, he would write, "As to myself, in endeavoring after . . . temporal and spiritual peace, I humbly desire to say, if I perish, I perish. It is but a shadow vanished, a bubble broke, a dream finished. Eternity will pay for all." [7]

In the end, Williams evokes genuine sorrow from the Christian reader, because his life could have counted for so much more. As it was, he did accomplish far more than even he himself realized. He would have pointed with pride to the long list of books, sermons and treatises which he had published, yet even his staunchest modern defenders will have to admit that these writings (the fruit of his rightness) are stupefyingly dull to read.

No, it is ironic that his greatest accomplishment turned out to have been on the heart level—not the head. In his late-blooming humility, he befriended the hostile Narragansetts, becoming a trusted friend of their chief, and leading many of them to Christ. Because of his missionary work to them, Rhode Island was the only colony spared from all Indian uprisings, and he was able to send the intelligence which saved Massachusetts from being taken by surprise in a terrible massacre.

With the passing of years, God had indeed succeeded in humbling Roger Williams to the point where He could make significant use of him. And Winthrop, Cotton, Hooker, and the others never lost their personal fondness for the windmill that once blew among them.

If Rogers Williams succumbed to one of the two great temptations for Christians—adamant, intellectual self-righteousness—Anne Hutchinson succumbed to the other: total infatuation with the experiential.

Mrs. Hutchinson and her husband arrived at Boston in 1636, and immediately joined John Cotton's church, for she had been an admirer of Cotton's when he had been preaching at Saint Botolph's in England. She admired him even more now, and for a while everything was sweetness and light. Mrs. Hutchinson had an extremely quick mind and a charming personality, in such potent combination that no one in New England had seen her like on their side of the ocean. And as for Cotton, never had he met anyone who was so enthusiastic about the Gospel, or who had such a quick grasp of the deeper things of the Spirit. She, in turn, could not praise him enough for his illumination of practically every subject on which he happened to preach.

When a man is gifted with a strong intellect, as Cotton was, there is an equally strong temptation which goes along with it: pride. In Mrs. Hutchinson he had finally found someone who appreciated—who really understood—the most profound points which he was trying to make. Not only did she understand them, but she even received insights of her own which were compatible with what he was preaching. Cotton began to look forward to his meetings with her after his sermons.

Her own enthusiasm now reached the point where she started inviting women to her home after church, to discuss the high points of Cotton's sermons. The meetings grew rapidly, and now some men began coming too. Gradually—imperceptibly—Mrs. Hutchinson began sharing some of her own beliefs, which were not entirely in line with what was being taught by Cotton—or anyone else for that matter. Not that any of the other New England ministers mattered to her at all: she subtly and indirectly proceeded to put each one of them down in her comments (though never to their faces), and always denied it if anyone were ever to ask her about it.

Heresy begins when one takes a basic truth and pushes it slightly out of balance with the rest of the body of truths which together comprise the essence of the Christian faith. Anne Hutchinson was teaching that a Christian was saved by faith alone. That much is true, but she went on to state that therefore, no amount of sanctification or good works could be taken as proof of salvation. While that is technically true, she maintained that the corollary was also true: The absence of santification and good works was no sign that a person *was not* saved. How *could* one tell, then? According to Mrs. Hutchinson, the Holy Spirit entered bodily into a person when he became saved. And anyone who had the Holy Spirit in him could tell whether someone else had the Spirit in him, too.

For individuals who are caught up in the heady intoxication of profound spiritual experiences, it is so easy to slip into error. Not that there is anything wrong with such experiences per se, but spiritual experience is only one leg of a three-legged stool. Unless it is balanced by the Word of God through Scripture and through other Christians, as well as the daily living of a life of self-denial, obedience and repentance, the stool will topple.

Satan is a master counterfeiter, who is able to imitate every spiritual experience which a Christian can have, including the "inner voice" of the Holy Spirit. Time after time we have seen cases of an especially "anointed" personality, who will lead a flock of gullible sheep into the strangest heresies, because the sheep have not yet learned to know their Shepherd's voice, and follow Him. Not nearly enough has been preached under the title: "Beware the Christless Pentecost."

What keeps the stool in balance? Facing the reality of our own egos, being willing to be corrected and shown where we are wrong, and choosing to stand against the demands of self. This is the Way of the Cross—to have self *decrease*, that He in us might *increase*—the only way a disciple can go. It was a way that neither Roger Williams nor Anne Hutchinson chose to go.

Without the Cross, error could only multiply, and soon Mrs. Hutchinson was claiming that the direct revelation of what she called the Holy Spirit was superior to "the ministry of the Word." This meant that whenever her personal revelation was in basic conflict with the ministers' interpretation of the Bible, they were wrong. Believing that she was always in direct communication with the Holy Spirit, she therefore felt that she did not need to submit to the rest of the Body of Christ in order to hear God. If anyone ever dared to openly question whether the inner voice she heard was indeed of God, she would grow fanatical, and wither the person with the power and eloquence of her response.

Understandably alarmed at such increasingly bizarre teaching, the ministers of the Bay Colony were also concerned with John Cotton's attitude toward Anne Hutchinson. For Cotton, normally their spokesman, could not bring himself to censure the woman; indeed, he seemed to be under her spell. And now her Sunday meetings had grown to number sixty to eighty people on a regular basis, including members of their own congregations. And she, waxing more bold in her rapidly growing popularity, was now not so subtly suggesting that none of them (save Cotton) was fit to preach the Gospel, because the Holy Spirit was telling her that none of them was truly saved!

The showdown came on that inevitable day when she was summoned to appear before the magistrates to answer to the charge of heresy. The courtroom was packed. Every minister within two days' ride was there, plus all the deputies, assistants, and Governor Winthrop. When she was challenged, in full confidence she exclaimed, "Take heed what you go about to do unto me . . . for I know that for this you go about to do to me, God will ruin you! And your posterity! And this whole State!"

How, the Court asked her, did she know it was God who revealed these things to her, and not Satan? And with that, fire fairly blazed from her eyes, and suddenly the roles were reversed: *she* was the interrogator, and the Court was the defendant:

MRS. H: How did Abraham know that it was God that bid him offer his son, being a breach of the sixth commandment?
COURT: By an immediate voice.
MRS. H: So to me by an immediate revelation!
COURT: How an immediate revelation?
MRS. H: *By the voice of His own Spirit to my soul!* [8]

And then she went on to threaten all of them with what God was telling her that He would do to them, even as she stood there in court.

The Court needed only a short deliberation to decide upon banishing her and those who would not disavow her beliefs, as "unfit for society." Where would she go? Where else? Only, by the time she departed for Rhode Island, her following had shrunk to a mere handful, and these were already arguing among themselves.

Mrs. Hutchinson's husband died the following year, and the badly deformed child which she was carrying at the time of her exile died at birth. Whereupon, she decided to leave Rhode Island and moved the remainder of her family to a lonely settlement in the Dutch Colony of New Netherlands, near a place called Hell's Gate (now Pelham). There, in September 1643, she and her family were cut down on their doorstep, the first victims of a local Indian uprising.

There is an even more macabre footnote to the Anne Hutchinson story which, the Puritans were convinced, bore out all the other evidence that she was a mouthpiece for Satan. We would not mention it, except for the fact that Winthrop himself felt that it merited a detailed account in his history of New England. In the same year that Anne Hutchinson had given birth to her grotesquely deformed stillborn child, so did her chief protégée, Mary Dyer. No description of the Hutchinson child exists, and the mothers endeavored to bury both babies without entering them into the town records. But word got out about Mary Dyer's baby—that it was a monster—and Winthrop, together with another magistrate and a church elder questioned the midwife who had been present at its birth.

Winthrop's detailed description of the creature's deformities is too revolting to reproduce here. He went on:

The Governor, with advice of some other of the magistrates and of the elders of Boston, caused the said monster to be taken up, and though it were much corrupted, yet most of those things were to be seen, as the horns and claws, the scales, etc. When it died in the mother's body (which was about two hours before the birth), the bed whereon the mother lay did shake, and withal there was such a noisome savor, as most of the women were taken with extreme vomiting and purging and were forced to depart. And others of them, their children were taken with convulsions (which they never had before or after), and so were sent home, so as by these occasions, it came to be concealed.[9]

It should be kept in mind that this is not *Rosemary's Baby* or *The Exorcist;* the bed-shaking, the stench, the convulsions, the vomiting—and the spawn of evil itself—actually *happened;* Governor Winthrop is too mature a witness to suspect him of distortion or exaggeration. If anything, his presentation would be conservative. And perhaps the Puritans, who somberly regarded it as a sign of Satan's authorship of Mrs. Dyer's and Mrs. Hutchinson's teachings, were not that far wrong.

The banishment of Roger Williams and Anne Hutchinson might best be summed up in these words from the Old Testament:

. . . My beloved had a vineyard on a very fertile hill. He digged it and cleared it of stones, and planted it with choice vines . . . and he looked for it to yield grapes, but it yielded wild grapes (Isaiah 5:1, 2).

Thus did the Vinedresser remove two aberrant shoots that were producing wild grapes.

The same year in which Williams left the Bay Colony saw the Lord remove another branch, but this one was a cutting specially chosen to be transplanted. It was a pruning that Governor Winthrop resisted at first, because he felt that the loss could hurt, even cripple the colony. The Reverend Thomas Hooker was a man of God who was in rare balance, who had been going the Way of the Cross for many years. Indeed, he had arrived at a point where he could write—and live—what amounted to the synthesis of the highest Puritan ideals.

Of the Way of the Cross, he had much to say, and we found ourselves wishing we had room to reprint large selections from his *Sum of Church Discipline* and *The Christian's Two Lessons: Self-Denial and Self-Trial*. This small sample will have to give the flavor of the rest:

We must lay down self . . . Therefore, because it is not in us to help ourselves, let us lay all at the feet of Christ, and expect nothing from self-sufficiency, but all from Christ . . . because that Christ and self-service cannot stand together, to have self in anything is to put out Christ; no man can serve two masters . . . .

Thus you have seen the first means [of becoming disciples], viz, self-denial. Now we come to the second; take up the cross. You must not think to go to heaven on a featherbed; if you will be Christ's disciples, you must take up His Cross, and it will make you sweat. By Cross, we understand troubles, because the death of the Cross was the bitterest and most accursed; therefore, it is put for all misery, trouble, affliction and persecution. [A man] must take up his cross, because it is his own . . . We must not bring misery on ourselves; there is no credit or comfort in this. The text does not say, "Let him make his cross," no, it is made already. So long as we have the world and our own corrupt hearts, and as long as there are devils in hell, there are troubles enough . . . .

Shall I not drink the cup which my Father gives? There is the force of the argument. God prepares it, therefore drink it, so the Apostle [Paul] reasons . . . God would have us live. If the patient be persuaded [that] the Physician has the skill, he will be willing to receive the potions prescribed by Him.[10]

There are some Christians today who are so resistant to denying themselves anything, and so committed to maintaining an atmosphere of artificial, self-generated joy that they would like to think that the man who wrote those lines must have been a pretty miserable fellow. Quite to the contrary, Thomas Hooker led an exceedingly positive and fulfilled life, and made in many ways an even greater contribution towards the birth of American democracy than Winthrop did.

Here was a man who, seeing himself as a totally needy sinner, was able to come to Christ daily with openness and humility. Thus he was a Christian who had profound inner peace and balance, upon whom God could rest heavy responsibilities, and through whom He created a new vine for His Vineyard. For Hooker listened to God, trusted Him, and obeyed Him.

Cambridge-trained, and an extremely gifted and compassionate pastor, Thomas Hooker was probably the most popular Puritan preacher in all England. As such, he was also number one on Laud's "hit" list, as soon as the latter became Archbishop. He barely escaped the King's soldiers, as he embarked for Holland in 1630. Three years later, God called him to New England, where a body of Christians, who called themselves "Mr. Hooker's company," had come over the year before and were waiting for him.

In Hooker, Winthrop found the first person he had met who fully shared his vision of what God was doing in New England! And yet despite his fame and popularity, Hooker had a humble spirit, and cheerfully and quickly fitted into the work at Massachusetts Bay. The two men enjoyed one another's company; and Winthrop saw Hooker as the ablest leader of all the clergy to come to America, and began to increasingly rely on him.

Since both men were intellectually creative, and could argue dispassionately, they spent much of what little free time they had in discussion. And exchanges such as the following might well have taken place that winter of 1633–34.

"Can you really be serious," we can image Winthrop saying to him one evening, seated by the hearth with Margaret spinning nearby (for she had joined him now), "about extending the vote? Government by the consent of the governed is one thing, but every man with a vote? And all the magistrates elected?"

He got up and stood with his back to the fire. "You're inviting anarchy, you know, or worse. Just because an idea happens to be momentarily popular with 51 percent of the people does *not* make it necessarily right. How often are God's strong dealings that popular? If the Kingdom of God were a democracy, how long do you think God would remain in office? That's why we've set the Bay's government up so that responsible leadership will not be encumbered by irresponsible legislation."

Hooker sipped his mulled wine and looked into the fire. "I have no quarrel with government by responsible and caring men, but tell me something: where are the checks and balances in the Massachusetts Bay system, to ensure against the corruption in leadership which so often accompanies absolute power? Don't you see that the people themselves must be allowed to help create the laws which govern them? Mind you," he thoughtfully tapped the rim of his pewter mug, "nothing would make me happier, John, than to have you continue in office until the Lord returns. But you're not going to, and we both know that. What if your successor turns out to be a bad apple? What if the magistrates start creating laws which line their own pockets or subvert the common good? How do we pluck them out, before they ruin the barrel?" He paused. "You *know* that can happen. And just how quickly it can happen," he added, when his host remained silent.

Winthrop poked a log into better position, creases forming on his brow. "But I say, you cannot trust most men to have the necessary wisdom to elect governors and assistants and magistrates. You'll have them putting their cronies in, for favors, or putting in golden-tongued charmers who will promise the world and all, and deliver nothing. I tell you, you'll wind up with more bad apples in your barrel than you ever dreamed of!'' And he started back to his chair. ''Government is best off in the hands of a few men who are totally dedicated to the work at hand—God's work. I am not advocating an aristocracy, you know that. I do not care what a man's background is, so long as he is totally surrendered to God and really means to *serve* his fellowman—*and* has the brains and pluck to do the job.''

''I know,'' said Hooker, looking up at him. ''But it is not a question of trusting the voters' judgment; it is a question of trusting the Holy Spirit to work through them. After all, wasn't one of the main purposes of the Reformation to restore to believers the responsibility for their own spiritual government? And isn't democracy really just an extension of the Reformation into civil government?'' He rubbed his chin. ''I know there's a risk. Yet it's the risk of the alternative that worries me even more.''

But Winthrop balked at the thought of trusting every man with the responsibility of government. And so they reached an impasse—one which would occur again and again, until finally Hooker and his church at Newton (Cambridge) requested permission to leave the Bay Colony and settle over on the Connecticut River.

Winthrop was loath to let him go. Hooker had been of more service to the Commonwealth and provided more leadership than all the other ministers combined. And even that was not his main contribution. For Hooker was a peacemaker. He would take two men with seemingly irreconcilable differences and would gently remind them what—and Who—was more important. And through his ministrations reconciliation would often come. To Winthrop, this was a commodity more precious than a year's supply of food or a shipload of new farming equipment. And then, too, if he left, how many good men would go with him?

And yet Hooker was not just independently leaving; he was asking the Governor's permission. And soon Winthrop came to see that if it *were* God's will, as Hooker seemed so sure that it was, instead of weakening the Bay Colony as he feared, it would eventually somehow strengthen it. Indeed, the two settlements could well prove to be mutually supportive. And this is, in fact, what happened. For God had given Hooker the vision of the next step in the evolution of American civil government, which had been born in the Reformation, actualized in the Pilgrim's church covenant and the Mayflower Compact, and further developed by Winthrop's (working) model of Christian charity.

Hooker felt strongly that all civil government in God's New Israel must be based on a voluntary submission to the same kind of covenant in civil terms which was the essence of their Puritan churches: "There must of necessity be a mutual engagement, each of the other, by their free consent, before by any rule of God they have any right or power, or can exercise either, each towards the other." [11] In 1638, in a letter to Winthrop, Hooker further crystallized his views on the magistrates' being elected for life and thus remaining virtually unchecked by the people in their exercise of authority: "I must confess, I ever looked at it, as a way which leads directly to tyranny, and so to confusion, and must plainly profess, if it was in my liberty, I should choose neither to live, nor leave my posterity, under such a government." [12] It was not yet the final form of American democracy, but it was getting close.

The *Fundamental Orders of Connecticut* were drafted a year later, and evolved quite naturally out of Hooker's beliefs. This constitution (for that was what it was) differed from the Bay Colony's system in four respects: first, there was no religious qualification for one to be able to vote. Second, definite restrictions were placed on the authority of the magistrates. Third, though the "inhabitants" (servants, etc.) could not vote for the governor and other officers as could "freemen" (landholders), nonetheless they had the legal right to elect deputies to the court. Fourth, the governor was sharply limited in power, and could not seek immediate re-election.

Finally, in *The Sum of Church Discipline*, Hooker took the opportunity to add his personal conviction that it was impossible to overemphasize the importance of the horizontal aspect of the covenant:

Mutual covenanting and confederating of the saints in the fellowship of the faith according to the order of the Gospel, is that which gives constitution and being to a visible church . . . It is free for any man to offer to join with another who is fit for fellowship, or to refuse . . . by mutual reference and dependence they are joined each to the other . . . .

In all combinations there is and will be some common end . . . [But] if each man may do what is good in his own eyes, proceed according to his own pleasure, so that none may cross him or control him by any power, there must of necessity follow the distraction and desolation of the whole, when each man hath liberty to follow his own imagination and humorous devices, and seek his particular, but oppose one another and all prejudice the public good . . . [Therefore] mutual subjection is, as it were, the sinews of society, by which it is sustained and supported.[13]

It is hard to say whether Hooker had Roger Williams and Anne Hutchinson specifically in mind. In any event, as was often to be the case, Hooker was speaking for all the Puritans. And no one had better stated the case for a covenanted society, as opposed to either aristocratic rule or the chaos of the arch-individualists. For "they had come to New England to build a City upon a Hill, not to erect a Tower of Babel." [14]

Thus would Connecticut become legendary for her "steady habits," and her government would indeed serve as the model for other colonies, and eventually for a union of colonies. And Hooker? The leaders of the Bay Colony continued to seek his wise counsel even after he had moved to Connecticut, and he found himself frequently invited back to Massachusetts to help them liberalize their own body of laws.

The new vine, although still young, was already producing some of the choicest grapes in God's vineyard. But as healthy as the vineyard now appeared, within the span of a generation the yield of all the vines would seriously decline.

11

God's Controversy
With New England

One of the greatest mysteries that we faced in our search was the question of what finally became of the Puritans. They had seemed to be prospering in every way—the hard times were behind them, there was plenty of good land and plenty to eat, spacious houses, and they were living in peace with the Indians. Spiritually, for the most part, they were deeply committed, obedient, and fulfilling the terms of the covenant. And God was blessing them beyond all measure . . . . Then, like a fire slowly dying down, the spiritual light began to dim, until, by the beginning of the 1700s, what had been a blazing light of the Gospel of Christ had become only a faint glow from smoldering embers. What had gone wrong?

The more we read, the more the question plagued us, for our research was beginning to indicate that the Covenant Way was the way in which God had intended America to go. If that were true, then the answer to the question of why the Puritans went wrong might very well provide the answer for us today.

We found our answers mostly between the lines of a number of sad accounts of such compromises as the Half-Way Covenant, and increasingly vehement sermons which fell on increasingly deaf ears. And we found something else: countless recorded instances of what the Puritans called Divine Providence—the extraordinary intervention of God on behalf of His people when they are in covenant with Him. Time after time, God would pour out His grace and mercy on the Puritans and protect them from dangers they could not foresee.

But we also discovered some sobering examples of Divine Justice, when those who had been in covenant openly scorned their commitment by word and deed. And we gained a better understanding of the judgments of God—those major and minor calamities which a loving Father permits in order to get the attention of His wayward children and cause them to turn back to Him. For the Puritans saw God's interventions, for weal or for woe, as distinctly as had their spiritual ancestors in ancient Israel:

Behold, I set before you this day, a blessing and a curse: the blessing, if you obey the commandments of the Lord your God . . . and the curse, if you do not obey the commandments of the Lord your God . . . (Deuteronomy 11:26–28).

So numerous were the blessings that God set before His people of the new Israel who were seeking to obey His commandments, that Cotton Mather's *Magnalia* devotes hundreds of pages to chronicling just some of the occurrences of Divine Providence. One marvelous account of God's supernatural care for His children occurs in Book II of the *Magnalia:*

For instance, an honest carpenter being at work upon a house where eight children were sitting in a ring at some childish play on the floor below; he let fall accidentally from an upper story a bulky piece of timber just over these little children. The good man, with inexpressible agony, cried out, "O Lord, direct it!" and the Lord did so direct it, that it fell on end in the midst of the little children and then canted along the floor between two of the children, without touching one of them all. But the instances of such things would be numberless.[1]

Another instance of God's taking a personal hand in the saving of Puritans' children is described by John Winthrop in his journal. It involved his two daughters, who, in February of 1632, "were sitting under a great heap of logs, plucking of birds, and the wind, driving the feathers into the house, the Governor's wife caused them to remove away. They were no sooner gone, but the whole heap of logs fell down in the place, and had crushed them to death, if the Lord, in His special providence, had not delivered them."[2] Had that wind sprung up a minute later, or been blowing in any other direction . . . .

"They that go down to the sea in ships . . . these see the works of the Lord and his wonders in the deep" (Psalms 107:23, 24 KJV). Thus begins one of the most intriguing sections in the *Magnalia:*

eleven tales of miraculous deliverances from the sea. Here are the highlights of two of them. On September 10, 1676, Ephraim Howe, his two sons and three other men, set sail from Boston for New Haven. Contrary winds and a storm blew them far out into the Atlantic and held them captive. Their exposure to the elements was lethal and with little in the way of victuals aboard, one by one they began to die.

First, Ephraim lost his two sons, as had his biblical namesake before him. But the storm raged on, finally driving them ashore on a desolate island near Cape Sable. The other men died after a few weeks, because there was nothing to eat but an occasional fish, or gulls which they could shoot (they had rescued some gunpowder). Ephraim survived alone.

Month after month went by, and although he could see fishing vessels on the horizon, none ventured near.

The good man, while thus deserted, kept many days in prayer, with fasting [sic], wherein he confessed and bewailed the many sins which had rendered him worthy of these calamities, and cried out to God for his deliverance. But at last it came into his mind that he ought very solemnly to give thanks unto God for the marvelous preservations which he had hitherto experienced, and accordingly he set apart a day for solemn thanksgiving unto God, his gracious preserver, for the divine favors which had been intermixed with all his troubles. *Immediately* [italics Mather's] after this, a vessel belonging to Salem did pass by that island, and seeing this poor servant of God there, they took him in. And so he arrived in Salem, July 18, 1677.[3]

[Less than two months shy of a year from the day he had departed!]

Our favorite of these sea stories involves *two* ships in distress. The first, under the mastery of William Laiton, was out of Piscataqua and bound for Barbados, when, some thousand miles off the coast, she sprang a leak which could not be staunched. Her crew was forced to take refuge in their longboat. It happened that they had a plentiful supply of bread, more than they could possibly eat, but so little water that after eighteen days of drifting, they were a teaspoon per man per day.

Meanwhile, another ship, captained by one Samuel Scarlet, was having its own difficulties, being "destitute of provisions, only they had water enough, and to spare." They spied the drifting longboat, but as Scarlet made ready to take them aboard, his men

. . . desired that he would not go to take the men in, lest they should all die by famine. But the captain was a man of too generous a charity to follow the selfish proposals thus made unto him. He replied, "It may be these distressed creatures are our own countrymen, and [anyway] they are distressed creatures. I am resolved I will take them in, and I'll trust in God, who is able to deliver us all." Nor was he a loser by this charitable resolution, for Captain Scarlet had the water which Laiton wanted, and Mr. Laiton had the bread and fish which Scarlet wanted. So they refreshed one another, and in a few days arrived safe to New England.

But it was remarked that the chief of the mariners who urged Captain Scarlet against his taking in these distressed people, did afterwards, in his distress at sea, perish without any to take him in.[4]

One seldom tires of hearing new accounts of God's wondrous faithfulness toward those who love and seek to remain faithful to Him. The same Psalm 107 with which Mather opens his sea accounts also contains these words: "Oh that men would praise the Lord for his goodness, and for his wonderful works to the children of men!"

But for those whose hearts were so hardened that they had nothing but scorn for the covenant, God's divine interventions took the form of judgments. And the Puritans expected no less, for as His new Chosen People, they knew that He would deal with them more strictly, precisely because of their call.

One of the grimmest tales of God's strict justice is recorded by John Winthrop. It happened in August of 1633.

Two men servants to one Moody of Roxbury, returning in a boat from the windmill, struck upon the oyster bank. They went out to gather oysters, and, not making fast their boat, when the flood [tide] came, it floated away, and they were both drowned, although they might have waded out on either side. But it was an evident judgment of God upon them, for they were wicked persons. One of them, a little before, being reproved for his lewdness and put in mind of Hell, answered that if Hell were ten times hotter, he had rather be there than he would serve his master.[5]

And so his wish was fulfilled.

An even more pointed example of God's judgment—and a moving, last-minute gift of repentance—took place in Boston in 1686. Condemned murderer James Morgan, who had in the days before his execution responded to the counseling help of Cotton Mather and given his life to Christ, turned on the gallows steps and addressed the crowd:

I pray God that I may be a warning to you all . . . In the fear of God, I warn you to . . . mind and have a care of that sin of drunkenness, for that sin leads to all manner of sins and wickedness . . . For when a man is in drink, he is ready to commit all manner of sin, till he fill up the cup of the wrath of God, as I have done by committing that sin of murder.

I beg of God, as I am a dying man and to appear before the Lord within a few minutes, that you may take notice of what I say to you . . . O that I may make improvement of this little, little time, before I go hence and be no more. O let all mind what I am saying now [that] I am going out of this world. O take warning by me, and beg God to keep you from this sin, which has been my ruin.

[And as the noose went round his neck] O Lord, receive my spirit! I come unto thee, O Lord, *I come unto thee!* [6]

There must have been more than a few people in that crowd who were deeply convicted of the need for a significant amendment of their own lives. But sad to say, the likely response of the majority of those present was one of indifference to his message, for a very subtle and dangerous change was taking place in the heart attitude of Puritan New England.

The ministers could see it coming, and Sunday after Sunday they had warned their congregations with such passages from the Word of God as:

Take heed lest you forget the Lord your God, by not keeping his commandments and his ordinances and his statutes . . . lest, when you have eaten and are full, and have built goodly houses and live in them, and when your herds and flocks multiply, and your silver and gold is multiplied, and all that you have is multiplied, then your heart be lifted up, and you forget the Lord your God . . . . Beware lest you say in your heart, "My power and the might of my hand have gotten me this wealth." You shall remember the Lord your God, for it is he who gives you power to get wealth; that he may confirm his covenant which he swore to your fathers, as at this day. And if you forget the Lord your God and go after other gods and serve them and worship them, I solemnly warn you this day that you shall surely perish (Deuteronomy 8:11–14; 17–19).

And this was exactly what was beginning to happen in God's New Israel, just one generation after the arrival of the first comers. For faith was not something that could be passed on from generation to generation, or imparted by baptism or the partaking of Holy Communion. In order for faith to come to flower, it must be planted in the soil of gratitude.

But being born into town situations instead of having to carve them out of the wilderness, the succeeding generations would not know desperate need. They would grow up never knowing what it meant to be persecuted for one's faith; to be mocked and scorned or even imprisoned merely because they loved God enough to attempt to put Him and His will before all else. The sons of the fathers would never know what it was like to have no land and no work and no say in how they were governed. They would have no indelible memories etched into their minds of ten, twelve, sixteen weeks of wet misery on the open seas—of living in tents or holes in the ground, while cold and sickness took one in two—of starving times which saw them on their hands and knees, looking for ground nuts or grubbing for mussels to stay alive—and all for the sake of their combined faith in the vision of a Promised Land.

Therefore they would not be inclined to put all their trust in God. It was by His grace that they and their parents were being blessed. And while they might give lip service to His grace, the truth was that since they had never known anything else, they could hardly share the gratefulness of their parents.

And what of those parents? As their common condition of great need gradually shifted to one of decided affluence, was their commitment to the covenant as absolute as it once had been? Or was having more than enough to eat, more than adequate shelter, and more than enough land, already beginning to take its toll? How quickly fade the pangs of harder times! Would America's affluence—the very gifts of a loving Father in response to the obedience of loving children—dim that Light of Christ which had seemed so dazzling? As a homestead of three acres became thirty and then three hundred, would greed replace need?

It is also human nature that one generation which has gone through a time of great tribulation will do all in its power to preserve and protect its offspring from the same deprivations. As the Puritan fathers and mothers became wise in the ways of living close to the land, they passed on to their sons and daughters an endless and priceless compendium of frontier knowledge—how to shoe a horse, when the wheat is ready for harvest, the finer points of carding and spinning wool.

And if, before each lesson, they forgot to stress the need to pray first and commit it all to God, and to know that it is His grace which was solely responsible for anything turning out well, the golden gift of resourcefulness would transmute itself to the lead of self-reliance. *My* land, *my* team of horses, "with the might of *my* hand . . . ." As the fathers began to think this way, they raised a generation of strong, well-adapted and supremely capable—and self-reliant—Yankees.

When a man can look at his own two hands and know what they are able to do—on the handles of a plow or an axe or the stock of a gun—when he knows what they can fashion with an awl or a plane or an adze—when he knows that they can tell by touch how soon a mare will foal or how fertile the soil is—when a man knows these things, he may well think that he does not need God as much. And then it will follow that he does not need other men, either.

Thus began one of the strongest and most revered of American traits: independence. The lone pioneer, carving out his homestead with his own family—that image occupies a most favored place in our cultural heritage. It carries on into the present time, with the glorification of the loner, the easy rider, and the rebel. The media extol him, the older generation relives youthful illusions through him, and their children believe in him and leave home to try to be King of the Road themselves—finding out too late that the dream is a nightmare.

It is a nightmare because God did not intend man to live alone. He intended man, and especially His children who are called by the name of His Son, to live as a body, to help and support one another. And God does His work of nurturing Christians primarily through other Christians. Indeed, the process of maturation (which the Bible calls sanctification) cannot be accomplished alone.

But a number of the first Americans had forgotten this, as had even more of their sons and daughters. They still went to church, if there was a church within an hour's ride, but their minds were often back on the spread, or the place or the plantation. (Next Sunday, the corn would have to go in, and church would have to wait.)

Those who did make it to their pews were treated to increasingly vehement calls to repentance from the ministers. This type of sermon was preached so often that it would eventually become known as a *jeremiad*, in honor of the Old Testament prophet who had thundered at a complacent Israel, and from whose writings the Puritan ministers frequently took their inspiration. Sunday after Sunday, they inveighed from their pulpits, and all across New England, meetinghouse rafters rang with the likes of Jeremiah 8:5, 6: "Why then has this people turned away in perpetual backsliding? They hold fast to deceit, they refuse to return. I have given heed and listened, but they have not spoken aright; no man repents of his wickedness, saying, 'What have I done?' "

But a man can become hardened to so strong a word as this. After all, the preachers had been saying the same thing for years, but the land was still fertile, the climate favorable, and the Indians peaceable, and God helped those who helped themselves, didn't He?

And so their grandsons helped themselves to more land and moved still further away, to establish their own life on their own land. There was no bothering now to gather a church first, no laws on the books which forbade inhabitants to live more than half a mile from the meetinghouse of a settled town, as there once had been. A man was free to go and do as he pleased, or as the Book of Judges puts it, "whatever was right in his own eyes."

Bradford, not too surprisingly, had foreseen it before anyone else, and it had broken his heart. Because he *knew* what God had intended.

No man now [1632] thought he could live, except he had cattle and a great deal of ground to keep them; all [were] striving to increase their stocks. By which means they were scattered all over the bay quickly, and the town in which they lived compactly till now was left very thin and in a short time almost desolate. And if this had been all, it [would have] been less, though too much. But the church must also be divided, and those that had lived so long together in Christian comfort and fellowship must now part and suffer many divisions . . . . And this, I fear, will be the ruin of New England, at least of the churches of God there, and will provoke the Lord's displeasure against them.[7]

A dozen years later, as more Pilgrims were anxious to get out on Cape Cod before all the best land was taken, Bradford would write:

But such as were resolved upon removal . . . went on notwithstanding, neither could the rest hinder them . . . And thus was this poor church left, like an ancient mother, grown old and forsaken of her children (though not in their affections), yet in regard of their bodily presence and personal helpfulness. Her ancient members being most of them worn away by death, and these of later time like children translated into other families, and she like a widow left only to trust in God. Thus she that had made many rich became herself poor.[8]

Cotton Mather, writing many years later, put it more bitingly: "Religion begat prosperity, and the daughter devoured the mother." [9] And in the same blunt vein, speaking of all New England, Judge Sewall wrote to Daniel Gookin, "Prosperity is too fulsome a diet for any man . . . unless seasoned with some grains of adversity." [10]

Was God wrong, then, to honor the obedience of His beloved children with blessings? Of course not! But, as John Danforth preached, ". . . to turn blessings into idols is the way to have them clapped under a blast. If the Lord loves His people, He will deliver the weapons out of their hands, that they are obstinately resolved to fight Him with . . . Better is it that Israel be saved and prosperity lost, than that prosperity be saved and Israel lost!"

God *would* clap them under a blast, as events would shortly demonstrate. But with all His heart, He was reluctant to do so, being patient far beyond the patience of men. And meanwhile, those men who knew the heart of God tried to alert their countrymen of the dire peril which they were surely bringing upon themselves. For God was now warning them directly, with droughts, with plagues of locusts and caterpillars, with smallpox epidemics, and with all the myriad and seemingly unconnected things which start to go wrong when grace is lifted.

Perhaps the most extraordinary chastisement in this vein was the rain of caterpillars which Winthrop reported in the summer of 1646.

Great harm was done in corn (especially wheat and barley) in this month by a caterpillar, like a black worm about an inch and a half long. They eat up first the blades of the stalk, then they eat up the tassels, whereupon the ear withered. It was believed by divers good observers that they fell in a great thunder shower, for divers yards and other bare places where not one of them was to be seen an hour before, were presently after the shower almost covered with them, besides grass places where they were not so easily discerned. They did the most harm in the southern parts, as in Rhode Island, etc., and in the eastern parts in their Indian corn. In divers places the churches kept a day of humiliation, and presently after, the caterpillars vanished away. [11]

The astonishing end to this plague is borne out by the Roxbury church records: ". . . much prayer there was made to God about it, with fasting in divers places, and the Lord heard and on a sudden, took them all away again in all parts of the country, to the wonderment of all men. It was the Lord, for it was done suddenly." [12]

For further corroboration, we have the account of the irrepressible Johnson:

Also the Lord was pleased to awaken us (to our sinful neglect of the Sabbath) with an army of caterpillars that, had He not suddenly rebuked them, they had surely destroyed the husbandman's hope. Where they fell upon trees, they left them like winter-wasting cold: bare and naked. And although they fell of fields very rarely, yet in some places they made as clear a riddance as the harvest-man's hand, and uncovered the gay green meadow ground. But indeed the Lord did, by some plots, show us what He could have done with the whole, and in many places cast them into the highways, that the cartwheels in their passage were painted green with running over the great swarms of them. In some fields they devoured the leaves of their peas and left the straw with the full crop, so tender was the Lord in His correction.

This [re]minded all these Jacobites of the end [purpose] of their coming over, but chiefly the husbandmen, whose over-eager pursuit of the fruits of the earth made some of them many times run out so far in this wilderness, even out of the sweet sound of the silver trumpets blown by the laborious ministers of Christ, forsaking the assembly of the Lord's people, to celebrate their Sabbaths in the chimney-corner, horse, kine [cattle], sheep, goats and swine being their most dear companions . . . ." [13]

While Johnson, Winthrop and a few others had sufficient discernment to see at that early stage what was happening, and spoke of it in no uncertain terms, they were as voices crying in the wilderness. Few listened. And so God, in His great love, had to follow the caterpillars with chastenings and warnings progressively more severe. Repeatedly, His people would turn back to Him, and pray and call His name and humble themselves, and He would gladly relent and return their blessings. But each time they were a little more quick to turn away again and each time their repentance was a little more perfunctory—a going through the motions, with not everyone bothering to observe the fast days or attend the services. And while there may indeed have been repentance in the hearts of many, it did not reach deeply enough to affect an amending of lives, for their hearts were turning hard and dry like Israel's of old. And so the droughts did not lift so quickly, nor did the pests entirely disappear.

The tragedy was poignantly expressed by Bradford, who stood at the end of his life, like old Jacob weeping for his sons gone into Egypt, looking back and measuring what might have been, by what they had actually had in the beginning. In 1655, two years before he died, as he reviewed the history which he had written of the Plymouth plantation, he came to the letter that Pastor John Robinson and Elder William Brewster had written from Leyden to Edwin Sandys in London. The letter brimmed with the confidence that, although other attempts at colonization had failed miserably, their situation was unique and unprecedented because of the proven strength of their covenant relationship. Indeed, they were "knit together as a body in a most strict and sacred bond and covenant of the Lord, of the violation whereof we make great conscience and by virtue whereof we do hold ourselves straitly tied to all care of each other's good, and of the whole by every one and so mutually." [14]

Reading that, Bradford lost his customary composure, and in a moment of rare and overwhelming anguish, poured out his heart on the back of that particular page in his manuscript: "O sacred bond, whilst inviolably preserved, how sweet and precious were the fruits that flowed from the same! But when this fidelity decayed, then their ruin approached. O that these ancient members had not died or been dissipated . . . or else that this holy care and constant faithfulness had still lived and remained with those that survived! . . ."

No one, not even Bradford, was denying that the settlement of the wilderness to the west was part of God's plan. But that was the ministers' whole point: *it should be carried out as part of His plan*, in accordance with His perfect will and timing. It should *not* be done willy-nilly, by isolated individualists, who could not care less about being in God's will, where a new stretch of bottom land was concerned. Heedless of the covenants they had sworn, without bothering to submit their decision to the elders of their churches, let alone obtain the permission of the civil authorities, they simply departed.

One preacher who responded more in anger than in sorrow was John Cotton:

But when men thus depart, God usually followeth them with a bitter curse: either taking their lives away from them, or blasting them with poverty, or exposing them to scandal where they come, or in entertaining them with such restless agitations that they are driven to repent of their former rashness, and many times return to the church from which they had broken away.[15]

It was an awesome thing in those days for a man of God to invoke such a solemn imprecation, but John Cotton's prophecy was to prove more true than even he might have expected.

Another symptom of the general spiritual malaise was the fact that the younger generation was not getting converted. The sons of the fathers, and especially *their* sons were not coming into the same saving relationship with Jesus Christ which their parents and grandparents had known.

The brunt of the responsibility had to rest squarely on the shoulders of the Puritan parents. For they were the ones who first eased up on their commitment to the Covenant Way. The Puritans had been called as a body to be so filled with the Light of Christ in their own lives that they would be "a city set on a hill" and "a light to lighten the Gentiles." This meant that unless there was *daily* repentance and a humbling of oneself before God, unless there was a continued willingness to be wrong and take correction, the inevitable result might be expressed by the unspoken motto "If you can't *be* good, look good." A shorter description of it is hypocrisy—the sin the Puritans seemed to hate so passionately in others, and yet came to practice themselves with ever-growing self-deception.

And thus the parents were on the horns of a dilemma: if they continued to be as hard on their children's sin as they had formerly been on their own, their hypocrisy would become manifest, and their children would have good cause to want no part of the Covenant Way. On the other hand, if they eased up on their children's sin, as they were doing on their own, they would be guilty of idolatry, and their children would have no awareness of their own need for Jesus Christ, let alone be drawn to the Covenant Way.

In truth, there was no need for a dilemma. If they had been willing to live once again according to the terms of the covenant which they had originally accepted, God would hear their prayers and heal their land. But once we lay down His Cross, our fallen nature is such that it strongly resists taking it up again.

Thus did the Puritans lay down their cross. They stopped their ears and refused to listen to their ministers, and they ceased to correct and admonish one another and their children, choosing instead, greed, privacy, independence, and idolatry.

The Light of Christ grew steadily dimmer. It was attracting hardly any of the children now. And thus the Puritan churches faced a further dilemma: what to do about the children of members who had never been converted to Christ themselves, but who now wanted to have their own children baptized in the church? In the end, they came up with what was dubbed the "Half-Way Covenant." This extended partial membership to such parents and enabled them to have their children baptized, but did not permit them to take Holy Communion. It was the best solution that they could come up with, and it fairly well defined the place they had come to: a half-way covenant for half-way committed Christians.

The preface to the *Magnalia* sums up the first half-century of God's New Israel:

Now one generation passeth away, and another cometh . . . and these have had the managing of the public affairs for many years, but are apparently passing away, as their fathers before them. There is also a third generation, who are grown up and begin to stand thick upon the stage of action . . . Much more may we, the children of such fathers, lament our gradual degeneracy from that life and power of such fathers that was in them, and the many provoking evils that are amongst us. (For these evils) have moved our God severely to witness against us, more than in our first times, by His lesser judgments going before, and His greater judgments following after.[16]

Greater judgments following after . . . their troubles mounted to the point that, in 1670, the government of Massachusetts conducted a special investigation to determine why God was so afflicting the people with sickness, poor crops, and shipping losses. But nothing came of it. The settlers followed their accustomed ways, and their hearts grew ever more hardened to the voices of their clergy, now warning that the blast John Danforth had predicted was imminent.

Actually, the government could have saved the time and cost of the investigation, if they had read with their hearts the poem of Michael Wigglesworth, which had already become a favorite in Puritan classrooms. Aptly entitled "God's Controversy With New England," three of its thirty-one verses read as follows:

> Our healthful days are at an end
> and sicknesses come on
> From year to year, because our hearts
> away from God are gone.
> New England, where for many years
> you scarcely heard a cough,
> And where physicians had no work,
> now finds them work enough.
>
> Our fruitful seasons have been turned
> of late to barrenness,
> Sometimes through great and parching drought,
> sometimes through rain's excess.
> Yea now the pastures and corn fields
> for want of rain do languish;
> The cattle mourn and hearts of men
> are filled with fear and anguish.

The clouds are often gathered
  as if we should have rain;
But for our great unworthiness
  are scattered again.
We pray and fast, and make fair shows,
  as if we meant to turn;
But whilst we turn not, God goes on
  our fields and fruits to burn.[17]

12

"As a Roaring Lion"

Like the drawing back of a mighty war bow, tension mounted in the early summer of 1675. There was one way in which God's blast of judgment might descend on a complacent, greedy, self-oriented people which was so ominous that no one dared think about it, let alone put it into words: a general, coordinated Indian uprising.

Prior to this, the Indians' ancient tribal rivalries had run so deep that there had never been a serious possibility of a massed uprising. And because God's people were living in obedience to their covenant with Him, His providential grace so covered them that such incidents as the one in 1639 which Winthrop relates were not unusual:

At Kennebeck, the Indians wanting food, and there being stores in the Plymouth trading house, they conspired to kill the English there for their provisions. And some Indians, coming into the house, Mr. Willet, the master of the house, [was] reading in the Bible, his countenance more solemn that at other times, so as he did not look cheerfully upon them, as he was wont to do. Whereupon they went out and told their fellows that their purpose was discovered. They asked them, how could it be? The others told them, that they knew it by Mr. Willet's countenance, and that he had discovered it by a book he was reading. Whereupon they gave over their design.[1]

But settler/Indian relations had been deteriorating for some time, and Metacomet, the son of Massasoit, sachem of the Wampanoags (to whom the settlers had given the Christian name Philip), was rumored to have been talking to chiefs of other tribes. And with the rush of events in early June, people were being forced to think the unthinkable.[2]

The arrow had been fitted to the bowstring back in January. Early one morning, some men passing by a large frozen pond in the settlement of Middleborough (about fifteen miles southwest of Plymouth) happened to notice something out on the surface of the pond. It looked like a man's hat, and there was something else nearby which appeared to be a musket. Since neither item was the sort of thing which a man would leave behind him, particularly in the dead of winter, and since the ice was clearly strong enough, they went out on the pond to take a closer look.

Sure enough, it was a hat and a gun. Suddenly, one of the men gave a cry: there, beneath the clear ice, was a face, its eyes open wide, staring upward, its dark hair billowed out around it! One of the men ran to get an ax, and the body which they chopped out of the ice was that of John Sassamon, a Christian Indian from the nearby Indian settlement of Nemasket. Presumably he had drowned while crossing, before the ice had fully hardened.

But something was wrong. Sassamon was an Indian; he would have known better than to try something so foolhardy. Closer examination revealed an acute swelling on the side of his head, which could have come from a blow, and no water had come out of the body to indicate death by drowning. But the most telling piece of evidence was that his neck was broken. Whatever else might happen to a man going through the ice, he would not break his neck. It began to look as if John Sassamon had been murdered, and the crime had been made to look like an accident.

The probability of murder became even more likely, when one considered the facts of John Sassamon's life. He had been reared in a community of Christian Indians at Natick, fifteen miles west of Boston, and had studied at Harvard. But then, perhaps in a crisis of identity, he had rejoined his native Indians in the wilderness, serving as the aide of the sachem Philip. John Sassamon was a bright and quick young man, as fluent in English as in his native tongue. As such, he must have been invaluable to Philip—until his Christian conscience began to trouble him. God's Spirit increasingly convicted him, to the point where he finally returned to Natick, where he was readmitted and became such a model convert that he was given the responsibility of instructing other Indians. Thus, when the Indian community at Nemasket sent for a native preacher, John Sassamon was the logical choice.

All of which could only have infuriated Philip, who was well known for his thinly veiled hatred of Christianity, and especially of the Christian missionaries who were pulling away some of his best warriors. In this hostility he was fully supported by the *powaws*, or medicine men, who saw their own power and influence being drastically undercut by the white man's religion. To Philip, John Sassamon would have appeared to be a turncoat of the vilest sort. That much was known.

What was not generally known was that shortly before his death, John Sassamon had come to Governor Winslow of the Plymouth Colony and his magistrates and secretly informed them that Philip and the Wampanoags were organizing a general conspiracy against the settlers. The Governor and his associates seemed to have discounted the warning at the time, even though John Sassamon had emphasized that he was risking his life to bring them that intelligence. But what they had persisted in taking lightly then, they were not taking lightly now.

Incredibly, an eyewitness to Sassamon's murder was found, an Indian who had observed the whole thing from the top of a nearby hill, which was close enough for him to recognize all three assailants, one of whom was a chief lieutenant to Philip. These men were apprehended, and the trial was set for June. To ensure the utmost fairness, there would be *two* juries: one composed of settlers, the other of the wisest Indians in the colony. Although the three defendants insisted upon their innocence throughout the trial, the verdict of both juries was unanimous: *guilty as charged*.

The sentence was death by hanging, and the war bow was drawn fully taut. Philip was furious. He insisted that the witness was lying and was in collusion with the settlers, in an obvious attempt to besmirch his honor (for if they were guilty, there could be no question as to who had given the order). Such was his insistence and also that of the defendants, who, even as they stood on the gallows, hotly denied that they had been at all involved with John Sassamon's death, that there might have been real doubt in future years. Indeed, that would have been almost a certainty, had it not been for an incredible instance of Divine Providence. As the trap door beneath the last of the three Indians was sprung, the rope broke! The Indian fell to the ground, and in the terror of the moment, chose to talk. He confessed that all three of them had done exactly what they had been convicted of, and although he maintained that he only watched while the other two had done the actual killing, he was re-hanged, and this time the rope did not break.

But Philip's patience did. Now large bands of armed Indians were seen moving through the countryside, and many settlers abandoned their far-flung homesteads and moved into more densely populated areas guarded by fortified houses called strong-houses. One wonders if perhaps they were reminded of the Scripture verse in 1 Peter 5: ". . . your adversary the devil, as a roaring lion, walketh about, seeking whom he may devour."

Fear stalked the land; the tip of the arrow on the war bow was seeking its aiming point. A few of the abandoned houses were looted and burned by the Indians, and armed bodies of militia went into the woods seeking the culprits, but returned in frustration, having chased shadows. Some shots were fired and returned, but the enemy was never seen. All through the first three weeks of June, a terrified populace held its breath.

One can imagine the scene on the outskirts of the settlement of Swansea in the Plymouth Colony, when the drawstring was finally loosed.[3] In the half-light before dawn, on the cool, clear morning of June 21, the blast came. It would have been guided by the feathers of a wild turkey—feathers attached not to the tail of a plump fowl, but to a lean willow shaft. At the other end of the shaft was a head of pointed flint, and as the silent missile traveled towards its mark, from well-concealed positions more than a hundred pairs of eyes followed its flight. On and on it flew, till it landed with a *thunk* in the stout oak door of the home of a settler we will call Isaac Trowbridge.

Hearing that sound, and no other, Trowbridge opened the door. His eyes widened as he saw the arrow, but before he could move to slam the door shut, a second arrow sank into his chest, and a third pierced his throat. His oldest son took the fourth, as he tried to drag his father inside. At that moment, the surrounding woods erupted in an unholy din, as scores of braves gave vent to hatreds stored up for decades. The middle son barricaded the door and put the family table up against the front window, while the youngest loaded their father's long-barreled flintlock. But it was futile, and the little family knew it. And before long, an ugly column of black smoke was rising in the still morning air.

That day Indians from Philip's nearby base at Mount Hope burned all the houses of Swansea, slaughtering and mutilating their inhabitants. When the colonial troops finally arrived, they were shocked and sickened at the horror of the scene which confronted them. The main street of the little village was strewn with the dismembered corpses of men, women, and children. So hideous was the sight that it did not even register at first that it could have been done by human beings. Satan had unleashed his fury on New England.

Dartmouth was the next settlement to come under the tomahawk, a day later, and then Taunton and Middleborough, and Sudbury. Fifty men were massacred in Lancaster, and forty homes were put to the torch in Groton. The Indians now prepared to move on Marlborough, with King Philip himself taking personal command of some fifteen hundred braves, a greater army than the colonists themselves had ever been able to muster.

New England was totally unprepared, strategically, mentally, and spiritually. A company of local militia would be hastily called out and dispatched to the relief of a beleaguered town or hamlet, only to be cut to pieces by a well-placed ambush waiting for it. A second column would be sent to the aid of the first, only to blunder into a separate ambush set for *it*. And so it went, until the settlers were afraid to go into the woods, let alone vigorously pursue the enemy. Throughout New England, morale had sunk to its nadir, for into the towns not yet under attack came the survivors—some in hysterics, others dumbstruck by atrocities beyond the human mind's capacity to assimilate.

Almost immediately a fast day was declared in Massachusetts, but no sooner had the service ended, than reports of fresh disasters arrived. Clearly this time God's wrath was not going to be turned aside by one day's worth of repentance.

Increase Mather and his son Cotton sounded the note that other clergymen soon picked up. They preached the most powerful sermons of their lives, based on Scriptures like:

> Behold, I am bringing upon you . . . a nation whose language you do not know . . . . Their quiver is like an open tomb, they are all mighty men. They shall eat up your harvest and your food; they shall eat up your sons and your daughters . . . they shall eat up your vines and your fig trees; your fortified cities in which you trust they shall destroy with the sword . . . . They lay hold on bow and spear, they are cruel and have no mercy, the sound of them is like the roaring sea . . . they [are] set in array as a man for battle, against you, O daughter of Zion. (Jeremiah 5:15–17; 6:23).

It was manifestly clear to the Mathers that God was not going to be satisfied with superficial or temporary change. What He now demanded was what He had been calling for all along: nothing less than a complete amendment of life. This would necessitate a rooting out of sin and a dealing with it to a degree which had not been seen on the eastern coast of America for nearly fifty years.

At first, the people, frightened and badly shaken though they were, still did not take the Mathers and their fellow ministers seriously, for they had heard it all so many times before. But, the war news got steadily worse. And it *was* war now, there was no question about that; practically every Indian tribe in New England had donned warpaint and was collecting scalps.

Finally, the people began to heed their ministers. The Bay Colony's churches filled, and people who had not attended church in years stood in the aisles and joined in the prayers.

For the battle was a spiritual one; there was no question about that, either, and even the most pragmatic among them was coming to accept that. God's patience with the colonists' hypocritical ways had come to an end. He was not about to relent and restore the saving grace, which had so long protected them and which they had so long taken for granted, unless the whole fledgling nation had a change of heart.

In the meantime, it was now the forces of Light which were reeling in confusion and disarray, and falling back on all fronts. As Samuel Cooke would preach a century later, "Satan, whom the Indians worshipped . . . [raised] armies of fierce, devouring beasts . . . ." [4] The Prince of Darkness had waited patiently for the seeds of greed to do their work. And now he laughed in triumph as his counterattack reached the peak of its fury, and his own obedient servants did their savage best to make up for all the ground lost and the insults taken. They fought with abandon and with the courage of knowing that this was their last chance. For they could not be pushed any further west by the advancing settlers. Their backs were to the Hudson River, beyond which the exceedingly hostile and powerful Iroquois nations held undisputed territorial rights. The time had come to push the white man back into the sea!

Many of those families and settlements which were now being hardest hit had long before removed themselves far from the churches, physically as well as spiritually. Moreover, many of these families had incorporated themselves into towns without first gathering a church. And the Mathers were making it abundantly clear that their misfortune was no coincidence. John Cotton's prophecy was coming home to roost!

But where even the most isolated settlements *had* striven to keep faith with God and with one another, God kept faith with them. According to a history of the town of Sudbury, the reason that Sudbury rather than Concord was chosen by the Indians as their next point of attack was that the Indians feared the influence that Concord's minister, Edward Bulkely, had with the Great Spirit. The history quotes an old Indian chronicle as follows: "We no prosper if we burn Concord," said they. "The Great Spirit love that people. He tell us not to go there. They have a great man there. He great pray." [5]

Another case in point is the siege of Brookfield. There, by the grace of God, the townspeople had time to gather into their block-house, where with their muskets they were able to hold off a vastly superior number of Nipmuck Indians. A scout named Ephraim

Curtis was among their number, and three times he tried to sneak through the Indian lines to get help. On the third attempt, he finally succeeded, crawling through the darkness on his hands and knees, expecting at any moment to be discovered and killed. He made it on foot to Marlborough, some thirty miles distant, where he collapsed, exhausted.

Meanwhile, back at the site of the blockhouse, the Nipmucks were strengthening their siege, occupying nearby barns and pouring musket fire into the windows of the blockhouse, which continued to hold out. Now the Indians resorted to bonfires, shooting flaming arrows into the roof of the house. But the people inside cut holes in the roof and extinguished the flames before they could spread. Next the Indians piled hay against a corner of the house and set it afire, but some of the settlers were able to dash out and quench the blaze.

Frustrated, the warriors built a mobile torch, using wheels from the farm vehicles, a barrel full of combustibles, and two extremely long shafts, made of poles spliced together. But just as this contraption was about to be set in motion, a sudden downpour drenched the combustibles and rendered it useless!

The siege had been underway for almost forty-eight hours, when word finally reached Major Samuel Willard, who was on his way to Lancaster with a strong force of mounted troopers. The force wheeled about and rode at the gallop to Brookfield, where the Indians were making such a tumult besieging the blockhouse that they did not hear the shouts or warning shots of their sentries, who had sighted the fast-approaching horsemen. After a brief, hot skirmish, the Indians vanished. And when the bullet-riddled door swung open, the troopers received the welcome of their lives!

Even in New England's darkest hour, God's judgment could be seen to be tempered with mercy on behalf of his faithful. It was a miracle that Curtis got through, another that the cloudburst came when it did, a third that Willard's force just happened to be within reach and ready for combat when the word came.

There were many other recorded instances of God's mercy in the form of Divine Providence throughout this war. But perhaps none was so moving as the narrative of Mary Rowlandson, who was taken alive by the Indians when they raided Lancaster. Her husband, the local pastor, was in Boston on business when the attack came, and she and thirty-six others were in one of the village's stronghouses, which the Indians succeeded in setting on fire.

Then I took my children and one of my sister's to go forth and leave the house, but as soon as we came to the door and appeared, the Indians shot so thick that the bullets rattled against the house as if one had taken a handful of stones and thrown them, so that we were fain to give back . . . The Lord hereby would make us the more to acknowledge His hand and to see that our help is always in Him. But out we must go, the fire increasing and coming along behind us, roaring, and the Indians gaping before us with their guns, spears and hatchets to devour us. No sooner were we out of the house, but my brother-in-law fell down dead, whereat the Indians scornfully shouted and hallooed, and were presently upon him, stripping off his clothes. The bullets flying thick, one went through my side, and the same through the bowels and hand of my dear child in my arms. One of my elder sister's children, named William, had then his leg broken, which the Indians perceiving, knocked him on the head. Thus were we butchered by those merciless heathen, standing amazed, with the blood running down to our heels . . . .[6]

They took her captive.

. . . but God was with me, in a wonderful manner, carrying me along and bearing up my spirit, that it did not quite fail. One of the Indians carried my poor wounded babe on a horse . . . I went on foot after it, with sorrow that cannot be expressed. At length, I took it off the horse, and carried it in my arms till my strength failed, and I fell down with it. [They put her and the child on a horse, until they made camp.] And now I must sit in the snow, by a little fire, and a few boughs behind me, with my sick child in my lap, calling much for water, being now through the wound fallen into a violent fever . . . Oh, may I see the wonderful power of God, that my spirit did not utterly sink under my affliction. Still the Lord upheld me with His gracious and merciful Spirit, and we were both alive to see the light of the next morning.

For nine days Mary Rowlandson struggled on, as she was taken with the roaming band, until finally her child died. But her awesome faith in God remained undiminished: "I have thought since of the wonderful goodness of God to me, in preserving me in the use of my reason and senses in that distressed time, that I did not use wicked and violent means to end my own miserable life." [7]

This was particularly meaningful as many of the women taken captive either went mad or committed suicide. For the Indians enjoyed inflicting mental torture almost as much as physical torture, and they never missed an opportunity to goad a captive whom they suspected of having a low threshold of self-pity. What was more, they seemed to recognize faith in Christ for what it was, and it either provoked them into a frenzy, or they left the Christian pretty much alone, possibly almost fearful of the Source of their inner strength. But other, less devout captives with only hope to sustain them, had precious little of that commodity. All New England was plunged into darkness, the likes of which had not been seen, even in the first terrible winters.

But the Light was never completely extinguished, and the darker it became, the fiercer burned the few lights which were left. Not in twenty years had Increase Mather preached so often to such capacity crowds. And for the first time in even longer than that, people were listening to every word—and not just hearing but heeding. In the face of the repeated successes of the Indians, the much-vaunted Yankee self-reliance and self-confidence melted away like a candle on a hot stove. A great many farmers and backwoodsmen knew the taste of fear for the first time in their lives, and got down on their knees, some also for the first time. By April of 1676, there was scarcely a man or woman in all of New England who was not diligently searching his or her own soul for unconfessed or unrepented sin. In fact, it became unpatriotic not to do so—as if one were not doing one's part for the war effort.

It was a time for poets to marshal their talents for the cause, as did Peter Folger, one of whose grandsons would be Ben Franklin:

> If we then truly turn to God,
>   He will remove His ire,
> And will forthwith take this His rod
>   And cast it in the fire.
> Let us then search what is the sin
>   that God doth punish for;
> And when found out, cast it away,
>   and ever it abhor.[8]

And it was a time for churches to renew their covenants. As one pastor put it, "We intend, God willing . . . solemnly to renew our covenant in our church state according to the example in Ezra's time . . . This is a time wherein the Providence of God does, in a knocking and terrible manner, call for it."

At last God's wrath began to abate. Mary Rowlandson observed from behind enemy lines, as it were,

. . . the strange providence of God in turning things about, when the Indians were at the highest and the English at the lowest. I was with the enemy eleven weeks and five days . . . [They] triumphed and rejoiced in their inhumane and many times devilish cruelty to the English. They would boast much of their victories, saying that in two hours' time they had destroyed such a captain and his company in such a place, and [would] boast how many towns they had destroyed, and then scoff and say [that] they had done them a good turn to send them to heaven so soon . . . .

Now the heathen begin to think all is their own, and the poor Christians' hopes [begin] to fail (as to man), and now their eyes are more to God, and their hearts sigh heavenward. And [they begin] to say in earnest, "Help, Lord, or we perish." When the Lord had brought His people to this, that they saw no hope in anything but Himself, then He takes the quarrel into His own hands. And though [the Indians] had made a pit in their own imaginations, as deep as hell for the Christians that summer, yet the Lord hurled themselves into it.[9]

Mary Rowlandson was miraculously released, shortly before the cessation of hostilities. And not only that, but her son and daughter, held captive elsewhere, were also released, and the family rejoined with her husband. "Thus hath the Lord brought me and mine out of that horrible pit, and hath set us in the midst of tenderhearted and compassionate Christians. It is the desire of my soul that we may walk worthy of the mercies received, and which we are receiving." [10]

The tide of war had begun to turn. Some modern historians, who are loath to give God credit for anything, point out that time and numbers were on the colonists' side, once they had regained their nerve. They had the weapons, and they had the supplies; all that was needed was for them to gain the courage to take the offensive. But the Puritans themselves knew from Whom that courage finally came. They knew Whom to thank, and they did, profusely.

It is one of the exquisite ironies of Divine Justice that the instruments with which God chose to turn the tide were ones which had, until the coming of the settlers, belonged to Satan. These were none other than the "Praying Indians"—those who had been converted to Christianity. These had remained loyal to the settlers, even though, in the initial shockwave of panic, they had been the focal point of much hatred. Badly frightened people had suddenly decided that the only good Indian was a dead Indian.

Had these Praying Indians not been courageously protected by the Reverend John Eliot (who would become known as the Apostle to the Indians), Daniel Gookin, Daniel Henchman, and William Danforth, it is almost certain that there would have been wholesale atrocities which would have redounded to our shame for the next three hundred years. As it was, many Christian Indians were interned on Deer Island in Boston's harbor for the duration of hostilities, with almost no shelter and wholly dependent on charity for their food. But they knew how to pray, and God looked after them.

When they were finally trusted enough to be given arms and combat assignments, these Christian Indians became scouts, the eyes and ears of the colonial forces whenever they had to maneuver in heavy cover, which was whenever they sought to carry the battle to the Indians. Now, instead of stumbling about helplessly, for the first time the colonials could move swiftly and with confidence through the densest forests. And it was the Christian Indians who made the difference. God used His newest sons, who had, until recently, been called "sons of the Devil" by those very settlers they were now helping to save.

The scouts taught the settlers to fight like Indians, who preferred to fight from cover wherever possible, who were content to harass and vanish until they were strong enough in numbers to risk an open confrontation, who put a greater premium on mobility than artillery—who, in short, by instinct followed all the dictates of modern guerrilla warfare. And now the settlers were learning the tactics that a century later would confound and utterly frustrate the British regulars under Howe and Burgoyne.

By the summer of 1676, the tide was definitely running in favor of the colonists. Now, instead of being fearful of going into the woods after their foes, the settlers were eager to close in combat with the enemy, wherever they were. For indeed, they believed that they were fighting the forces of hell themselves, and now that they had purged their own hearts of unconfessed sin, they felt that they could call on the Lord to join with them. "Pray for us, and we'll fight for you!" was their cheery cry to those who had to stay behind, and the Indians noted their new aggressive spirit with dismay.

So many people had sincerely and publicly repented of their sinful ways, so many lives were truly reformed, so many broken relationships were restored, and so many churches solemnly renewed their covenants, that God relented and poured out His mercy. There was a sense of freshness in the colonies, a sense of cleanness, and new hope. The colonies were united in a common cause, while Satan's house again divided against itself, along the lines of the ancient tribal rivalries. Now "luck" seemed to be running so much against the Indians that they began giving themselves up, in small bands, and then in droves.

On August 26, 1676, the decisive action took place. An embittered Wampanoag deserter, whose kinsman King Philip had ordered killed for suggesting that the Indians should make peace with the settlers, met with the Indian fighter, Captain Benjamin Church. He offered to lead Church and his company, who had been pursuing Philip all across southern New England, to the place where the renegade chieftain was encamped. For Philip had stolen back to the Wampanoag settlement at Mount Hope, on the peninsula of Bristol Neck, Rhode Island, where it had all begun.

In the dead of night, Church moved his men in canoes onto the peninsula, and set up an ambush. A detachment of men would approach the Indian settlement from the north, getting near and lying still all night. At dawn, they would rise up and attack, making as much noise as possible. Meanwhile, the main body of Church's force would have formed a wide perimeter to the south. As the Indians fled in silence, their attackers yelling behind them, the circle of Church's men, lying in wait, would pick them off.

The plan went like clockwork. At the first light of dawn the tremendous uproar terrified the Indians and sent them bolting in panic. The settlers shouted and whooped, the Indians ran as swiftly and quietly as deer. One, fleeter than the rest, nearly broke through the cordon before he was felled. It was Philip. For all intents and purposes, King Philip's War was over.

Why had Philip returned to the seat of his power? Why had he, who knew as much about ambushes as any man alive, failed to post lookouts? Was it deliberate—the Indian equivalent of a soldier's honorable death? Whatever the reason, it was over. The aftermath of the war which cost proportionately more lives than any other war in America's history, and loaded the survivors with crippling debt, nonetheless proved salutary. Prosperity was indeed lost, but God's New Israel was saved—for a season.

If God was trying to build a new Israel in America, Satan was doing everything he possibly could to thwart it. And the people who represented the greatest threat to him were those most dedicated to living the Covenant Way of obedience to the Saviour who had conquered him. These were the Puritans. We have just seen how Satan waited two generations until affluence had so softened the Army of Light that he had an excellent chance to destroy them physically. But his willing servants were defeated through God's providential intervention on behalf of *His* own repentant servants.

Scripture tells us that until Christ returns and destroys the Devil, he will continue to wage war against the Kingdom of God. Satan would bide his time for another sixteen years, before launching his second and last major assault against the Puritans. This time the battle would be waged not in terms of the flesh and blood of the physical realm, but in terms of the principalities and powers of the spiritual realm. For this final offensive, Satan would loose a concentrated attack of demonic spirits which in virulence has never been equaled in American history, before or since. We would rather not give it even this much recognition, since it was an episode which spanned only a few years in more than a century of American Puritan history. But it has been so grossly mishandled in modern treatment, and the parallels with what is happening in this country today are so striking, that it has to be included.

The Bible makes it clear that there are only two sources of supernatural power: God and Satan. And in the spiritual realm, as in geopolitics, there is no such thing as a power vacuum: where Light reigns, darkness is banished. But when the Light dims, the shades of night gather in the wings, waiting. The candle flame grows weaker still and begins to flicker; the darkness holds its breath.

Christianity is a power religion. Christ has the power to re-create men from the inside out, as every man who has ever met Him knows. And one of the early lessons a new Christian learns through experience is that the power of Christ is greater than the power of the Enemy. When Jesus shed His blood on the Cross, He broke the back of Satan's power, then, now and forever. One of the ways God teaches a Christian this is by letting Satan harass him, to the point where he calls out to his Saviour—and discovers that, in the name of Jesus, he has authority over the greatest powers of hell!

For that reason, Satan avoids open confrontations with seasoned Christians wherever possible. He will send his dupes and unwitting servants to do his dirty work, and he will indirectly concentrate his most cunning wiles on breaking down citadels of Light from within, on the ground of hidden sin. The only place where he can safely flaunt his power openly is where men do not know that he is a defeated foe—or where faith in Christ has grown dim.

As the seventeenth century drew to a close, so enfeebled had the affluent Christianity of the Puritans again become, that the supernatural manifestations of Satan's power—occultism, witchcraft, poltergeist phenomena (demons at mischief), and so forth, were coming out into the open. Witches began hanging out their shingles, as it were, letting it quietly be known that they could cure warts and straighten toes and mix love potions (all white magic, for the come-ons; the black magic—the hexing, the cursing, the spellbinding—would come later). And the gullible, the unwary, the hopeless turned to this source of power, and more and more people began to come to "the knowing ones" for advice and counsel.

As their influence grew, they became bolder, until there was almost an unacknowledged competition between them and the local pastors. And all the while, demonic activity increased to the point where scarcely a village existed which did not have at least one house that was bedeviled by "haunts."

Of the several contemporary accounts of this sudden holocaust of satanic activity, Cotton Mather's was the most comprehensive. This was not because he was obsessed with the occult (as modern anti-Puritans would have us believe), but simply because he was one of the few ministers strong enough in the faith to come against Satan and remain supremely confident of victory. And because of this, everyone came to him with his supernatural problems—as if he were the only fireman in a town of straw houses.

As we read these ancient accounts of some of the things that happened, we were frankly stunned: cases of demonic possession or poltergeist phenomena were nothing new to us, but never had we heard of whole towns literally infested with invisible beings, or anything to compare with the intensity of their malevolence. And God had allowed it, as a warning, and to shake the Christian settlers out of their acute spiritual apathy.

Typical were the goings-on in the house of William Morse at Newberry, described here by Cotton Mather:

In the night, he [Morse] was pulled by the hair and pinched and scratched . . . and blows that fetched blood were sometimes given him . . . A little boy belonging to the family was the principal sufferer of these molestations, for he was flung about at such a rate, they feared his brains would have been beaten out . . . all the knives which belonged to the house were one after another stuck into his back, which the spectators pulled out . . . The poor boy was divers times thrown into the fire, and preserved from scorching there, with much ado . . . once the fist beating the man was discernible, but they could not catch hold of it . . . and another time, a drumming on the boards was heard, which was followed with a voice that sang, "Revenge! Revenge! Sweet is revenge!" At this, the people being terrified, called upon God, whereupon there followed a mournful note, "Alas, alas, we knock no more, we knock no more!" and there was an end of all.[11]

And the instances of possession were as violent and tenacious as any we had ever read or heard of. The thirteen-year-old daughter of John Goodwin of Boston was such a difficult case that it actually took weeks of battling to gain her deliverance. And the final struggle was won only after several ministers fasted and prayed at length together. Mather relates:

When we went into prayer, the demons would throw her on the floor at the feet of him who prayed, where she would whistle and sing and yell to drown out the voice of prayer, and she would fetch blows with her fist and kicks with her foot at the man that prayed. But still her fist and foot would always recoil when they came within an inch or two of him, as if rebounding against a wall . . . At last the demons put her upon saying that she was dying, and the matter proved such that we feared she really was, for she lay, she tossed, she pulled, just like one dying . . . and then one particular minister . . . set himself to serve them [the Goodwin family] in the methods prescribed by our Lord Jesus Christ. Accordingly, the Lord being besought thrice in three days of prayer, with fasting on this occasion, the family then saw their deliverance perfected. And the children afterwards, all of them, not only proved themselves devout Christians, but unto the praise of God, reckoned these their afflictions among the special incentives of their Christianity.

Things finally reached the point where the Puritans felt that broad action had to be taken, as the Bible commanded that it must. Cotton Mather, in *The Wonders of the Invisible World*, comments aptly on the state of affairs:

The New Englanders are a people of God, settled in those which were once the Devil's territories, and it may easily be supposed that the Devil was exceedingly disturbed, when he perceived such a people here accomplishing the promise of old made unto our blessed Jesus—that He should have the utmost parts of the earth for His possession . . . The Devil, thus irritated, immediately tried all sorts of methods to overturn this poor plantation . . . Wherefore the Devil is now making one attempt more upon us—an attempt more difficult, more surprising, more snarled with unintelligible circumstances than any that we have hitherto encountered . . . The houses of the good people there are filled with the doleful shrieks of their children and servants, tormented by invisible hands with tortures altogether preternatural.[12]

One of the most diabolical things about this onslaught of demons and hell's angels was that apparently they often assumed the form of innocent good people in the town as they went about their foul practices, "framing" them, as it were, giving rise to accusations against these innocents, and fomenting all manner of jealousies and hatred. This became so great a problem that Increase Mather and a conclave of ministers warned civil judges throughout the Bay Colony not to accept such testimony as the basis for conviction of witchcraft.

For there was certainly no doubt in any Puritan's mind that a massive frontal attack of witches and wizards, in league with one another, was indeed afoot. Mather reports that more than 120 then in custody freely confessed that the Devil had appeared to them with a book in his hand for them to sign, agreeing to serve him.

In light of the modern tendency to judge the Puritans as sin-obsessed bigots, who went berserk hunting imaginary ghosts and executing innocent people on trumped-up charges of witchcraft, it should be kept in mind that many contemporary accounts of this period document dozens of cases similar to those extracted above. Indeed, under such tremendous pressure from the Enemy, the real wonder is that the Puritans acted with as much restraint as they did. During the five months in which the furor lasted, from May of 1692 to October of that same year, twenty people were actually executed for witchcraft before the trials at Salem were brought to a halt. While in that same year in Europe, many hundreds of witches were put to death.[13]

The witchcraft trials were stopped when the clergy prevailed upon Governor William Phips to curtail them. They were convinced that the proceedings were not in God's will, and that the whole land had become gripped by a spirit of vengeance.

Nevertheless, the atmosphere of fear, dread and insidious fascination was not completely dispelled until Samuel Sewall, who had been one of the judges at the Salem trials and a devout Puritan all his life, interpreted the death of his daughter four years later and the birth of a stillborn son, as God's displeasure with the role he had played. Fearful that he might have condemned some innocents to death at Salem, he did the only thing a committed Christian under heavy conviction can do: he publicly repented for what he had done.

PETITION PUT UP BY MR. SEWALL ON THE FAST DAY

January 14, 1697

Samuel Sewall, sensible of the reiterated strokes of God upon himself and family, and being sensible that as to the guilt contracted upon the opening of the late Commission of Oyer and Terminer at Salem, he is, upon many accounts, more concerned than any that he knows of, desires to take the blame and shame of it, asking pardon of men, and especially desiring prayers that God, who has unlimited authority, would pardon that sin and all his other sins, personal and relative. And according to His infinite benignity and sovereignty, not visit the sin of him or of any other, upon himself or any of his, nor upon the land. But that He would powerfully defend him against all temptations to sin for the future, and vouchsafe him the efficacious, saving conduct of His Word and Spirit.[14]

This petition was like a breath of fresh air through the whole of New England, as if someone had thrown open the front door and let the air and sunshine in. Others were led to make similar public repentances, and New England shuddered, as if she had awakened from a bad dream.

But sadly, she then closed her eyes, and went back to sleep again. The voices of the Mathers and a few others did their best to get her to bestir herself, but she would not budge. As the years passed, the voices grew fainter, until at last they died away. And a new generation of ministers, who knew their theology but for the most part did not know their Lord, were content to let her sleep.

13

A Sunburst of Light

One of the things which most puzzled us in our search for evidence of God's hand in our nation's history was what seemed to us to be the prolonged lull which seemed to settle over America between the end of the Puritan era and the first stirrings of independence. The only significant spiritual development in this span of more than half a century was that sunburst of light in the middle of this period, which historians call the Great Awakening. The problem was that this tremendous outpouring of the Holy Spirit, which Richard Niebuhr has referred to as our national conversion,[1] seemed to be a flash in the pan—which came and then died away after just a few years.

If God is indeed the Great Economist, and if He indeed had a plan and a timetable for the establishment of His new Israel, where was the continuity in His handiwork? How did this nova of light connect with the dying embers of the Puritan era on the one hand, and the unlit torch of the Revolutionary War on the other?

We came to see that the Great Awakening was actually a *re-awakening* of a deep national desire for the Covenant Way of life. This yearning did not die with the passing of the Puritan era, but only went dormant. It was a desire which would produce a new generation of clergymen who would help to prepare America to fight for her life.

It is a hunger so deeply engrained in the American national psyche that it can never die, although it can go fast asleep and lie dormant for years. God reawakened that desire in the 1740s—and what He has reawakened once, He can reawaken again.

Along the southern perimeter of Cape Cod Bay, large sand flats extending about a mile are exposed at low tide. Once a year or so, a summer lightning storm will pass over these flats. The sky quickly grows very dark, and low, heavy clouds are tinged with an ominous yellow-green. Then the wind picks up, flattening the dune grass, and suddenly the sky is illuminated by a jagged bolt of lightning, streaking earthward and blasting the wet sand of the flat. A cracking burst of thunder follows almost immediately, for the lightning is close to shore, Another bolt arrows down, and another and another, until the thunderclaps cannot be separated, and the ground fairly shakes under the multiple impact.

Similar lightning storms of the Spirit of God have fallen in different places throughout history. And God has said that He would do this: "And in the last days it shall be, God declares, that I will pour out my Spirit upon all flesh, and your sons and your daughters shall prophesy, and your young men shall see visions, and your old men shall dream dreams; yea, and on my menservants and my maidservants in those days, I will pour out my Spirit . . ." (Acts 2:17, 18).

In 1734, the lightning began to strike America. And indeed, nothing short of a series of lightning bolts could have awakened this slumbering Christian giant who had eaten so much prosperity pudding, washed down with goblet after goblet of the wine of self-satisfaction.

As the place for the first bolt to fall, God chose Northampton, Massachusetts, the little town of the most learned and respected theologian which America had yet produced. Jonathan Edwards was a brilliant, but reserved and dry, Puritan preacher, who delivered his sermons in a monotone, with his eyes never straying from the back wall of the church.

Perhaps God chose Edwards's parish because he had recently been preaching ever-bolder sermons against the popular notion that man, by his own efforts, can accomplish the purposes of God, rather than solely by the enabling of His grace. Possibly it was because the world would have to take seriously Edwards's account of what was about to happen. Other theologians could not put it down to an overactive imagination, and anyone who knew him personally, would know that these phenomenal events could not have been the product of his own personality! For whatever reason the lightning did fall, and no one was more astonished than Edwards himself.

Nevertheless, he was a well-trained observer, and did a first-class job of reporting God's lightning storm in his *Narrative of Surprising Conversions:* [2]

And then it was, in the latter part of December, that the Spirit of God began extraordinarily to . . . work amongst us. There were, very suddenly, one after another, five or six persons who were, to all appearance, savingly converted, and some of them wrought upon in a very remarkable manner.

Particularly I was surprised with the relation of a young woman, who had been one of the greatest company-keepers in the whole town. When she came to me, I had never heard that she was become in any ways serious, but by the conversation I then had with her, it appeared to me that what she gave an account of was a glorious work of God's infinite power and sovereign grace, and that God had given her a new heart, truly broken and sanctified . . . .

God made it, I suppose, the greatest occasion of awakening to others, of anything that ever came to pass in the town. I have had abundant opportunity to know the effect it had, by my private conversation with many. The news of it seemed to be almost like a flash of lightning upon the hearts of young people all over the town, and upon many others . . . .

Presently upon this, a great and earnest concern about the great things of religion and the eternal world became universal in all parts of the town and among persons of all degrees and all ages. The noise of the dry bones waxed louder and louder . . . . Those that were wont to be the vainest and loosest, and those that had been the most disposed to think and speak slightly of vital and experimental religion, were not generally subject to great awakenings. And the work of conversion was carried on in a most astonishing manner and increased more and more; souls did, as it were, come by flocks to Jesus Christ . . . .

This work of God, as it was carried on and the number of true saints multiplied, soon made a glorious alteration in the town, so that in the spring and summer following, Anno 1735, the town seemed to be full of the presence of God. It never was so full of love, nor so full of joy . . . there were remarkable tokens of God's presence in almost every house. It was a time of joy in families on the account of salvation's being brought unto them, parents rejoicing over their children as new born, and husbands over their wives, and wives over their husbands.

The goings of God were then seen in His sanctuary, God's day was a delight and His tabernacles were amiable. Our public assembles were then beautiful; the congregation was alive in God's service, everyone earnestly intent on the public worship, every hearer eager to drink the words of the minister as they came from his mouth. The assembly in general were, from time to time, in tears while the word was preached, some weeping with sorrow and distress, others with joy and love, others with pity and concern for their neighbors.

There were many instances of persons that came from abroad, on visits or on business . . . [who] partook of that shower of divine blessing that God rained down here and went home rejoicing. Till at length the same work began to appear and prevail in several other towns in the country.

In the month of March, the people in South Hadley began to be seized with a deep concern about the things of religion, which very soon became universal . . . About the same time, it began to break forth in the west part of Suffield . . . and it soon spread into all parts of the town. It next appeared at Sunderland . . . About the same time it began to appear in a part of Deerfield . . . Hatfield . . . West Springfield . . . Long Meadow . . . Enfield . . . Westfield . . . Northfield . . . In every place, God brought His saving blessings with Him, and His Word, attended with His Spirit . . . returned not void.

When God pours out His Spirit in a major way, He seldom concentrates on just one area . . . . In 1733, an eager and ebullient English lad of nineteen named George Whitefield, whose widowed mother kept an inn in Gloucester, went down to Oxford to begin the first year of his advanced education. Determinedly devout, George was busily engaged in visiting prisoners and poorhouses, to earn God's approval. At Oxford, he was drawn to the circle of pious believers around John and Charles Wesley, and they, in turn, welcomed this good-humored and charmingly innocent fellow into their "Holy Club." Under John Wesley's dour and often imperious leadership, the club put great emphasis on a disciplined spiritual life. Due to what their critics considered to be their methodical ways, they were dubbed Methodists. And like so many other anti-Christian slurs, the name eventually became appropriated.

George Whitefield read voraciously. In his quest for a closer relationship with Christ, he was led to an obscure, slim volume, *The Life of God in the Soul of Man*, by a forgotten Scot named Henry Scougal. Whitefield was nonplused to discover that all of the good things which he had been doing to earn God's favor were of no account. What he needed, he learned, was to have Christ formed *within* him; in short, he needed to be "born again."

He thereupon embarked on a rigorous program of self-imposed asceticism, giving up everything he enjoyed, even the Holy Club, to bring himself closer to Christ. Nothing he tried seemed to work, yet he drove himself harder and harder until at last his health began to give away. His friends were deeply concerned, but nothing would dissuade him from his determined course. In the end, when nothing he could do, or pray, or think seemed to make any difference, he threw himself on his bed and cried out, "I thirst!" According to John Pollock, in his superb, popular biography of George Whitefield,[3] it was the first time in his life that he had ever called out in utter helplessness. Pollock goes on to describe what happened next:

> He became aware that he was happy, as he had not been happy for nearly a year. Instinctively he knew why. He had thrown himself, at long last, blindfolded and without reserve, without struggle or claim, into God's almighty hands. And Someone . . . seemed to say, "George, you have what you asked! You ceased to struggle and simply believed—and you are born again!"
>
> The sheer simplicity, almost the absurdity, of being saved by such a prayer made George Whitefield laugh. At that laugh, the flood-gates burst. "Joy—joy unspeakable—joy that's full of, big with glory!"

And he rushed out of the room, to share the Good News that Jesus Christ had come for sinners, and that all a sinner needed to do was repent, accept Jesus' atoning death for him, and spiritually throw himself into God's hands.

Thus began the ministry of the greatest evangelist of the eighteenth century, one of the handful of men in the history of Christendom to be used by God to change the course of nations through the power of His Spirit.

George Whitefield was ordained on June 20, 1736, at the age of twenty-two. In the first three cities in which he preached, Bath, Bristol, and Gloucester, revival broke out in the wake of his sermons. But Whitefield did not tarry to continue the harvest which God had begun.

His call, he felt, was to General Oglethorpe's new colony in America, where the Wesleys had already gone and were now urging him to join them. He left with visions of evangelizing the Indians, and arrived to find even more enthusiasm for his message of the New Birth. Before long, it seemed that all Georgia was vibrating to the deep, resonant, far-carrying tones of the remarkable "boy preacher," who had the ability to capture the hearts as well as the minds of his hearers.

In the meantime, John Wesley, who had returned in disillusionment to England, had his famous experience in Aldersgate Street, London. He felt his heart "strangely warmed. I felt that I did trust in Christ, Christ alone, for salvation; and an assurance was given to me that He had taken away my sins, even *mine* . . . ." [4]

The lightning had struck again. And now another pastor was enthusiastically proclaiming the message of the New Birth (though his ministry would never attract the throngs of people that Whitefield's did).

Whitefield himself returned to England after a few months, but only temporarily, to implore the trustees of the colony to provide land and approval for an orphanage, for he now regarded America as his home. Back in England, he found that the revival which his preaching had ignited in the Bristol-Gloucester area had continued unabated. It was a revival which cut across all class distinctions, for young Whitefield now found himself invited to address the nobility, in some of the most exclusive drawing rooms in England. However, the results of this were mixed, for although many lords and ladies truly repented and received Christ, at least as many more were outraged at the suggestion that they were sinners, and that they might have even a greater need of Christ than the common people.

Someone was needed in England to be God's agent for the furthering of the revival. Whitefield now urged Wesley to assume this role, and Wesley readily agreed. But here they ran into the first of many obstacles, and God began to show them how He would overcome them. Whitefield was continuing to preach, but now found the pulpits of Bristol closed to him by jealous pastors, who deplored his "enthusiasm." God's solution: preach in the open.

His first congregation was made up of coal miners on the outskirts of Bristol—and very much on the outskirts of society. For the colliers were almost more animals than men. Wholly uneducated and cruelly exploited, they perfectly fit the dictum of Thomas Hobbes, in that their lives, which were ruled by "continual fear and danger of violent death . . . [were] solitary, poor, nasty, brutish and short." [5] Respectable citizens were terrified by their violent ways, and they shocked even hard-bitten sailors by digging up the corpse of a murderer whose suicide had robbed them of public execution—and then holding a high festival around it.

Whitefield felt a deep burden for them, and as they had no church—indeed, had never heard a preacher—he resolved to bring them the Gospel of Jesus Christ in the open air. Accordingly, he found some high ground, near the exit of the mines, and as they began to appear, he began to preach on the Sermon on the Mount. Before long several hundred miners were standing before him, listening to his words about a Saviour who came, not for the righteous but for sinners. He told them of Jesus' love for them—so great a love that He gave Himself over to His persecutors to be crucified, and that as the nails were driven into His hands and feet, His only thought was for them—for each man standing there that day. And as they raised Him up, and He hung there hour after hour in unspeakable agony, He was suffering for them, that they might be forever freed from their sins. Because He loved them that much.

Suddenly Whitefield noticed pale streaks forming on faces black with grime on that of a young man on the right, an old bent miner on his left, and two scarred, depraved faces in front—more and more of them, as he preached on, "white gutters made by their tears down their black cheeks." [6]

Three days later he was summoned before the chancellor of the diocese, who forbade him to preach in Bristol again. But the next day, he was back preaching to the colliers, and this time there were two thousand listening. The following Sunday, there were *ten* thousand, for by now there were far more townspeople than colliers. And on Sunday, March 25, 1739, the crowd was estimated by *Gentleman's Magazine* at twenty-three thousand!

The Spirit led Whitefield all over England that summer, and wherever he went, storms of holy lightning followed, until by the time he sailed for Philadelphia on August 15, "George Whitefield had preached to more people than any man alive, probably more than any one man in history." But he was anxious to get back to America, for "he dared to trust that his preaching might help create one nation under God—thirteen scattered colonies united with each other . . . ." [7]

Whitefield's reception in Bristol was almost cool in comparison with the welcome which awaited him wherever he rode or sailed, up and down the eastern seaboard. We have seen what vast crowds Billy Graham's Crusades can draw, and the real conversions of so many thousands of Americans in the major cities in which they are held. We have seen the endless throngs of enthusiastic Christians who would flock to Kathryn Kuhlman meetings. And we have read the old-time reports of even greater numbers convening for Billy Sunday, of entire towns converted on a single night in the preaching and healing ministry of Dr. Alfred Price. Even so, we were not prepared for the impact of George Whitefield on America.

The lightning had already begun to fall in several locations on this side of the Atlantic. In New Jersey and Pennsylvania, William Tennent and his four sons were enthusiastically carrying the word of the New Birth to the Presbyterians. Fed up with the resistance of the administrations of Yale and Harvard to the enthusiasm of the new evangelical preachers (known as the "New Lights"), he had founded a school to train preachers. Derisively dubbed the "Log College," it would lead to the formation of what is now Princeton University. His son, Gilbert, became the most famous American-born evangelist of the Great Awakening.

In New Jersey, Theodore Frelinghuysen was proclaiming the light throughout the Dutch Reformed Church. In Virginia, it was borne by the Presbyterian minister and hymn-writer Samuel Davies. In the backwoods of Pennsylvania, Connecticut, and New Jersey, the lightning was falling among the Indians, its conductor being a missionary named David Brainerd. Riding on horseback, under the auspices of the Presbyterian Church, Brainerd was in open awe of the power of God which fell on one village after another as he preached. Indians would change so dramatically that skeptical whites would come to the meetings to mock, only to be converted themselves! Best of all, the Indians would tell their friends, and the Light spread on its own—an "irresistible force of a mighty torrent or swelling deluge," Brainerd would write.[7] He drove himself unmercifully, often preaching three times a day, for hours at a stretch, and he died of tuberculosis at the age of twenty-nine. Jonathan Edwards's biography of him made him an example to all who were considering a call to the mission field, and it was by far the most popular book Edwards ever wrote. Of him, Wesley said, "Find preachers of David Brainerd's spirit, and nothing can stand before them . . . Let us be followers of him, as he was of Christ, in absolute self-devotion, in total deadness to the world, and in fervent love to God and man."

These early reformers performed yeoman's service within their denominations or geographic locales, but it was Whitefield whom God used to tie it all together. Everywhere he went, revival accompanied him. And those who had been bearing the Light before he arrived, unanimously welcomed him as an answer to prayer. In Northampton, where the revival of 1735–37 had died down, Jonathan Edwards offered him his pulpit and was moved to tears by his preaching. Edwards's wife Sarah wrote to her brother in New Haven: "It is wonderful to see what a spell he casts over an audience by proclaiming the simplest truths of the Bible . . . Our mechanics shut up their shops, and the day laborers throw down their tools to go and hear him preach, and few return unaffected." [8]

In Philadelphia, William Tennent saw Whitefield as the prophet who would fan the embers which he had lit so long before, while Whitefield regarded the elder Tennent as "the aged standard-bearer who had been through the battle and had more to teach, if he [Whitefield] could find the time to listen." [9]

That first night in Philadelphia, Whitefield preached from the courthouse steps, with William Tennent standing by his side. The streets were jammed, but the people stood perfectly still.

"Father Abraham," cried Whitefield, "whom have you in heaven? Any Episcopalians?"

"No!" Whitefield called out, answering his own query.

"Any Presbyterians?"

"No!"

"Any Independents or Seceders, New Sides or Old Sides, any *Methodists?*"

"No! No! No!"

"Whom *have* you there, then, Father Abraham?"

"We don't know those names here! All who are here are *Christians*—believers in Christ, men who have overcome by the blood of the Lamb and the word of His testimony."

"Oh, is that the case? Then God help me, God help us all, to forget having names and to become *Christians* in deed and in truth!"

Whitefield met another man in Philadelphia, who was not a man of God; who, in fact, remained a confirmed agnostic, despite all Whitefield's persuasion. Nevertheless, Ben Franklin became his fast friend. Then in his thirties, the well-known writer and publisher of *Poor Richard's Almanac*, was astonished by "the extraordinary influence of [Whitefield's] oratory on his hearers." And on one occasion Franklin found himself putting four gold sovereigns, all the money he had on him, in the collection plate, when he had firmly intended to part with no more than a shilling. (Wherever he spoke, Whitefield raised money for the orphanage in Georgia.) "It was wonderful to see the change soon made in the manners of our inhabitants," Franklin recorded. "From being thoughtless or indifferent about religion, it seemed as if all the world were growing religious, so that one could not walk through the town in an evening without hearing psalms sung in different families of every street."

Franklin, the first truly scientific observer of lightning, listened to Christ's twenty-five-year-old lightning rod preaching from the courthouse steps, and was amazed at the carrying power of his voice. Retracing his steps backwards down Market Street until he could at last no longer hear him, the amazed Franklin computed that in an open space, Whitefield's words could be heard by thirty thousand people!

And on more than one occasion, they were. Even when he came unexpectedly to a town, there was an astonishing turnout. For example, there was the time he felt God wanted him to change his itinerary at the last minute and preach at Middletown, Connecticut. The moment they knew he was coming, riders galloped down all the roads ahead of him, spreading the word that the man who had preached in Philadelphia "like one of the old apostles" would soon be preaching in front of the meetinghouse. Farmers dropped their hoes and left their plows, grabbed their wives and mounted their horses. One observer described a sound like distant thunder, and he saw a great cloud rising along the road—everyone was riding as fast as he could down the dirt road to Middletown. When Whitefield arrived, several thousand horses had been tethered in long lines at the back of a vast crowd of dust-covered farmers. It looked as if an entire cavalry division had dismounted and was awaiting him!

"If George Whitefield wished to set America ablaze for God, he must win New England." [10] writes Pollock, and that meant Boston. Of New England's chief city, Whitefield wrote on October 12, 1740:

Boston is a large populous place, and very wealthy. It has the form of religion kept up, but has lost much of its power. I have not heard of any remarkable stir for years. Ministers and people are obliged to confess that the love of many is waxed cold. Both seem too conformed to the world . . . I fear many rest in head-knowledge, are close pharisees, and have only a name to live. It must needs be so, when the power of Godliness is dwindled away, where the form only of religion is become fashionable amongst people . . . .[11]

Whitefield laid the blame squarely on the clergy: "I am persuaded [that] the generality of preachers talk of an unknown and unfelt Christ. The reason why congregations have been so dead is because they had dead men preaching to them. How can dead men beget living children?" [12] That aroused a storm of antipathy, and he was roundly denounced from one famous pulpit after another (though it seemed to have no diminishing effect on the huge numbers of people who flocked to hear him). But other ministers, who went to his meetings, heard God Himself in what he said, and no less than twenty ministers in Boston alone openly acknowledged George Whitefield as the instrument of their conversion.

Whitefield's heart responded to the people of Boston, even as theirs did to him: "Yet Boston people are dear to my soul. They were greatly affected by the Word, followed night and day, and were very liberal to my dear orphans . . . I promised, God willing, to visit them again, when it shall please Him." [13]

It was around this time that a New England sailor, as drunk as he could be (and still walk), happened upon him one evening. "Well, Reverend Whitefield! S'good to see you again! I (hic) . . . ."

"I do not know you, sir," Whitefield replied, bemused.

"Don't *know* me! Why, you converted me at _____ ten years ago!"

"I should not wonder. You look like one of *my* converts. If the Lord had converted you, you would have been a sober man!" [14]

And so it went, year after year, up and down the East Coast, and as far inland by canoe and horseback as civilization extended. For Whitefield loved the frontier, and next to actually preaching, he was happiest in the saddle, seeing new terrain and new people, red and black, as well as white. In the summer of 1754, he wrote to Charles Wesley,

My wonted vomitings have left me, and though I ride whole nights and have frequently been exposed to great thunders, violent lightnings, and heavy rains, yet I am rather better than usual, and as far as I can judge am not yet to die. O that I might at length begin to live! I am ashamed of my sloth and lukewarmness, and long to be on the stretch for God. [15]

It is a true mark of his spirit, that George Whitefield should be ashamed of his sloth and lukewarmness in the same year in which he preached a hundred times in six weeks, riding the main roads and throughout the backwoods of New England, covering nearly two thousand miles in five months! It is a miracle that he did feel so healthy, because, as any preacher knows, preaching two, three and sometimes even *four* times a day (and usually for more than an hour or two per sermon) is a punishing schedule. And to do so, straight through for *six weeks* . . . !

But this was the measure of how given to Christ George Whitefield was. He had cheerfully elected to go the Way of the Cross, and counted it nothing but gain to have the privilege of picking up his cross daily. And he did pay a fearful toll in health. He drove himself unmercifully. No matter how sick he was, as long as he had the strength to stand and the breath to speak, he would preach, and trust God to sustain him through the sermon and to provide the power and the anointing.

The Lord never failed him. Friends would beg him to stay in bed, but Whitefield would have none of it; like his Lord, he set his face towards Jerusalem. Some might say that this was not good stewardship of God's gift of health. But the power of the Holy Spirit of God fell practically every time he preached, and one wonders if it was not given to him in response to his obedience and his willingness to put himself "on the stretch for God." If he had driven himself any less hard, if he had gone easy on himself (as most of us would have in the same circumstances), would the tremendous work which God purposed through him have been accomplished?

The Lord, through the preaching of this covenanted man, *was* uniting the thirteen colonies—on a level so deep that few people even realized at first what was happening. But wherever Whitefield went, he was preaching the same Gospel. The same Holy Spirit was quickening his message in people's hearts, and Presbyterians, Congregationalists, Episcopalians, Catholics, Quakers, Moravians—all were accepting the same Christ in the same way. In so doing, as Pollock points out, Whitefield "was the first man to cut across denominational barriers. He rejected the solution of earlier reformers, who encouraged followers to drop previous loyalties and form a 'purer' sect—and thus increase the barriers that divide." [16]

In Charleston, people were discovering that Jesus died for their sins, that He could and would forgive sin, and that they need not continue any longer under the bondage of sin. And in New Haven, and Providence, and Peekskill, and Baltimore, they were making the exact same joyous discovery. And because this was so important—indeed, because it was so much *more* important than anything else in their lives—geographical barriers became no more significant than denominational ones. They were still there, but they were inconsequential alongside the magnitude of their shared experience.

They were beginning to discover a basic truth which would be a major foundation stone of God's new nation, and which by 1776 would be declared self-evident: that in the eyes of their Creator, all men were of equal value. By the sovereign act of Almighty God, and through the obedience of a few dedicated men, the Body of Christ was forming in America.

Through the almost universal, almost simultaneous experience of the Great Awakening, we began to become aware of ourselves as a *nation*, a body of believers which had a national identity as a people chosen by God for a specific purpose: to be not just "a city upon a hill," but a veritable citadel of Light in a darkened world. The Pilgrims had seen it, especially Bradford; so had such Puritans as Winthrop and Hooker and the Mathers. But they had all died away, and the vision of the covenant relationship had seemed to die with them.

Now, through the shared experience of coming together in large groups to hear the Gospel of Jesus Christ, Americans were rediscovering God's plan to join them together by His Spirit in the common cause of advancing His Kingdom. Furthermore, they were returning to another aspect of His plan—that they were to operate not as lone individualists, but in covenanted groups.

Still another facet of this great awakening was its emphasis on action—to believe in Jesus Christ meant not merely discussing theology, but making life-changing decisions and acting upon them. As Jonathan Edwards emphasized about David Brainerd, the true Christian is the one who spends his life *acting* in service to the common good. Thirty years later, that would become a vital necessity.

Thus, by a divine lightning storm, the land had been awakened again. Only now it was not just a sprinkling of settlers around Cape Cod and Massachusetts Bay; now the land was a giant. Yet it was a growing giant still, and here again we marveled at the depth of wisdom reflected in God's timing. For it would need a full thirty years—time enough to raise up a whole new generation of evangelical ministers and laity to carry the Light to the westernmost settlements—before the young giant was spiritually tough enough to face its supreme test.

Far from there being a prolonged lull after the sunburst of Light, the watchword of this period was action. Whitefield and the others would ride and ride, and preach till their lungs practically gave out. (All together, Whitefield preached more than eighteen thousand sermons between 1736 and 1770!)

We wondered, as we came to the closing pages of Whitefield's story, if part of the tremendous urgency he felt at the end of his life was not Spirit-given—if indeed God was not requiring of him a superhuman effort to spread the Light as far and as quickly as possible. In 1770, his health now broken and his breathing tormented by asthma attacks, he drove himself as never before. He reached Boston on his last visit, on August 15, five months after British troops had fired on a mob of civilians, killing five, in what would come to be known as the Boston Massacre. Never had the crowds been larger, nor "the word received with greater eagerness than now. All opposition seems, as it were, for a while to cease." [17]

The next month found him up in New Hampshire, where the ministers of Exeter begged him for a sermon. But when the time came, he could barely breathe, and one of them said to him, "Sir, you are more fit to go to bed, than to preach."

"True, sir," gasped Whitefield. Then, glancing heavenward he added, "Lord Jesus, I am weary *in* Thy work, but not *of* it. If I have not finished my course, let me go and speak for Thee once more in the fields, and seal Thy truth, and come home and die!"

And the Lord granted his request. The entire district seemed to have converged on the Exeter green that Saturday afternoon. At first, Whitefield could hardly be heard, and his words were rambling, as if he could not focus his mind. He stopped and stood silent. Minutes passed. Then he said, "I will wait for the gracious assistance of God. For He will, I am certain, assist me once more to speak in His name."

Then, according to Jonathan Parsons, the minister of Newburyport, he seemed to be rekindled by an inner fire. His voice now strong and clear, for an hour he preached with such tremendous power that Parsons could write, "He had such a sense of the incomparable excellencies of Christ that he could never say enough of Him." On and on he went, into the second hour, seeming to look right into heaven: ". . . he felt the pleasures of heaven in his raptured soul, which made his countenance shine like the unclouded sun."

Nearly two hours had passed, when he cried out: "I go! I go to rest prepared. My sun has arisen and by the aid of heaven has given light to many. It is now about to set . . . . *No!* It is about to rise to the zenith of immortal glory . . . O thought divine! I shall soon be in a world where time, age, pain and sorrow are unknown. My body fails, my spirit expands. How willingly I would ever live to preach Christ! But I die to be *with* Him!"

That night he was put to bed in the Parsonses' home and had a fitful sleep. In the early morning, despite a crushing pain in his chest, he nonetheless pulled himself out of bed and made his way over to the window, to see the dawn's early light. George Whitefield died, just as the first rays of the sun caught the waters of the bay below. The new day would soon break across the nation. His dream had come true: America was a nation now—one nation under God.

14

"No King But King Jesus!"

When does tyranny become tyranny? Is there a time when it is not only morally correct but the will of God for one to resist legally constituted authority? When does the "Lord's anointed" lose his anointing? When did it become God's will for America to throw off the yoke of Britain? Was it God's will at all?

Of all the questions we faced, this last was the one we dreaded the most. For a strong case could be made against America's ever having come out from under the mother country's authority. If God did intend this land to be a new Israel, then each major step in the implementation of this plan would have to conform with His righteousness. A holy end, no matter how sublime, could never justify unholy means.

The more we debated this, the more mired down we became. So we prayed to be shown the way out of this mental swamp. And that same morning in Florida, in which we had been unable to discern the true nature of the Puritans' call, the Holy Spirit went on to show us why America *had* to resist—why, for them to do anything less would have been the gravest disobedience. This part of the revelation began with a verse of Scripture coming to Peter's mind, which, when we looked it up, was Galatians 5:1, and which proved to be the key to all that followed:

> For freedom, Christ has set us free; stand fast, therefore, and do not submit again to a yoke of slavery.

One nation under God—this was the political as well as spiritual legacy of the Great Awakening. All America had now in some

254

measure experienced the Scriptural truth that, in Christ, all men are brothers. Highborn or commoner, great merchant or poor farmer, magistrate or soldier—all were equal at the foot of the Cross. Eternal heaven was open to all who accepted Jesus as their Lord and Saviour, and it mattered not what their station in life was or how wealthy they were, or who their parents were.

The same things were true wherever His Kingdom was established on earth. Thus, as the equality of believers was emphasized more than ever in American churches, it was only natural that it would extend into civil government as well. Here then, was the seed of that democracy which would be embodied in the Constitution of the United States: of the political understanding that all men were equally entitled to the vote, and that, in the sight of God, a farmer was as good as King George. For God was no respecter of persons: His laws applied equally to all men.

It is difficult for us, with ten generations of democracy behind us, to appreciate just how radical were the words of the Declaration of Independence that "all men are created equal." Never before in history had the world actually *believed* in the equality of man. That is why, beginning with the Mayflower Compact, a century and a half earlier, the American system of government under God had been so unique. *Under God*—that was the key. Democracy would be subsequently tried in many places through the next two centuries, but only in nations where the one true God was worshiped would it succeed. For the study of man's history shows that equality, without the unifying hand of Almighty God, inevitably breeds chaos and anarchy.

"The Brotherhood of Man" which takes the Brotherhood of Christ and tries to leave Christ out of it, is one of the most destructive lies which Satan has ever perpetrated. A decade after the American Revolution, the French, whose so-called Age of Reason philosophers are too often given the credit for first conceptualizing democracy, attempted to establish their version of the Brotherhood of Man. But it was without Christ. The resulting carnage horrified the world. Within a single generation, France was back under the yoke of tyranny, bowing to the Emperor Napoleon.

Liberty, equality, fraternity—these are qualities of spirit that are God's alone to give, and cannot be won by force. *But once given,* they are man's to preserve and protect, and to defend with his life's blood, if necessary. This was the concept which began to form in America during the Great Awakening. This fruit had appeared on the vine before, but it could not come into full maturity until the colonies became the Colonies—not just the separate entities of Massachusetts and Virginia, the Carolinas, and the others.

The first settlers who came to America had known that they were separated unto God and called out for a special purpose. We have seen how carefully they treasured every privilege of self-governing autonomy, and how liberally they interpreted the rights of self-regulation granted them by the Crown. They were careful not to provoke that Crown into any action which might in any way diminish their precarious autonomy. Although they claimed the rights of Englishmen whenever it was convenient to do so, and paid lip service to the Crown, from the very beginning they thought of themselves as Americans, not Englishmen.

Some contemporary historians dispute this, emphasizing how the colonies depended upon England for their very survival, especially in the beginning. But our research has not borne this out; in fact, in New England, quite the contrary was the case. In 1634, one visitor was positively incensed that he could not find the English flag flying anywhere in Boston! [1] Reports were constantly coming back to England about how independent the Puritans were in deed, word, and attitude.

The reason for this independence was that their ultimate dependence was on God, not on England. And thus it was that the Pilgrims, who had almost nothing of their own, learned in their very first year that God would see them through anything. And the Puritans, who were a little better off, from the beginning trusted God to show them how to take care of themselves. He never failed them. Early Virginia, on the other hand, never did put her trust in God, with the result that *she* was totally dependent on England for almost forty years.

There was another factor contributing to an attitude of Yankee independence. Within thirty years of their founding, these colonies were being run by men who had been born in America. They had never experienced what it was like to live under a king, and had, indeed, never known anything *but* republican democracy, in its purest, town-meeting form.

So the Colonies' tradition of independence was an established reality more than a century before England decided to put an end to it. Their resistance came to the surface only when England would apply pressure. Indeed, what made it so unique in man's long history of resistance and revolution was the amount of wisdom mixed with it.

The colonists tried to do nothing to incite England, avoiding all

antagonism, complying whenever possible. Yet they also did nothing to encourage the military presence of England on their side of the ocean. When King Philip's War broke out and it appeared that the Indians might drive them back into the sea, even then, they did not do the obvious thing, and beseech the mother country for help. Though the war would take a fearful toll in lives and burden them with horrendous debts, they knew that they had to fight it out alone. For to invite British troops onto their soil might mean that they would never be rid of them.

Interestingly, in the late seventeenth and early eighteenth centuries, most of New England's ministers were solidly behind the discreet resistance of the colonies. For they firmly believed that acceptance of the Church of England's official doctrine of passive submission to monarchy would be nothing less than a repudiation of all that God had been building in America, ever since He had first called them to His new Canaan.

It is at this point that we had to face a nagging question: if Jesus Himself, and Saint Paul, both taught the importance of submission to civil authority, how could the American Revolution be justified? Romans, chapter 13, could hardly be more clear:

> Let every person be subject to the governing authorities. For there is no authority except from God, and those that exist have been instituted by God. Therefore he who resists the authorities resists what God has appointed, and those who resist will incur judgment. (Romans 13:1, 2).

Other minds two centuries ago must have been similarly troubled, because the ministers themselves (we found, as we read their sermons) had begun providing the answers. America was a new event in the history of man. Never before had God taken a body of Christians and planted them in a land where there was no immediate civil authority, where, by the guidance of the Holy Spirit, they were to establish their own civil authority. *This* was why the Spirit-inspired pattern of the early Pilgrim church was so crucially important.

For freedom, Christ has set us free; stand fast therefore, and do not submit again to a yoke of slavery. That would be exactly what the new Americans would be guilty of, if, having been given their freedom by God, they voluntarily gave up their authority to govern themselves. It would be like the Israelites—after all God had done for them to bring them out of Egypt—turning around and inviting

Pharaoh to bring his troops to Canaan and put them back under servitude.

Their resistance, however, did not go unnoticed. Nearly a century before the Revolution, Charles II's advisors warned him that "the ministers were preaching freedom," and urged him either to regulate them or to replace them with Episcopal priests. The matter came to a head in 1682: Charles II demanded that Massachusetts either swear allegiance to the Crown, administer justice in the King's name, repeal their restrictions on suffrage (only church members could vote), and allow Episcopal clergy to form churches—or relinquish its charter. The Bay colonists informed him, as tactfully as possible, that they would not do the former, and could not do the latter. (After all, they considered that to surrender their charter would be to "give up the ark of the Lord!" [2])

Informed of this, Charles II demanded the return of the charter, decreeing in 1683 that Massachusetts "make a full submission and entire resignation of their charter to his pleasure." [3]

Now they were really in trouble, for there was no way the Bay Colony alone could conceivably stand up to the greatest military power on earth. The Yankees faced the darkest crisis since the General Sickness had struck the Old Colony and the Bay Colony in their first winters. There seemed to be no alternative but to give up all that their fathers and grandfathers had lived and died for, all that they themselves had been taught to revere since they were old enough to understand.

At this crucial time, the leadership of Puritan New England gravitated, as it had eight years before during the Indian uprising, to one man: Increase Mather. And as he had previously, he turned directly to heaven for his guidance. Then he carefully prepared his decision.

To submit and resign their charter would be inconsistent with the main end of their fathers' coming to New England . . . [Although resistance would provoke] great sufferings, [it was] better to suffer than sin. (Hebrews 11:26, 27). Let them put their trust in the God of their fathers, which is better than to put confidence in princes. And if they suffer, because they dare not comply with the wills of men against the will of God, they suffer in a good cause and will be accounted martyrs in the next generation, and at the great day.[4]

Early in January, 1684, Mather attended an emergency town meeting in Boston, convened to consider what Boston's response would be to the King's declaration. One can imagine the Old South

Meetinghouse packed to the doors with freemen, the crowd standing shoulder to shoulder in the aisles, as the stern, upright Puritan ascended to the pulpit. He then outlined the Scriptural references supporting resistance, recalling the story of Jephthah and Naboth, who refused to give away the inheritance of their fathers, and of David, who wisely chose to fall "into the hands of God, rather than into the hands of men." If we refuse to submit, argued Mather, we keep ourselves in God's hands, and who knows what He may do for us? And he closed by declaring that giving up the Charter would be a sin against God, and who "would dare to be guilty of so great a sin"?

The entire assembly was in tears. The vote not to submit was unanimous, and that unequivocal stand strongly influenced the other towns in the colony to do likewise.

When word reached Charles II, he was in a rage. He determined to send Colonel Percy Kirk and five thousand troops to bring Massachusetts to heel once and for all, and his choice sent shudders through even the King's advisers. For "Bloody Kirk," the notorious governor of Tangier, was known to stop at nothing to crush opposition. As this news preceded the dispatching of Kirk, New England was plunged into despair.

Increase Mather reports that when the news reached him in February of 1685, he shut himself in his study, and spent the day on his knees, in fasting and prayer about the colony's burdens. At length, the heaviness that he had felt in his heart left him, and was replaced by joy. Without any proof, except the inner conviction of his spirit, he knew that God was assuring him of Massachusetts' deliverance.[5] Two months later, word arrived that Charles II had died of apoplexy. His brother James II had succeeded him, and Kirk would not be coming after all! The joyous news spread throughout the Colonies. As Mather worked back the date of Charles's death, and found it to be the very day that he had spent in prayer and fasting, his jubilant attitude changed to awe.

Though James II did not send Kirk, he did send Sir Edmund Andros, who sought to impose the authority of the Crown in no uncertain measures. His orders: strike at the heart of the resistance which had become ingrained in the New England colonists. And since even the Crown recognized that the resistance had begun with their religion, *that* was where it had to be broken. Accordingly, one of Andros's first official acts was to order that Episcopal services be held in the Old South Meetinghouse.

If there had ever been any doubt among the Puritans that "resistance to tyranny was obedience to God,"[6] that doubt was effectively removed. It was now clear to even the most undiscerning Puritan that passive, docile submission to English rule would mean the reimposition of the oppressive authority of the Church of England from which God had delivered their forefathers. The struggle *was* spiritual.

But political freedoms were also involved, for Andros peremptorily revoked the charters of all the Colonies. His agents arrived to collect Connecticut's charter at the meetinghouse in Hartford, one evening after dark. In the candlelit room, the cherished document was laid out on a table. At the moment the King's men formally ordered that the charter be handed over to them, the candles were suddenly snuffed out. There was a great hubbub, and when light was restored, the charter had disappeared! It had been secreted away and hidden in the hollow trunk of an old oak tree. (Andros never did find the document, though he proceeded to carry out his orders without it.)

His next measure was the strict enforcement of the Navigation Acts of 1651 and 1663, which required all colonial trade to be carried exclusively in British ships manned by British crews. In effect, this meant that the Colonies could trade only with England, and it was the first of a series of increasingly oppressive, greed-motivated measures which Britain would impose on the Colonies in the ensuing century.

When does tyranny become tyranny?

By Scripture, it happens when a ruler breaks the commandment of 2 Samuel 23:3 (KJV): *He that ruleth over men must be just, ruling in the fear of God.*

By Puritan interpretation, constructed before the first Pilgrims and Puritans embarked for America, it is when a ruler knowingly and deliberately contravenes the will of God, thus making it impossible for his subjects to follow that divine will.

By the Magna Carta, which established English common law, it is when a ruler ceases to act under that law and denies his subjects their rights, as guaranteed by that law.

By pronouncement of James I: "A king ceases to be a king, and degenerates to a tyrant, as soon as he leaves off to rule according to his laws." [7]

By Parliamentary interpretation, it is when Englishmen have measures imposed upon them, such as taxation, without their consent or even representation.

By every one of these definitions, James II's attitude toward the Colonies was tyrannical. As the Puritans saw it, *he* was the rebel,

for he was using the power of his office, not to serve the people but to oppress them. Therefore he was in direct disobedience to the will of God, as delineated in both Testaments of the Bible.

Yet the personal experience of living under God's discipline, as well as a thoughtful reading of history and the careful study of Scripture, teach the absolute necessity for submission to authority—to God, of course, but also to those civil and spiritual leaders whom He has put in authority over us. Since all authority originates with God (however it might subsequently become perverted), a case can be made for blind submission, no matter what. But on the other hand, when should a person *not* submit?

Like so much of the Christian walk, there is no clear-cut, *a priori* answer; it is a matter of one's own heart attitude and the guidance of the Holy Spirit. In the case of a people submitting to a ruler, this is how it finally seemed to us to settle out: Resistance is a matter of the utmost gravity, and should be entered into only after every other legal, political, and diplomatic recourse has been exhausted. Moreover, the *vast majority* of the Body of Christ involved should be convinced in their hearts that resistance is now the only remaining way in which it is possible to continue in God's will. And this heart attitude is the key: *It should be entered into only with the greatest reluctance.*

Two excellent biblical examples of this reluctance are the attitudes of David and Daniel. Saul, insanely jealous of David's good standing with God and His people, was pursuing him through the length and breadth of Israel. And David, of course, resisted Saul's desire to kill him by fleeing. Twice God allowed Saul to fall into David's hands. But on both occasions David refused to slay the man whom God had once raised up to be King of Israel, saying, "The Lord forbid that I should . . . put forth my hand against him, seeing he is the Lord's anointed" (1 Samuel 24:6).

When Darius became king of the Medes and Persians, he made Daniel, who was obviously more capable and more submitted to him than was anyone else, the chief administrator of the land. All the other satraps and administrators were so jealous that they sought high and low to find something with which to discredit him to the King. But to no avail; Daniel's record of service was impeccable.

Nevertheless they were able to devise a scheme to destroy him. Knowing Daniel to be a devout believer in God, they tricked Darius into issuing an edict which stated that anyone praying to any god or man other than Darius himself, would be thrown into the lions' den.

When Daniel learned of the edict, he was faced with a difficult choice, for to resist it could cost him his life. But his life had been given to him by God in the first place, to be used as God saw fit. If God now required it of him as a pledge of his faith, so be it; in God he trusted. And so he disobeyed the command of his earthly authority, in order to keep the commandment of his Ultimate Authority. (It is interesting that here Darius was as reluctant as Daniel—and both were overjoyed and praised God, when He delivered Daniel.)

In 1689, word reached the Colonies that the mills of God were still grinding: James II had been overthrown by William and Mary, in the "Glorious Revolution." Andros was apprehended, as he tried to escape capture disguised in women's clothes. And five weeks later, William and Mary's Declaration of Indulgence arrived. This did not reinstate New England's charters, but did return their rights as freeborn Englishmen—albeit under Crown-appointed governors, who were to accept the advice and counsel of the Colonies' elected representatives. Peace of a sort returned, and lasted until well after the Great Awakening. England was largely preoccupied with its European wars, until the coming to power of George III in 1760.

Here was a monarch whose ego demanded total submission to the throne. For a long time he had been waiting for an opportunity to deal with the independent spirit of America. Scarcely had England concluded a peace treaty with France, than George decided that the time had come. His first step was to increase the size of the British force garrisoned in America (left there to discourage a fresh outbreak of the French and Indian War), from 3,100 men to 7,500. The Colonies saw no need for this increase, but then, the Colonies had no say in the matter.

The cost of garrisoning these troops was going to be approximately 200,000 pounds sterling per annum, a staggering sum. The Crown decided the Colonies would pay for this indirectly, by imposing various acts and duties. First came the Molasses Act of 1733: the Colonies could buy molasses for the making of sugar and rum only from British interests in the West Indies.

Then the old Navigation Acts were strictly enforced. To accomplish this, Customs Commissioners were sent to collect duties, but the commissioners turned out to be appallingly corrupt. Consequently, all the revenues raised went to pay the salaries of the commissioners themselves, and their large, self-appointed staffs of political cronies. The cost of garrisoning had not even begun to be met.

New tariffs were then imposed, the most galling of which was the Stamp Act of 1765: every legal document had to have a stamp of the British Government on it in order to be official. Infuriating as this was, it was nothing compared to the Townshend Acts of 1767, imposing duties on glass, lead, tea, paper, and so forth. There was no longer any pretense of paying the cost of the British garrison; this was for the purpose of raising revenues to pay for England's global adventures. The mood in America was ugly, and getting uglier. At the request of the commissioners, who began to fear for their physical safety, General Thomas Gage and two more regiments of troops were dispatched to Boston in 1768.

A year later, the hated Townshend Acts were repealed, all save the one on tea. But two years after that, the East India Tea Company, then on the verge of bankruptcy, was excluded from these duties. This meant the end of many American tea companies and precipitated the Boston Tea Party. The King demanded that the culprits be apprehended and prosecuted to the limit of the law—in England! And when no culprits could be found, he decided to punish the entire city of Boston by closing her port to all commerce in 1774. But what was meant to be a warning to all the Colonies of what would happen to those who resisted, soon had precisely the opposite effect.

As usual, American opinion on this mounting crisis was strongly shaped by the ministers. Those men of God who were American-born and not in Crown Colonies (such as Georgia and Virginia) were becoming nearly unanimous in their support of resistance. Thanks to the Great Awakening, there was now a new generation of committed clergymen salted throughout America, many of them men of considerable spiritual depth and maturity. As the list of "intolerable acts" mounted, so did their remonstrations. It was almost as if they had George III in the front row of their congregations, and were trying to make him see the error of his ways. But if the King saw any of their sermons, he took no notice: Like Pharaoh (unto whom many sermons likened him), his heart was hard and growing harder.

Americans were now being taxed for the mother country's own revenue, and at the same time denied the basic right of all Englishmen to representation in the government which was levying the taxes. For the King to ignore this right which was guaranteed by the Magna Carta, meant that he was putting himself above the law. And that settled it.

Still, despite the exhortations of firebrand believers like Samuel Adams of Boston, and political opportunists like Patrick Henry of

Virginia, Colonial resistance remained reluctant, and minimal. Men of wisdom on both sides of the Atlantic could foresee the inevitable fruit of the Crown's present policy, and were praying that this fruit would not come to pass.

Even among the hierarchy of the Anglican Church, which stood only to gain from the suppression of American resistance, there were men of conscience who were courageous enough to risk all, to speak out on behalf of the Americans. Jonathan Shipley, Bishop of Saint Asaph, had this to say to his colleagues in the House of Lords in 1774:

At present we force every North American to be our enemy, and the wise and moderate at home must soon begin to suffer by the madness of our rulers . . . It is a strange idea we have taken up, to cure their resentments by increasing their provocation . . . Now the spirit of blindness and infatuation is gone forth. We are hurrying wildly on, without any fixed design, without any important object. We pursue a vain phantom of unlimited sovereignty which was not made for men, and reject the solid advantages of a moderate, useful and intelligent authority. That just God, whom we have all so deeply offended, can hardly inflict a severer national punishment than by committing us to the natural consequences of our own conduct. Indeed, in my opinion, a blacker cloud never hung over the island.[8]

In America, as we have indicated, resistance to oppression had been a favorite topic in Yankee pulpits for more than a century. Indeed, a quarter of a century before Paul Revere's night ride, one of its most articulate (albeit increasingly liberal) proponents, Jonathan Mayhew of Boston, preached:

It is blasphemy to call tyrants and oppressors God's ministers . . . When [magistrates] rob and ruin the public, instead of being guardians of its peace and welfare, they immediately cease to be the ordinance and ministers of God, and no more deserve that glorious character than common pirates and highwaymen.[9]

Fifteen years later, the hated Stamp Act brought forth this response from Mayhew:

The king is as much bound by his oath not to infringe the legal rights of the people, as the people are bound to yield subjection to him. From whence it follows that as soon as the prince sets himself up above the law, he loses the king in the tyrant. He does, to all intents and purposes, un-king himself by acting out of and beyond that sphere which the con-

stitution allows him to move in, and in such cases he has no more right to be obeyed than any inferior officer who acts beyond his commission. The subject's obligation to allegiance then ceases, of course, and to resist him is no more rebellion than to resist any foreign invader . . . it is making use of the means, and the only means, which God has put into their power for mutual and self-defense.[10]

And when the Stamp Act was repealed shortly thereafter, Mayhew had more to say:

God gave the Israelites a king in His anger, because they had not sense and virtue enough to like a free commonwealth, and to have Himself for their king. That the Son of God came down from heaven to make us "free indeed," and that "where the Spirit of the Lord is, there is liberty," this made me conclude that freedom was a great blessing . . . And who knows, our liberties being thus established, but that on some future occasion, when the kingdoms of earth are moved and roughly dashed one against another . . . we, or our posterity, may even have the great felicity and honor to "save much people alive," and keep Britain herself from ruin!

Nor was Mayhew the first to prophesy that one day Americans might be the salvation of the mother country that was seeking to oppress them. Cotton Mather put it in spiritual terms in his *Magnalia:*

But behold, ye European churches, there are golden candlesticks in the midst of this outer darkness; unto the upright children of Abraham, here hath arisen light in darkness. And let us humbly speak it, it shall be profitable for you to consider the light which from the midst of this outer darkness is now to be darted over unto the other side of the Atlantic Ocean.[11]

As George III and his ministers relentlessly increased the pressure calculated to bring the Colonists to their knees, the rhetoric from American pulpits also increased. In 1767, Josiah Quincy's sermon was printed in the Boston *Gazette:*

In defense of our civil and religious rights, with the God of armies on our side, we fear not the hour of trial; though the hosts of our enemies should cover the field like locusts, yet the sword of the Lord and Gideon shall prevail.[12]

The tempo was building. The whole world watched with rapt attention the mortal battle which was shaping up between Britain and the foremost jewel in her crown of Empire. As Du Chatelet, France's ambassador in England, wrote confidentially to his Minister of Foreign Affairs in March of 1768:

I please myself with the thought that [open conflict] is not so far off as some imagine . . . The ties that bind America to England are three-fourths broken. It must soon throw off the yoke. To make themselves independent, the inhabitants want nothing but arms, courage and a chief . . . Perhaps this man exists; perhaps nothing is wanting but happy circumstances to place him upon a great theatre.[13]

Even as these words were being written, in Virginia a veteran colonel and gentleman farmer named George Washington quietly said at Mount Vernon, his beautiful home on the Potomac, "Whenever my country calls upon me, I am ready to take my musket on my shoulder."

And the following month, from New York, came this word from a well-known lawyer named William Livingston:

Courage, Americans . . . The finger of God points out a mighty empire to your sons. The savages of the wilderness were never expelled to make room for idolators and slaves. The land we possess is the gift of heaven to our fathers, and Divine Providence seems to have decreed it to our latest posterity . . . The day dawns in which the foundation of this mighty empire is to be laid, by the establishment of a regular American Constitution . . . before seven years roll over our heads, the first stone must be laid.

(This quote appeared in the New York *Gazette* in April, 1768; in April, 1775, "the shot that was heard round the world" was fired on Lexington green.)

In September of 1768, it was the Boston *Gazette*'s turn: "If an army should be sent to reduce us to slavery, we will put our lives in our hands and cry to the Judge of all the earth . . . Behold—how they come to cast us out of this possession which Thou hast given us to inherit. Help us, Lord, our God, for we rest on Thee, and in Thy name we go against this multitude." [14]

At this juncture, the Townshend Acts were repealed, and for the next three years there was something akin to peace. The vast majority on both sides was still hoping that it would not come to war. Yet the peace was not a real peace, born of a desire for reconciliation, or the resolution of points of difference. It was as fleeting and deceptive as the calm before the storm.

In reality, nothing had changed. In 1772, a Rhode Islander, traveling in England, wrote to his friend Ezra Stiles, rector of Yale

College: "You will often hear the following language, 'Damn those fellows! We shall never do anything with them till we root out that cursed Puritanic spirit!'" [15]

And now town meetings all over New England were preparing and issuing declarations, in a veritable litany of protest. Nor did smallness of size mitigate against boldness of sentiment. Tiny Chatham, out on the "elbow" of Cape Cod, declared in December, 1772, that its townspeople held their "civil and religious principles to be the sweetest and essential part of their lives, without which the remainder was scarcely worth preserving." [16]

In like spirit, the new year of 1773 was rung in by the men of Marlborough. "Death," they proclaimed unanimously on the first of January, "is more eligible than slavery. A free-born people are not required by the religion of Jesus Christ to submit to tyranny, but may make use of such power as God has given them to recover and support their laws and liberties . . . [we] implore the Ruler above the skies, that He would make bare His arm in defense of His Church and people, and let Israel go."

It is interesting to note that a pivotal change had taken place in American rhetoric: no longer were the exhortations coming exclusively from the pulpits and a few zealous "patriots"; the broad mass of the people themselves had taken up the torch and were carrying it forward on their own.

And now even a governor, Jonathan Trumbull of Connecticut, spoke out openly in defense of freedom: "It is hard to break connections with our mother country, but when she strives to enslave us, the strictest union must be dissolved . . . 'The Lord reigneth; let the earth rejoice; let the multitudes of isles be glad thereof' — the accomplishment of such noble prophecies is at hand." [17]

But most Crown-appointed governors remained submitted to their king, and one wrote to the Board of Trade in England: "If you ask an American, who is his master? He will tell you he has none, nor any governor but Jesus Christ." [18] Which may have given rise to the cry which was soon passed up and down the length of America by the Committees of Correspondence: *"No king but King Jesus!"* [19]

Sam Adams had urged implementation of the Committees for the purpose of keeping all the Colonies abreast of the latest resistance developments. Yet despite the Committees and America's growing unity of spirit, she remained disjointed and compartmentalized in terms of any concerted action. A political cartoon of the day reflected this, picturing a snake in thirteen sections, with the caption DON'T TREAD ON ME!

This is exactly what a willful, obtuse and vindictive Crown did. The Patriots, as they called themselves, had almost given up on ever finding an event which would catalyze and/or catapult them into union. The event was handed to them when the British decided to punish Boston for her Tea Party. This closed the most prosperous port in America to all incoming and outgoing trade, thereby not only ruining Boston financially, but imposing on her near-siege conditions.

Stunned outrage and commiseration swept America! The first to send physical aid were the people of South Carolina, who shipped two hundred barrels of rice to the port nearest to Boston, and pledged eight hundred more. At Wilmington, North Carolina, the sum of two thousand pounds was raised in a few days. A vessel was donated to carry provisions, and the crew volunteered to sail her without pay. Lord North, the British Prime Minister, had scoffed at the idea of American union, likening it to a rope of sand. "It is a rope of sand that will kill him," said the people of Wilmington. Windham, Connecticut, sent 258 sheep, and Delaware was so earnest that plans were made for sending relief annually. Maryland and Virginia contributed liberally, George Washington personally subscribing fifty pounds (approximately thirty-five hundred 1977 dollars).[20]

By August, the men of Pepperell, Massachusetts, had already sent many loads of rye. Their leader, William Prescott, must have summed up the feelings of a great many Americans, when he wrote to the men of Boston:

We heartily sympathize with you, and are always ready to do all in our power for your support, comfort and relief, knowing that Providence has placed you where you must stand the first shock. We consider that we are all embarked in [the same boat] and must sink or swim together. We think if we submit to these regulations, all is gone. Our forefathers passed the vast Atlantic, spent their blood and treasure, that they might enjoy their liberties, both civil and religious, and transmit them to their posterity. Their children have waded through seas of difficulty, to leave us free and happy in the enjoyment of English privileges. Now if we should give them up, can our children rise up and call us blessed? . . . Let us all be of one heart, and stand fast in the liberty wherewith Christ has made us free. And may He, of His infinite mercy, grant us deliverance out of all our troubles.[21]

In October, Massachusetts held a Provincial Congress, the President of which, John Hancock, declared:

We think it is incumbent upon this people to humble themselves before God on account of their sins, for He hath been pleased in His righteous judgment to suffer a great calamity to befall us, as the present controversy between Great Britain and the Colonies. [And] also to implore the Divine Blessing upon us, that by the assistance of His grace, we may be enabled to reform whatever is amiss among us, that so God may be pleased to continue to us the blessings we enjoy, and remove the tokens of His displeasure, by causing harmony and union to be restored between Great Britain and these Colonies.

Two things stand out here: first, that the basic Puritan response of seeking for sin at the outset of hard times was still intact among men who had truly given themselves to God. Second, that these same men still hoped and prayed for a peaceful resolution, and would enter into active resistance only with the greatest reluctance.

Once committed, however, their commitment was total. That same Congress addressed the inhabitants of Massachusetts Bay as follows: "Resistance to tyranny becomes the Christian and social duty of each individual . . . Continue steadfast, and with a proper sense of your dependence on God, nobly defend those rights which heaven gave, and no man ought to take from us." [22]

So, the dawn broke on the year 1775. The nation responded as one body to the ringing words of Patrick Henry's famous speech, given on March 23 in the Virginia House of Burgesses:

There is no longer room for hope. If we wish to be free, we must fight! An appeal to arms and to the God of Hosts is all that is left us!

They tell me that we are weak, but shall we gather strength by irresolution? We are not weak. Three million people, armed in the holy cause of liberty and in such a country, are invincible by any force which our enemy can send against us. We shall not fight alone. God presides over the destinies of nations, and will raise up friends for us. The battle is not to the strong alone; it is to the vigilant, the active, the brave . . . .

Is life so dear, or peace so sweet, as to be purchased at the price of chains and slavery? Forbid it, almighty God! I know not what course others may take, but as for me, give me liberty or give me death!" [23]

15

"If They Want to Have a War . . ."

As we began to delve into the actual events of the Revolutionary War itself, looking for examples of God's intervention, we again found ourselves up against the generally accepted modern view: that we Americans had outsmarted the British—Yankee ingenuity, bravery, tactics (and Washington's "luck") had combined to defeat the most powerful nation on earth. These popular assessments never even consider the possibility that God had anything to do with the war at all!

And yet, if it *was* God's will for America to break forcibly with her mother country, then there should be ample evidence of His not only having supported her endeavors, but also His having directly intervened on her behalf—as dramatically and conclusively as He did in the days of the Old Testament. For if there is one thing that the Bible teaches, it is that God honors obedience with His blessing. He does not honor disobedience. We did find this evidence—in such abundance that we no longer needed to be concerned about "shoehorning coincidences" to fit our theory. We found that even the British began to rue the fact that Divine Providence appeared to be favoring the American cause. But let the evidence speak for itself. (And ironically, there is even one episode in which America played the part of the invading aggressor, and in which God most decidedly acted on behalf of the British!)

"Stand your ground!" Captain John Parker called out to the seventy-odd Minutemen hastily forming a line on the Lexington green. "Don't fire unless fired upon. But if they want to have a war, let it begin here!" [1]

A few men must have cheered, but probably most did not look up from their preparations. They were tamping down powder charges with wadding, rolling musket balls down the three-foot-long barrels of their muskets, and securing them with more wadding. With the exception of the church bell which was sounding the alarm, and the drummer boy who was beating "to arms," it was strangely quiet. Men were too busy to talk.

Jonas Parker, the captain's first cousin, took his position. With deliberation he put his tricornered hat on the ground in front of him, and filled it with musket balls and flints. He had told his friends that he was resolved "never to run from before the British troops," and he was about to prove it. On his left, Isaac Muzzey was topping up his powder horn from the open keg which was being brought down the line. On his right, Jonathan Harrington was trying to look relaxed, conscious that his young wife was watching him from the upstairs window of their house by the green.

The light of early dawn might have played through the limbs of the shade trees on the green, that nineteenth day of April, in the spring of 1775. The trees were already coming to bud, three weeks ahead of season, due to an uncommonly warm April. They would have thrown long shadows across the green towards the men. It had started off to be another warm day—a beautiful one, with no wind, a clear sky, and a soft haze which seemed to give everything an idyllic, dreamlike quality . . . .

"*Here they come!*" came the cry, and all eyes turned to the east corner of the triangular green. Coming up the road in the distance could be seen the first ranks of a column of British regulars—approaching on the double. There were far more than Captain Parker had anticipated—several hundred, in fact. From his experience in the French and Indian Wars, he knew what had to be done. "Disperse, you men!" he commanded up and down the line. "Do not fire. Disperse!"

To make a stand now, in the face of such overwhelming odds, would be nothing but a stupid, pointless waste. Instead, they would fall back, melt away into the countryside and beat the British to Concord. Revere and the other express riders would have already roused all the towns within three hours' march, and at Concord, there would be enough other Minutemen and militia to make a fight of it. So Captain Parker and most of his band turned away from the onrushing British and started to leave the green.

But now blood-lust swept through the British forces. Months of bitter frustration, combined with supreme arrogance, exploded at the sight of these rebel bumpkins daring to oppose them. Venting their rage in long battle shouts and huzzahs, the Redcoats broke ranks and charged onto the green, redoubling their efforts as they saw most of the Minutemen turning away, apparently full of fear. Major John Pitcairn, the officer in command of the British, sensed that he was losing control of his men. He spurred his horse forward and yelled out to them: "Soldiers, don't fire! Keep your ranks! Form and surround them!" And then to the Minutemen, he shouted, "Throw down your arms, and you'll come to no harm!"

But other, younger British officers were caught up in the same excitement which gripped the troops. A pistol shot rang out, and then another (and the only pistols on the green that day were carried by British officers). Two or three nervous shots followed, mixed with confused cries of "Fire!" and "Hold your fire!" Finally, a junior officer in the van of the charge yelled, "Fire, fire, damn you, fire!" and waving his sword in a sweeping circle around his head to signal a volley, he pointed it at the Minutemen.

A volley crashed across the green, and everyone stopped. It was as if both sides were startled at this development, and each looked at the other, to see what had happened. None of the Minutemen were hit, which was not surprising, considering that the British had not stopped to take aim. And the Redcoats themselves were obscured behind a cloud of powder smoke. The British regulars, composed of light infantry and grenadiers, the fastest and strongest of Gage's expeditionary force, were seasoned professionals. They were the first to come to their senses, and now they quickly formed into crisp, even lines and re-loaded.

"Throw down your arms, damn you!" A British officer on horseback called out. "Why don't you rebels lay down your arms?"

As if in answer, several Minutemen fired then, and the officer swung his sword and shouted to his men, "Fire, by God, *fire!*" And a second volley, this one well aimed, tore into the Minutemen who were standing on the green. Jonas Parker, who had stood his ground, fell, badly wounded, and unable to get up, struggled to re-load his musket where he lay. On his left, Isaac Muzzey was killed instantly; on his right, Jonathan Harrington was hit in the chest. He stumbled away towards his house, fell, got up and fell again. He crawled the last of the way, gushing blood from the hole in his chest. His horrified wife ran downstairs to help him in. As she opened the door, he reached out to her and died at her feet. Behind him, Jonas Parker was run through with a bayonet, as he tried to raise his musket.

The only Minutemen now left on the green were the dead and the wounded. Some of the light infantry, again out of control, were chasing fleeing rebels. The main body of British, however, gave three triumphant huzzahs to celebrate their victory, and then marched off down the road towards Concord. As their fifes and drums receded in the distance, quiet returned to the green. The Battle of Lexington had lasted less than a quarter of an hour. But for the British, a long day—the first of an eight-year nightmare—was just beginning.

Down the country lanes pounded express riders like Paul Revere, urging their horses onward. And in the fields, farmers would stop their plowing and listen to the approaching hoofbeats. Then the rider, covered with dust, his horse lathered, would appear. "To arms, to arms! The war's begun! They're heading for Concord!" was all he had time to shout, as he passed. And farmers to the north and east for miles around would leave their plows in mid-furrow, grab their muskets and powder horns, fill their pockets with musket balls and be gone, racing down the road to their assembly points.

The seven hundred British regulars were also moving fast, covering the twenty miles from Cambridge to Concord in seven hours—including the action at Lexington. But by the time they reached Concord (approaching 11:00 A.M.), the powder, cannon, and weapons which they were going to confiscate had all been removed and hidden. The main body of Redcoats stayed in Concord, while search parties went off in different directions. Thanks to Tory spies, they had a general idea of where to look.

The largest contingent continued on up the road toward North Bridge, where they left a hundred men behind and went on. Scarcely were they out of sight than the rebel column which had been shadowing them now filed down towards the bridge. Hastily pulling back across the bridge, a few of the British panicked and fired, and the officer in charge ordered a volley. This cut down several of the Minutemen, who finally fired a volley of their own, dropping four Redcoats.

The British soldiers were shocked. These farmers had not scurried away at the first volley, as those at Lexington had seemed to. Here they stood their ground and calmly returned fire. And they could shoot! As the first British squad knelt to reload, the second took aim behind them. At that instant, the second squad became aware that there was no third squad behind *them*. The third squad had run. Immediately, the second and first squads ran after them, including a number of men who had led the charge across Lexington green. Panic now gripped them as strongly as excitement had at the beginning of the day. Their officers tried to rally them, but it was no use; their withdrawal soon became a footrace to see who could get back to Concord the fastest.

When they rejoined the main body of troops in Concord, the officers decided to get everyone back to Charlestown as fast as they could go, hoping that the reinforcements which had been requested (after the resistance at Lexington) had been dispatched. From that point on, they were running the bloodiest gauntlet that British troops had ever experienced—or would experience, until the Light Brigade charged at Balaklava. All along the way, the Minutemen kept up a steady fire on their flanks, well-concealed behind stone walls, hedges, and screening woods. The increasingly frustrated British hardly ever saw more than a dozen in one body.

The Minutemen would take cover ahead of them, aiming carefully and firing, re-loading while lying down, and then running ahead to get in another shot. Finally, the British were forced to send out large bodies of flankers to sweep the woods and fields on either side of the road. Now the Minutemen began to take casualties too. But the flankers, who had to push through underbrush and ford creeks, quickly tired and had difficulty keeping ahead of the column.

Exhaustion was taking its toll in the ranks, as well. The British had gotten no sleep the night before and had been making a forced march all day—twenty miles to Concord, and thus far, nine miles back. They had been toiling under a hot sun most of the way—and hot musket fire for the last three hours. Increasingly, men were dropping by the wayside, knowing that the rebels were scooping up all the stragglers, but unable to take another step.

The most critical concern of the British officers was that the men were no longer responding to orders which did not suit them. And more ominous, they were starting to abandon their wounded. As they approached Lexington, where nine long hours earlier they had raised their shouts of triumph, the harassing fire became so intense that the column slowed almost to a halt. Maddened by a foe they could not see, and their own ammunition nearly expended, the British regulars were close to the "every-man-for-himself" stage.

If that happened, their senior officers knew, the retreat would become a rout.

The officers were all on foot now, their horses having been killed. In desperation, they ran to the front of the column and threatened the men with sword and pistol, to keep them from breaking and scattering. If they could be held, they would at least block the way of the others. Just beyond Lexington green, under the heaviest fire of the day, the troops sullenly began to form into a line of defense, letting the remainder of the column pass through. Among them, they had perhaps three volleys left . . . .

A skirl of bagpipes came over the musket fire. "It's the first brigade!" came the shout from the rear. "We're saved!" All heads turned, and there, coming up the road from Cambridge was the relief column—Brigadier General Percy at the head of a thousand men. Stunned by the conditions that he found, Percy ordered the two field-pieces he had brought with him to the head of the column, where they were immediately discharged into the thickening Minutemen.

This stopped their pursuers, who had never faced cannon before. Percy took the opportunity to form a defensive square, in the middle of which the exhausted light infantry and grenadiers lay on the ground, panting and trying to get their breath back. Percy gave them forty minutes, then ordered the column back to Charlestown, where they would have the cover of the British warships in the harbor. The harassing fire continued, stinging like hornets. But the fresh troops were now sent out as flankers, and the cannon kept the rebels at bay.

It was well after dark before they reached Bunker Hill and safety. That day over 250 British had been killed or wounded. (And in those days a wound by a three-quarter-inch musket ball often proved fatal.) The Minutemen had suffered nearly a hundred casualties themselves, but the victory was clearly and gloriously theirs.

The effect of Lexington and Concord on the Americans was to send their confidence soaring. They had stood up to the best British troops and had given them a fearful drubbing. Of its roughly four hundred thousand population, Massachusetts estimated that, counting every man from sixteen to sixty, they should be able to field one hundred and twenty thousand men! The war would be over in time to get the crops in! And as express riders fanned out through the Colonies, the rest of America joined Massachusetts in her exuberance.

No sooner had word reached New Haven, than a young aggressive and ambitious captain of militia named Benedict Arnold assembled his men and headed for Concord, the seat of the Massachusetts Provincial Congress. He had a daring plan: the taking of Fort Ticonderoga, which controlled Lake George and Lake Champlain. The fort's brass cannon would provide the American forces around Boston with the one vital ingredient they lacked, and Massachusetts warmly welcomed him and his men. They made Arnold a colonel and, authorizing him to recruit up to four hundred men, they dispatched him immediately.

At the same time, however, leaders in Connecticut had also decided to take Fort Ticonderoga, to block a possible thrust down Lake Champlain by British General Guy Carleton in Canada. Captain Edward Mott and his band of militia were sent from Hartford to commission Ethan Allen and his Green Mountain Boys, foresters and roustabouts roaming the New Hampshire Grants, to take the fort.

By the time Colonel Arnold had caught up with Colonel Allen on May 9, the latter was already leading a force of some 240 men. Arnold insisted that he should have sole command, but Allen ignored him. Finally they reluctantly agreed to share the command. At the shore of Lake Champlain boats were assembled, and carried some 83 men over in the first crossing, including both colonels. Allen decided not to risk losing the advantage of surprise by waiting for the rest. As they crept forward through the gray fog of early morning, to their astonishment, they saw that the wicket gate of the fort was open. In rushed Allen and Arnold, side by side, the rest following as fast as they could. A startled sentry raised his musket, aimed it at Allen at point-blank range and pulled the trigger, but the gun did not fire.

A few Redcoats appeared and were quickly overwhelmed, while Allen stormed up the stairs which led to the quarters of the fort's commander, Captain Delaplace. He thumped on the door, and (according to a British witness) bellowed a stream of backwoods profanity at the fellow he heard skulking about inside. Eventually Delaplace opened the door, to look up at a six-foot-four giant who roared at him: "Deliver this fort instantly!"

"By what authority?" Delaplace pluckily replied.

"*In the name of the great Jehovah and the Continental Congress!*" Allen thundered, and raised his sword over Delaplace's head. The captain ordered his forty-man garrison to lay down their arms, and the gateway to New York was now securely in American possession.[2]

Speaking of Jehovah, the reader at this point may well find himself wondering where God's hand was in all this? It was there—in the fort's main gate being inexplicably left open, and the sentry's weapon misfiring, so that the fort was taken without the loss of a single life. But the wine of victory is sweet—and heady. Under its influence, nothing is easier to forget than God. And the next glass would prove to be the headiest of all.

Whenever His people begin to take pride in their own strength or accomplishments, God will move heaven and earth to call them back to Himself before their hearts harden. As He has since the dawn of recorded history, He usually does this through concerned believers—the prophets of old and some of the most outspoken (and therefore least popular) Christian leaders. In 1775, no one was more concerned than the committed clergy. For all their patriotic enthusiasm, the most mature among them never lost sight of the importance of submitting to God's will, and giving Him all the thanks and all the glory. As long as Americans stayed in that heart attitude, they were safe; God would continue to surprise them with His blessings and protection.

And a surprising number of the rank and file knew this. Amos Farnsworth, Yankee farmer turned militiaman, would write in his journal about an exchange with the British on one of the islands in Boston harbor: "About fifteen of us squatted down in a ditch on the marsh and stood our ground. And there came a company of regulars on the other side of the river . . . And we had hot fire, until the regulars retreated. But notwithstanding the bullets flew very thick, there was not a man of us killed. Surely God has a favor towards us . . . . thanks be unto God that so little hurt was done us, when the balls sung like bees round our heads."[3]

On May 31, three weeks after the taking of Fort Ticonderoga, the Reverend Samuel Langdon, President of Harvard College, was invited to address the Provincial Congress of Massachusetts on election day. Knowing that his sermon would be printed and read throughout America, Langdon framed his text carefully. No matter how unpopular his message might be, he was determined to say what he felt God was impressing upon him.

We have rebelled against God. We have lost the true spirit of Christianity, though we retain the outward profession and form of it. We have neglected and set light by the glorious Gospel of our Lord Jesus Christ and His holy commands and institutions. The worship of many is but mere compliment to the Deity, while their hearts are far from Him. By many the Gospel is corrupted into a superficial system of moral philosophy, little better than ancient Platonism.

What Langdon was specifically aiming at was the drift towards Deism, which was undermining the bedrock of a Trinitarian understanding of Christianity. This trend would ultimately lead to Unitarianism, a watered-down belief in God as an impersonal Higher Being who was the God of Nature, which denies the deity of Christ, let alone the necessity of His atoning sacrifice on the Cross.

Now Langdon turned his attention to the war.

Wherefore is all this evil upon us? Is it not because we have forsaken the Lord? Can we say we are innocent of crimes against God? No, surely it becomes us to humble ourselves under His mighty hand, that He may exalt us in due time . . . . My brethren, let us repent and implore the divine mercy. Let us amend our ways and our doings, reform everything that has been provoking the Most High, and thus endeavor to obtain the gracious interpositions of providence for our deliverance . . . .

If God be for us, who can be against us? The enemy has reproached us for calling on His name and professing our trust in Him. They have made a mock of our solemn fasts and every appearance of serious Christianity in the land . . . May our land be purged from all its sins! Then the Lord will be our refuge and our strength, a very present help in trouble, and we will have no reason to be afraid, though thousands of enemies set themselves against us round about.

May the Lord hear us in this day of trouble . . . we will rejoice in His salvation, and in the name of our God, we will set up our banners . . . .[4]

A fortnight later, the Patriots were setting up their banners atop the newly dug earthworks on the southern projection of Bunker Hill known as Breed's Hill, located on Charlestown peninsula across the Charles River from Boston. Providentially, on June 15, they learned of Gage's plan to occupy these heights and those on Dorchester peninsula to the south. The following day, after a prayer service conducted by Dr. Langdon, they moved onto the heights and proceeded to lay out earthworks. All through the night they worked to prepare the substantial fortifications which greeted the British on the sunrise of the seventeenth.

As soon as Gage was informed, he ordered a massive frontal assault. At last the British had what they wanted! The rebel cowards who had behaved so despicably on the Lexington-Concord road were going to stand still and fight like men, instead of skulking about through the woods like a pack of wild savages. The officers fairly rubbed their hands together in anticipation. Now these rebels were going to have a real battle—European-style, against the finest, best disciplined troops in the world!

And the troops themselves felt the same way. Many were still smarting from the humiliation they had received two months before, which had affected the attitudes of even the Tory women towards them. Wait till these farmers got a taste of cold steel (the eighteen-inch bayonets on the end of "Brown Bess," the standard army musket). Then we'd see who would run! Yankee Doodle would suddenly remember some urgent plowing that needed to be done on the back forty! Quite a few old scores were going to be settled that afternoon.

Gage, perhaps even more than the American leaders, sensed how important was the impending engagement.[5] He could not be sure how many men the Americans had—spies and sympathetic Loyalists indicated that, spread out in a wide perimeter around Boston, there were perhaps as many as fifteen thousand—but their numbers were increasing all the time. As Boston at that time was situated on a peninsula, Gage could hold the city against a superior force by heavily fortifying the landward approach over Boston Neck and relying on the British fleet to protect his flanks. Nevertheless, a decisive victory now would do much to deflate the rebel cause. On the other hand, if they *did not* win a major victory . . . but that did not bear thinking about. Gage committed twenty-two hundred men to the action—a full third of his entire force, which now included two thousand newly arrived reinforcements. As field commander, he named his own second-in-command, General William Howe, who had fought on the Plains of Abraham at Quebec under Wolfe, the conqueror of Canada.

At about two in the afternoon, the cannon fire from the British ships in the harbor intensified. On the Boston side of the Charles, long columns of Redcoats were queuing up and embarking in a flotilla of small boats. In charge of the thousand men in the redoubt on top of Breed's Hill was William Prescott of Pepperell. Even though his men had been digging all night, he had them keep at it, deepening and strengthening the redoubt, until it was a veritable fortress of earth.

The bombardment from the ships increased, as the British came ashore and began to form into long-lined detachments. General Howe stationed himself in front of his corps on the right wing, calling to the men: "I do not expect any one of you to go any further than I am willing to go myself."[6] And with that, as the church bells struck three, he unsheathed his sword and started up the long undulating hill towards the Patriot position. Behind him, two lines of Redcoats, stretching all the way across the peninsula, began to advance up the open slope.

From Copp's Hill in Boston, General John Burgoyne, known to his friends and troops as "Gentleman Johnny," was as elegant in prose as he was in dress:

And now ensued one of the greatest scenes of war that can be conceived. If we look to the heights, Howe's corps, ascending the hill in the face of the entrenchments, and in a very disadvantageous ground, was much engaged. To the left, the enemy poured in troops by the thousands, over the land, and in the arm of the sea our ships and floating batteries cannonaded them. Straight before us a large and noble town was in one great blaze—the church steeples, being timber, were great pyramids of fire above the rest. Behind us [in Boston], the church steeples and heights of our own camp covered with spectators; the enemy all in anxious suspense; the roar of cannon, mortars and musketry . . . [Howe's forces looked] exceedingly soldier-like . . . in my opinion, it was perfect.[7]

On and on came the thin red lines, supremely confident, and puzzled by only one thing: the complete silence on the part of their foes. Not a shot was fired, and they were well within range. What were they waiting for?

What they were waiting for was the command to fire. For Prescott was a veteran of the French and Indian Wars, and he knew the value of the saying, "Don't fire until you see the whites of their eyes." Finally the command was given: *"Fire! "* The whole top of the hill suddenly erupted in a sheet of flame. The effect was devastating: great swaths were cut in the ranks of the Redcoats, as the rest withdrew in disorder. Company after company in the front ranks would report losses of six, eight, even nine out of ten, as Howe struggled to reform his lines.

He managed to do so in remarkably short order, which spoke well of both his generalship and the truly impressive discipline of the British regulars. Once again, the drums beat out the call to advance, and once again the thin red lines began to move. Back up the hill they marched, their ranks tight and even, their eyes straight ahead, as they stepped over the redcoated bodies that covered the hillside.

This time, Prescott let them get twice as close as before—less than thirty yards away—before he swung down his sword and cried out, *"Fire! "* Practically the entire British front rank was destroyed in the first volley. And again, after stubbornly hanging on in the face of the subsequent murderous fusillade, the British broke and ran down the hill to the boats. Colonel Prescott told his men that their enemies "could never be rallied again, if they were once more driven back." [8]

Although several of his aides had been shot dead on his right and left, Howe was nevertheless quite collected, as he sent for reinforcements, and prepared to mount a third attack. But now he changed his tactics. Feinting another wide frontal attack, he ordered a bayonet charge on the redoubt, first having his men discard their 120-pound field packs.

Up in the redoubt, Prescott's men had gotten so low on powder that they broke open old artillery shells and shared what scanty amount was there. The third assault was a repeat of the first two, but this time the powder did not hold out. Though the British line was stunned and staggered, it did not break and fall back as before.

Now the Redcoats came on the run, their eighteen-inch bayonets leveled, and the ragged fire of the last few Yankee rounds was not enough to stop them. As the first wave came over the parapet, Prescott shouted to all those of his men who had bayonets to meet them, while those who had any powder left were to go to the rear of the redoubt, where they would have room to take aim. Those with neither bayonets nor powder used their muskets as clubs.

Finally, as they were about to be overwhelmed, Colonel Prescott gave the order for retreat, and was himself one of the last to leave. Burgoyne later attested, in a letter to British authorities, that "the retreat was no rout; it was even covered with bravery and military skill." [9]

Two enlisted men also wrote accounts of that action. The first was our friend Amos Farnsworth, who was now a corporal in the Massachusetts militia and whose diary entry for that day reads:

We within the entrenchment . . . having fired away all [our] ammunition and having no reinforcements . . . were overpowered by numbers and obliged to leave . . . I did not leave the entrenchment until the enemy got in. I then retreated ten or fifteen rods. Then I received a wound in my right arm, the ball going through a little below my elbow, breaking the little shellbone. Another ball struck my back, taking a piece of skin about as big as a penny. But I got to Cambridge that night . . . Oh, the goodness of God in preserving my life, although they fell on my right hand and on my left! O may this act of deliverance of thine, O God, lead me never to distrust thee; but may I ever trust in thee and put confidence in no arm of flesh! [10]

The other account is also by a believer, who knew how much God's hand had been in the afternoon's proceedings, and who had an equally grateful heart. This is by Peter Brown, in a letter to his mother:

The enemy . . . advanced towards us in order to swallow us up, but they found a chokey mouthful of us, though we could do nothing with our small arms as yet for distance, and had but two cannon and nary a gunner. And they from Boston and from the ships a-firing and throwing bombs, keeping us down till they got almost round us. But God, in His mercy to us, fought our battle for us, and although we were but few and so were suffered to be defeated by them, we were preserved in a most wonderful manner, far beyond expectation, to admiration . . . .

Had Howe pressed on after the retreating New Englanders, he could easily have taken Cambridge (which lay only two miles away) and thousands of Patriot prisoners. Indeed, everyone expected Howe to follow through, and General Sir Henry Clinton urged him to do so, but Howe concluded he should not pursue any further. His men were "too much harassed and fatigued to give much attention to the pursuit of the rebels," he later reported to General Gage.[11] (It is interesting to note that British blindness in missing golden opportunities to turn costly victories into decisive routs would become a characteristic of their military operations during the Revolution.)

So, despite the fact that the British had wound up in possession of the hill by the end of the day, the victory of Bunker Hill had exacted a fearful price, as even the British command would privately admit. Of the 2,200 British soldiers engaged, Gage informed Lord Dartmouth, nearly half—1,054 officers and men—had been killed or wounded! "A dear-bought victory," General Clinton observed. "Another such would have ruined us." And Gage himself admitted, "The loss we have sustained is greater than we can bear." [12]

On the other hand, the Americans, who had lost 441 men out of around 3,000 who saw combat, knew just as surely that they had won. Wrote Sam Adams from Philadelphia to James Warren: "I dare say you would not grudge them every hill near you, upon the same terms." [13] They had proven to the British, and even more importantly to themselves, that they could also stand and fight with the best of them, trade volley for volley, and give as good as they got. If the wine of victory had caused America to get a bit tipsy before, it very nearly ruined her now.

What was desperately required was a mature, sober head and a steady hand to assume the leadership of the military. And as always, God had just the man in mind. Fortunately, John Adams had made the same choice. Adams was known for his shrewd judgment of character, and along with Franklin, he was one of the most persuasive members of Congress. The man whom Adams wanted to have as commander-in-chief of the new Continental Army was the only qualified man who did not want the job. As Adams put it, "Mr. Washington, who happened to sit near the door, as soon as he heard me allude to him, from his usual modesty darted into the library room." [14] But to Adams's mind, that very selflessness and abhorrence of position were two of the things which most recommended him.

The motion was formally presented and George Washington was unanimously chosen. In accepting the position, he declared that he would serve without pay. Characteristically, he closed his brief acceptance remarks with: "I beg it to be remembered by every gentleman in this room that I this day declare with the utmost sincerity that I do not think myself equal to the command I am honored with."

On the morning of June 23, as word of the victory of the Battle of Bunker Hill was about to reach Philadelphia, a throng of admirers assembled around Washington. He was about to leave to take command of the Continental Army at Cambridge. His extraordinary popularity with ordinary people was a phenomenon which would remain constant throughout Washington's life in public service. He was a quiet man, not given to easy back-slapping friendships. And his popularity, when he was made aware of it at all, surprised and astonished him—which only served to draw people to him all the more.

Because of this humility and this popularity, and because of a truly supernatural gift of wisdom, he evoked jealousy from his colleagues in Congress and in the military. But the affection of the people never wavered. And this morning, the tall, firm-jawed, blue-eyed Virginian was positively resplendent in his brand-new general's uniform with its blue coat and cream-colored breeches and waistcoat. Embarrassed at the fuss being made over him by the gathering of officers and delegates and the band playing in his honor, Washington quickly swung up into the saddle, waved good-bye, and set off at a brisk trot.

Who *was* this statuesque horseman who was riding off into the destiny of every American? Much controversy among historians has raged about him, but in the hearts of ordinary Americans, he has shared the place of top affection with only one other President. Surprisingly little is known about Washington's boyhood, and stories like the one about the cherry tree seem to be apocryphal attempts to fill the void. We were especially curious about him, in light of the controversy which we found in the history books of the nineteenth century. Some enthusiastic Christians claimed that Washington was a committed Christian, while arch-conservatives pointed out that these enthusiasts were prone to claim that anyone who had ever alluded to God was a believer. They noted that Washington referred to God in such general terms as Divine Providence and Heaven, which smacked to them of the Deism that was at that time making such incursions.

It was an important question, because in the three centuries of American history which this book covers, only three other men played as pivotal a role as that of George Washington—Columbus, Winthrop, and Whitefield. In the lives of all three, the measuring rods of their ability to carry out their divine callings had been: *trust in Him, sacrifice,* and *selflessness.*

"By chance" we stumbled across an old book, out of print for more than half a century, which provided many of the answers. We found it on a rainy Tuesday, in the stacks of the Yale Divinity School Library. It was written by a man named William Johnson, and it bore the title, *George Washington, the Christian.*[15]

What we came upon inside ranked in excitement with the discovery of Columbus's heaven-sent rebuke. When he was about twenty, George Washington filled twenty-four pages of a little manuscript book with some of the most beautiful prayers we have ever read. All of them were written out in his own hand, and he titled the little book *Daily Sacrifice.* The first entry was subtitled *Sunday Morning,* and contained these words:

> Let my heart, therefore, gracious God, be so affected with the glory and majesty of (Thine honor) that I may not do mine own works, but wait on Thee, and discharge those weighty duties which Thou requirest of me . . . .

And in the next entry, *Sunday Evening,* are these words:

> O most glorious God . . . I acknowledge and confess my faults, in the weak and imperfect performance of the duties of this day. I have called on Thee for pardon and forgiveness of sins, but so coldly and carelessly that my prayers are become my sin and stand in need of pardon. I have heard

Thy holy word, but with such deadness of spirit that I have been an unprofitable and forgetful hearer . . . . But, O God, who art rich in mercy and plenteous in redemption, mark not, I beseech Thee, what I have done amiss; remember that I am but dust, and remit my transgressions, negligences and ignorances, and cover them all with the absolute obedience of Thy dear Son, that those sacrifices (of sin, praise and thanksgiving) which I have offered may be accepted by Thee, in and for the sacrifice of Jesus Christ offered upon the Cross for me.

In *Monday Morning*'s entry, young Washington had written:

Direct my thoughts, words and work, wash away my sins in the immaculate Blood of the Lamb, and purge my heart by Thy Holy Spirit . . . daily frame me more and more into the likeness of Thy Son Jesus Christ.

And in *Monday Evening*'s:

Thou gavest Thy Son to die for me; and hast given me assurance of salvation, upon my repentance and sincerely endeavoring to conform my life to His holy precepts and example.

The man who wrote these words was no Deist, but a very devout Christian.

His mother had been a strong source of spiritual life in his early years. On the day he left home to begin a lifetime of serving his country, she said to him: "Remember that God only is our sure trust. To Him, I commend you," and then she added, "My son, neglect not the duty of secret prayer." [16] The extensive notes on the margins of his prayer-filled notebook indicate that Washington heeded this advice. His discipline of private prayer was to stand him in good stead in the years to come.

Entering the Virginia militia as a young officer, Washington distinguished himself in combat during the French and Indian Wars. One of the campaigns in which he served included the Battle of the Monongahela, July 9, 1755. In this action, the British forces were decimated, and his commanding officer, General Edward Braddock, was killed. Fifteen years after this battle, Washington and his life-long friend Dr. Craik were exploring wilderness territory in the Western Reserve. Near the junction of the Kanawha and Ohio Rivers, a band of Indians came to them with an interpreter. The leader of the band was an old and venerable chief, who wished to have words with Washington. A council fire was kindled, and this is what the chief said:

I am a chief and ruler over my tribes. My influence extends to the waters of the great lakes, and to the far blue mountains. I have traveled a long and weary path, that I might see the young warrior of the great battle. It was on the day when the white man's blood mixed with the streams of our forest, that I first beheld this chief. I called to my young men and said, "Mark yon tall and daring warrior? He is not of the red-coat tribe—he hath an Indian's wisdom, and his warriors fight as we do—himself alone is exposed. Quick let your aim be certain, and he dies." Our rifles were leveled, rifles which, but for him, knew not how to miss . . . 'Twas all in vain; a power mightier far than we shielded him from harm. He cannot die in battle. I am old, and soon shall be gathered to the great council fire of my fathers in the land of shades, but ere I go, there is something that bids me speak in the voice of prophecy: Listen! The Great Spirit protects that man, and guides his destinies—he will become the chief of nations, and a people yet unborn will hail him as the founder of a mighty empire.[17]

Confirmation of this episode can be found in Bancroft's definitive nineteenth-century history of the United States. And at that same battle, according to other sources, as well as Washington's journal, the twenty-three-year-old colonel had two horses shot out from under him and four musket balls pass through his coat.[18] There was nothing wrong with the Indians' marksmanship!

"Death," wrote Washington to his brother, Jack, "was leveling my companions on every side of me, but by the all-powerful dispensations of Providence, I have been protected." [19] This conviction was further shared by Samuel Davies, the famous Virginia clergyman, who wrote, "To the public I point out that heroic youth . . . whom I cannot but hope Providence has preserved in so signal a manner for some important service to his country." Indeed, such was Washington's fame that across the ocean, Lord Halifax was to ask, "Who is Mr. Washington? I know nothing of him, but that they say he behaved in Braddock's action as bravely as if he really loved the whistling of bullets."

This was God's man, chosen for the hour of America's greatest crisis.

General George Washington rode hard for Cambridge that June of 1775, compelled by a sense of urgency. Though he did not know it, God's Spirit was urging him on, for America's intoxication from the wine of victory had slid from tipsy self-confidence into boastful arrogance. Arnold and Allen, who had taken Fort Ticonderoga, now wanted to take all of Canada. Each was convinced *he* was the man to do it, and Congress, caught up in the exuberance of successive victories, reversed its policy and gave its approval. America was about to undertake its first campaign of territorial acquisition. Responsible and God-fearing leadership of the army was needed immediately.

16

"Give 'Em Watts, Boys!"

It had been raining torrentially for three straight days when Washington rode into Cambridge on July 2. It had taken him only seven days to get there from Philadelphia, almost as fast as an express rider could make it. The rain had turned the camp into a quagmire, yet in no way did it dampen the enthusiasm of the troops for their new Commander-in-Chief. Due to his earlier exploits, Washington was already something of a legend; the men whom he now commanded would soon find that the legend was grounded on very real bedrock.

Washington was stunned by the utter lack of discipline among the thirteen thousand troops casually encamped around Boston. Companies of militia had arrived from all over the Colonies, and more were coming in all the time. These were brave men, Washington knew, and eager to serve. And they were also woods-savvy, physically fit, and expert marksmen.

Just how expert had been demonstrated by the First Maryland Rifles at Fredericktown, where they paused on their way to Cambridge. A number of the backwoodsmen displayed their skill by repeatedly hitting a piece of paper the size of a silver dollar at a distance of up to thirty yards. As for their fitness, on their way to Cambridge, the Virginia Rifles covered the six hundred miles in three weeks, without losing a man.[1] (That is an average of twenty-nine miles a day—*every* day!)

But they had not the first idea of soldiering, and neither had their officers. Indeed, the officers, Washington swiftly concluded, were the greatest problem. For almost all the militia companies were comprised of hometown units serving under their own officers. It was easy to see that an officer who had grown up with his men—who had farmed with them and drunk with them and voted with them—was not likely to cut across old, deep friendships for the sake of enforcing discipline. Consequently, serious offenses received mild rebukes, and minor offenses were ignored. The resultant atmosphere at Cambridge was more like that of a jamboree than a military establishment.

The cumulative impact of it all came as a massive shock to Washington. He had not sought this assignment, had accepted it only because his colleagues had pressed it upon him, and he had felt it his duty to respond. Even so, there would be several times that he would write his wife, Martha, or his brother, Jack, and freely confess that he would like to leave it all and go and live on his land in the Western Reserve. This was the first of those times.

But leaving was impossible, and Washington knew it. For he was a man under authority—God's and Country's—and his life was not his own.

Because he had spent his life under authority, Washington knew firsthand the value of discipline and obedience. He had been disciplining himself for years, and now, by the example he set, it was clear that he expected his officers to do the same. That meant that officers were expected to be present at all inspections, assemblies, meals, and other functions on time, and in correct uniform. And while he did not require them to rise at 4:30 A.M., as he sometimes did, they were to curb their own foul language forthwith.

One result of Washington's insistence upon proper military behavior was that a number of officers were court-martialed that summer. Many were broken in rank and more than a few were cashiered out of the Army. Nor was it any different for the generals. Washington had requested, and been granted, the authority to hand-pick the four major-generals and four brigadiers who would be his immediate subordinates. Where possible, he filled these positions with men of experience who had proven their reliability and resourcefulness under pressures of combat. For Washington had a healthy appreciation of just what it could cost to have the wrong person in a key position at a time of crisis. To have a commander on your flank who was paralyzed by the fear of being wrong, or who was emotionally unstable and prone to panic, was to court disaster.

But there were nearly two dozen men in Cambridge already possessing ranks of brigadier and above, veterans of the French and Indian Wars, or in the militias of their various colonies. A few of these were on Washington's list of eight; most were not. Washington was no people-pleaser; he did not hesitate to jump capable junior officers over men of far greater seniority. And he did this knowing that these men had influential friends in Congress, and might spend the rest of their careers doing their best to under-cut him (as several did). But he was willing to do whatever he felt God would have him do, regardless of what it would cost him in reputation or popularity.

Thus the change in the attitude of the Continental Army, that summer of 1775, was rapid and dramatic. The day after Washington formally took command, the following general order was issued:

The General most earnestly requires and expects a due observance of those articles of war established for the government of the army, which forbid profane cursing, swearing and drunkenness. And in like manner, he requires and expects of all officers and soldiers not engaged in actual duty, a punctual attendance of Divine services, to implore the blessing of Heaven upon the means used for our safety and defense.[2]

William Emerson, pastor of the church on Harvard Square, in whose house Washington first stayed, wrote to a friend:

There is great overturning in the camp, as to order and regularity. New lords, new laws. The Generals Washington and [his adjutant, Charles] Lee are upon the lines every day. New orders from His Excellency are read to the respective regiments every morning after prayers.

One of those new orders read:

The General orders this day [July 20, the first national fast day] to be religiously observed by the forces under his Command, exactly in manner directed by the Continental Congress. It is therefore strictly enjoined on all officers and soldiers to attend Divine service. And it is expected that all those who go to worship do take their arms, ammunition and accoutre-ments, and are prepared for immediate action, if called upon.

They were to be like Gideon's men, drinking of the water watch-fully, or like the Pilgrims, marching to their Sunday service with blunderbusses shouldered.

Discipline, and more discipline—that was the rule that summer. Men learned how to march and drill, but more importantly, they learned how to obey. And an astonishing transformation took place: the Continental Army began to become an army in fact, as well as in name. And all, save a few passed-over senior officers whose egos could never forgive him or who lusted after his posi-tion, gave the credit to Washington. He, in turn, was quick to give it to God, Whom he knew was responsible.

Others knew it, too. Throughout America, certain committed ministers were reminding their congregations that it was only through God's continuing mercy that America had fared as well as she had, and that repentance, not strength of arms, would decide the outcome. Typical was the very strong message that William Gordon, pastor of the Third Church of Roxbury, preached to the Continental Congress on the day before the national fast:

Our degeneracies, we must conclude from the light of nature and revelation, have contributed to bring us under the present calamities . . . We are now in an unusual way called upon to wash ourselves, to make ourselves clean, to put away the evil of our doings from before our eyes, to cease to do evil, to learn to do well, and to seek every kind of judgment.[3]

In most of these sermons, not only was there a strong emphasis on the need for individual repentance before God, but there was also a clear call on Americans to renew their covenant commitment to one another. Increasingly, reference was being made to the curse on the city of Meroz (Judges 5:23, KJV):

Curse ye, Meroz, said the angel of the Lord, curse ye bitterly the inhabitants thereof; because they came not to the help of the Lord, to the help of the Lord against the mighty.

Preaching after the battles of Lexington and Concord, William Stearns had said:

We trust that all whose circumstance will admit of it will go, that none such will refuse to enlist in defense of his country. When God, in His providence, calls to take the sword, if any refuse to obey, Heaven's dread artillery is leveled against them, as you may see . . . *Cursed be he that keepeth back his sword from blood!* (Jeremiah 48:10). Cursed is the sneaking coward who neglects the sinking state, when called to its defense—O then flee this dire curse—let America's valorous sons put on the harness, nor take it off till peace shall be to Israel.[4]

Nor were the exhortations of their ministers confined to words. These men did not hesitate to put their own lives on the line. During the battles of Lexington and Concord, Chelsea's minister, Philips Payson, captured two British supply wagons single-handedly.[5] John Craighead raised a company of militia from his parish and himself led them off to join Washington in New Jersey, where it was recorded that he "fought and preached alternately." [6] So numerous, in fact, were the fighting pastors that the Tories referred to them as "the black regiment," and blamed them for much of the resurging zeal of the Colonial troops. One of the most colorful examples is what happened in a staid Lutheran church in the Shenandoah valley of Virginia, one Sunday morning in 1775. The thirty-year-old pastor, Peter Muhlenberg, delivered a stirring sermon on the text, "For everything there is a season, and a time for every matter under heaven" (Ecclesiastes 3:1).

He reached the end of his sermon and said a solemn prayer—and then continued to speak. "In the language of the Holy Writ, there is a time for all things. There is a time to preach and a time to fight." He paused, and then threw off his pulpit robe to reveal to the startled congregation the uniform of a colonel in the Continental Army. *"And now is the time to fight!"* he thundered and then he called out, "Roll the drums for recruits!" The drums rolled, and that same afternoon he marched off at the head of a column of three hundred men. His regiment was to earn fame as the 8th Virginia, and Muhlenberg was to distinguish himself in a number of battles, rising to the rank of brigadier general, in charge of Washington's first light infantry brigade.[7]

But for sheer poignancy, one episode surpasses all the rest. Early in June of 1780, in support of a British advance, Hessian General Wilhelm von Knyphausen crossed from Staten Island to New Jersey with five thousand men. At the little village of Springfield, just west of Union, he encountered unexpected resistance and was forced to withdraw. In the course of this action, the wife of the Reverend James Caldwell, a mother of nine, was shot in her home, while her husband was away. Whether or not it was intentional (Caldwell had a price on his head and later that same day his house was burnt to the ground), the incident inflamed the townspeople. When Knyphausen's force returned two weeks later, even though reinforced by British General Clinton himself, he was again stopped, this time in furious action. At the height of the shooting, the Patriots, taking cover behind a fence that was adjacent to Caldwell's church, ran out of the paper wadding needed to hold powder and ball in place in their muskets. Caldwell gathered up all the copies of *Watts Psalms and Hymns* he could carry, and rushed out to the crouching riflemen. Tearing pages out of the hymnals, he passed them out, shouting, "Put Watts into 'em, boys! Give 'em Watts!" [8]

As the fall of 1775 drew on, spirits continued high outside Boston. Within, however, they could hardly be much lower. The memories of Bunker Hill were too searing to be easily forgotten . . . not just of the devastation of that afternoon, but of the streets of Boston so filled with wounded crying out in agony that the city itself became an open-air field hospital. Nor was there any transportation to move the wounded to what little medical help was available, which meant that hundreds died unattended. There were so many funerals that General Gage ordered that the church bells not be tolled.

And now the city was in a veritable state of siege, reduced to eating salt pork and dried peas, and whatever the marauding British warships might be able to commandeer. Gage had been recalled in disgrace and succeeded by Howe. But even with their losses replaced, and their numbers increased by another thousand reinforcements, the British Army was still outnumbered by nearly two to one. Against such odds, Howe felt, offensive operations were out of the question.

And across the Charles River, despite the high morale in the American ranks, Washington was frustrated by a Congress which seemed insensitive to his army's most basic needs: gunpowder and cannon. He had enough powder for only nine rounds per man, which would provide for about five minutes of heavy combat. This was hardly sufficient to launch an offensive against Boston, and there was no artillery to batter down the British defenses, even if he did have the powder. In addition, although he had more men than the British, his lines were so much longer that it was almost impossible to assemble a sufficient striking force in one place and still protect his flanks. As a result, Washington, who had been assured that he would have twenty-two thousand men (but who would never, at any time during the war have more than fourteen thousand on the rolls), was left to try to provoke the British into sallying forth.

In the meantime, the preliminary stages of the Canadian invasion had begun in earnest. The main body of the attack force, under General Philip Schuyler, was at Fort Ticonderoga, with his field commander, Colonel Richard Montgomery, and under him, Ethan Allen. From the beginning, America's first campaign of territorial conquest seemed dogged with misfortune. *Everything* went wrong. They were supposed to have been halfway to Montreal by mid-October, but General Schuyler's sickness had forced him to turn over command to Montgomery. In addition, short supplies, torrential rains, and continual debates over Montgomery's orders slowed their progress to a crawl.[9]

But that was nothing compared to what was happening to the other prong of the attack. Benedict Arnold was leading a thousand

men up the Kennebec River, straight into the heart of Maine's vast wilderness, with the first frosts of winter already setting in. He had persuaded Washington to let him plan and carry out a daring surprise attack on Quebec, from a direction they would never expect. But a written request from Arnold to a friend in Quebec for information was intercepted before they had even reached their halfway point. From that point on, the British knew they were coming, and their greatest advantage, the element of surprise, was gone. But the men on the trek hardly cared, because the operation was soon reduced to a grinding ordeal of nightmare proportions.

The bateaux, or river boats, had been made hurriedly out of green wood, and the consequent leaking had ruined quantities of provisions and ammunition. Vicious, icy rapids took a steady toll of the bateaux, and grueling portages delayed them still further. On October 18, the last two remaining oxen were slaughtered for meat. The next morning, the weather, which had never been good, became horrendous. Four days and nights of relentless, driving, downpour raised the river ten feet. More bateaux and supplies were lost, as what had been a difficult, dangerous route before now became a raging, malevolent torrent.

By October 25, the rain had turned to snow and had brought the army to a halt, and in Christopher Green's detachment the men were eating their candles to stay alive. Mutiny became more than a possibility, as the officers of the Connecticut men forced Roger Enos, their commander, to withdraw them from the folly and take them back to Cambridge.[10] His effective force now reduced by a third, Arnold struggled on, but the worst was yet to come.

The most frightening thing about the vast Maine wilderness is how easy it is to get lost. As they reached Lake Mégantic, much of Arnold's remaining force, misled by inaccurate maps, became trapped in endless delta swamps that seemed hopelessly similar. For three unbelievable days and nights, four companies of men stumbled aimlessly through the frozen wastes with nothing to eat. As Dr. Isaac Senter, the army physician, said: "We wandered through hideous swamps . . . with the conjoint addition of cold, wet and hunger, not to mention our fatigue—with the terrible apprehension of famishing in this desert . . . . We proceeded with as little knowledge of where we were, or where we should get to, as if we had been in the unknown interior of Africa or the deserts of Arabia."[11] Men died here, often from sheer exhaustion. George Morrison of the Pennsylvania Rifles described it: "At length the wretches raise themselves up . . . wade through the mire to the foot of the next steep and gaze up at its summit, contemplating what they must suffer before they reach it. They attempt it, catching at every twig and shrub they can lay hold of—their feet fly from them—they fall down—to rise no more." [12]

The first few days of November along the Chaudière River held further experiences of smashed bateaux, drowned riflemen, and starvation. Next to be eaten were the company dogs and shaving soap; lip salve, leather boots, and cartridge boxes soon followed. But finally, on November 8, the 650 remaining men of Arnold's ill-fated army reached Point Lévis, opposite Quebec on the Saint Lawrence River. They were as exhausted as if they had been through eight weeks of unbroken combat. And the British had not yet even been encountered.

By this time, their whereabouts were well known to the brilliant British General Guy Carleton, who had ample opportunity to strengthen Quebec's defenses, and was expecting an attack at any moment. Arnold got his men across the river on November 13, the day Montreal fell to Montgomery. But nineteen more days were to pass before Montgomery was able to join Arnold, and then he could bring only three hundred men with him. Moreover, the enlistment time of most of his men was about to run out. Montgomery knew they had to attack quickly, and together they decided they could not wait any longer. But they felt they needed a stormy night to "cover" their maneuvers up the precipices of Quebec. On December 30, they got their cover in the form of a blinding snowstorm.

Montgomery and Arnold attacked from two different directions. In the first fusillade at close quarters, Montgomery and all his best senior officers were all killed outright. This left his force without effective leadership, and the commissary officer, who suddenly found himself to be the senior officer present, promptly ordered a retreat.

Meanwhile, having heard nothing, Arnold and his men continued their attack alone. Arnold, whose indomitable will and ravenous ego made him a brilliant but erratic commander, was badly wounded in their own first skirmish and taken back to the camp. His men, confused and lost in the storm, fought on gamely in small groups. But they were finally forced to surrender, and the fiasco of the Canadian invasion was mercifully over. In the space of a few moments, all the weeks of sacrifice and agony had come to nothing. The Americans had suffered thirty dead, forty-two wounded, and more than four hundred men taken prisoner. The British lost seven killed and eleven wounded.

Arnold and the other survivors held out on the south side of the

Saint Lawrence until spring, but their ranks were further decimated by an outbreak of smallpox. With the coming of spring, and the arrival of two British warships, they finally gave up and started south for Lake Champlain. Back on American soil, wracked with dysentery and smallpox, they staggered into Fort Ticonderoga.

To read the story of the invasion of Canada is to experience a wrenching tragedy. For these men had given everything, in total, unhesitating commitment—and for nothing. It was enough to break a Patriot's heart.

How often do we ourselves pour all our energies and resources into something which seems so right or so good—only to see it come to nothing? Bitter and frustrated, it might not ever occur to us that the reason is that our endeavor, no matter how noble it appears or how sincere our commitment, has been totally out of God's will.

During the Canadian expedition, Divine Providence, it seemed, was dispensed—or withheld—in direct relationship to how close an individual or body of men was to the center of God's perfect will. As Abraham Lincoln would respond, during another period of grave national crisis: "Sir, my concern is not whether God is on our side; my great concern is to be on God's side." [13]

The annexation of Canada was clearly not in God's plan for the United States. And as the pursuing British for once pressed their advantage and came after the fleeing Americans, we wondered when Divine Providence would again favor the Patriot cause.

Down Lake Champlain came the Union Jack flying in more than a score of makeshift gunboats, led by a flagship of eighteen guns which had been disassembled and transported overland. Nothing stood between them and Fort Ticonderoga—nothing except a ragtag fleet of bateaux and sailboats that Arnold had desperately improvised in an attempt to check the British advance.

Trading them broadside for broadside, the little American fleet fought on until their last bateau was destroyed. Arnold and a few of his men managed to make it to shore and get back to the fort. The first American "navy" was annihilated, but the stiff resistance they had put up was so unexpected that it at last elicited the more typical British response of putting caution before zeal. General Carleton decided to build a proper fleet, and as winter was coming on, construction was postponed until the following spring. Thus did Arnold's daring counterstroke purchase a whole year in which America was able to strengthen her northern defenses.

It was fascinating to see how abruptly the tide had turned, as soon as the battered Patriot remnant was back on American soil and defending it! It was as if God had a different plan for Canada, that endless northern wilderness which had been so dearly bought and paid for by the blood of French martyrs—a plan separate and distinct from His plan for America. And His plan for America quite obviously did *not* include territorial acquisition. Through the lifting of His grace, God was delivering a strong rebuke, not merely to Arnold and the others involved, but to the nation which had sent them with its blessings.

What happened to a small body of men in Canada was but a reflection of the dangerous spiritual condition of pride and self-confidence which was permeating the colonies. Many ministers sensed it, and called for repentance. Through their urging, Congress acknowledged that the war could be won only through a continuing willingness to face up to and deal with sin, both personal and national. Hence, a second day of fasting, humiliation, and prayer was declared by Congress for May 17.

When the national day of repentance arrived, strong sermons were preached from every pulpit in the country. Perhaps the most widely reprinted was that of Dr. John Witherspoon, President of the College of New Jersey (Princeton):

> While we give praise to God, the supreme disposer of all events, for His interposition on our behalf, let us guard against the dangerous error of trusting in, or boasting of, an arm of flesh . . . I look upon ostentation and confidence to be a sort of outrage upon providence, and when it becomes general, and infuses itself into the spirit of a people, it is a forerunner of destruction . . . but observe that if your cause is just, if your principles are pure, and if your conduct is prudent, you need not fear the multitude of opposing hosts.
>
> What follows from this? That he is the best friend to American liberty, who is most sincere and active in promoting true and undefiled religion, and who sets himself with the greatest firmness to bear down on profanity and immorality of every kind. Whoever is an avowed enemy of God, I scruple not to call him an enemy to his country.[14]

Throughout the war, committed ministers remained acutely aware of the nation's tendency towards pride and self-confidence. As Samuel West, Dartmouth's minister, would preach in Boston two months later:

> Our cause is so just and good that nothing can prevent our success but only our sins. Could I see a spirit of repentance and reformation prevail throughout the land, I should not have the least apprehension or fear of

being brought under the iron rod of slavery, even though all the powers of the globe were combined against us. And though I confess that the irreligion and profaneness which are so common among us gives something of a damp to my spirits, yet I cannot help hoping, and even believing, that Providence has designed this continent for to be the asylum of liberty and true religion.[15]

With the winter of 1775 coming on, the outlook around Boston seemed nearly as bleak as that within. Due to the almost total lack of gunpowder and cannon, Washington was powerless to attempt even minor sorties, let alone launch any kind of major offensive. Indeed, he could do little more than sit and watch his army dribble away, like sand running out of an hourglass. The problem was not desertion, which Washington had chosen to handle with the threat of disgrace rather than by the British method. The Redcoats had already hanged two men in Charlestown for desertion, although their customary penalty was a thousand lashes. (This almost invariably resulted in death long before the count was completed.) Washington, however, prescribed thirty-nine lashes, to be followed by a general assembly to witness the deserter being drummed out of the army. The shame was lifelong.

The American problem was a hopeless mishmash of short-term provincial enlistments, some of which ran for only a month's duration! To be sure, Washington had sent many officers back to their respective Colonies in order to recruit a new army, based on long-term (one year) enlistments, to begin January 1. But initial indications were that this program was going to fall far below projected quotas. As a result, Washington—and Washington alone, as it turned out—felt a compelling urgency that some sort of significant action take place while he still had the manpower left to achieve it. Powder was finally beginning to come in, though still only at a trickle. Yet even if they had the powder they needed, without cannon to prepare and support an engagement, and specifically to smash down the British defenses on Boston Neck, there was no hope of success.

The Canadian Expedition was a harrowing example of what could happen when God withheld His blessing. But by contrast, the Continental Army and its praying General continued to be favored by the intervention of Divine Providence. For instance, in the course of one of the countless, fruitless discussions of the need for artillery:—"If only we had a dozen howitzers, or a dozen mortars, or a dozen twelve-pounders, or a dozen *anything* . . ."— somebody happened to remember the guns at Fort Ticonderoga, and that Arnold had once proposed to bring them to Cambridge. But that had been back in April, when the roads were dry. It was the dead of winter now: the roads were either muddy sinks or covered with ice. Yet Washington sensed the hand of God in the suggestion, and turned the scheme over to Henry Knox. It was farfetched, but if anyone could make it work, Knox could.

Henry Knox was a two-hundred-fifty-pound, twenty-five-year-old amateur engineer, who had learned what he knew of gunnery from books in the Boston bookstore he once owned. On the face of it, his youth and lack of any firsthand experience with artillery made him a most unlikely candidate, but once again Washington heeded his inspired intuition. In the early months of the war, he had come to rely upon Knox, a deft and skillful improvisor, for solutions to his thornier problems.

There were upwards of fifty pieces of artillery at Ticonderoga. Knox's assignment: bring them to Cambridge as quickly as possible. His solution was a novel one—sleds! And Divine Providence provided the necessary snow. When his bizarre caravan arrived in Cambridge January 18, Washington was overjoyed. Disregarding the unanimous counsel of his generals, he had set his will on taking and fortifying the heights on the Dorchester peninsula—the only site, other than Bunker Hill, from which Boston could be brought under effective bombardment.

Provided that enough gunpowder could ever be collected, only one obstacle remained: the ground was frozen so hard that it was impossible to dig any fortifications. And without protection, the first cannonade would blow any defenders off the summit like flicking sweat off a brow.

Here again, God's hand could be seen in the solution. Later on the same night on which Washington had presented the problem to some of his officers, young Rufus Putnam, another amateur engineer, happened to be passing Brigadier General William Heath's quarters. The thought came to him to pay a visit. He did, and while there, among Heath's volumes, he spied a book on field engineering. In the book, Putnam noticed a diagram and description of a "chandelier"—a piece of French equipment new to him. It was a sectional wooden framework, designed to hold in place "fascines"—large, tightly bound bundles of sticks. Joined with other chandeliers, it made a barrier as effective as a trench. *Voilà!* As the magnitude of his discovery registered, he ran to tell General Washington.

At once the General gave the command to start constructing hundreds of chandeliers and fascines. Then was added an ingenious—purely Yankee—touch: barrels full of stones, to be laid end to end in front of the chandeliers, and chocked in place. As the British lines came up the hill, the chocks would be knocked loose, and the barrels sent trundling down into their ranks with devastating effect.

Powder was now the only lacking ingredient, and supplies had finally built up to the point where there was enough for thirty cartridges per man. This was barely half the standard British combat issue, but Washington decided it would have to suffice. Accordingly, on the night of March 4, the Americans commenced a heavy bombardment. To this the British responded in kind, and thus was attention diverted away from what was taking place on Dorchester Heights.

The Continental Army could have waited a year and not experienced more ideal weather conditions than those which occurred that night: a ground mist completely covered their operations at the base of Dorchester Heights, while the weather was perfectly clear on the top of the hill, well lit by a nearly full moon. The final touch was a breeze blowing inland to carry the noise of their work away from the British. Some eight hundred men labored to place the pre-assembled chandeliers in position and load them with fascines, all of which were brought up the hill by three hundred amazingly quiet teams and drovers. Silently these men worked hour after hour in the moonlit darkness, following plans which Knox had laid out with such precision that the whole line fit together as if it had been set up that way many times before.

But the greatest evidence of how much the grace of God was involved was the fact that *nothing went wrong*. No chance slip of the tongue, no wandering Tory passerby, no lowing ox or breaking cart spoiled the perfect surprise.

And at dawn, the reaction of the British was stunned incredulity. Captain Charles Stuart wrote that the fortifications "appeared more like magic than the work of human beings." And the British Army's engineer, Captain Archibald Robertson, said, ". . . a most astonishing night's work that must have employed from 15,000 to 20,000 men." Vice-Admiral Molyneux Shuldham informed Howe that he "could not possibly remain in the harbor under the fire of the batteries from Dorchester Neck." And Howe himself could only say, "The rebels have done more in one night than my whole army would have done in months." [16]

The honor of the British Army demanded an immediate attack on the new rebel position, and accordingly Howe called a council of war. He gave orders for two forces of two thousand men each to be assembled for embarkation on the next tide, and down to the longboats went the files of redcoated infantry.

But as they waited for the tide, a storm came up out of nowhere. It was no ordinary storm: "A wind more violent than any I had ever heard," wrote one British soldier.[17] Approaching near-hurricane velocity, it drove thick snow laterally across the water, rendering any amphibious operation out of the question.

The storm continued all night. As it died away in the morning, Howe (greatly relieved) could now declare that the rebels had thus been given too much time to strengthen and solidify their positions, so that a frontal attack would be the height of foolhardiness.

Boston was now untenable for the British. A fortnight later, when the Americans fortified and set up a battery on Nob Hill, Dorchester's nearest promontory, the British abruptly evacuated Boston, giving up the city which they had held for a year and a half.

Washington readily recognized that the storm represented "a remarkable interposition of Providence . . . But . . . I can scarce forbear lamenting the disappointment." [18] For he had three thousand men atop Dorchester Heights, far more than had defended Bunker Hill. And for once they had all the powder they could use! What was more, many had been seasoned under fire, and morale could not have been higher. In addition, he had prepared a surprise for Howe: the moment the British troops were committed on Dorchester Heights, with two-thirds of their effective force out of the city, Washington planned to land an additional four thousand men on Boston itself. His plan was that this body was to have raced to the heavily defended neck. Taking the defenders from behind, it was to have broken open a passage, letting in another force that would have been waiting beyond. In this single stroke, the British would have been finished. In sum, it would appear that Washington had good cause to lament.

Yet, as it worked out, the city of Boston was turned over to the Americans without the loss of a single life on either side, which would certainly be the way God would prefer it. In addition, we found a well-reasoned article which points out that the whole amphibious operation depended entirely on the element of surprise, with no contingency for withdrawal had anything gone wrong.[19]

The result could easily have been as great a strategic blunder as the storming of Quebec. Supposing four thousand men had been lost, or "merely" taken prisoner? At a time when re-enlistments had never been more crucial, the American spirit would have been shattered—and so would confidence in Washington's ability to command. In fact, it seems more than likely that he would have been relieved of command, thus removing the man God had chosen to unite the Continental Army—and the nation. The title of the article: "Providence Rides a Storm."

As the Americans poured into Boston, and the citizens cheered their welcome, they discovered to their shock something which confirmed a point their ministers had been emphasizing all along: that the battle which they were fighting was basically a spiritual one. The Old South Church had been desecrated, wantonly and calculatedly. "Gentleman Johnny" Burgoyne had turned it into a riding academy for the cavalry of his regiment! "The pulpit and all the pews had been taken away and burned for fuel, and many hundred loads of dirt and gravel were carted in and spread upon the floor. The south door was closed, and a bar was fixed, over which the cavalry were taught to leap their horses at full speed. A grog shop was erected in the gallery . . . ."[20]

Nor was this an isolated incident: throughout the northern Colonies, dissident (i.e. non-Anglican) churches were systematically abused, in a spontaneous manifestation of anti-Christian feeling. The Presbyterian church at Newtown, Long Island, had its steeple sawed off, and was used as a prison and guardhouse. Later, it was torn down completely, and its boards used for the construction of soldier' huts. In New Jersey, the church at Princeton was stripped of its pews and gallery for fuel, and the churches at Elizabeth and Mount Holly were burned. In New York City, the Presbyterian churches were made into prisons, or used by British officers for stabling their horses. All told, more than fifty churches throughout the country were totally destroyed, and dozens of others were damaged or otherwise misused.[21]

Thus, in the sessions of Congress that spring and early summer of 1776, the fundamental spiritual aspect of the struggle with Great Britain was becoming more and more the hinge on which debate turned. Should America seek to retain the security of her earlier relationship with the mother country? Should she put her trust in the vaunted "rights of Englishmen"? Should she seek reconciliation, and return to the peace of former years at whatever price?

Yes, was the opinion which then prevailed in Philadelphia, where an almost fantasy-like refusal to accept the reality of what had already taken place seems to have held the colonial representatives firmly in its thrall. So strong was it, that they spent much time carefully drafting a conciliatory appeal addressed directly to King George. (When it was presented to him, he disdained to even look at it.)

The situation was reminiscent of the Israelites in the wilderness, convincing one another that they had been better off in Egypt, and daily growing more and more certain that the only thing to do was to go back. For out in the wilderness they were forced to face the unknown and to put their entire trust in God. There was no one else *to* trust! Gone was the memory of the slave pits, of the grinding, hopeless existence before the Lord God of Hosts had delivered them. Now all they could remember was that there had been a peace of sorts in knowing where one's next meal was coming from, even if it had been only a crust. And there had been security in knowing where one would sleep the following night, even if the cold earth had been one's pillow.

It may well have been the unknown, and *having* to trust in God because there was nowhere else to turn, that was causing many delegates to Congress in 1776 to turn their thoughts to the past, wishing that they could go back to the 1730s, or forties or fifties. It is startling to see how deeply this aura of unreality had permeated Congress—until one realizes that it is not much different from our national attitude today.

If we look at the nostalgia craze which has been sweeping America during the past few years, has our national preoccupation with the 1930s, or the forties or the fifties not been deeper than a passing fad? Could it not stem from the same root as the Continental Congress's yearning to go back to a less perilous time? We escape into the past, where things "made sense" and life "meant something" and "values still mattered," and where there was still spiritual life at the national core. Or we escape into the future, and among those who are still young enough to have most of their stake in the future, the science-fiction craze is every bit as strong as the nostalgia escape. But escape is the byword—forwards, backwards, or sideways—into alcohol, busy-ness, good works, passivity, fantasy, or even madness. For the reality of the present and the immediate future seem even more frightening today than they were in Philadelphia two hundred years ago. They, at least, knew that they had God to trust in.

There were a few realists then in Congress, men like the Adamses and two or three others, who were not trying to escape reality. John Adams—one of the most persevering realists—had the private comfort of knowing that his wife, Abigail, stood with him. As she wrote to her husband on June 18:

I feel no anxiety at the large armament designed against us. The remark-able interpositions of heaven in our favor cannot be too gratefully acknowledged. He who fed the Israelites in the wilderness, who clothes the lilies of the field and who feeds the young ravens when they cry, will not forsake a people engaged in so righteous a cause, if we remember His loving kindness.[22]

These few realists saw clearly that things had progressed beyond the point of no return, and that to go back now would be to go back under England's terms—a far-from-benevolent dictatorship. For despite the support of the most eloquent and noble-minded Members of Parliament, the prevailing sentiment there reflected the King's own intransigence (as well it might, since George III's personal patronage had bought the majority of seats). In his eyes the only way to deal with rebellion was to crush it. To show any mercy was only to invite its reoccurrence in the future.

When hearts are thus hardened, the most compelling persuasion in the world cannot move them. Nine plagues in a row had failed to soften Pharaoh's heart, and the comparison between him and George III was now being made in more sermons than ever. Nevertheless, famous parliamentarians like Pitt, Burke, and Fox, in rising for the cause of America, reached heights of oratory seldom heard since the days of Rome.

The Bishop of Saint Asaph had summed up the position of the pro-American minority and set the tone, when he said: "My Lords, I look upon North America as the only great nursery of freedom now left on the face of the earth . . . we seem not to be sensible of the high and important trust which Providence has committed to our charge. The most precious remains of civil liberty that the world can now boast of are lodged in our hands, and God forbid that we should violate so sacred a deposit." [23]

Pitt, England's great former Prime Minister, put it in strictly civil terms:

The spirit which now resists your taxation in America is the same which formerly . . . established the great fundamental, essential maxim of your liberties—that no subject of England shall be taxed but by his own consent. This glorious spirit . . . animates three millions in America, who prefer poverty with liberty, to gilded chains and sordid affluence, and who will die in deference of their rights as men, as freemen.

When your lordships look at the papers transmitted us from America, when you consider their decency, firmness and wisdom, you cannot but respect their cause, and wish to make it your own. For myself, I must declare and avow that in all my reading and observation . . . for solidity of reasoning, force of sagacity, and wisdom of conclusion, under such a complication of difficult circumstances, no nation or body of men can stand in preference to the general Congress at Philadelphia.

And this was the considered opinion of the foremost British statesman of the eighteenth century! Did it make any impression on King George? He dismissed it contemptuously, calling Pitt "a trumpet of sedition."

Nor was the debate over the fate of America confined to Parliament. All of England, to say nothing of Scotland and Ireland, seemed to feel more intensely about it than anything since the Glorious Revolution, nearly a century before. The highest officers in both the army and navy refused to serve. Lord Jeffrey Amherst, the Crown's greatest general in the French and Indian Wars, rejected the King's repeated offers of an active command. And General Henry Conway, only slightly less famous, not only refused to take any part in the war, but openly opposed it at every point.

The same held true at the bottom of the military establishment. By his willingness to enlist, the British commoner traditionally expressed his approval or disapproval of his nation's wars, and in the case of the American rebellion, it was the latter. Never in all of Great Britain's history had she experienced such difficulty in raising an army! In the Seven Years' War with Spain, three hundred thousand Britons had responded to the call of the recruiting drum; now she could not find fifty thousand. Recruiting officers were stoned in Ireland, tarred and feathered in Wales. Even the extensive use of press-gangs could not meet the navy's needs.

In the end, a furious George III was forced to hire mercenaries from abroad. However, even there he was rebuffed; Catherine of Russia did not bother to reply to his personal request written in his own hand; Frederick the Great of Prussia curtly refused him. Johan Derk van der Capellen of Holland let George III know exactly where he stood, as he expressed his opinion to his fellow countrymen: "But above all, it must appear superlatively detestable to me, who think the Americans worthy of every man's esteem and look upon them as a brave people, defending in a becoming, manly and religious manner those rights which, as men, they derive from God, not from the legislature of Great Britain." [24]

And in England, there were those to whom the immunity of Parliament did not extend, who were not afraid to express their own outspoken opinions. The Lord Mayor and Aldermen of London made so bold as to petition the King:

As we would not suffer any man, or body of men, to establish arbitrary power over us, we cannot acquiesce in any attempt to force it upon any part of our fellow subjects. We are persuaded that, by the sacred, unalterable rights of human nature, as well as by every principle of the constitution, the Americans ought to enjoy peace, liberty and safety, [and] that whatever power invades these rights ought to be resisted. We hold such resistance, in vindication of their constitutional rights, to be their indispensable duty to God, from whom those rights are derived to themselves.[25]

George III was finally able to locate, among the lesser princes of Germany, three who would sell him the use of their soldiers—three princes who, in the words of Edmund Burke, "snuffed the cadaverous taint of lucrative war." [26] Altogether, he was able to buy the services of thirty thousand German mercenaries, which comprised more than half the King's total force.

Of all those in sympathy with the American cause, the most impressive address came not from the House of Lords, but from the House of Commons. There, Mr. George Johnstone spoke in terms so ringing that he might have been standing alongside Samuel Adams or Patrick Henry.

I maintain that the sense of the best and wisest men in this country are on the side of the Americans, that three to one in Ireland are on their side, that the soldiers and sailors feel an unwillingness to serve . . . I speak it to the credit of the fleet and army: they do not like to butcher men whom the greatest characters in this country consider as contending in the glorious cause of preserving those institutions which are necessary to the happiness, security and elevation of the human mind . . . .

To a mind who loves to contemplate the glorious spirit of freedom, no spectacle can be more affecting than the action on Bunker Hill. To see an irregular peasantry commanded by a physician, inferior in number, opposed by every circumstance of cannon and bombs that could terrify timid minds, calmly waiting the attack of the gallant Howe leading on the best troops in the world, with an excellent train of artillery, and twice repulsing those very troops who had often chased the chosen battalions of France, and at last retiring for want of ammunition, but in so respectable a manner that they were not even pursued—who can reflect on such scenes and not adore the constitution of government which could breed such men! Who is there that can dismiss all doubts on the justice of the cause which can inspire such conscious rectitude?

The conduct of the people of New England for wisdom, courage, temperance, fortitude and all those qualities that can command the admiration of noble minds, is not surpassed in the history of any nation under the sun. Instead of wreaking our vengeance against that colony, their heroism alone should plead their forgiveness.[27]

But neither the King nor any of his Ministers or Members of Parliament seemed to hear. That same day he had announced his decision to crush the rebellion by force of arms, including the use of mercenaries. When the ensuing debate was finally over, the House of Lords voted in favor of the King's address, 76 to 33, and Commons voted 278 to 108 in favor. England had declared war.

Still, even seven months later, as the first week of June, 1776, drew to a close, the majority of men in Congress in Philadelphia were hoping against hope that some eleventh-hour formula for reconciliation would be found. They knew how much it would cost them personally to cast their votes with those few who were advocating an open declaration of independence. Such a move would close the door forever to any possibility of rapprochement with the Crown. Down on their necks would come the full military might on land and sea of the greatest power on earth. Even if they were truly united, they could not hope to stand up to such a force for very long. All their debates over the past weeks had indicated how sorely separated and individualistic these thirteen Colonies still were. It would take more than a miracle to bring them into unity . . . . Dare they commit the Colonies they represented to such peril?

Though none of the delegates openly spoke of their personal jeopardy, this was surely on the minds of more than a few. For the men who signed such a declaration would, in the likely event of America's defeat, be held personally responsible. And the penalty for instigating rebellion against the Crown was death. As Ben Franklin put it succinctly, "We must indeed all hang together, or most assuredly we will all hang separately." [28]

But in a sense, it was already too late. On May 10, town meetings all over Massachusetts had unanimously voted in favor of independence.[29] On May 15, the Virginia Convention voted for independence. And on June 7, documented evidence arrived of the treaties which George III had made with the German princes, purchasing the use of their mercenaries in America. In the face of that, Richard Henry Lee of Virginia formally proposed that Congress make a declaration of independence, stating that these united Colonies are, and of a right ought to be, free and independent states. John Adams immediately seconded the proposal. After a day's debate, Congress adjourned for three weeks to let the doubtful representatives of the middle Colonies go home to sound out the will of their constituents.

In the meantime, Franklin, Adams, Sherman of Connecticut, Livingston of New York, and young Jefferson of Virginia hurried to draw up a draft of the proposed declaration.

We hold these Truths to be self-evident, that all Men are created equal . . . . We, therefore, the representatives of the UNITED STATES OF AMERICA, in General Congress, Assembled, appealing to the Supreme Judge of the World for the Rectitude of our Intentions, do, in the Name and by the Authority of the good People of these Colonies, solemnly Publish and Declare, That these United Colonies are, and of Right ought to be, Free and Independent States . . . . And for the support of this Declaration, with a firm Reliance on the Protection of divine Providence, we mutually pledge to each other our Lives, our Fortunes, and our sacred Honor.

Jefferson did most of the final composing, borrowing heavily from the phraseology of popular sermons of the day—except for the two phrases, "appealing to the Supreme Judge of the World for the Rectitude of our Intentions" and "with a Firm Reliance on the Protection of divine Providence." These Congress insisted upon including, over Jefferson's strenuous objection, for he was a confirmed "enlightened rationalist," soon to become privately a Unitarian.[30] So resentful was Jefferson at their tampering with his prose that he sent copies of his original draft to his personal friends, that they might better appreciate his unedited effort.

June 28: The convention of Maryland voted for independence. Word reached Philadelphia that New Jersey had dismissed her old delegates and was sending new ones, who were instructed to vote for independence.

July 1: Congress entered what John Adams called "the greatest debate of all." Dickinson of Pennsylvania spoke eloquently and at length against independence. When he had finished, there was a long and thoughtful silence. Adams kept hoping that someone "less obnoxious" than himself, who was "believed to be the author of all the mischief," would rise to answer. But none did, and so, reluctantly, Adams rose. And he spoke with such quiet power and conviction that not a man present remained unmoved, especially as he reached his conclusion:

Before God, I believe the hour has come. My judgment approves this measure, and my whole heart is in it. All that I have, and all that I am, and

THE LIGHT AND THE GLORY

all that I hope in this life, I am now ready here to stake upon it. And I leave off as I began, that live or die, survive or perish, I am for the Declaration. It is my living sentiment, and by the blessing of God it shall be my dying sentiment, Independence now, and Independence for ever! [31]

No one spoke. Just then, the door swung open and in strode a mud-spattered figure with two others behind him. It was Dr. John Witherspoon, at the head of the New Jersey delegation. Apologizing for being late, he said that although he had not heard the debate, he had not lacked sources of information on the various issues. "Gentlemen, New Jersey is ready to vote for independence. In our judgment, the country is not only ripe for independence, but we are in danger of becoming rotten for the want of it, if we delay any longer." [32]

The Congress proceeded to the vote, and nine of the thirteen Colonies voted with New Jersey that day: Pennsylvania and South Carolina voted *no*, and New York abstained. Delaware was split, one delegate to one.

Since Congress was, in effect, only acting as a committee on behalf of the whole country, any decision on the Declaration would have to be unanimous. It was decided that debate would resume the next morning, to be followed by another vote. In the meantime, to resolve the Delaware deadlock, which could well decide the outcome, an express was dispatched to Dover, the capital of Delaware, to fetch their third delegate, Caesar Rodney.

A Patriot of deep conviction, Rodney had been summoned home on urgent business. But now the express rider arrived at his farm at two in the morning, bearing word that debate would resume in less than seven hours, after which the final vote would be taken. Taking his best horse, Rodney galloped off into the pitch-black, stormy night. It was eighty-nine miles to Philadelphia, over stretches of road which were difficult under the best of conditions, and this night the conditions could not have been worse. Streams which were normally fordable with ease had become swollen torrents, and the rain had turned one portion of the road into a quagmire so deep that Rodney had to dismount and lead his horse through it, to avoid its being crippled.

Unable to obtain a fresh change of horses until dawn, Rodney nevertheless arrived at the State House by 1:00 P.M. just as the final vote was being taken. Half-carried into the assembly room, he was barely able to speak: "As I believe the voice of my constituents and of all sensible and honest men is in favor of independence, my own judgment concurs with them. I vote for independence." [33]

The Delaware deadlock was broken, and the other delegations voted the same way, save New York, which abstained. The decision was twelve to none. The Colonies had just become the United States of America.

In the silence that followed the announcement of the vote, the late afternoon sun cast its soft rays through the tall windows—on a brass candlestick standing on a green felt table-covering, a carved eagle over the door, a pair of spectacles lying on a polished desk. The magnitude of what they had done began to weigh upon them, and they realized that they and their countrymen were no longer Englishmen, but citizens of a fledging nation barely a few minutes old. Many stared out the window. Some wept openly. Some, like Witherspoon, bowed their heads and closed their eyes in prayer.

John Hancock broke the silence: "Gentlemen, the price on my head has just been doubled!"

A wry chuckle followed, and then Samuel Adams rose: "We have this day restored the Sovereign, to Whom alone men ought to be obedient. He reigns in heaven and . . . from the rising to the setting sun, may His Kingdom come." [34]

17

The Crucible of Freedom

As the news of the Declaration spread abroad in the newborn nation, Americans everywhere were delirious with joy—cheering, waving, ringing church bells, wasting gunpowder. Samuel Adams wrote: "The people, I am told, recognize the resolution as though it were a decree promulgated from heaven." [1] And John Adams was so elated he wrote Abigail twice on the same day. In the first letter, he took a sobering look at the reality of what lay immediately ahead:

It is the will of heaven that the two countries should be sundered forever. It may be the will of heaven that America shall suffer calamities still more wasting and distresses yet more dreadful. If this is to be the case, it will have this good effect, at least: it will inspire us with many virtues which we have not, and correct many errors, follies and vices, which threaten to disturb, dishonor and destroy us . . . The furnace of affliction produces refinements in states, as well as individuals. [2]

In his second letter, however, he looked prophetically into the future of the nation, saying that the day on which the Declaration was passed:

. . . will be the most memorable . . . in the history of America. I am apt to believe that it will be celebrated by succeeding generations, as the great anniversary festival. It ought to be commemorated, as the Day of Deliverance, by solemn acts of devotion to God Almighty. It ought to be solemnized with pomp and parade, with shows, games, sports, guns, bells, bonfires and illuminations, from one end of this continent to the other, from this time forward forevermore.

You will think me transported with enthusiasm, but I am not. I am well aware of the toil and blood and treasure that it will cost to maintain this

310

Declaration, and support and defend these States. Yet through all the gloom I can see the rays of ravishing light and glory. I can see that the end is worth more than all the means.

America's euphoria died away quickly enough. On the same day that the Declaration was passed in Philadelphia, General Howe landed on Staten Island with the first of what would ultimately amount to an invading force of fifty-five thousand men. The American recruiters doubled their efforts, and soon farmers and tradesmen began to sign up for a whole year, for word of what had happened at Sullivan's Island was just beginning to reach the northern states.

Directed at Charleston, South Carolina, on June 28, a combined British land and sea assault was intended to seal off the South's principal seaport, and provide the British with an excellent base for future operations. But "luck" had run so heavily against the British that it was almost laughable. Fort Sullivan, guarding the entrance to Charleston's harbor, hardly deserved the designation "fort." It was a dirt-and-palmetto-stake affair with a great morass of mud in its middle.

But these humble ingredients worked in the defenders' favor, as the British warships narrowed the range and opened fire. Cannon balls that hit it made little impression on the sixteen-foot-thick earthworks, and those shells which landed inside disappeared into the mud without exploding. The British overcharged their mortars for greater range—and blew them up. The narrow gap of water behind the fort proved even narrower than General Clinton's reconnaissance had indicated. A British ship which tried to negotiate it soon ran aground and had to be abandoned. On into the darkness, the fleet pounded the fort, and the fort pounded the fleet.

About 9:30 in the evening, the guns finally stopped firing. Weighing the balance, Admiral Peter Parker and General Clinton, who had already landed a ground force on an adjacent island, elected to disengage. Dawn revealed that although the fort was badly battered, the fleet had fared even worse. Two of the British ships, the *Bristol* and the *Experiment*, each suffered upwards of a hundred men killed or wounded, two ships were sunk, and many others were severely damaged. (The American casualties were twelve killed and twenty-four wounded.) [3] The Americans, by the manifold grace of God, had again stood their ground against seemingly overwhelming odds.

The fleet, with its army, sailed north to join the main body of

British on Staten Island. There, during the next two months, thirty-two thousand invading troops gathered under Howe, nine thousand of whom were German mercenaries. As Washington had anticipated, the British considered control of New York pivotal to their suppression of the uprising. New York controlled the Hudson River, the gateway to the north, which also effectively split the Colonies in half. Only one obstacle stood in the enemy's path: the American-held town of Brooklyn, on the western end of Long Island.

On the morning of August 22, fifteen thousand British troops were landed on the southeast shore of Brooklyn without opposition. Three days later they were reinforced by an additional five thousand Hessians. Facing them were barely eight thousand Americans under Washington, half of them untrained. In fact, only three weeks before, there had been less than five thousand. But in response to a sincere appeal from Washington, revealing how desperate the American plight was, Connecticut's Governor Jonathan Trumbull had called for nine more regiments of volunteers, in addition to the five that Connecticut had already sent.

Be roused and alarmed to stand forth in our just and glorious cause. Join . . . march on; this shall be your warrant: play the man for God, and for the cities of our God! May the Lord of Hosts, the God of the armies of Israel, be your leader.[4]

In five days, the British had nearly surrounded the Americans, just north of the Flatbush region, when the order for attack was given on August 27. The Americans left and center were overwhelmed and fell back to the final defensive perimeter around the northern tip of Brooklyn. The right, under William Alexander (known as Lord Stirling because of his Scottish ancestry), was cut off and trapped. While Stirling and the Delawares held a ridge, their colors flying, five times the Marylanders flung themselves at Cornwallis's lines, trying to break through to rescue them. The last time they almost succeeded. But fresh British reinforcements stopped them, though the British reported that Stirling, personally leading his men, "fought like a wolf." [5]

Washington and his generals had observed the entire action through field telescopes. Several of his generals had speculated that Stirling would give up his hopeless position without a fight. When it was over, according to an eyewitness, General Washington wrung his hands in anguish and cried out, "Good God, what brave fellows I must this day lose!"

All that afternoon, the Americans held their breath, waiting for the final British assault which would surely finish them. They were outnumbered by more than three to one, low on powder (as always), and would soon have the British fleet in the mouth of the East River at their back. Dark thoughts must have gone through the minds of many of them . . . it had been a noble, even glorious revolution, for there *had* been days of glory . . . . No matter what happened in the next few hours, the British could never take away from them the memory of Lexington and Concord, of Bunker Hill, Fort Sullivan . . . . Freedom—it had been a cause worth dying for . . . .

But now they had to face the grim reality of how great the odds were against them. Many must have thought they were mad to have even considered that they had the faintest chance of success. "Put your trust in God," their ministers had said. "He is with us; He will see us through." Well, where was He now?

And so they waited . . . and waited. And waited. And never knew that God was with them all the time. For Howe, against all military logic, was once again failing to follow up his all-too-obvious advantage. And this was not a dull general! His surrounding maneuver of the night before had been brilliantly conceived and flawlessly executed, taking the Americans entirely by surprise. As afternoon became evening, and the night wore on silently and peacefully, it gradually became apparent that Howe was not going to attack. Unbelievable! A miracle, a few would begin to say. Yet Howe's unaccountable delay was only the opening curtain on what would be the most amazing episode of divine intervention in the Revolutionary War.

The morning of the twenty-eighth dawned overcast and threatening—but quiet; there was still no movement from the British positions. All that day, the Americans continued to wait, tense, exhausted, for the inevitable barrage which would precede the final action. But the British guns remained silent. In the late afternoon, a cold pelting rain began to fall and kept on falling into the night, soaking the tentless, lightly clothed, and hungry Americans. But the rain came on a northeast wind, and that wind prevented Howe's fleet from entering the East River.

And now Washington had a plan. It was a desperate gamble, dependent upon so many unlikely intangibles that it hardly deserved to be called a plan. But it was better than a suicidal defense, and surrender was out of the question. If only God's grace continued to favor them . . .

Washington called a council of war and informed his senior

officers that he had decided to take the entire army off Brooklyn by small boat. They would rejoin the main body of American forces (some twelve thousand additional men) at the foot of Manhattan Island, behind Knox's major batteries. Immediately his generals pointed out that it was a full mile across the East River. All of them knew what the British fleet would do to a flotilla of small boats filled with infantry, the moment they spotted them. Better to die in the trenches—at least there, they could sell themselves dearly.

But Washington had made up his mind. Even so, in his heart he must have been praying much, for only God could prevent the enemy from discovering what they were up to.

The first thing they needed was boats and men to handle them. By "coincidence," the last reinforcements to have come over from Manhattan were John Glover's company of Marbleheaders. All of these were expert oarsmen, who had practically grown up in small boats on the shores of Massachusetts Bay! Washington now called upon them to locate the small boats they would need, and they were soon joined by the 27th Massachusetts—Salem men with the same skills. All night long, these men made the treacherous, two-mile round trip. At first they had to fight the wind and stormy chop. Then, after midnight, the wind died away, so they had to quietly glide through the still waters. Dipping their oars deftly and silently into the water, they pulled them through without a wash and raised them out clean, ready for another stroke.

While the flat calm enabled them to take much heavier loads—so that the gunwales were barely above the surface—the danger was much greater now. For there was no storm or rain to cover any accidental noise. Now they could ill afford the squabbles which had broken out earlier in the evening, as the men had waited in line to be taken off the beach. The officers were vigilant to shut off any argument in its earliest stages. And the impossible evacuation (reminiscent of the miracle of Dunkirk) continued.

With the clearing of the night, it became crucial to maintain a screen of men in the front positions so that the British would not suspect a withdrawal. Shortly after two in the morning, however, the two Pennsylvania battalions under newly promoted Brigadier General Thomas Mifflin received orders, apparently from Washington, to quit their positions and proceed to the boats forthwith. Obediently they had done just that, when their withdrawal happened to be discovered by the one man who could have known for certain that there had been a mistake: Washington himself. All night long he had been riding along the lines and the shore, and now he quickly redressed the situation and got the Pennsylvanians back to their posts. Perhaps a full half-hour had passed, during which there had been not a single defender visible anywhere on the American lines, and the night was so clear and well lit by moonlight that the enemy could be clearly seen, extending his trenches toward the American lines. The British must have been blind!

And now came the greatest peril of all: dawn. As the first hints of pink began to illumine the eastern horizon, the embarkation was far from over. At least three more hours would be needed to get the last man across, and the sky above was cloudless. It would be a dazzlingly clear day. Now all American eyes were fixed on the eastern sky, as it began to redden, and the darkness shrank westward. Though the men remained silent, one could sense their anxiety mounting as the covering of night began to recede and leave them naked.

What happened next should be told by one who saw it: "As the dawn of the next day approached," Major Ben Tallmadge would write, "those of us who remained in the trenches became very anxious for our own safety, and when the dawn appeared there were several regiments still on duty. At this time a very dense fog began to rise [out of the ground and off the river], and it seemed to settle in a peculiar manner over both encampments. I recollect this peculiar providential occurrence perfectly well, and so very dense was the atmosphere that I could scarcely discern a man at six yards distance . . . we tarried until the sun had risen, but the fog remained as dense as ever." [6]

Virtually every man who kept a diary that day recorded that fog, and most of them made a point of giving the credit where it was due. The fog remained intact until the last boat, with Washington in it, had departed. Then it lifted, and the shocked British ran to the shore and started firing after them, but they were out of range. Nearly eight thousand men had been extricated from certain death or imprisonment without the loss of a single life! The Continental Army had suffered a severe defeat, with some fifteen hundred casualties. Yet, thanks to a storm, a wind, a fog, and too many human "coincidences" to number, there still *was* a Continental Army!

Once again, Howe inexplicably waited before crossing to Manhattan, this time making the Americans a precious gift of two full weeks in which to recuperate, replenish supplies, and reposition themselves. Washington had learned the invaluable lesson of withdrawal before vastly superior forces, and it was a lesson which would earn him the grudging respect of the enemy, who would refer to him as a cunning fox. But he still had much to learn about tactics and the strategic placement of troops.

Washington had divided his forces. His main body was stretched in a line across upper Manhattan, along the Harlem Heights. But he had left Knox and his best artillery, along with four thousand men under Putnam, in the Battery, their heavily fortified position at the foot of the island. The east side of the island, opposite which there was increasing British activity, was thinly held by local militia. When the attack came, it came there. The militia broke and ran, scrambling north for the safety of the main lines.

The British landed with comparative ease at Kip's Bay, their officers proceeding to Murray Hill. There Howe was invited to take refreshment at the home of Mrs. Robert Murray, a prominent hostess of New York, who had often entertained British Governor William Tryon. Unknown to Howe, Mrs. Murray was a secret friend of the American cause. Howe was thoroughly charmed by her, and lingered over Mrs. Murray's madeira—while another priceless opportunity slipped between his fingers.

As he had been proceeding up the east side of Manhattan, Putnam and Knox had been making their own way up the west side, without either column being aware of the other! At one point, they were even on the same road, headed towards one another, when . . . but let Dr. James Thacher, surgeon with the Continental Army, tell it:

Most fortunately, the British generals, seeing no prospect of engaging our troops, halted their own and repaired to the house of Mr. Robert Murray, a Quaker and a friend of our cause. Mrs. Murray treated them with cake and wine, and they were induced to tarry two hours or more, Governor Tryon frequently joking her about her American friends. By this happy incident, General Putnam, by continuing his march, escaped an encounter with a vastly superior force, which must have proved fatal to his whole party. One half-hour, it is said, would have been sufficient for the enemy to have secured the road at the turn, and entirely cut off General Putnam's retreat. It has since become almost a common saying among our officers that Mrs. Murray saved this part of the American army.[7]

God works in mysterious ways, His wonders to perform . . . .

The pattern of Washington tarrying too long, but Howe tarrying even longer, was to repeat itself a number of times that fall. The Continental Army withdrew from Manhattan and began a long retreat down the length of New Jersey, finally forming a thin line on the far side of the Delaware. Cornwallis had bragged that he would catch Washington in New Jersey "as a hunter bags a fox," [8] but the fox proved more elusive than he had anticipated. As one British officer described the campaign: "As we go forward into the country, the rebels fly before us. And when we come back, they always follow us. 'Tis almost impossible to catch them. They will neither fight, nor totally run away, but they keep at such a distance that we are always a day's march from them. We seem to be playing at bo-peep."

The game ended Christmas night, 1776. Once again, Washington faced the imminent prospect of a vanishing army. Most of the men sent from New York to reinforce him had not re-enlisted, and their enlistments all came up at the end of the year. If Washington was going to make a bold stroke, and take the offensive, it would have to be before then. And a bold stroke was desperately needed: the whole nation's morale had never been lower. Key men in Congress, with no appreciation of Washington's brilliant husbanding of every man, bullet, and ounce of powder, were frustrated at an army that refused a "manly" fight. There had even been a conspiracy of jealous generals and Congressmen afoot, to replace Washington with General Charles Lee. Lee was a vastly overrated egocentric who had just recently (and providentially) been captured by the enemy, while going for a ride in front of the American lines.

The stroke was to be a surprise attack on Trenton. Once again, the Americans had the unseen aid of their strongest Ally. Rapidly developing the shrewd discernment for which he would be justly famous, Washington decided to attack in the predawn hours of December 26. The Hessian garrison in winter quarters there could be counted upon to be most heavily asleep, particularly if the schnapps had flowed as liberally as was customary on Christmastide. As his troops loaded into the small boats on their side of the Delaware, a violent snow and hailstorm suddenly came up, reducing visibility to near zero. This ensured that any sentries outside would be doing their best to stay inside, or at least get as much under cover as possible.

The Hessians were so totally surprised, that they could not believe what was happening. Henry Knox was there, and as he described it in a letter to his wife, "The hurry, fright and confusion of the enemy was not unlike that which will be when the last trump will sound." [9] In forty-five minutes of fighting, almost a thousand prisoners were taken. American casualties: two men frozen to death on the march; three men wounded. And the surprise to the young nation was also total. Washington had taken the offensive, in a stunning victory! "Never were men in higher spirits than our whole army is," wrote Thomas Rodney, and he spoke for much of the rest of America, as well.

Was it a fluke, as Washington's detractors, now themselves in disfavor, muttered? Or was it, as Knox wrote, that "Providence seemed to have smiled upon every part of this enterprise"?

Cornwallis, in charge of the British campaign in New Jersey, had been convinced that the front had stabilized for the winter and was about to sail for England to see his ailing wife, when news came that Trenton was lost. He was ordered south with heavy reinforcements. When he reached Trenton on January 2, he rejected the advice of his officers to attack Washington at once, observing that he could just as well "bag the fox" the next morning. His quartermaster general retorted, "My Lord, if you trust those people tonight, you will see nothing of them in the morning." [10]

Leaving his campfires burning, and muffling his artillery wheels, Washington slipped away to Princeton. While driving back a support column which was on its way to join Cornwallis, he deliberately rode in front of his troops to within thirty yards of the British line, in order to steady his force of wavering recruits. Washington was six feet, three inches tall (which, compared to the five-foot-five-inch average height of the Continental soldier, would be like his being six feet, six inches today) and yet miraculously he survived the first volley of both sides! The Americans rallied and went on to take the town and hold it, until Washington learned that Cornwallis was approaching.

This victory, following so closely on Trenton, made up the minds of those colonial Americans still wondering about whether or not to volunteer. As Nicholas Cresswell, caustic British traveler and gentleman would note, "Volunteer companies are collecting in every county on the continent, and in a few months the rascals will be stronger than ever. Even the parsons, some of them, have turned out as volunteers and pulpit drums—or thunder, which you please to call it—summoning all to arms in this cursed babble. Damn them all!"

The following summer proved to be a repeat of the game of bo-peep, with Washington never having enough men to launch a major offensive, yet all the while wearing down and frustrating the British. It was a race against time, for once again, America's patience with her General was wearing thin.

It wore a lot thinner with the loss of Fort Ticonderoga on July 8. Burgoyne was pushing down from Canada, planning to effect a union with forces which Howe was supposed to have dispatched up the Hudson from New York. But Howe had other plans. In an effort to deal a heavy blow to the rebels, he struck out for Philadelphia, their largest city, the seat of the American government, once again moving with ponderous slowness and badgered by Washington all the way. So Burgoyne was left up in New York to force his way through the wilderness. In the end, finding himself outmaneuvered and surrounded, he was finally captured by Arnold. It was all over at Saratoga on October 17: Burgoyne and seven thousand men surrendered, in the greatest single victory of the war!

But the one bright moment soon passed, and shrouds of gloom returned to encircle the American cause. A month earlier, the Continental Army had been badly mauled at Brandywine, as they had tried in vain to stop the British march towards Philadelphia. But more than twice as many fresh enemy troops as had been captured at Saratoga had since arrived in the Colonies, and America's chief city had now become an armed British camp. Liberty and independence, once seemingly within grasp, were becoming a forgotten dream. For the first time, Americans as a whole were confronted with the hard facts of their circumstances. Locked in a desperate struggle for survival, they were slowly being backed towards the precipice of surrender by a more powerful adversary. Though they were contesting every inch of ground, there was now some question as to how long America's will to endure would hold firm.

Such were the thoughts that may have weighed on Washington's mind as he sat on his big gray horse and watched his men file silently past, that cold and dismal December 19. They were on their way into Valley Forge, the site he had chosen for their winter encampment. He had decided that Trenton was too dangerous, and Wilmington, Lancaster, or Reading would have afforded the British access to too much territory unmolested. Valley Forge was barely fifteen miles from Philadelphia, yet because it lay in the fork where Valley Creek ran into the Schuylkill River, it was easily defensible. With open fields nearby for drilling and ample wood for fuel and shelter, strategically Washington could not have chosen a better location.[11]

Few of the men who shuffled past him through the snow had ever heard of Valley Forge—a name that would be chiseled in the cornerstone of this nation's history. Nor did they care; they were exhausted, hungry, freezing—and had long since given up hope of meat for supper, a warm bed, a dry pair of stockings. Many did not have a pair of stockings left. Their footgear consisted of strips of blanket wound around their feet. All too quickly the blanket would wear through, and they would be walking through the snow barefoot. In the entire dwindling army of eleven thousand men, there may have been less than a dozen properly equipped for the terrible winter that lay ahead.

As they passed by, their heads down in protection against the icy wind, no drumbeat marked the cadence of their steps, only the rattle of leafless branches overhead. There were no complaints, no greetings, nor did their General attempt to encourage them with hearty words. They knew he was there, and that was enough.

Though he did speak, the tall figure on the still horse, whose own shoulders were hunched against the cold, was grieving for his men. As the pale afternoon light faded and gave way to a moonless, starless night, perhaps he sensed that they were marching into the dark night of the young nation's soul. For now came the time of testing, the time that sooner or later seemed to come to every covenanted body of Christians on this continent. The first Pilgrims and Puritans had faced their starving times; their grandsons had suffered through the horror of a massed Indian uprising. And now it was Valley Forge—the ordeal which, in later centuries, would become known as our "crucible of freedom."

Snow fell early that winter—and stayed. Extreme low temperatures saw the Schuylkill freeze over, and preserved every inch of snow that lay on the ground, till the roads were clogged with drifts several feet deep. Shelter now became a matter of desperate urgency.

Washington himself had designed the huts they would sleep in—log cabins of the simplest construction. Sixteen feet long, fourteen feet wide and six feet high, these cabins would be easy to heat, and could shelter a dozen men on four triple-decker bunks. With shake shingles, no windows, no flooring, and holes under the eaves for ventilation, they were so simple that they could be gotten up quickly by men not possessing woodsmen's skills.

Practically every able-bodied man at Valley Forge was put to work on them, and upward of seven hundred cabins were erected in less than a month. Not until the last man was thus quartered, did Washington quit his own leaky tent for the relative comfort of Isaac

Potts's house, which was to serve as his headquarters. Doctor Thacher and the General's staff must have been immensely relieved at this move, having dreaded to think what would become of the army—and the nation—were their leader to be felled by influenza. And disease was taking a fearful toll of their numbers; they would lose one in four that winter, to flu, smallpox, typhus, and exposure.

But Washington did not spare himself. Early in the morning, he would begin making the rounds of the camp, and would spend most of the day riding from one regiment to the next, talking with the men. As Dr. Thacher commented: "The army . . . was not without consolation, for his excellency the commander-in-chief . . . manifested a fatherly concern and fellow-feeling for their sufferings and made every exertion in his power to remedy the evil and to administer the much-desired relief." [12]

Yet there was precious little that even the General of the Army could do. Congress, comfortably ensconced some ninety miles to the west in York, no longer benefited from the leadership of the best men in America. Men like Adams, Franklin, Jay, Hancock, and Livingston were all vitally employed elsewhere, and their places had been filled by lesser men, who were consumed with petty bickering and united in their jealousy of Washington. They convinced each other that his needs were exaggerated. Instead of sending the wagons of victuals and winter clothing for which he pleaded, they would merely print more paper money. With this he was supposed to pay his troops and purchase what he needed. They chose to remain oblivious to the reality of the situation, which was that after several months of both armies feeding off the land, the countryside was exhausted. What scant provender did remain was finding its way into Philadelphia, where the British paid in gold.

From the beginning, life in Valley Forge was grim. The huts were smoky and dark, and the newest men in each hut were given the bottom bunks closest to the door—the ones that got cold first, when the night fire burned low. In the morning, the men took turns taking the bucket and padding down to the frozen creek, to fetch cooking water. Meal after meal, their food consisted of "firecake"—wheat or cornmeal poured into a kettle of water, mixed, and ladled out on a big stone in the middle of an open fire, where it baked. Sometimes, there was a bit of salt pork, too, or some dried fish, when the wagons got through. As for winter clothing, it was in such scarce supply that Washington had to issue a general order threatening punishment to anyone cutting up a tent to make a coat out of it, for they had to save every tent they could for next summer.

As the winter wore on, and the list of sick and dead mounted higher, life in Valley Forge became an unbearable nightmare. Now there were men who were literally naked, because they did not have even rags to wrap around them. A committee from Congress (they finally sent one in the middle of February) was shocked to find how many "feet and legs froze till they became black, and it was often necessary to amputate them." [13] Exposure to the elements combined with the starvation diet to insure optimum conditions for the diseases which now ravaged the camp.

Washington himself, throughout his life given to understatement, wrote:

No history now extant can furnish an instance of an army's suffering such uncommon hardships as ours has done and bearing them with the same patience and fortitude. To see men without clothes to cover their nakedness, without blankets to lie on, without shoes (for the want of which their marches might be traced by the blood from their feet) . . . and submitting without a murmur, is a proof of patience and obedience which in my opinion can scarce be paralleled.[14]

Yet the nightmare grew worse. When, in mid-February, the entire camp was down to their last twenty-five barrels of flour, Washington wrote: "I am now convinced beyond a doubt that unless some great and capital change suddenly takes place . . . this army must inevitably be reduced to one or other of these three things: starve, dissolve or disperse, in order to obtain subsistence." [15]

And on February 16, a civilian named John Joseph Stoudt would write in his diary:

For some days there has been little less than a famine in the camp . . . Naked and starving as they are, we cannot enough admire the incomparable patience and fidelity of the soldiery, that they have not been excited ere this by their suffering, to a general mutiny and dispersion. Indeed, the distress of this army for want of provisions is perhaps beyond anything you can conceive . . . .[16]

This, then, was the miracle of Valley Forge. That the men endured was indeed amazing to all who knew of their circumstances. But the reason they endured—the reason they believed in God's deliverance—was simple: they could believe, because their General *did* believe.

Washington made no secret of his Christian faith. In his general order calling for divine services every Sunday, he said: "To the distinguished character of a Patriot, it should be our highest glory to add the more distinguished character of a Christian." [17] And others, such as the pastor of a nearby Lutheran church, Henry Muhlenberg, would note his faith with approval:

I heard a fine example today, namely, that His Excellency General Washington rode around among his army yesterday and admonished each and every one to fear God, to put away the wickedness that has set in and become so general, and to practice the Christian virtues. From all appearances, this gentleman does not belong to the so-called world of society, for he respects God's Word, believes in the atonement through Christ, and bears himself in humility and gentleness. Therefore, the Lord God has also singularly, yea, marvelously, preserved him from harm in the midst of countless perils, ambuscades, fatigues, etc., and has hitherto graciously held him in His hand as a chosen vessel. [18]

When it came to prayer, however, Washington preferred to pray in private, and it is doubtful that he ever prayed more fervently than he did that winter. One of the number of accounts of people accidentally discovering him in prayer involved the General's temporary landlord, Isaac Potts.

Potts was a Quaker and a pacifist, who one day noticed Washington's horse tethered by a secluded grove of trees, not far from his headquarters. Hearing a voice, he approached quietly and saw the General on his knees at prayer. Not wanting to be discovered, he stood motionless until Washington had finished and returned to his headquarters.

Potts then hurried to return to the house himself to tell his wife Sarah, "If George Washington be not a man of God, I am greatly deceived—and still more shall I be deceived, if God do not, through him, work out a great salvation for America." [19]

Something else happened that winter which says much about the quality of Washington's faith. A turncoat collaborator named Michael Wittman was captured, and at his trial, it was proven that he had given the British invaluable assistance on numerous occasions. He was found guilty of spying and sentenced to death by hanging. On the evening before the execution, an old man with white hair asked to see Washington, giving his name as Peter Miller. He was ushered in without delay, for Miller had done a great many favors for the army. Now he had a favor to ask of Washington, who nodded agreeably.

"I've come to ask you to pardon Michael Wittman."

Washington was taken aback. "Impossible! Wittman has done all in his power to betray us, even offering to join the British and help destroy us." He shook his head. "In these times we cannot be lenient with traitors; and for that reason I cannot pardon your friend."

"Friend! He's no friend of mine. He is my bitterest enemy. He has persecuted me for years. He has even beaten me and spit in my face, knowing full well that I would not strike back. Michael Wittman is no friend of mine!"

Washington was puzzled. "And you still wish me to pardon him?"

"I do. I ask it of you as a great personal favor."

"Why?"

"I ask it because Jesus did as much for me."

Washington turned away and walked into the next room. Soon he returned with a paper on which was written the pardon of Michael Wittman. "My dear friend," he said, placing the paper in the old man's hand, "I thank you for this." [20]

Such charity did not weaken him in the army's eyes; the men loved him for it, as did his officers. No one who had served with him could understand why there were generals and Congressmen who wanted to see him replaced. But then, the latter did not know how it was at Valley Forge. "The greatest difficulty," said the young Marquis de Lafayette, "was that, in order to conceal misfortunes from the enemy, it was necessary to conceal them from the nation also." [21]

Despite the necessity for secrecy, across the nation pastors were beginning to catch the spirit of the tremendous spiritual struggle that was being waged at Valley Forge. More and more sermons were likening Washington to Moses. There were the obvious parallels, of course, but there was also the similarity in his choosing to partake of the same hardships as his men: "By faith Moses, when he was come to years, refused to be called the son of Pharaoh's daughter; Choosing rather to suffer affliction with the people of God, than to enjoy the pleasures of sin for a season; Esteeming the reproach of Christ greater riches than the treasures in Egypt . . ." (Hebrews 11:24–26 KJV). Thus did Washington covenant himself with his men in the suffering of Valley Forge, while a day's ride away, the British sat warm and full-bellied, enjoying after-dinner brandy by the fireside.

In the crucible of freedom, God was forging the iron of the Continental Army into steel. And now there was a new strength and determination in the camp, as revealed in this piece by an anonymous Valley Forge soldier, which appeared in the *Pennsylvania Packet:* "Our attention is now drawn to one point: the enemy grows weaker every day, and we are growing stronger. Our work is almost done, and with the blessing of heaven, and the valor of our worthy General, we shall soon drive these plunderers out of our country!" [22]

The soldiers who came through Valley Forge were tempered into the carbon-steel core around which an army could be built.

In the tempering process, God sent almost as unlikely an agent as Squanto had been to the Pilgrims—a ruddy-cheeked, bemedaled German with a passion for drill, and a twinkle in his eye. This was Friedrich Wilhelm Augustus Baron von Steuben, a former captain in the Prussian army and staff officer of Frederick the Great. Well recommended by Ben Franklin in Paris, von Steuben volunteered his services to the American cause. Washington quickly recognized his expertise, and assigned him the task of making a professional army out of the Continentals. [23]

Von Steuben proceeded with typical Prussian thoroughness. There was no drill manual, so he set about to write one. Then one company of men was trained until they responded almost instinctively to the various commands. With these men, he demonstrated to the rest of the companies how to drill.

In musketry, this by-rote precision was especially important. "Prime firing pans . . . charge muskets . . . remove ramrods . . ."—there were many steps to firing a musket, and if, in the heat of battle, one step were overlooked, there would be a gap in the volley. (There were, for example, instances of soldiers forgetting to remove their ramrods from their barrels and actually firing them at the enemy. A flying ramrod had been known to kill a man, but the soldier's musket was useless thereafter.) By the time spring came, von Steuben had drilled the men to the point where they could produce a crisp volley every fifteen seconds.

Arising at 3:00 A.M. and on the parade ground by sunrise, the Prussian was a demanding drillmaster. He had a saving sense of humor, however, and his oaths were frequently punctuated by laughter. When driven to distraction by the repeated fouling up of one company or another, he would swear at them in German till he was out of breath, then call on his interpreter to carry on in English. His perseverance bore fruit: as March turned into April, the Continental Army began to march as one. And their newly acquired precision was more than a little responsible for their steadily improving morale.

From this time forth, Washington never needed to worry about another year-end enlistment lag; men were now signing up for three-year tours. But regardless of the contracted length of their tour, the veterans of Valley Forge were in for the duration, and would not think of leaving until the job was done. And when hardest assignments came—the frontal attacks, the bayonet charges, the flanker details—the Valley Forge men were the ones invariably chosen.

On the first of May, intelligence reached the American camp that France, having become convinced that the Colonial army could stand up to the full might of the British military establishment, was at last coming into the war on the side of America. The dark night was over; the French were allies! With that news, volunteers and supplies began pouring in from all over the country. And now, thanks to Valley Forge, there was an army—a *real* army—ready to receive them.

Historians generally credit Washington as having achieved his greatest feat in holding the army together at Valley Forge. But Washington himself credited God. In announcing the French decision to his joyous troops, he said:

It having pleased the Almighty Ruler of the universe to defend the cause of the United American States, and finally to raise up a powerful friend among the princes of the earth, to establish our liberty and independence upon a lasting foundation, it becomes us to set apart a day for gratefully acknowledging the divine goodness, and celebrating the important event, which we owe to His divine interposition.[24]

In Philadelphia, less than two weeks later, a farewell party was held for Howe, who had asked to be recalled, and had turned his command over to Clinton. It was a costume fête, and in extravagance it rivaled the Court of Louis XIV, showing more imagination than the entire British expeditionary force had at any time since coming to America!

It was followed by new orders from London, returning Clinton to New York. Because the few ships available were crammed with Tory refugees, Clinton's troops and artillery would have to go by land, back up through New Jersey. That meant a long, strung-out column with exposed flanks . . . .

It was an attack-commander's dream: to hit from the side, with a sharp, compacted force—the damage they could inflict was incalculable. And they could hit again and again, as the British column reformed. It would be the retreat from Concord all over again, but on a much broader scale! And now they would be ready!

Yet, as the British commenced their march on the morning of June 18, there was dissension in Washington's war council. His second-in-command, General Charles Lee (recently returned in a prisoner exchange) was "passionately opposed" to an attack on Clinton. To Lee, who cut Washington down behind his back at every opportunity, it was the crudest naïveté to believe that mere Americans could stand up to British regulars. The thing to do, he repeatedly counseled, was to do nothing, to stay where they were and see what developed. And many senior and junior officers—amateurs all—came under the spell of this seasoned professional.

As long as Satan has men who have made total commitments to the magnification of their own egos, he seldom has to intervene directly. Men so given to serving self are serving him faithfully, since he is ego-incarnate. Hence, there was no need for satanic intervention at this crucial moment in the tide of Revolutionary affairs; Charles Lee was doing just fine.

Washington then turned to ask the opinion of a young and fiercely loyal Brigadier who had been with him, in fact and in spirit, all through New Jersey and Valley Forge. "Fight, sir!" was Anthony Wayne's reply, and Nathanael Greene, Lafayette, and John Cadwalader all closed ranks behind their commander-in-chief. But five precious days would pass before Washington would shake off the hypnotic grip of Lee's prestige and inform the officer corps that they were taking the offensive immediately.

The opportunity for a killing blow from the flank was now gone, but they could still catch them and deliver an attack to the rear of the British column, if they moved quickly. Once again their invisible Ally seemed to be doing His part; the weather suddenly turned almost tropical, with hundred-degree heat and sudden downpours, which only increased the humidity. The British column was strung out over twelve miles, and barely dragging along, for all the wells along the way had been filled and the bridges blown, in anticipation of their return to New York.

Military etiquette dictated that Charles Lee be given field command of the attack force—which he spurned as unworthy of him. Vastly relieved, Washington gratefully turned the command over to Lafayette and Wayne, whom he knew he could count on to press the attack. And at last the Continental Army swung out of Valley Forge and onto the trail of the British. This was a different army than had come down that road six months before, leaving a trail of bloody footprints in the snow. Now there was a sharpness to the beat of the field drums, and a bite to the music of the fifes, which added a couple of inches to each stride—and an extra half-mile to the distance covered in an hour. And when the pipers lit into "Yankee Doodle," the soldiers grinned and grips tightened on the stocks of long-barreled rifles. As the sergeants called out cadence and marching orders, there was a precision and crispness to the response. The Americans were an army now. In training and toughness they were second to none, as they were about to demonstrate.

They caught up with the British at Monmouth, and Charles Lee, who had changed his mind and demanded that he be given the field command after all, permitted Wayne to engage the enemy. But as soon as the British turned to fight, Lee ordered a general retreat.

Furious, Washington spurred to the front of his own column, summarily relieved Lee of command, and rescued his forces from impending disaster. Back and forth he rode on his big gray, calmly urging the men to re-form, and giving them the example of his own quiet courage in the midst of withering fire. No man could look at him that day and not take heart. The troops stopped, turned, and fought the British to a standstill, causing them to grudgingly fall back. There was no clear-cut victor at Monmouth that day, but from that time forth, the British never again made the mistake of underestimating their opponents.

In the wake of the British withdrawal, the military command of Philadelphia was turned over to Arnold. Benedict Arnold—the very name has become synonymous with the depths of betrayal and infamy. In that context it is a name as familiar to Americans as the name of Judas Iscariot. Yet with the exception of Washington himself, Arnold was the most courageous and intrepid commander in American uniform, which only makes the well-known tale the more tragic.

There is a part of Arnold's story which is pertinent to the role which divine intervention played in the Revolutionary scheme of things. Arnold's contact was Clinton's adjutant, Major John Andre. Disguised as a civilian (and hence, by military definition, a spy), it was André's bad "luck" to encounter an American patrol as he was about to re-enter the British lines above New York. Mistaking the patrol for British, André let slip that he was a British officer. He was immediately searched, and in the heel of his shoe were discovered secret plans for the fortification of West Point, along with a pass signed by Arnold, the commander of the fort.

The officer in charge, failing to put two and two together, sent André under guard to explain to Arnold just how he happened to be in possession of the pass and the plans. At this point, Major Ben Tallmadge, Washington's Chief of Intelligence, by "coincidence" happened to be in the area and heard about the capture of the apparent spy. He *did* put two and two together, for he had been privately concerned about Arnold for some time. Although he was too late to stop the news from getting to Arnold, he did have his men hold the spy, and when he interrogated him, it all came out.

Arnold narrowly escaped, but West Point was saved. Had the patrol not met André, had he not mistaken them for British soldiers, had the one man most likely to comprehend quickly the enormity of the plot not been in precisely the right place at the right time . . . .

In announcing the discovery of Arnold's infamy to the country, Washington said: "Treason of the blackest dye was yesterday discovered . . . . The providential train of circumstances which led to it affords the most convincing proofs that the liberties of America are the object of divine protection." [25]

A poignant epilogue to this sad narrative is that Arnold's last request, as he lay dying in England, was to be dressed in his American uniform.

Monmouth marked the last time that the two main bodies of the British and American armies would be within striking distance of one another. For the next two years, the actions would mostly involve detachments and would be largely indecisive—fluid campaigns which swept the South and involved such names as Cowpens. King's Mountain and Guilford Courthouse. It was a frustrating war for both sides, since there never seemed to be enough time or men or supplies to decide the issue. The Americans were usually outnumbered and therefore in the familiar role of drawing the enemy ever further from its bases of supply. And it was here that General Greene summed up the war from the American point of view: "We fight, get beat, rise and fight again." [26]

The fact that they kept on rising was what finally took the heart out of the British effort; the Americans would not stay down. And they gave every indication that they were prepared to go on fighting and getting beat and rising and fighting again until the Lord Himself returned. That kind of perseverance wore the British down; they began to make mistakes.

The biggest mistake of all was a compounded one—an accumulation of misjudgments, human errors, and the handiwork of God, which wound up with Cornwallis and six thousand British troops bottled up in Yorktown. In the fall of 1781, hoping to be evacuated by the British fleet under Graves and transported to rejoin Clinton in New York, Cornwallis had brought to a close his southern campaign. He had fought well and his men had done all that could be expected of them. Yet now he was here, and the fox he was going to bag five summers before had him under siege.

But Graves continued to exhibit the same shortcoming which had become a British habit throughout the Revolutionary War: tardiness. Terribly slow in getting under way, Graves arrived at Chesapeake Bay one day too late. The French fleet under de Grasse had beaten him to it, and had put the cork in Cornwallis's bottle. Graves immediately formed a line of battle, and the French came out to meet him, rather than risk being trapped in the bay.

As they sailed out of the Chesapeake, beating into an offshore headwind, they were easy targets for the British. But Graves failed to press his advantage, and allowed them the precious time to form their own battle line. As they closed, there was confusion in the signals along the British line, with the result that the French were able to outmaneuver them and inflict substantial damage. Graves finally decided to break off and return to New York, to refit his ships—thus sealing Cornwallis's fate.

The end was now inevitable, and both sides knew it. Pressing their advantage, the Americans brought their heaviest artillery to bear on Yorktown and the British lines. On the night of October 14, 1781, four hundred Frenchmen stormed Redoubt #9, and four hundred Americans simultaneously stormed Redoubt #10. (The charge was led by a young Lieutenant Colonel named Alexander Hamilton.) In fifteen minutes of furious hand-to-hand fighting it was all over. The Americans made these two British outposts the right anchor of their new siege line, which brought their cannon almost within point-blank range.

In the meantime, Cornwallis had planned one last, desperate gambit, to escape the ever-tightening American noose. He would use the exact same surprise evacuation tactic which had miraculously extricated the American army from Brooklyn Heights. On the night of the sixteenth, he began ferrying his troops across the York River in small boats, under cover of darkness. But instead of being favored by the elements, this small-boat evacuation was disrupted by them. Cornwallis had actually succeeded in getting a third of the army across undetected, when a sudden violent storm of wind and rain came up out of nowhere, driving the boats downriver and making further passage impossible. By the time the storm subsided, too many hours had been lost to complete the evacuation, so Cornwallis ordered the troops on the far side of the river to be brought back. As the last boats returned at daybreak, they came under the heaviest American artillery fire yet. As General Banistre Tarleton said: "Thus expired the last hope of the British Army." [27]

That morning, as the sun rose, the newly dug forward batteries opened fire with a relentless bombardment. Cornwallis raised the white flag before noon.

Doctor Thacher was there:

The whole of our works are now mounted with cannon and mortars. Not less than one hundred pieces of heavy ordnance have been in continual operation during the last twenty-four hours. The whole peninsula trembles under the incessant thunderings of our infernal machines. We have leveled some of their works in ruins and silenced their guns. They have almost ceased firing. We are so near as to have a distinct view of the dreadful havoc and destruction of their works . . . .[28]

Although the war would drag on for another two years, the generals on both sides sensed that it was over. The formal surrender was set for two o'clock on the afternoon of the eighteenth. In an open field behind Yorktown, the American and French forces formed two long lines, down the middle of which the British were to march in a column of fours. The French, with fresh uniforms and new, black-leather leggings, looked resplendent in the soft October sunlight of a warm fall day. The Americans, in buckskins, homespun shirts or faded blue-and-white Continentals, seemed more like militia than an army, except that their lines were just as straight, their posture as erect.

Silence hung over the field as a gentle breeze stirred leaves that were just beginning to turn color. Then, in the distance came the sound of the British marching drums—slurred, erratic, not at all crisp and precise, as they were famed to be. The drummers, like many of the men, had prepared themselves with rum. The officers came first, on horseback.

Cornwallis, it turned out, could not bring himself to turn over his sword to Washington in person, and so had pleaded "indisposition" and instructed his deputy to do so. Washington refused to deal with Cornwallis's deputy himself, and sent Benjamin Lincoln, his deputy of comparable rank, to accept the sword.

And then the soldiers came, marching to the popular tune of

"The World Turned Upside Down." (As indeed it was!) Down the files they came, some angry, some weeping; the Americans said not a word, but looked straight ahead. Six years seemed to pass with the slow tread of the red-coated infantry and grenadiers. Lexington, Concord, Bunker Hill, Dorchester Heights, Brooklyn Heights, Trenton, Princeton, Saratoga—Valley Forge—Monmouth, the Southern Campaign, Yorktown . . . it seemed so much longer, a lifetime at least . . . .

"Ground muskets!" each British officer commanded his men when they reached the end of the file, and they did so sullenly, flinging their Brown Besses on the ground in front of them. Some of the British were seen to crack the butts of their muskets on the ground as they threw them on a pile; some of the regimental musicians staved in the heads of their drums. When it was finally finished, a tremendous roar of joy went up from the Americans—a roar that would be heard throughout the country and around the world. There were prayers that day, too—not as loud perhaps, but which carried even further.

Washington ordered a thanksgiving service to be held the day after the surrender:

> The Commander-in-chief earnestly recommends that the troops not on duty should universally attend with that seriousness of deportment and gratitude of heart which the recognition of such reiterated and astonishing interposition of Providence demands of us.[29]

This was a theme which was very much on his mind in later days; as he would say to Brigadier Nelson, "The hand of Providence has been so conspicuous in all this, that he must be worse than an infidel that lacks faith, and more than wicked, that has not gratitude enough to acknowledge his obligations." [30]

But the best word on Yorktown was spoken by one of the most famous ministers of that day, Timothy Dwight. In a sermon "occasioned by the capture of the British Army under the command of Earl Cornwallis," he preached on Isaiah 59:18, 19:

> According to their deeds, accordingly he will repay, fury to his adversaries . . . to the islands, he will repay recompence. So shall they fear the name of the Lord, from the west, and his glory from the rising of the sun. When the enemy shall come in like a flood, the spirit of the Lord shall lift up a standard against him (KJV).

In the sermon itself, he said:

Who, but must remember with hymns of the most fervent praise, how God judged our enemies, when we had no might against the great company that came against us, neither knew we what to do? But our eyes were upon Him. Who, but must give glory to the infinite Name, when he calls to mind that our most important successes, in almost every instance, have happened when we were peculiarly weak and distressed? While we mark the Divine hand in the illustrious event we are now contemplating. can we fail to cry out, "Praise the Lord, for He is good, for His mercy endureth forever." [31]

The assembled senior officers of the Continental Army, dressed in the best uniforms which they could manage, seemed to have no interest in the sumptuous fare on the gleaming white tablecloth before them. There was a heaviness in the room, and halfhearted conversations died away into silence. They were gathered at Fraunce's Tavern, in Lower Manhattan, on December 4, ten days after General Clinton and all the British had quit the city. It had been two years since the Battle of Yorktown, and word had recently arrived of the signing of the long-awaited peace treaty with the British. They were awaiting General Washington, and the occasion was a farewell luncheon at which the General would take leave of those of his senior officers who were still in uniform. Ben Tallmadge, now a brevet Lieutenant Colonel, was there and kept record of all the details.

The General arrived, prompt as always, and from his face, he was as deeply moved as any of them. Most of them had been with him since Valley Forge, and a few, like Henry Knox, had been with him from the beginning. But now it was over. This was the last time that they would ever be together like this again.

Looking around and noticing that no one had approached the elegant buffet, with its several wines and choices of succulent meats, puddings and pies, the General took a plate and absently helped himself to a small portion. Taking a glass of wine, he encouraged the others to do likewise. One or two moved to do as he had bid them, but then the General mercifully spoke to what was so heavy on all their hearts.

"With a heart full of gratitude," he began, his voice breaking, "I now take leave of you." He made a maximum effort to control his emotions. "I most devoutly wish that your latter days be as prosperous and happy as your former ones have been glorious and honorable." He raised his glass, and one or two made a faltering attempt at a reply.

The General, his eyes glistening, spoke again. "I cannot come to each of you but shall feel obliged if each of you will come and take me by the hand." The first to come to him was Henry Knox. The two men looked at one another and said nothing. The tears streaming down their faces said it all. They shook hands, embraced, and parted. One by one, the remaining officers, among them old von Steuben, embraced their Commander-in-Chief and silently parted.

"Such a scene of sorrow and weeping," Tallmadge wrote, "I had never before witnessed, and hope I may never be called to witness again . . . . Not a word was uttered to break the solemn silence . . . or to interrupt the tenderness of the scene. The simple thought that we were then about to part from the man who had conducted us through a long and bloody war, and under whose conduct the glory and independence of our country had been achieved, and that we would see his face no more in this world, seemed to me to be utterly insupportable." [32]

The moment their farewells were completed, the General begged leave, and he departed, passing through a corps of light infantry at attention. He walked to the waterfront, where a barge waited to take him to the Jersey shore, and his officers followed behind him in saddened silence. A large crowd had gathered to wish him good-bye, and one wondered if his mind cast back to that bright June morning in Philadelphia, in 1775, when a throng had gathered to wish Godspeed to the new Commander-in-Chief. As soon as he was seated, the barge cast off, and the tall figure in its stern raised his hat in final farewell.

But the General's ordeal of honor was not over. One more parting was required: the formal resignation of his commission before Congress. The Government was now temporarily headquartered at Annapolis, Maryland (which was fortunately on his way to Mount Vernon). Thomas Mifflin, the same brigadier who had inadvertently withdrawn his covering troops from the line at Brooklyn Heights, was now President of Congress. He addressed the General with respect born of the awareness of the moment: "Sir, the United States, in Congress assembled, are prepared to receive your communications."

The General rose and bowed to the members. From his pocket he drew a paper which shook noticeably in his hand. He congratulated Congress, and then, speaking of the war, commended to them the officers who had served him so faithfully and well. At this point, as he recalled some of the individual men who had performed with unusual distinction—men like Nathanael Greene, Daniel Morgan, Henry Lee, and of course his own staff—his emotions again threatened to overwhelm him. He now held the paper in front of him with both hands, to quiet its trembling. "I consider it an indispensable duty to close this last solemn act of my official life by commending the interests of our dearest country to the protection of Almighty God, and of those who have superintendence of them to His holy keeping."

The General choked, and there were many who could scarcely see the tall speaker through their own tears. "Having now finished the work assigned me, I retire from the great theatre of action, and bidding affectionate farewell to this august body under whose orders I have so long acted, I here offer my commission and take my leave of all the employments of public life."

And so saying, from the inside breast pocket of his uniform coat, he drew forth his commission and handed it to President Mifflin. At last, nothing stood between him and Mount Vernon, far from the demands and pressures of public life.

18

"Except the Lord Build the House . . . ."

The search was almost over. We had seen how miraculously God would intervene to preserve and protect His covenanted people. And He continued to do so, even though they did not always live up to their end of the covenant. We saw how He brought them by His grace to final victory. At last all that God had purposed for His new Israel seemed to be within reach. America was now free to be that "city on a hill" which John Winthrop had envisioned.

But instead, a sad trend toward a de-emphasis of the Covenant Way had already begun. Even as the newborn republic was inscribing its money with IN GOD WE TRUST, that trust was lessening. For the first time in more than a century and a half, America's ministers were no longer her most influential leaders. We needed to find out why.

And we did find out. But we also discovered something else: that despite the spiritual decline, God made certain that those same covenant promises which He made to our forefathers when He brought them here, would always be a viable possibility in the United States of America. We saw how He ensured that, no matter what happened in intervening generations, we Americans would still be able to avail ourselves of those promises, and re-enter a covenant relationship with Him *as a nation*.

The state of the nation was one of exhilaration. For America, the United States of America, *was* a nation—totally free and independent for the first time in the nearly two centuries since the English ships had sailed up the James River to settle Jamestown, and the three centuries since Columbus had glimpsed the low coastline of San Salvador. *America, America, God shed His grace on thee . . . .*

"Great indeed is the salvation He hath shown! And great the obligations we are under to praise!" preached George Duffield in Philadelphia, reflecting the sentiment of the majority of the nation's ministers. For Duffield, the destiny of the Redeemer Nation, of the City set on a Hill, was now fulfilled. God's Kingdom on earth was now established.

With Israel of old, we take up our song: "Blessed be the Lord, who gave us not as a prey to their teeth. Blessed be the Lord, the snare is broken and we are escaped." . . . Here also shall our Jesus go forth conquering and to conquer, and the heathen be given Him for an inheritance, and these uttermost parts for a possession. The pure and undefiled religion of our blessed Redeemer—here shall it reign in triumph over all opposition! [1]

But Duffield's words were premature. While this promise was indeed bright, it had not happened yet. And David Tappan, in his pulpit at Newbury, Massachusetts, was one of the first of the minority to sound a more cautionary note. He reminded his hearers that God had delivered America *in spite of* her national traits—not *because* of them.

Let us beware that we do not impute these signal divine appearances in our favor to any peculiar excellence in our national character. Alas, the moral face of our country effectually confutes such a vainglorious statement. Crimes of the blackest hue, countless multitudes of abominations, mark the visible character of this great, this highly favored community, and still provoke the great displeasure of heaven . . . Let us remember that for His own sake, He hath done these great things, not for any righteousness in us . . . But that His own name might be exalted, that His own great designs . . . extending the kingdom of His Son, may be carried into effect. [2]

John Rodgers, in New York, preached a whole sermon on the remarkable instances of Divine Providence in the war just concluded. Among other things, he pointed out that if the British had first struck in the South, rather than at Boston, three Colonies in all likelihood would not have joined the union. He speculated on what would have happened had a lesser man assumed the generalship of the army, and on the unlikelihood of such total surprise as that which accompanied the attacks on Trenton and at Princeton. He noted the extraordinary timing of the arrivals of de Grasse, de Barras and Washington at Yorktown, which sealed Cornwallis's fate.

Lastly, God has done great things for us, by that honorable, and may I add, glorious peace, by which He has terminated the late unnatural war . . . There is not an instance in history, within my recollection, of so great a revolution being effected in so short a time, and with so little loss of life and property, as that in which we this day rejoice.[3]

With few exceptions, it seemed to the ministers of America that the Light, which had been brought by the first Christ-bearers, had at last been joined by the glory of His Kingdom Come—or soon coming. The greatest exception was unquestionably Timothy Dwight, grandson of Jonathan Edwards. This candid and persuasive clergyman was shortly to become the President of Yale College, and the leading advocate of his age for evangelical Christianity. Dwight was looking for the imminent arrival of God's Kingdom.

God brought His little flock hither and placed it in this wilderness, for the great purpose of establishing permanently the church of Christ in these vast regions of idolatry and sin, and commencing here the glorious work of salvation. This great continent is soon to be filled with the praise and piety of the Millennium. [He would preach this on a future fast day.] But here is the seed, from which this vast harvest is to spring.[4]

Dwight was convinced that a return to Puritan ideals and *priorities* was the only thing that would ensure the coming of the kingdom that God had clearly intended to create here. And one of the old themes which he repeatedly hit upon was the need for a re-establishment of the covenant relationship which their forefathers had entered into with God, and with one another. He was not averse (as were most of his colleagues) to looking at the duality of the Old Testament concept of covenant, at what would happen if they did *not* keep their end of the bargain.

"Nothing obstructs the deliverance of America," he had preached in 1777, "but the crimes of its inhabitants." Only if

America honored the vertical and horizontal aspects of the covenant would "independence and happiness [be] fixed upon the most lasting foundations, and that Kingdom of the Redeemer . . . . [be] highly exalted and durably established on the ruins of the Kingdom of Satan." [5]

So there it was, once again, back to the same basic truth: the glory that could be America's depended upon her living up to the Light which she had been given. Nothing had changed since men like William Bradford and John Winthrop and Thomas Hooker had accepted their personal calls and given definition to the corporate call on God's people. As far as God was concerned (if Dwight were hearing Him correctly), the covenant was still in effect.

Dwight was not the only one gravely concerned about the need for a spiritual binding together. Washington wrote the Governor of each of the thirteen States, upon his disbanding of the army:

I now make it my earnest prayer that God . . . would incline the hearts of the citizens . . . to entertain a brotherly affection for one another, for their fellow-citizens of the United States at large, and particularly for their brethren who have served in the field. And finally that He would most graciously be pleased to dispose us all to do justice, to love mercy, and to demean ourselves, with that charity, humility and pacific temper of mind, which were the characteristics of the Divine Author of our religion, and without an humble imitation of whose example in these things, we can never hope to be a happy nation.[6]

Just how united *were* the United States? The dire peril of the war which had threatened them all had forced a semblance of the covenant on the States. For there would have been no suing for peace, no conditional surrender; it would have been either victory or subjection of the most ruthless sort, which was how Great Britain traditionally dealt with uprisings—with the gibbet or the headsman's axe.

America had known this in her heart. So, when Boston's harbor had been shut down, all the colonies had responded spontaneously; after the battle of Lexington, Virginia and Maryland riflemen had marched for Cambridge. And when Cornwallis had cut into the heart of Virginia, there were many Massachusetts men who had come down to avenge her. For eight years the States had fought and bled and cared for one another, almost as if they had covenanted before God to do so.

Yet even with all the prayer and the sacrifice, Congress still had to beg the States for money to support the war effort. Nor was it empowered to impose a draft, with the result that the Continental Army was trying to attract recruits at the same time that soldiers were going for several months without getting paid. But what really belied any covenant heart-attitude—what really *proved* that the horizontal aspect of the covenant was not possible outside of Christ—was what happened as soon as the war was over, and the pressure was lifted. Fallen man's utter selfishness came roaring back with a vengeance—and what a contrast to the selflessness of the Pilgrims! States that had, throughout the war, avoided contributing their fair share, now simply refused to pay at all. Massachusetts wound up paying more of the war's expenses than any other state—about as much as Pennsylvania, New York, Virginia, and Maryland combined—though her population was only 13 percent of America's total.[7]

The disputes between the states accelerated and deepened with a rapidity which was disheartening, to say the least. Some states were willing to cede their western holdings to Congress; others refused to do so. Some states had worked hard to pay off their war debts; others wanted Congress to assume them. The Articles of Confederation—an emergency, stopgap solution intended to provide some form of unified, legal government—were woefully inadequate. They provided no executive or judicial branches, no national power to compel, indeed little more than a national citizenship. The only power Congress had was the power to make war and peace, draft treaties, and maintain a postal service. Yet some of the states thought that even this was too much, and refused to ratify the Articles.

The quarrels between the states finally grew deep-set and vindictive, with each state raising or lowering tariffs and coining its own money. Several states even sent their own ambassadors abroad to make trade agreements in competition with each other and with the United States Government! In a word, "the union" was a mess. And many of the most responsible, realistic men in America were seriously beginning to question whether it would ever work at all.

George Washington, who passionately wanted no more of public life, now felt compelled to do all he could to save the union. He started a letter-writing campaign to the men who were in a position to most shape opinions in America. Pleading from deep conviction and with great dignity for the salvation of the nation, and exerting all of his own considerable influence, he declared that "something must be done, or the fabric will fall, for it is certainly tottering." [8]

That "something" turned out to be the Constitutional Convention in Philadelphia, in May, 1787. Originally convened to patch up the holes in the Articles of Confederation, it was soon redirected to the framing of a whole new constitution. Washington was hoping that he would not have to go, but the State of Virginia would hear none of it. She insisted that he be among her delegates. And once he got to Philadelphia, he was the unanimous choice to chair what should have been an awesome and momentous occasion. For it was the first time in history that men had ever had the opportunity to freely write a new constitution for their own government.

It started out instead to be the stormiest convention ever held on American soil. The northern states insisted that representation be apportioned on the basis of population; the southern states (less densely populated) said no. They felt it should be on the basis of land under cultivation. And the small states feared a ganging up by the larger states, both northern and southern. There was a great deal of heat and very little light being generated; in fact, historians are in general agreement that it was only the dignity of Washington's presence and demeanor which preserved the convention at all. God's placing of the right man in the right role at the most critical moments is a thing of never-failing astonishment.

To cite a recent appraisal of Washington by Page Smith, whose superb two-volume history, *A New Age Now Begins*, does for the Revolution what Bruce Catton has done for the Civil War:

His genius was the ability to endure, to maintain his equilibrium in the midst of endless frustrations, disappointments, setbacks and defeats . . . George Washington became the symbol of the [American colonists'] determination to endure. He was bound to create and sustain a Continental Army and in the process to destroy or at least mute the deep-rooted parochialism of the states. So he not only symbolized the will of the Americans to persevere in the cause of liberty, he symbolized the unity of the states; he embodied the states united, or the United States . . . If Washington's army had disintegrated, as it seemed so often on the verge of doing, Congress might well have followed suit . . . If Congress had disbanded, the problem of creating a viable nation out of thirteen disparate and jealous provinces would have been infinitely more difficult. Above all, if Washington had not, in his splendid erectness . . . and his presence, *embodied* the union, it is doubtful that unification could have been accomplished on the practical political level . . . .

In a sense it was Washington's restraint, more than Washington's actions, that determined his greatness . . . Greatness consists, as we have said before, in being appropriate to the requirements of the hour. By this measure Washington, as Commander-in-Chief of the Continental Army and perhaps even more as the first President of the United States, was a very great man.[9]

Mr. Smith does not comment on the source of Washington's ability to endure, but Washington himself commented on it often enough, giving all the credit to God and expressing his own neediness through prayer. As for his restraint, which is another word for self-denial, never did it bear more fruit than at the Constitutional Convention of 1787. As deeply as he personally felt about the issues at hand, he denied himself, and would not enter into the on-the-floor debating. He remained scrupulously impartial in the manner in which he presided, and restricted himself to sharing his beliefs in between the floor sessions.

Nevertheless, the mood eventually reached an ugly pitch, and it became painfully apparent to all present that the convention—and the union—was about to break up. "And thy neighbor as thyself"—the horizontal aspect of the covenant, which Timothy Dwight and a few others were calling for—was a myth. What was here being required of the States was the same relinquishing of self-interests and individual rights which the Pilgrims and Puritans had so willingly surrendered, as they entered into covenant with God and one another. But the States were unwilling to give up enough of their "sovereign rights" to let come into being the nation which God intended.

And now, with debate over representation hopelessly deadlocked and growing increasingly bitter (part of the New York delegation had already gone home in disgust and others were preparing to follow), God once again had mercy on the affairs of America. This time He used perhaps the least likely (and therefore most arresting) vehicle—the eighty-one-year-old *philosophe* who had, some forty years before, good-humoredly rejected the efforts of his friend George Whitefield to convert him.

At this crucial moment, when there was not a man present who had any real hope of finding an effective solution, it was Ben Franklin who rose to speak. This elder statesman, who was also one of the most prominent physicists of his age, quietly said:

In the beginning of the contest with Britain, when we were sensible of danger, we had daily prayers in this room for Divine protection. Our prayers, Sir, were heard, and they were graciously answered. All of us who were engaged in the struggle must have observed frequent instances of a superintending Providence in our favor . . . . And have we now forgotten this powerful Friend? Or do we imagine we no longer need His assistance?

I have lived, Sir, a long time, and the longer I live, the more convincing proofs I see of this truth: "that God governs in the affairs of man." And if a sparrow cannot fall to the ground without His notice, is it probable that an empire can rise without His aid?

We have been assured, Sir, in the Sacred Writings that except the Lord build the house, they labor in vain that build it. I firmly believe this. I also believe that, without His concurring aid, we shall succeed in this political building no better than the builders of Babel; we shall be divided by our little, partial local interests; our projects will be confounded; and we ourselves shall become a reproach and a byword down to future ages. And what is worse, mankind may hereafter, from this unfortunate instance, despair of establishing government by human wisdom and leave it to chance, war, or conquest.

I therefore beg leave to move that, henceforth, prayers imploring the assistance of Heaven and its blessing on our deliberation be held in this assembly every morning before we proceed to business.[10]

That speech—and the sober reflection in the silence which followed—marked the turning-point. Their priorities rearranged by Franklin's startling admonition, the delegates, nearly all of whom were believers of one kind or another, got on with the business of crafting a new constitution. Under Washington's careful shepherding, the Constitution, complete with its Bill of Rights, came into being. And the union was assured.

"We, the people of the United States . . . ." Thus begins what has become the oldest written constitution still in effect today. One of Britain's great Prime Ministers, William Gladstone, called it "the most wonderful work ever struck off at a given time by the brain and purpose of man." [11] And the greatest legal minds of two centuries have continued to marvel at it as being almost beyond the scope and dimension of human wisdom. When one stops to consider the enormous problems the Constitution somehow anticipated and the challenges and testings it foresaw, that statement appears more understated than exaggerated. For not even the collective genius of the fledgling United States of America could claim credit for the fantastic strength, resilience, balance, and timelessness of the Constitution. And most of them knew it.

The proof of its magnitude is how well it *works*—better than its framers ever dared hope. In vivid, recent memory, we have seen just how well the intricate system of built-in checks and balances—and its awesome self-cleansing ability—does work. Through due process of law, the body politic purged itself—so smoothly and effectively that many of us took it for granted.

Why does it work so well? Aside from the divine origin of its inspiration, the Constitution was the culmination of nearly two hundred years of Puritan political thought. The earliest church covenants started with the basic, underlying assumption which was central to their faith: the sinfulness of man's fallen nature, in which "dwells no good thing." That may appear depressing or negative to anyone who wants to believe in the innate goodness of man. But the fact is, it is only depressing to someone who has not yet learned the full reality of the truth that Jesus Christ came to save sinners, and that only He can be our righteousness.

As we have seen, the Puritans were not a dour, introspective, lifeless lot, no matter how certain modernists would like to paint them. They were joyful and prodigiously productive, but serious when it came to dealing with sin. And they were absolute realists about the dark nature of man, when the Spirit of Christ was not operative within him. Therefore, they anticipated the possibility of the very worst happening in their church and civil governments, and planned contingencies accordingly, so that when the worst occasionally did occur, the blockage, rather than the system, would be eliminated.

The Constitution was conceived and framed on exactly this principle. To persuade New York to ratify it, Alexander Hamilton, John Jay, and James Madison wrote the *Federalist Papers*, which were based on the assumption that "the primary political motive of man was self-interest, and that men, whether acting individually or collectively, were selfish and only imperfectly rational." [12]

Madison focused on the chief obstacle inherent in the democratic system—"a factious spirit":

There are two methods of curing the mischiefs of faction: the one, by removing the causes; the other, by controlling its effects.

There are again two methods of removing the causes of faction: the one, by destroying the liberty which is essential to its existence; the other, by giving to every citizen the same opinions, the same passions, and the same interests.

It could never be more truly said than of the first remedy that it was worse than the disease. Liberty is to faction what air is to fire, an element without which it instantly expires. But it could not be less folly to abolish liberty, which is essential to political life, because it nourishes faction, than it would be to wish the annihilation of air, which is essential to animal life, because it imparts to fire its destructive agency.

The second expedient is as impracticable as the first would be unwise. As long as the reason of man continues fallible, and he is at liberty to exercise it, different opinions will be formed. As long as the connection subsists between his reason and his self-love, his opinions and his passions will have a reciprocal influence on each other . . . The latent causes of faction are thus sown in the nature of man.[13]

The alternative to removing the causes of faction was to control its effects, and this was what the Constitution was all about. It is interesting to note that the major contemporary alternative to democracy—communism—*does* attempt to remove the causes of faction by removing liberty, and as much as possible, freedom of thought. And through intensive indoctrination of the very young, it also attempts to impose a sameness of opinion.

It is even more interesting to note that in American Christian community life of the early seventeenth century, the cause of faction was much reduced, because so many men sincerely wanted God's will more than their own. In God's will there was a oneness, and those who sincerely sought it, usually found it. Hence, there was the dynamic tension of a general uniformity of opinion, while at the same time the liberty always existed to choose the way of self over the way of God.

And so the Constitution, this institutionalizing of the covenant's legacy, was constructed on the realistic and Scriptural assumption that the natural self-interest and self-love of man has to be checked. The checks and balances were ingenious: there would be three separate branches of government—legislative, executive, and judicial. The legislative branch would make the laws, but the executive branch had the power of veto. The executive branch appointed the members of the Supreme Court, but the appointments were subject to the approval of the legislative branch. On the other hand, these appointments were for life, where the other two branches were subject to frequent elections. And the judicial branch had a unique power: judicial review—the power to decide that a law is unconstitutional. There are many more examples, of course, but the amazing thing is how smoothly such an elaborately interwoven and interdependent system works. And (aside from God's grace and inspiration) it works for one reason: it takes into account what the Puritans termed "the utter depravity of man."

By contrast, in less than two years, another revolution was to take place, this one also by a people desiring to rule their own lives in a free and democratic society. But the difference was that the French Revolution was based on the enlightened philosophy of the Age of Reason. Popularized by Voltaire and Rousseau, who emphasized the innate *goodness* of man (and de-emphasized the need for dependence on God or the redemption of Christ's shed blood), what did this equally sincere belief produce? A democracy, to be sure—but one which almost immediately devolved into a Reign of Terror, the likes of which for sheer rapaciousness and cruelty, has seldom been seen in the history of man.

But to an agnostic, who has no Redeemer, no Saviour, no Comforter, no source of grace or forgiveness or Providential intervention, the concept of the utter depravity of man is so depressing that he *has* to believe in the basic goodness of man—or go into despair. Such a man simply blinds himself to the bankruptcy of his philosophy, and goes through life carefully avoiding a head-on confrontation with reality, all the while affirming the nobility of "the brotherhood of man."

Such a man was Thomas Jefferson, who was so blind to the forces being unleashed by the French Revolution that in describing it in a letter from France, he would glowingly write: "The mass possesses such a degree of good sense as to enable them to decide well." In this he was diametrically opposed by the realism of Alexander Hamilton, who said, "Take mankind in general, they are vicious." [14]

Because the new Rationalism, or Enlightenment, of the Age of Reason soon found its way into the most fashionable salons on this side of the Atlantic, preachers such as Dwight and Witherspoon were terribly concerned, particularly since the epidemic seemed to be gaining such a foothold on their respective campuses. But many other ministers were actually duped by its subtle blandishments, for it flattered the ego by exalting the intellect. The explosion of "light" progressed so rapidly that soon the Enlightenment held that science would eventually find the answer to every problem (an idea that has gone bankrupt only within the past two decades). Moreover, there were certain demonstrable natural laws, as immutable as the Scriptural laws of the Old and New Testaments. And so in the sermons of the day God's place began to be shared equally with the "law of nature."

How could so many ministers have been taken in? The Puritan tradition in America had put great emphasis on the importance of a well-trained and disciplined mind—as a tool to be placed at God's disposal and totally submitted to His will and glory. As we have seen, most of the first colleges in America were founded in order to give American-born future ministers educations equal to those heretofore obtainable only at Oxford and Cambridge. And the ministers were further encouraged to continue their studies after college, for the one thing the Puritans despised was a "dumb dog" for a clergyman in the pulpit.

But the intellect is one of Satan's prime harvesting grounds for reaping the fruit of pride, and without the strong check and balance of an awareness of the dangers of self-righteousness, it can soon become an instrument for the glorification of self, not God. Many ministers were being led astray into Enlightenment thinking. Indeed, things got to the point that, in some ministerial circles (much like today), it became rather naïve and even a trifle primitive to think of God in such intensely intimate and personal terms as had been the case in first-century Christianity. The "French Infidelity" caught on quickly, and many ministers became the unwitting progenitors of rational Deism. They had forgotten what the early Puritans had known so well: that ultimately, it was not the mind but the *will* that mattered—the willingness to put down one's own will for God's will.

And so, for the first time, the ministers lost touch with the people. For the better part of two centuries, they had provided the spiritual, moral, and intellectual leadership for the nation. But now that mantle had passed to statesmen, politicians, educators, publishers, and prominent laymen. The nation was spiritually adrift, and the ministers had no one to blame but themselves.

The people, however, still retained enough of a relationship with the Lord to know when their hearts were not being reached. And the people stayed away from church in droves. In 1788, when the ministers of Connecticut published a rebuke to the people for the neglect of their worship, the newspapers spoke some strong truth to the ministers in a reply on the editorial pages. "We have heard your animadversions upon our absence from Sabbath meetings," said the New Haven *Gazette*,[15] "and we humbly conceive that if you wish our attendance there, you would make it worth our while to give it. To miss a sermon of the present growth, what is it but to miss an opiate? And can the loss of a nap expose our souls to eternal perdition?"

This attitude was symptomatic of the general feeling throughout the land. There were still many sermons about the Kingdom of God being established in America, but relatively few were dealing bluntly with what that Kingdom was going to cost personally. The problem was that the ministers themselves were no longer willing to pay the price. At the moment when the Light which had so overcome the darkness in America should have been at its brightest, ready to burst into glory, it was beginning to dim. America had been complacent before, or affluent or self-reliant or greedy, but never had she been so adrift from her spiritual moorings.

However, the Constitution was her safeguard. For the surprising truth about it is that it is nothing less than the institutional guardian of the Covenant Way of life for the nation as a whole! Two centuries later, it still guarantees the possibility of our one day re-entering as a nation our covenant with God, whenever we might choose to do so. As long as the Constitution, with its attendant Bill of Rights ("Article I: Congress shall make no law respecting an establishment of religion, or prohibiting the free exercise thereof . . ."), remains the law of the land, the choice will still be there.

The Constitution is the finest contract ever drawn by man for his own self-government. But as precious as the Constitution is, it is nonetheless a secularizing of the spiritual reality of the covenant. It can thus never be the substitute for a covenant life totally given to the Lord Jesus Christ. And there is an enormous difference between the two, as Richard Niebuhr points out: "Contract always implies limited [commitment], covenant unlimited commitment. Contract is entered into for the sake of mutual advantages; covenant implies the presence of a cause to which all advantages may need to be sacrificed." [16]

And now, God took the next vital step, for America was ready to consider who should be her first President. God's candidate was already so popular that even those who jealously sought to tear him down dared not provoke the public's wrath by saying aught against him. When the electors from the thirteen States gathered, only one name commanded the respect of the States-Rightists as well as the Federalists. It mattered not to them that he sincerely did not want the honor, and only wanted to be left in peace. No other name was put forward, and an express was sent to Mount Vernon, to request George Washington's presence.

A visit to Mount Vernon at the end of April, when the dogwoods are in full bloom, is a memorable experience. It is a beautiful and well-cared-for estate, with outbuildings in good repair, pointing up the traditional conservative lines of the main house. But from the moment one sets foot on the long brick walk, one is struck by the incredible sense of peace about the place. If it is possible to tell anything of a man's personality from the feel of his home, then this was the home of a man who was at rest in his inner man.

Spacious and graceful, it is complete with a small formal garden and a greenhouse for experiments with growing oranges and peppers and other exotic plants. Blending harmoniously as it does with its natural surroundings, Mount Vernon reflects a heart in tune with its Creator. Standing on the porch with its tall colonnade, gazing out over the smooth green lawn and the swaying willows to the peaceful Potomac, one might conclude that this was God's gift to an obedient servant, and that Washington appreciated it as such.

But "to whom much is given, of him much will be required." And when the messenger from the electoral college arrived, Washington knew that he had to heed the call.

He reached New York in time to be inaugurated on April 30, 1789. Stepping out onto the outdoor balcony of Federal Hall, in full view of the assembled multitude, he requested that a Bible be brought. Having placed his right hand on the open book, he took the oath of office. And then, embarrassed at the thunderous ovation which followed, the pealing church bells, and the roaring of artillery, the new President went inside to deliver his inaugural address to Congress.

Speaking with a gravity which verged on sadness, his voice deep and tremulous, he went further than he had ever gone before in stressing the role of God in the birth of the nation:

It would be peculiarly improper to omit, in this first official act, my fervent supplication to that Almighty Being, who rules over the universe, who presides in the councils of nations, and whose providential aids can supply every human defect, that His benediction may consecrate to the liberties and happiness of the people of the United States . . . No people can be bound to acknowledge and adore the invisible hand which conducts the affairs of men more than the people of the United States. Every step by which they have advanced to the character of an independent nation seems to have been distinguished by some token of providential agency . . . We ought to be no less persuaded that the propitious smiles of Heaven can never be expected on a nation that disregards the eternal rules of order and right, which Heaven itself has ordained.[17]

The next eight years saw the sober, prayerful judgment of this man imparted upon the governing of the new nation. Thanks to God, the United States was getting off on the right step.

But there was another spirit rising in those first eight years, a spirit which was a further refinement of the new rationalism. It held that although religion had played its part, yet it was most definitely not the wellspring of morality which devout Christians claimed. Indeed, it had exerted entirely too much influence on the running of the country and the affairs of men. When this spirit cried out for the separation of Church and State (which were already separated), what it was really calling for was a drastic de-emphasis of religion's

influence in all areas of national life. Religion was no longer necessary, for it called men to believe in myths, and it had no right to a
major role in the shaping of men's lives. If some people wanted to
indulge in it, that was their own business, but other people should
not have to be exposed to it.

The man who came to personify this spirit also came from Virginia, from an estate three days' ride from Mount Vernon. It was
an estate which was also beautiful in its way—an exquisite monu-
ment to the intellect of its owner, Thomas Jefferson. As
Washington's Secretary of State and later as President, Jefferson
was very careful to conceal his Deism and never commit himself
publicly on the subject of Christianity, beyond stating that in his
opinion Christ was the greatest moralist who had ever lived. For,
as modern historian Russell Kirk points out, "were his Deism (including his rejection of Christ as supernatural Redeemer) fully
known, he and his party would be in deep difficulty with popular
opinion." [18]

But it was what Jefferson did *not* say that gave his position away.
Those ministers who were still in close touch with the Lord, and
still had an appreciation of His call upon the nation, were incensed
that Jefferson would be given such national responsibility. None
was more outspoken than Timothy Dwight, whom Jefferson's
inner circle sarcastically referred to as "the pope in New Haven."

The battle lines were drawn: throughout the country there were
religious leaders who believed with Dwight that "where there is no
religion, there is no morality" and that "with the loss of religion . . . the ultimate foundation of confidence is blown up, and
the security of life, liberty and property buried in ruins." [19]

On the other hand, the movement around Jefferson maintained
that man had progressed to the point where he could be responsible
for his own morality, without the benefit of intrusive, restrictive,
narrow-minded religion. The rationalists would affect a posture of
marvelous toleration. As Puritan Nathaniel Ward said, "Nothing is
easier than to tolerate when you do not seriously believe that differences matter." [20]

But Jefferson's true feelings were to finally come to light, upon
the posthumous publication of his personal correspondence. Here
he revealed himself to be a private champion of Unitarianism, who,
during his own term in the office of President, compiled the "Jefferson Bible." This was a retelling of the story of Jesus, pointedly
leaving out every reference to the miraculous, or the divine origin
of the Saviour. His purpose:

The establishment of the innocent and genuine character of this benevolent moralist, and the rescuing it from the imputation of imposture, which has resulted from artificial systems invented by ultra-Christian sects, e.g. the immaculate conception of Jesus, his deification, the creation of the world by him, his miraculous powers, his resurrection and visible ascension, his corporal presence in the Eucharist, the Trinity, original sin, atonement, regeneration, election, orders of Hierarchy, etc." [21]

Since such a list includes practically every tenet of the Christian faith, what Jefferson was really calling for was an end to Christianity.

Unitarianism was just coming into being, and as he confidentially wrote to Benjamin Waterhouse, "That doctrine [Unitarianism] has not yet been preached here to us [in Charlottesville], but the breeze begins to be felt which precedes the storm, and fanaticism is all in a bustle, shutting its doors to keep it out." In Boston, however, Jefferson would write to Thomas Cooper, "Unitarianism has advanced to so great strength as now to humble this haughtiest of all religious sects [Presbyterianism]." And finally, in one of his last letters, to Waterhouse he would write: "I rejoice that in this blessed country of free inquiry and belief, which has surrendered its creed and conscience to neither kings nor priests, the genuine doctrine of only one God is reviving, and I trust there is not a young man now living in the United States who will not die a Unitarian."

Why so much concern about bringing finally to the light exactly where Jefferson really stood? Because he, more than anyone else, was responsible for initiating the de-emphasis of religion which is gaining so much momentum in our time. For Jefferson's attitude towards the independence of morality—his refusal to accept that it not only stems from committed Christianity, but it cannot long exist without it—is reflected with almost mirror-like verisimilitude today.

The conflict finally embroiled even Washington. For eight years, the first President had been led to preserve the dignity of his office by refusing to get entangled in the gut-level fighting that was going on, permitting himself to comment on it only upon the occasion of his leaving office. In his Farewell Address, Washington said:

Of all the dispositions and habits which lead to political prosperity, Religion and Morality are indispensable supports . . . And let us with caution indulge the supposition that morality can be maintained without religion . . . reason and experience both forbid us to expect that national morality can prevail in exclusion of religious principle.[22]

A generation later, the great French historian Alexis de Tocqueville would spend a year traveling in the United States and make the following observations:

It is their mores, then, that make the Americans . . . capable of maintaining the rule of democracy . . . The importance of mores (above that of law and the influence of geography) is a universal truth to which study and experience continually bring us back. I find it occupies the central position in all my thought; all my ideas come back to it in the end.[23]

And then, speaking of the American people as a whole, he would write:

I do not know whether all Americans have a sincere faith in their religion—for who can search the human heart—but I am certain that they hold it to be indispensable to the maintenance of republican institutions.[24]

Washington's last day in office was not the ordeal of honor that his previous leave-takings had been. He was immensely relieved to be at last stepping down. Sixty-four years old now, the eight years in office had taken a tremendous physical and emotional toll. The people had begged him to take a third term, but he was too tired; he had taken the second only at their absolute insistence. Perhaps he sensed that His Maker would soon be calling him home, and he wanted to see one more spring and summer come to his beloved retreat on the Potomac.

He had just come from the swearing-in ceremonies at Congress Hall, where John Adams had delivered a moving inaugural address and taken the oath of office. Washington had stopped by his quarters to clear his desk, before paying the new President a visit at his rooms in the Francis Hotel. There is no account of these last moments at his desk, but from what we know of the man, and the circumstances surrounding his departure, it is not difficult to imagine them.

On his desk were drafts of the last two personal letters he had written as President—to Henry Knox, offering his condolences on the death of three of his children; and to his friend Jonathan Trumball, who as Governor of Connecticut, had once raised nine companies of riflemen in response to the General's urgent personal appeal. Also on his desk was a large pile of letters from friends and well-wishers, and some clipped-out editorials, most of them full of praise—except for a vitriolic attack by Tom Paine. He had done his best to smear the reputation of the departing President, and hence the Federalists, which Washington and Adams and Hamilton had led.

It was only politics, Washington might have told himself. But Paine's comments hurt, as they were intended to, and the General knew that there was more to them than just politics. Paine had privately asked him for the job of Postmaster General, and when Washington, after much consideration, had turned him down as not sufficiently qualified, Paine had flown into a rage, calling him "treacherous in private friendship and a hypocrite in public life." [25]

But the public did not know that—and probably never would, unless Washington chose to reveal it. If he were to expose what lay behind Paine's vicious personal attack on him, the latter's career as a pamphleteer and editorialist might well be finished. But Washington merely shook his head and looked out the window. In another month, the dogwoods would be out at Mount Vernon, he might have mused. Or perhaps he prayed and commended the nation into the hands of the God who had shepherded them so amazingly to this point. Then, slowly and stiffly, he got up from the familiar desk, gathered the papers into a letter case, took a last look around, and left.

Outside, he did not seem to notice the handful of people, waiting at a respectful distance, as he turned and headed down Chestnut Street towards the Francis Hotel. The people followed discreetly behind him, without speaking. Others joined them, as they recognized the tall, slightly bent figure, until by the time he reached his destination, there was a sizable throng assembled. On the steps of the hotel, he turned and took note of them standing there, from all trades and all walks of life. They said not a word, but as he noted how many eyes were glistening with tears, his own suddenly brimmed. He bowed silently, and quickly went inside.[26]

"Good-bye, Mr. President," someone called after him, "God bless you!"

The Search Ends

Two years after Washington assumed the Presidency, a Southern Methodist preacher named Francis Aspinwall made a pilgrimage to New England, where the groundwork of God's New Israel had first been laid.

I rode over rocks and hills, and came to Wilton . . . My horse is very small, and my carriage inconvenient in such rocky, uneven, jolting ways . . . We are now in Connecticut, and never out of sight of a house . . . I do feel as if there had been religion in this country once, and I apprehend there a little form and theory left. There may have been a praying ministry and people there, but I fear they are now dead.[1]

America, America, God shed His grace on thee . . . .
From the very beginning, God did abundantly answer this nineteenth-century prayer we have sung so often. And there is really no way to measure how much the grace which God has poured out on this nation is a direct result of the obedience and sacrifice of those first Franciscan and Dominican missionaries, the Jesuit martyrs, and the earliest generations of nameless Americans who chose the Covenant Way.

Yet even as His grace continued, our hearts grew harder, to the point where we took it so much for granted that we made a joke of it, "God looks after fools, drunks, and the United States." In the face of such callous indifference, God could not bless us indefinitely, and now the grace has begun to lift. Francis Aspinwall's summation of Connecticut in 1791 could well apply to the whole nation today.

The opening pages of this book mentioned some social indicators of the lifting of God's grace—the rapidly decaying morality, the disintegrating American family, the acceptance of rebellion and violent crime as the norm for modern life. But recent natural phenomena also seem to bear witness to it. There have been earthquakes, and droughts and floods; there have been untimely frosts, a slight but significant drop in the average mean temperature, and freak weather conditions which have lately seen hurricanes in California, and more snow in northern Florida than on Cape Cod, and the worst winter in the east in our history. Add to this the new strains of crop blight and infestation, which technology seems no longer able to check and, to borrow a phrase from the Puritans, it would seem that God's Controversy with America has begun in earnest.

Entering into covenant with us, God has called the people of this country to be "a city set on a hill." And since we have repeatedly betrayed this covenant, it should hardly come as a surprise that His dealings with America are now severe. Yet even in the midst of God's judgment can be seen His mercy, for while He does deal with His people more strictly than with others, He does not reject them. When He enters a covenant, it is forever. The promises which He made to the early comers to His New Israel remain intact and unmodified, though now a far greater amendment of our lives is required in order to fulfill our end of the bargain.

For a whole nation to return to the Covenant Way seems impossible. But it is not impossible; it has been done before. And we have the biblical example of Nineveh to prove it. The biggest and most powerful city of its age had reached such a state of corruption that God was on the verge of destroying it, as he had Sodom and Gomorrah. But through His reluctant prophet, Jonah, He gave the people of Nineveh one last chance. And Nineveh repented. The entire city, from its simplest inhabitants to its most sophisticated, left their old ways—and were spared.

We are not saying that America is at the Nineveh-point—yet. Indeed, our demise could well be a more gradual, drawn-out affair, to allow us as much time as possible to repent. If God continues to lift His grace as He has begun to, it will not be long before we will be in a hell very much of our own making. But whether the end comes with a bang or a whimper, we are nearly at our corporate Point of No Return, beyond which it will be too late for America, as a nation, to turn back.

Yet such is God's mercy, that He does not even require the whole nation to repent. It is enough if only the Christians, those who truly know Him, will do this. He told us as much in 2 Chronicles 7:14 (italics added):

If *my* people, who are called by *my* name, shall humble themselves, and pray and seek my face, and turn from their wicked ways, then I will hear from heaven and will forgive their sin and heal their land.

But herein lies a dilemma, for many Christians believe that they are already fulfilling these dictates. They *are* praying and seeking His face, living a Christian life, fellowshiping with other Christians, tithing, helping the poor and needy, witnessing to nonbelievers, and so forth. In fact, their response might well be an angry, "What *more can* we do?"

Many hoped that electing a Christian President would do the job. But as Dwight Eisenhower once said, "Never let yourself be persuaded that any one Great Man, any one leader, is necessary to the salvation of America. When America consists of one leader and 158 million followers, it will no longer be America." [2] It is the most dangerous kind of corporate self-delusion to think that a President, regardless of how much he heeds God, can reverse the bent of the national will, once it is set in a certain direction. And when it becomes apparent that he cannot, he (and the Christianity he professes) will become the next scapegoat.

All of which seems to put the responsibility directly upon each of us who has a personal relationship with our Saviour—much as we might like to blame the immorality of others for the precipitous rate of decline. But the responsibility is *ours*, and it always has been. When Solomon Stoddard once challenged Increase Mather on this very point, pointing out that the covenanted Christians in seventeenth-century New England were only a fraction of the population, Mather retorted that, nonetheless, that fraction was sufficient to "stand for the entire land" and "redeem the whole." [3]

But what *can* we Christians do, that we are not already doing? The answer is there in that familiar verse from 2 Chronicles. It is a phrase that we have seen so often that we scarcely give it any thought: "If my people shall *humble* themselves . . . ." What does that really mean? It means to have done with the things of self and ego, to battle them with the same determination and tenacity which were the hallmark of the early Pilgrims and Puritans, as they strove to go the Covenant Way.

There is a great movement of the Spirit of God abroad in our land now, full of promise and encouragement and new life in Christ. In response to it, Christian roots are shooting out laterally in all directions, yet while these feeder roots are vital to rapid growth, what is now desperately needed is a simultaneous deepening of the tap root. For without it, the first great storms of tribulation are going to wreak a terrible destruction.

Jesus said, "I am the Way, the Truth, and the Life." The Chris-

tian walk begins with the discovery that He *is* the Way. The believer next learns, through Bible study and teaching, that He is the
Truth. But our Lord does not intend us to stop there, but to move
on into the third phase of our walk, the daily experience of Him as
our Life. This third phase, which so many Christians are loath to
enter into, is the one which develops the tap root.

Why are so many Christians reluctant to move into a deeper
relationship with Christ? Because the way to deepening in Christ is
the Way of the Cross: the way of self-denial—*of unconditional
surrender of one's own will to God's will, and of true covenant
commitment to one another.* This is the Way to which He has
called all serious Christians ("If any man would come after me, let
him deny himself and take up his cross daily and follow me"—
Luke 9:23), and from all that our Christian experience shows us, it
is the *only* way to spiritual maturity.

It also is the only way that we Christians can yet fulfill our
nation's call. Individually—and corporately—we need to re-enter
the covenant relationship which our forefathers had with God and
with one another.

As we have seen, the vertical aspect of the Covenant Way requires that we each consider ourselves to be soldiers in Christ's
army, to be sent when and where He directs, for whatever purpose
He might have, and to receive our orders cheerfully and without
murmuring, setting our wills to carry them out to the best of our
abilities.

Our forefathers, from the Pilgrims and Puritans to those who
resisted the tyranny of George III, understood that the call on our
nation was a call to personal and corporate freedom in Christ. "For
freedom Christ has set us free; stand fast therefore, and do not
submit again to a yoke of slavery" (Galatians 5:1). They also understood that this freedom was not license to do as they pleased,
but freedom to do the will of God. In short, they chose to live by
what we, their modern descendants, have tended to ignore—Paul's
strong warning to the Galatians a dozen verses further on:
". . . do not use your freedom as an opportunity for the flesh, but
through love be servants of one another. For the whole law is
fulfilled in one word: 'You shall love your neighbor as yourself.' "

In other words, the true measure of our commitment to Christ is
revealed in the *horizontal* aspect of our covenant: How willing are
we Christians to be servants of one another? Enough to become
deeply involved in others' lives? *To have them involved in ours?*
How much do we really care about our neighbors—at home, at
work, or at church?

Sad to say, most of us do not care that much. Even where our fellow Christians are involved, we prize our personal independence too much to truly covenant with them. And yet, if we are ever to break out of our self-centeredness and become Christ-centered members of one body, this is what we *must* do. We must covenant with one another in a practical way—husband and wife, prayer partners, co-workers—to be open and honest with one another, and to care enough for one another to help each other grow out of self and mature in Christ.

For in Christ, we *are* called to be our brothers' keepers—to walk and live in the light with one another. As John said, "If we say we have fellowship with him, while we walk in darkness, we lie and do not live according to the truth; but if we walk in the light as he is in the light, we have fellowship with one another, and the blood of Jesus his Son cleanses us from all sin." (1 John 1:6, 7).

The Pilgrims knew the value of becoming one body. With the Mayflower Compact, they chose to relinquish their individual independence, and as a covenanted people, not only survived but established our basic American spiritual and civil institutions. The first Puritans knew it, too—that the very survival of their little towns depended upon the depth of their covenant relationship with one another. And surely this was what God was doing at Valley Forge, when He forged an army out of a disintegrating band of independent individuals.

In our hearts, we also know that God has called us Christians to a horizontal as well as vertical covenant. But the cost—of turning from our independent ways, of being willing to hear God speak to us through the lips of others, of coming into the light by exposing the hidden sins of attitude or thought, of humbling ourselves by admitting where we are wrong—is more than most of us care to pay.

Thus it was for many of the second-generation Pilgrims, too, as they broke covenant and moved away—and broke Governor Bradford's heart in the process. Later, many of the half-way covenanted Puritans were forcibly reminded by King Philip's War of how far they had strayed from their commitment. And a century later, the states' refusal to relinquish their independence nearly aborted the birth of our national republic.

"United we stand" is one of our nation's mottos, and "Out of many, one" is another. But these are true words only because a few of the first Americans were willing to pay the price.

So we modern Christians *must* humble ourselves and renew the horizontal as well as the vertical aspect of our covenant with God. If we do this, He *will* hear, and forgive our sins, and heal our land.

It can still happen. Our forefathers have broken the trail for us, and shown the way. Their call *is* our call. If just a fraction of us Americans choose to go the Covenant Way, it will suffice. Then each of our lives will be filled with the light of Him who said, "I am the light of the world." And if the candlepower of each covenanted Christian were to be joined to the whole, the result would truly be the blaze of glory which John Adams foresaw. America would yet become the citadel of light which God intended her to be from the beginning!

Source Notes

THE SEARCH

1. Columbus's *Book of Prophecies*, which is available only in Spanish, and has never been published in this country. Largely a compilation of all the teaching and prophecies in the Bible on the subject of the earth, distant lands, population movements, and undiscovered tribes, as well as similarly pertinent writings of the ancient Church fathers, much of this work has been privately translated by August J. Kling, who quoted these excerpts in an article in *The Presbyterian Layman*, October, 1971.
2. Sacvan Bercovitch, *The Puritan Origins of the American Self*, p. 28.
3. Cotton Mather, *Magnalia Christi Americana*, I, pp. 7–11.
4. Bercovitch, *Puritan Origins*, p. 51.
5. *Ibid.*, p. 52.

Chapter 1: CHRIST-BEARER

1. The original journal of Christopher Columbus has been lost, but much of it was retold by Bishop Bartolomé de Las Casas, a sixteenth-century historian who was with Columbus in Española on his third voyage. This passage is from the translation by Cecil Jane, *The Voyages of Christopher Columbus*, pp. 146, 147.
2. As recorded by Oviedo, official chronicler of the court of Ferdinand and Isabella, from subsequent interviews with the participants. However, the exact details—the dialogue, etc.—are a matter of conjecture. Since comparatively little source material on Columbus is available in English, we found we had to rely greatly on his two major modern biographers, Samuel Eliot Morison and Björn Landström, for the narrative details of his life. To these two discerning scholars we acknowledge our debt and our gratitude. This incident was referred to in Morison's *The European Discovery of America*, p. 60.
3. These figures are from the first four chapters of Björn Landström's *Columbus*. An ocean sailor himself, Landström brings his own navigational expertise to bear in his evaluation.
4. Samuel Eliot Morison, *Admiral of the Ocean Sea*, pp. 57–60.
5. Landström, pp. 37, 38.
6. Morison, *European Discovery of America*, p. 40.
7. *Ibid.*, p. 53. (The authors have given the literal Latin translation in the text.)
8. Morison, *Admiral*, p. 172.
9. This quote and those to follow are from Landström, pp. 66–75.

Chapter 2: "IF GOLD BE YOUR ALMIGHTY"

1. This quote and the following one are from Landström, *Columbus*, p. 103.
2. *Ibid.*, p. 106.

3. Christopher Columbus, *His Own Book of Privileges* (1893), facsimile edition of manuscripts in the Foreign Office in Paris. (This copy in the Beinecke Rare Book Library, Yale University, New Haven, Conn.)

4. Morison, *Admiral*, pp. 404, 405.

5. Landström, p. 133.

6. Morison, *Admiral*, pp. 523–526.

7. Landström, p. 152.

8. This quote and the following one are from Morison, *Admiral*, pp. 617–619.

9. This quote and the following one are from Jane, *The Voyages*, pp. 299, 304.

Chapter 3: BLESSED BE THE MARTYRS

1. Luther Weigle, *The Pageant of America*. (The author was for many years Dean of the Yale Divinity School, and was the chairman of the committee responsible for the Revised Standard Version of the Bible.)

2. An ethnological study now under way in Southern California indicates, from aerial surveys and extensive examination of ancient growing fields and watering systems, that the population of northern Latin America at the beginning of the sixteenth century was between 85 and 115 million. A reliable census, taken a century later by Spain's administrators in the New World, fixes the population at 10 million. If the study proves accurate, this means that the Conquistadors and their successors were responsible for the greatest demographic annihilation in history!

3. Landström, *Columbus*, p. 133.

4. This quote and the four which follow are from Weigle, pp. 24–30.

5. Charles E. Kistler, *This Nation Under God*, p. 18.

6. Weigle, p. 28.

Chapter 4: "DAMN YOUR SOULS! MAKE TOBACCO!"

1. George F. Willison, *Behold Virginia*, pp. 3, 10.

2. Alexander Brown, *The First Republic in America*, p. 31.

3. Brown, *The Genesis of the United States*, Vol. I, p. 53.

4. Willison, p. 13.

5. Edmund Morgan, *American Slavery—American Freedom*, p. 63.

6. Willison, p. 28.

7. *Book of Common Prayer*, p. 82.

8. Brown, *Genesis*, I, p. 256.

9. From John Smith's *Works*, as quoted by Perry Miller in "The Religious Impulse in the Founding of Virginia," *William and Mary Quarterly*, 3rd series, Vol. V, p. 494.

10. Willison, p. 54.

11. John Smith, *Travels and Works*, I, p. 152; and Barbour, *Jamestown Voyages*, II, p. 444, as quoted in Morgan, *American Slavery*, p. 73.

12. George Bancroft, *Bancroft's History of the United States*, 3rd edition, Vol. I, p. 133.

13. Morgan, *American Slavery*, p. 77.

14. Thomas J. Fleming, *One Small Candle: The Pilgrims' First Year in America*, p. 31.

15. Brown, *Republic*, p. 467.

16. This quote and the three which follow are from Willison, pp. 69, 79, 80.

17. Brown, *Genesis*, I, p. 369.

18. George Somers reported that he saw "an apparition of a little round light like a faint star, trembling and streaming along with a sparkling blaze, half the height upon the main mast, and shooting sometimes from shroud to shroud . . . running sometimes along the mainyard to the very end, and then returning" (Brown, *Republic*, p. 114).

19. Willison, p. 112.

20. Brown, *Genesis*, I, p. 339.

21. Willison, p. 106.

22. Morgan, p. 73.

23. Willison, p. 120.

24. Bancroft, I, p. 141.

25. John Demos, *Remarkable Providences*, p. 259.

26. Willison, p. 345.

Chapter 5: TO THE PROMISED LAND

1. William Bradford, *Of Plimoth Plantation*, Wright and Potter edition, p. 3. While there are several modern editions of this classic available, anyone seriously interested should be sure to get an unexpurgated edition, for at least one modern edition we know of has elected to leave out "irrelevant theological meditations."

2. *Ibid.*, p. 13.

3. *Ibid.*, p. 36.

4. Fleming, *One Small Candle*, p. 31.

5. Bradford, pp. 34, 35.

6. Jesper Rosenmeier, "Bradford's of Plymouth Plantation," in *Typology and Early American Literature*, edited by Sacvan Bercovitch, p. 76.

7. Bradford, pp. 41, 42.

8. Fleming, p. 36.

9. Bradford, p. 72.

10. This quote and the following ones from Robinson's letter are from *Ibid.*, pp. 76, 79–81.

11. Perry Miller and Thomas H. Johnson, *The Puritans*, Vol. I, p. 246.

12. This quote and the ones to follow, including Cushman's letter, are all from Bradford, pp. 85–89.

13. From a photograph of the original in Kate Caffrey's *The Mayflower*, p. 115.

14. This quote and the ones to follow are from Bradford, pp. 94–96.

Chapter 6: "GOD OUR MAKER DOTH PROVIDE"

1. This quote and the following story are from Bradford, *Of Plimouth Plantation*, pp. 101, 103.

2. From Bradford and Winslow's *Morte's Relation*, as quoted in Alexander Young's *Chronicles of the Pilgrim Fathers*, pp. 158, 159.

3. Fleming, *One Small Candle*, p. 133.

4. Bradford, p. 106.

5. Fleming, p. 136.

6. This quote and the following one are from Bradford, pp. 113, 114.

7. *Ibid.*, p. 492.

8. For many of the specific details of this remarkable story, we are indebted to Stanley E. Goodman's "Squanto" in *They Knew They Were Pilgrims*, edited by L. D. Geller, pp. 25–31.

9. Bradford, p. 117.

10. For the following details we are indebted to Fleming, pp. 208–213.

11. Bradford, p. 129.

12. From the original sermon, the first American sermon ever published. Robert Cushman, "The Sin and Danger of Self-Love," p. 33.

13. This quote and the following one are from Bradford, p. 162.

14. This quote and the following one are from Edward Winslow, quoted in Young's *Chronicles*, pp. 347–350.

15. Bradford, p. 171.

16. Young, p. 350.

17. "Emmanuel Altham to Sir Edward Altham," quoted in Sydney V. James, Jr.'s *Three Visitors to Early Plymouth*, pp. 23ff.

18. Fleming, p. 218.

Chapter 7: "THY KINGDOM COME"

1. Fleming, *One Small Candle*, p. 22.

2. Bercovitch, *Puritan Origins*, p. 17.

3. *Ibid.*, p. 18.

4. This quote and the two to follow are from the *Winthrop Papers*, Massachusetts Historical Society, Vol. I, pp. 196, 201.

5. William Warren Sweet, *The Story of Religion in America*, p. 48.

6. *Winthrop Papers*, II, pp. 138–143.

7. Edmund S. Morgan, *The Puritan Dilemma*, p. 47.

8. *Winthrop Papers*, II, p. 152.

9. Perry Miller, *Errand Into the Wilderness*, p. 11.

10. This quote and the following one are from Morison, "John Winthrop and the Founding of New England" in *Colonial America*, edited by Davis R. B. Ross, Alden T. Vaughan, and John B. Duff, p. 25.

Chapter 8: A CITY UPON A HILL

1. Edward Johnson, *The Wonder-Working Providences of Sion's Saviour in New England*, J. Franklin Jameson, editor (pub. 1653), Barnes and Noble edition, p. 61.

2. Morgan, *Dilemma*, p. 54.

3. *Winthrop Papers*, II, pp. 160, 161.

4. *Ibid.*, pp. 292–295.
5. Edward Johnson, pp. 46, 47.
6. Cotton Mather, *Magnalia Christi Americana,* Book II, as quoted in Bercovitch, *Puritan Origins,* p. 1.
7. Morgan, *Dilemma,* p. 58.
8. *Winthrop Papers,* II, p. 313.

Chapter 9: THE PURITAN WAY

1. Morgan, *Dilemma,* p. xi. In this quote the author was also speaking against the popular negative image of the Puritans.
2. Perry Miller and Thomas Johnson, *Puritans,* I, p. 284.
3. Edmund S. Morgan, *The Puritan Family,* p. 10.
4. This quote and the following one are from *Remarkable Providences,* edited by John Demos, pp. 222–239.
5. Winthrop, *History of New England,* II, pp. 12–13.
6. This quote and those immediately following are from Barrett Wendell, *Cotton Mather,* pp. 119, 198.
7. *Winthrop Papers,* III, pp. 223, 224.
8. This quote and the two following are from Morgan, *Family,* pp. 7, 19, 143.
9. W. De Loss Love, Jr., *The Fast and Thanksgiving Days of New England,* p. 104.
10. Edward Johnson, *The Wonder-Working Providences,* pp. 77, 78.
11. Morgan, *Dilemma,* p. 60.
12. This quote and the following one are from Love, pp. 105, 106.
13. Quoted in Sanford H. Cobb, *The Rise of Religious Liberty in America,* p. 162.
14. Alice Morse Earle, *The Sabbath in Puritan New England,* p. 68.
15. *Ibid.,* p. 315.
16. This quote and the following one are from Sweet, *The Story of Religion,* pp. 57, 58.
17. Earle, pp. 275–278.

Chapter 10: THE PRUNING OF THE LORD'S VINEYARD

1. Mather, *Magnalia,* II, p. 430.
2. Morgan, *Dilemma,* p. 116.
3. Roger Williams, *The Complete Writings of Roger Williams,* VII, p. 37, as quoted in Bercovitch, *Puritan Origins,* p. 110.
4. Bradford, *Of Plimouth Plantation,* p. 370.
5. *The Complete Writings of Roger Williams,* edited by John Russell Bartlett, Vol. VI, p. 141.
6. Clifford Shipton, "Puritanism and Modern Democracy," *The New England Historical and Genealogical Register,* July, 1947, p. 189.
7. Roger Williams, *Writings,* VI, p. 350.
8. Morgan, *Dilemma,* p. 152.
9. Winthrop, *History,* I, pp. 313–316.

10. Thomas Hooker, *The Christian's Two Chief Lessons*.

11. Perry Miller and Thomas Johnson, *The Puritans*, p. 188.

12. Perry Miller, *Errand*, p. 44.

13. Clinton Rossiter, "Thomas Hooker," *The New England Quarterly*, Vol. 25, pp. 479–481.

14. John C. Miller, *The Colonial Image*, p. 25.

Chapter 11: GOD'S CONTROVERSY WITH NEW ENGLAND

1. Mather, *Magnalia*, II, p. 306.

2. Winthrop, *History*, I, pp. 119, 120.

3. Mather, II, pp. 295, 296.

4. *Ibid.*, p. 300.

5. Winthrop, *History*, I, p. 126.

6. Mather, II, p. 356.

7. Bradford, *Of Plimouth Plantation*, as quoted in Stephen Foster, *Their Solitary Way*, p. 50.

8. Bradford, *Of Plimouth Plantation*, pp. 508, 509.

9. Mather, I, p. 63, as quoted in Foster, p. 121.

10. This quote and the following one are from Foster, pp. 124, 132.

11. Winthrop, *History*, II, p. 277.

12. Love, *The Fast and Thanksgiving Days*, p. 181.

13. Edward Johnson, *The Wonder-Working Providences*, p. 253.

14. This quote and the following one are from Rosenmeier, *Typology* by Bercovitch, p. 104.

15. Foster, p. 58.

16. Mather, *Magnalia*, I, pp. 7, 8.

17. Love, p. 191.

Chapter 12: "AS A ROARING LION"

1. Winthrop, *History*, I, pp. 387, 388.

2. For the sequence of these events we are much indebted to Douglas Edward Leach's excellent work, *Flintlock and Tomahawk*.

3. Although our scene is imagined, the place and the approximate date of Philip's opening attack can be ascertained from John Fiske's *The Beginnings of New England*, p. 214.

4. George N. Williams, *Wilderness and Paradise in Christian Thought*, p. 112.

5. *Old Sudbury*, p. 23.

6. Demos, *Remarkable Providences*, p. 287.

7. John Miller, *The Colonial Image*, pp. 260–262.

8. This quote and the following one are from Leach, pp. 195, 198.

9. Demos, p. 305.

10. John Miller, p. 289.

11. This quote and the following one are from Mather, *Magnalia*, II, pp. 392–403.

12. This quote and the following one are from John Miller, pp. 185, 186.

13. Sweet, *The Story of Religion*, p. 61. The author gives the figure of half a million witches executed in Europe from the fourteenth century to the eighteenth.

14. John Miller, p. 190.

Chapter 13: A SUNBURST OF LIGHT

1. H. Richard Niebuhr, *The Kingdom of God in America*, p. 126.

2. Jonathan Edwards, *The Works of President Edwards* (Isaiah Thomas, editor), Vol. III, pp. 14–19.

3. This quote and the following one are from John Pollock, *George Whitefield and the Great Awakening*, pp. 18, 19.

4. John Wesley, *Journal*, p. 64.

5. Thomas Hobbes, Leviathan, part I, Chapter 8.

6. This quote and the facts in the following two paragraphs are from Pollock, pp. 83, 112, 115.

7. This quote and the following one are from Russell T. Hitt, *Heroic Colonial Christians*, pp. 171, 198.

8. Pollock, p. 164.

9. These references to Whitefield's visit to Philadelphia are from Pollock, pp. 117–121.

10. *Ibid.*, p. 156.

11. From Whitefield's journal, as quoted by Peter Gomes in "George Whitefield in the Old Colony: 1740," in *They Knew They Were Pilgrims* (Geller, editor), p. 93.

12. Pollock, p. 162.

13. Whitefield's journal, quoted in *They Knew They Were Pilgrims*, p. 93.

14. Pollock, p. 250.

15. *Ibid.*, p. 246.

16. *Ibid.*, p. 248.

17. This quote and the following quotes are all from Pollock, pp. 268–270.

Chapter 14: "NO KING BUT KING JESUS!"

1. Perry Miller, *Orthodoxy in Massachusetts*, p. 220.

2. Fiske, *Beginnings*, p. 247.

3. Wendell, *Cotton Mather*, p. 46.

4. This quote and the following one are from David Lovejoy, *The Glorious Revolution in America*, pp. 154, 155.

5. *Ibid.*, p. 176.

6. This is the famous quote of John Bradshaw, president of the high court which had tried Charles I in 1649 (*Encyclopaedia Britannica*, Vol. 4, p. 60) as quoted in Foster, *Their Solitary Way*, p. 165.

7. *The Pulpit of the American Revolution*, edited by John Wingate Thornton, p. 74.

8. Printed in the Maryland *Gazette*, September 29, 1774, and quoted in Hezekiah Niles's *Principles and Acts of the Revolution in America*, p. 164.

9. Thornton, pp. 73, 74.

10. This quote and the following one are from Clinton Rossiter, *Seedtime of the Republic*, pp. 241–245.

11. Mather, *Magnalia*, I, p. 26, as quoted in A. W. Plumstead's introduction to his selection of Massachusetts Election Sermons, *The Wall and the Garden*, p. 28.

12. Bancroft, *History*, VI, p. 102.

13. This quote and the two following quotes are all from Bancroft, VI, pp. 140–142.

14. *Ibid.*, p. 195.

15. Edmund Morgan, "The Puritan Ethic and the American Revolution," *William and Mary Quarterly*, Vol. 24, p. 17.

16. This quote and the following one are from Bancroft, VI, pp. 440–442.

17. Kistler, *This Nation*, p. 56.

18. Niles, *Principles and Acts of the Revolution in America*, p. 198.

19. Cushing Stout, *The New Heavens and the New Earth*, p. 59.

20. Bancroft, VII, pp. 73, 74. One eighteenth-century pound sterling equaled sixteen ounces of silver, currently worth around $4.40 per ounce.

21. *Ibid.*, p. 99.

22. *Ibid.*, p. 229.

23. *Ibid.*, p. 274.

Chapter 15: "IF THEY WANT TO HAVE A WAR . . ."

1. For the events of April 19, 1775, we are indebted to the Boston *Globe*'s special section "The Lexington-Concord Alarm," March 9, 1975, pp. 39–71.

2. Boston *Globe*'s special section, "The Battle of Bunker Hill," June 8, 1975, pp. 15, 16.

3. Page Smith, *A New Age Now Begins*, p. 508.

4. Samuel Langdon, sermon reprinted in Plumstead, *The Wall*, pp. 364–373.

5. For the story of the battle for Bunker Hill, we are indebted to the Boston *Globe*, "Bunker Hill," pp. 20–39.

6. Winston S. Churchill, *A History of the English-Speaking Peoples*, Vol. III, Bantam Edition, p. 152.

7. Boston *Globe*, "Bunker Hill," p. 30.

8. *Ibid.*, p. 35.

9. *Ibid.*, p. 38

10. This quote and the following one are from *The Spirit of '76*, edited by Henry Steele Commager and Richard B. Morris, pp. 122–124.

11. George F. Scheer and Hugh F. Rankin, *Rebels and Redcoats*, p. 62.

12. *Ibid.*, pp. 62, 63.

13. Boston *Globe*, "Bunker Hill," p. 39.

14. This quote and the following one are from the Boston *Globe*, special section "Washington's First Victory," March 7, 1976, p. 5.

15. The following quotes are all from William Johnson, *George Washington, the Christian*, pp. 23–28.

16. *Ibid.*, p. 36.

17. *Ibid.*, pp. 41, 42.

18. Kistler, *This Nation*, p. 54.

19. This quote and the following two quotes are all from Bancroft, *History*, IV, p. 190.

Chapter 16: "GIVE 'EM WATTS, BOYS!"

1. Page Smith, *A New Age*, p. 572.

2. This quote and the following two quotes are all from William Johnson, *George Washington*, pp. 69, 70.

3. From the original printed sermon, Boston, 1775.

4. Philip Davidson, *Propaganda and the American Revolution*, pp. 205, 206.

5. Bancroft, *History*, VII, p. 307.

6. W. P. Breed, *Presbyterians and the Revolution*, p. 85.

7. From the fourth installment of George Cornell's series, "The Founding Faith," Associated Press, April 16, 1976.

8. Breed, pp. 80–82.

9. Bruce Lancaster and J. H. Plumb, *The American Heritage Book of the Revolution*, Dell edition, pp. 119, 120.

10. Boston *Globe*, "Washington's First Victory," March 7, 1976, p. 34.

11. *Ibid.*, p. 35.

12. Lancaster and Plumb, p. 123.

13. *The Encyclopedia of Religious Quotations*, edited by Frank S. Mead, p. 265.

14. From the original sermon, Princeton, May 17, 1776.

15. Thornton, *The Pulpit*, p. 311.

16. Boston *Globe*, "Washington's First Victory," p. 65.

17. James Thomas Flexner, "Providence Rides a Storm," American Heritage series, Vol. XIX, No. 1, p. 17.

18. *Ibid.*, p. 98.

19. *See* footnote 17.

20. H. Niles, *Principles and Acts*, p. 480.

21. J. Franklin Jameson, *The American Revolution Considered as a Social Movement*, pp. 91, 92.

22. *Adams Family Correspondence*, edited by L. H. Butterfield, Vol. II, p. 16.

23. This quote and the following one are from Commager and Morris, pp. 230–233.

24. *Ibid.*, pp. 265, 266.

25. *Ibid.*, p. 241.

26. *Ibid.*, p. 265.

27. *Ibid.*, pp. 260, 261.

28. *Annals of America*, Vol. II, *Encyclopaedia Britannica*, 1968, p. 276.

29. Actually, the first Americans to declare their independence were the citizens of Mecklenburg County, North Carolina, in May, 1775.

30. Russell Kirk, *The Roots of American Order*, pp. 342, 343, 404.

31. Dan Smoot, *America's Promise*, p. 6.

32. Edward Frank Humphrey, *Nationalism and Religion*, p. 85.

33. There is a moving footnote to this anecdote, for which we are indebted, as well as for the details of Rodney's ride, to Robert E. Lewis, for an article in Piedmont Airline's *Pace Magazine*, July/August 1976, p. 25. Caesar Rodney had cancer. It was disfiguring his face, and the only doctor in the world known to have any treatment for it was in England. Rodney had been planning a trip to England, to attempt to rid himself of this affliction. But by casting his vote for independence, he knew that the possibility of his being cured would be lost forever.

34. Kistler, p. 71.

Chapter 17: THE CRUCIBLE OF FREEDOM

1. Kistler, *This Nation*, p. 73.

2. This quote and the following one are from *Adams Family Correspondence*, II, pp. 28, 30, 31.

3. *Voices of 1776*, edited by Richard Wheeler, pp. 144–150.

4. Bancroft, *History*, IX, p. 79.

5. Scheer and Rankin, *Rebels and Redcoats*, p. 167.

6. *Ibid.*, p. 171.

7. Commager and Morris, *The Spirit*, p. 464.

8. This quote and the following one are from *Ibid.*, pp. 495, 496.

9. This quote and the following two are from *Ibid.*, p. 513.

10. This quote and the following one are from *Ibid.*, pp. 518, 519.

11. For these facts, and much of the description which follows, we are indebted to Henry Armitt Brown, *The Valley Forge Oration*, 1878, as reprinted in Verna M. Hall's *The Christian History of the American Revolution*, pp. 56–59.

12. Wheeler, *Voices*, p. 288.

13. Hall, *Revolution*, pp. 61, 62.

14. Douglas Southall Freeman, *George Washington*, Vol. IV, p. 621.

15. Hall, *Revolution*, p. 61.

16. John Joseph Stoudt, *Ordeal at Valley Forge*, p. 135.

17. William Johnson, *George Washington*, p. 112.

18. Henry Melchior Muhlenberg, *Notebook of a Colonial Clergyman*, p. 195.

19. Mason Weems in William Johnson, *George Washington*, p. 103.

20. *Ibid.*, pp. 108–110.

21. Wheeler, p. 287.

22. Stoudt, p. 146.

23. For these details and the ones to follow, we are indebted to Page Smith, *A New Age*, pp. 1008–1013.

24. Kistler, *This Nation*, pp. 74, 75.

25. Wheeler, p. 382.

26. Lancaster and Plumb, *The American Heritage*, p. 320.

27. Page Smith, p. 1704.

28. Wheeler, p. 454.

29. William Johnson, p. 134.

30. Paul F. Boller, Jr., *George Washington and Religion*, p. 106.

31. From the original sermon.

32. This quote and the following ones are all from Scheer and Rankin, *Rebels and Redcoats*, pp. 504, 506, 507.

Chapter 18: "EXCEPT THE LORD BUILD THE HOUSE . . . ."

1. *The Patriot Preachers of the American Revolution*, edited by Frank Moore, pp. 358–360.

2. *Ibid.*, pp. 305, 306.

3. *Ibid.*, pp. 334, 335.

4. From the original sermon, Boston, 1813.

5. Quoted in Stephen E. Berk, *Calvinism Versus Democracy*, p. 24.

6. From *The Washington Papers*, edited by Saul K. Padover, as quoted in *Decision* magazine, February, 1976.

7. Daniel Wait Howe, *The Puritan Republic of the Massachusetts Bay in New England*, p. 397.

8. Allan Nevins on Washington, in the *Encyclopaedia Britannica*, Vol. 23, 1970 edition, p. 243.

9. Page Smith, *A New Age*, pp. 1792–1797.

10. *In God We Trust*, edited by Norman Cousins, p. 42. Ben Franklin would write to Ezra Stiles three years later that, "as to Jesus of Nazareth . . . I have, with most of the present dissenters of England, some doubts as to his divinity, though it is a question that I do not dogmatize upon, having never studied it, and think it needless to busy myself with it now, when I expect soon an opportunity of knowing the truth with less trouble." But it was also Ben Franklin who wrote, while he was America's ambassador in Paris, "He who shall introduce into public affairs the principles of primitive Christianity will change the face of the world." (Kistler, *This Nation*, p. 83).

11. *Annals of America*, Britannica, III, p. 122.

12. Cecelia Marie Kenyon in the *Encyclopaedia Britannica*, Vol. 9, 1970 edition, p. 138.

13. *The Federalist Papers*, as quoted in *Annals of America*, III, pp. 216, 217.

14. *Time* magazine, Bicentennial Issue #2, "The New Nation," "September 26, 1789," p. 14.

15. July 31, 1788, as quoted in Esmond Wright, *Causes and Consequences of the American Revolution*, p. 183.

16. Richard Niebuhr, "The Idea of Covenant and American Democracy," in *Church History*, Vol. XXIII, p. 134.

17. Kistler, *This Nation*, p. 97, and William Johnson, *George Washington*, pp. 161, 162.

18. Kirk, *The Roots of American Order*, p. 343.

19. Charles Roy Keller, *The Second Great Awakening*, p. 36.

20. Quoted in Cushing Stout, *The New Heavens and New Earth*, p. 79.

21. This quote and the following three quotes are all from Cousins, pp. 149, 161–163.

22. William Johnson, p. 218.

23. Alexis de Tocqueville, as quoted in Kirk, p. 448.

24. Alexis de Tocqueville, *Democracy in America*, Vol. I, p. 391.

25. *Guideposts*, "A Letter From the President of the United States," May, 1975, pp. 16–18.

26. J. A. Carroll and M. W. Ashworth, *George Washington*, Vol. VII of the Douglas Southall Freeman biography, p. 438.

THE SEARCH ENDS

1. Chard Powers Smith, *Yankees and God*, pp. 289, 290.

2. *National Courier*, Sept. 3, 1976, p. 20.

3. Bercovitch, *Puritan Origins*, pp. 95, 96.

Bibliography

Adams, Amos, "A Concise Historical View of the Difficulties, Hardships and Perils which Attended the Planting and Progressive Improvements of New England," First Church of Roxbury, 1770

Adams Family Correspondence, Vol. II, L. H. Butterfield, Ed., Cambridge: Harvard University Press, 1963

Adams, Samuel, *The Rights of the Colonists*, Boston: Old South Leaflets, Vol. VII

Ahlstrom, Sydney E., *A Religious History of the American People*, New Haven: Yale University Press, 1972

American Heritage History of the Thirteen Colonies, New York: American Heritage Publishing Co., 1967

Andrews, Charles M., *The Rise and Fall of the New Haven Colony*, New Haven: Yale University Press, 1936

Angle, Paul M., *The American Reader*, New York: Rand McNally & Co., 1958

Balch, Thomas, "Calvinism and American Independence," Presbyterian Quarterly, July 1876

Baldwin, Alice M., *The New England Clergy and the American Revolution*, New York: Frederick Ungar Publishing Co., 1958

Bancroft, George, *Bancroft's History of the United States*, Vols. I–X, Third Edition, Boston: Charles C. Little & James Brown, 1838

Bartlett, Robert Merrill, *The Pilgrim Way*, Philadelphia: United Church Press, 1971

Bercovitch, Sacvan, *The Puritan Origins of the American Self*, New Haven: Yale University Press, 1975

Bercovitch, Sacvan (Ed.), *Typology and Early American Literature*, Cambridge: University of Massachusetts Press, 1972

Berger, Josef & Dorothy (Eds.), *Diary of America*, New York: Simon & Schuster, 1957

Berk, Stephen E., *Calvinism Versus Democracy*, Hamden, Ct.: Shoestring Press, Inc., 1974

Blodgett, John Taggard, "Political Theory of the Mayflower Compact," Publication of the Colonial Society of Massachusetts, Vol. 12, January, 1909

Boller, Paul F., Jr., *George Washington and Religion*, Dallas: Southern Methodist University Press, 1963

Boni, Albert & Charles, *Journal of First Voyage to America*, by Christopher Columbus, New York: 1924

Book of Common Prayer, Episcopal Church, New York: The Church Pension Fund, 1945

Boorstin, Daniel J., *The Americans: The Colonial Experience*, New York: Vintage Books, 1958

Bradford, Wm., *Of Plimoth Plantation*, Boston: Wright & Potter, 1901

Branscomb, Harvie, "The Contribution of Moral and Spiritual Ideas to the Making of the American Way of Life," Madison, Wis.: University of Wisconsin, 1952

Brauer, Jerald C., Church History, Vol. 27, "The Rule of the Saints in American Politics," Indiana: The American Society of Church History, 1958

Breed, Rev. W. P., *Presbyterians and the Revolution*, Philadelphia: Presbyterian Board of Publication, 1876

Breen, T. H., *The Character of the Good Ruler*, New Haven: Yale University Press, 1970

Brewer, David J., *The United States as a Christian Nation*, Philadelphia: John C. Winston Co., 1905

Bridenbaugh, Carl, *Vexed and Troubled Englishmen, 1590–1642*, New York: Oxford University Press, 1968

Brown, Alexander, *The First Republic in America*, Boston & New York: Houghton, Mifflin & Co., 1898

Brown, Alexander, *The Genesis of the United States*, Boston & New York: Houghton, Mifflin & Co., Vol. I, 1890; Vol. II, 1891

Bumgardner, Georgia B. (Ed.), *American Broadsides*, Barre, Mass.: Imprint Society, 1971

Caffrey, Kate, *The Mayflower*, New York: Stein & Day, 1974

Calder, Isabel MacBeath, *The New Haven Colony*, New Haven: Yale University Press, 1934

Carroll, Peter N. *Puritanism and the Wilderness*, New York: Columbia University Press, 1969

Cheever, George B., D.D., *The Journal of the Pilgrims at Plymouth in New England in 1620*, New York: John Wiley, 1848

Churchill, Winston S., *A History of the English-Speaking Peoples*, Vol. III, New York: Bantam Books

Clebsch, William A., *From Sacred to Profane America*, New York: Harper & Row, 1968

Cobb, Sanford H., *The Rise of Religious Liberty in America*, New York: MacMillan Co., 1902

Cohen, J. M. (Ed. & trans.), *The Four Voyages of Christopher Columbus*, Baltimore, Md.: Penguin Books, 1969

Columbus, Christopher, *His Own Book of Privileges*, 1893

Commager, Henry Steele & Morris, Richard B. (Ed.), *The Spirit of Seventy-Six*, New York: The Bobbs-Merrill Co., Inc., 1958

Cooke, Samuel, "A Sermon Preached at Cambridge, May 30, 1770," Boston: 1770

Cornelison, Isaac S., *The Relation of Religion to Civil Government in the United States of America*, New York: De Capo Press, 1970

Cornell, George W., "The Founding Faith," *The Daily Item*, Sunbury, Pa.: April 16, 1976

Cotton, John, "God's Promise to His Plantations," Old South Leaflets, Vol. III, Boston: Directors of the Old South Work, Old South Meeting House

Cousins, Norman, *In God We Trust*, New York: Harper & Bros., 1958

Crouse, Nellie M., "Causes of the Great Migration 1630–1640," *The New England Quarterly*, Vol. 5, Portland, Me.: Southworth Press, 1932

Cushman, Robert, *The First Sermon Ever Preached in New England, 1621*, New York: J. E. D. Comstock, 1858

Davidson, Philip, *Propaganda and the American Revolution*, Chapel Hill: University of North Carolina Press, 1941

Demos, John (Ed.), *Remarkable Providences*, New York: George Braziller Inc., 1972

Dillon, Francis, *The Pilgrims*, Garden City, N.Y.: Doubleday & Co., 1975

Dulles, John Foster, "The Power of Moral Forces," Washington, D.C.: General Foreign Policy Series 84, U.S. Dept. of State, 1954

Dwight, Timothy, *The Conquest of Canaan*, New York: AMS Press, Inc., 1971
Dwight, Timothy, "A Discourse in two parts, on the Public Fast," Boston; July 23, 1812
Dwight, Timothy, "A Discourse on Some Events of the Last Century," New Haven, January 7, 1801
Dwight, Timothy, *Greenfield Hill*, New York, 1794
Dwight, Timothy, "Sermon preached at Northampton on November 28th, 1781," Lamont Library Basement Microtexts, Harvard University
Dwight, Timothy, "Virtuous Rulers a National Blessing," Hartford: a sermon preached at the General Election, May 12, 1791
Earle, Alice Morse, *The Sabbath in Puritan New England*, New York: Scribners, 1891
Eddy, Sherwood, *The Kingdom of God and the American Dream*, New York: Harper & Bros., 1941
Edwards, Jonathan, *Thoughts on the Revival of Religion in New England*, New York: American Tract Society, 1740
Eliot, John, *The Christian Commonwealth or the Civil Policy: or The Rising Kingdom of Jesus Christ* (reprint of 1659 edition), New York: Arno Press, 1972
Encyclopaedia Britannica, Vols. 9, 23, Chicago, 1970
Encyclopaedia Britannica, *The Annals of America*, Vols II and III, 1784–1796, Chicago; 1968
Fiske, John, *The Beginnings of New England or the Puritan Theocracy in Its Relations to Civil & Religious Liberty*, Cambridge: Houghton, Mifflin & Co., 1900
Fleming, Thomas J., *One Small Candle: The Pilgrims' First Year in America*, New York: W. W. Norton & Co., Inc., 1963
Flexner, James Thomas, "Providence Rides a Storm," *American Heritage*, Dec., 1967, Vol. XIX, No. 1, New York: American Heritage Publishing Co.
Ford, Paul Leicester (Ed.), *Writings of Christopher Columbus*, New York: 1892
Foster, Stephen, *Their Solitary Way*, New Haven: Yale University Press, 1971
Freeman, Douglas S., *George Washington, A Biography*, Vols. I–VII, New York: Charles Scribner's Sons, 1948
Geller, L. D. (Ed.), *They Knew They Were Pilgrims: Essays in Plymouth History*, New York: Poseidon Books, Inc., 1971
Gordon, William, "Sermon to the Third Church of Roxbury," July 19, 1775
Gray, Stanley, "The Political Thought of John Winthrop," *New England Quarterly*, Vol. III, Portland, Me.: Southworth Press, 1930
Guideposts Magazine, "A Letter From the President of the United States," May, 1975, Carmel, N.Y.
Gutman, Judith Mara, *The Colonial Venture*, New York: Basic Books, Inc., 1966
Hall, David D., *The Faithful Shepherd: A History of the New England Ministry in the Seventeenth Century*, Chapel Hill: University of North Carolina Press, 1972
Hall, Verna M., *The Christian History of the American Revolution*, San Francisco: Foundation for American Christian Education, 1976
Hall, Verna M., *The Christian History of the Constitution of the United States of America*, San Francisco: Foundation for American Christian Education, 1975
Halliday, E. M., "Nature's God and the Founding Fathers," *American Heritage*, Vol. XIV, No. 6, New York: American Heritage Publishing Co., Oct. 1963
Hansen, Marcus Lee, *The Atlantic Migration 1607–1860*, Cambridge: Harvard University Press, 1940

Harris, John (Ed.), "Battle of Bunker Hill," *The Boston Globe*, June 8, 1975

Harris, John (Ed.), "Washington's First Victory," *The Boston Globe*, March 7, 1976

Harris, John (Ed.), "Lexington-Concord Alarm," *The Boston Globe*, March 9, 1975

Hart, Albert Bushnell (Ed.), *American History Told by Contemporaries*, New York: Macmillan & Co.
   Vol. I, Era of Colonization 1492–1689, 1900
   Vol. II, Building of the Republic 1689–1783, 1899

Heimert, Alan, "Puritanism, the Wilderness and the Frontier," *New England Quarterly*, Vol. 26, No. 3, September, 1953

Heimert, Alan, *Religion and the American Mind*, Cambridge: Harvard University Press, 1966

Hill, Douglas, *The English to New England*, New York: Clarkson N. Potter, Inc., 1925

Hitt, Russell T. (Ed.), *Heroic Colonial Christians*, Philadelphia: J. B. Lippincott Co., 1966

Hooker, Thomas, *The Christian's Two Lessons, Self-Denial and Self-Trial*, London: Printed by T.B. for P. Stephens and C. Meredith, at the Golden Lion in St. Paul's Churchyard, 1640.

Hosmer, James Kendall (Ed.), *Winthrop's Journal "History of New England,"* Vol. II, 1630–1649, New York: Barnes & Noble, 1908

Howe, Daniel Wait, *The Puritan Republic of the Massachusetts Bay in New England*, Indianapolis: Bowen-Merrill Co., 1899

Humphrey, Edward Frank, *Nationalism and Religion*, Boston: Chipman Law Publishing Co., 1924

James, Sydney V., Jr. (Ed.), *Three Visitors to Early Plymouth*, Plymouth, Mass.: Plimoth Plantation, Inc., 1963

Jameson, J. Franklin, *The American Revolution Considered as a Social Movement*, Princeton: Princeton University Press, 1926

Jameson, J. Franklin (Ed.), *Johnson's Wonder-Working Providence 1628–1651*, New York: Barnes and Noble, Inc., 1910

Jane, Cecil (Trans. & Ed.), *The Voyages of Christopher Columbus*, London: Argonaut Press, 1930

Johnson, William J., *George Washington, the Christian*, Nashville, Tenn.: Abingdon Press, 1919

Jones, Alonzo T., *Civil Government and Religion or Christianity and the American Constitution*, Chicago & New York & Calif.: American Sentinel, 1889

Jones, Rufus M., M.A., D.Litt., *The Quakers in the American Colonies*, New York: Russell & Russell, Inc., 1962

Keller, Charles Roy, *The Second Great Awakening in Connecticut*, New Haven: Yale University Press, 1942

Kirk, Russell, *The Roots of American Order*, LaSalle, Ill.: Open Court, 1974

Kistler, Rev. Charles E., *This Nation Under God*, Boston: Richard G. Badger, The Gorham Press, 1924

Kling, August J., "Columbus—a Layman 'Christ-bearer' to Uncharted Isles," *Presbyterian Layman*, October, 1971

Lancaster, Bruce & Plumb, J. H., *The American Heritage Book of the Revolution*, New York: Dell Publishing Co., Inc., 1958

Landström, Björn, *Columbus*, New York: The Macmillan Co., 1966

Leach, Douglas Edward, *Flintlock and Tomahawk*, New York: The Macmillan Co., 1958

Lewis, Robert E., "Listen My Children and You Shall Hear . . . ." *Pace Magazine*, July/August, 1976

Love, W. DeLoss, Jr., *The Fast and Thanksgiving Days of New England*, Boston & New York: Houghton, Mifflin & Co., 1895

Lovejoy, David S., *The Glorious Revolution in America*, New York: Harper & Row, 1972

Marty, Martin E., *Righteous Empire: The Protestant Experience in America*, New York: Dial Press, 1970

Mather, Cotton, *A Faithful Account of the Discipline Professed and Practised in the Churches of New England*, Boston: S. Gerrish, 1726

Mather, Cotton, Lecture in Boston, 1690—"The Present State of New England," New York: Haskell House Publishers, Ltd., 1972

Mather, Cotton, *Magnalia Christi Americana; or the Ecclesiastical History of New England*, Vols. I & II, Hartford: Silas Andrus, 1820

Mather, Increase, "An Earnest Exhortation to the Inhabitants of New England," Boston; 1676

Mather, Increase, *Remarkable Providences*, London: John Russell Smith, 1856

McLaughlin, Andrew C., *Foundations of American Constitutionalism*, New York: New York University Press, 1932

Mead, Frank S. (Ed.), *The Encyclopedia of Religious Quotations*, Westwood, N.J.: Fleming H. Revell Company, 1965

Mead, Sidney E., *The Lively Experiment, the Shaping of Christianity in America*, New York: Harper & Row, 1963

Miller, John C. (Ed.), *The Colonial Image*, New York: George Braziller, 1962

Miller, Perry, *Errand Into the Wilderness*, Cambridge: Belknap Press of Harvard University Press, 1956

Miller, Perry, "The Garden of Eden and the Deacon's Meadow," New York: *American Heritage*, Vol. 7, Dec. 1955

Miller, Perry, "The Marrow of Puritan Divinity," *Colonial Society of Massachusetts Publications*, Vol. 32, Feb. 1935

Miller, Perry, *Nature's Nation*, Cambridge: Harvard University Press, 1967

Miller, Perry, *The New England Mind*, New York: The Macmillan Co., 1939

Miller, Perry, *Orthodoxy in Massachusetts* 1630–1650, Boston: Beacon Press, 1959

Miller, Perry & Johnson, Thomas H. (Eds.), *The Puritans*, Vol. I, New York: Harper & Row, 1963

Miller, Perry, "The Religious Impulse in the Founding of Virginia: Religion and Society in the Early Literature," *The William and Mary Quarterly*, 3rd series. Vol. 5, Williamsburg: Institute of Early American History & Culture, 1948

Moehlman, Conrad Henry, *The American Constitutions and Religion*, Barre, Ind., 1938

Monsma, John Clover, *What Calvinism Has Done for America*, Chicago: Rand, McNally & Co., 1919

Moore, Frank (Ed.), *The Patriot Preachers of the American Revolution*, New York, 1860

Morgan, Edmund S., *American Slavery—American Freedom*, New York: W. W. Norton & Co., 1975

Morgan, Edmund S., "The Puritan Ethic and the American Revolution," *William & Mary Quarterly*, 3rd series, Vol. 24, No. 1

Morgan, Edmund S., *The Puritan Family*, New York: Harper & Row, 1944

Morgan, Edmund S., *The Puritan Dilemma*, Boston: Little, Brown & Co., 1958

Morgan, Edmund S., *Visible Saints: The History of a Puritan Idea*, New York: New York University Press, 1962

Morison, Samuel Eliot, *Admiral of the Ocean Sea*, Boston: Little, Brown & Co., 1942

Morison, Samuel Eliot, *The European Discovery of America*, New York: Oxford University Press, 1974

Morris, B. F., *Christian Life and Character of the Civil Institutions of the United States*, Philadelphia: George W. Childs, 1864

Muhlenberg, Henry Melchior, *The Notebook of a Colonial Clergyman*, trans. and ed. by Theodore G. Tappert and John W. Doberstern, Fortress Press, Philadelphia, 1975

Newman, Paul S., *In God We Trust*, Norwalk, Ct.: C. R. Gibson Co., 1973

Niebuhr, H. Richard, "The Idea of Covenant and American Democracy," read before the American Studies section of the American Historical Association, at Chicago, December 28, 1953

Niebuhr, H. Richard, *The Kingdom of God in America*, New York: Harper & Bros., 1959

Niles, H., *Principles and Acts of the Revolution in America*, Baltimore, 1822

Old Sudbury, Boston: Pinkham Press, 1929

Park, Edward A., *The Works of Samuel Hopkins*, Vol. I, Boston: Doctrinal Tract and Book Society, 1854

Pellman, Hubert Ray, *Thomas Hooker: A Study in Puritan Ideals*, Philadelphia: University of Pennsylvania Press, 1958

Perry, Ralph Barton, *Puritanism and Democracy*, New York: Vanguard Press, 1944

Plumstead, A. W. (Ed.), *The Wall and the Garden, Selected Massachusetts Election Sermons, 1670–1775*, Minneapolis: University of Minnesota Press, 1968

Pollock, John, *George Whitefield and the Great Awakening*, Garden City, N.Y.: Doubleday and Co., 1972

Pope, Liston, "Religion as a Social Force in America," Smith College lecture

Priestley, Herbert Ingram, *A History of American Life, Vol. I: The Coming of the White Man 1492–1848*, New York: Macmillan Co., 1929

Richey, Russell E., *American Civil Religion*, New York: Harper & Row, 1974

Robinson, Stewart M., *And . . . We Mutually Pledge*, New Canaan, Ct.: The Long House, Inc., 1964

Ross, David R. B., Vaughan, Alden T., and Duff, John B. (Eds.), *Colonial America: 1607–1763*, New York: Thomas Y. Crowell Co., 1970

Rossiter, Clinton, *Seedtime of the Republic*, New York: Harcourt, Brace & World, Inc., 1953

Rossiter, Clinton, "Thomas Hooker," *New England Quarterly*, Vol. 25

Russell, Francis, "Apostle to the Indians," *A Treasury of American Heritage*, New York: Simon & Schuster, 1954–60

Savage, James (Ed.), *A Review of Winthrop's Journal*, Boston: Dutton & Wentworth, 1854

Scheer, George F. & Rankin, Hugh F., *Rebels and Redcoats*, New York: The World Publishing Co., 1957

Shaw, Mark R., "The Spirit of 1740," *Christianity Today*, January 2, 1976

Shipton, Clifford K., "Puritanism & Modern Democracy," *New England Historical and Genealogical Register*, July, 1947

Simpson, Alan, *Puritanism in Old and New England*, Chicago: University of Chicago Press, 1955

Smith, Chard Powers, *Yankees and God*, New York: Hermitage House, 1954

Smith, James Ward & Jamison, A. Leland (Ed.), *Religion in American Life*, Princeton: Princeton University Press, 1961:

Vol. I, *The Shaping of American Religion*

Vol. II, *Religious Perspectives in American Culture*

Vol. IV, *A Critical Bibliography of Religion in America*, Nelson R. Bun (Ed.)

Smith, Page, *A New Age Now Begins*, 2 vols., New York: McGraw-Hill, 1976

Smith, William, *A Sermon on the Present Situation of American Affairs*, Philadelphia: James Humphreys, Jr., 1775

Smoot, Dan, *America's Promise*, Dallas, Tex.: The Dan Smoot Report, 1960

Stiles, Ezra, "Sermon Preached at the Anniversary Election, May 8, 1783," New Haven: Thomas & Samuel Green, 1783

Stoddard, Solomon, "The Way for a People to Live Long in the Land that God hath Given Them" (sermon), Boston: Bartholomew Green, 1703

Stoudt, John Joseph, *Ordeal at Valley Forge*, Philadelphia: University of Pennsylvania Press, 1963

Stout, Cushing, *The New Heavens and New Earth*, New York: Harper and Row, 1974

Sweet, William Warren, *The Story of Religion in America*, New York: Harper & Bros., 1950

Thomas, Elbert D., *This Nation Under God*, New York: Harper & Bros., 1950

Thomas, Isaiah, *Works of President Edwards*, Vol. III, Worcester: 1808

Thornton, John Wingate, *The Pulpit of the American Revolution*, Boston: D. Lothrop & Co., 1876

Time magazine, Special 1776 Issue, "Independence," July 4, 1776, Chicago: Vol 10J, No. 20

Time magazine, Bicentennial Issue #2, "The New Nation," September 26, 1789, Chicago: Vol. 107, No. 21

Tocqueville, Alexis de, *Democracy in America*, 2nd Edition, trans. by Henry Reeve, Francis Bowen (Ed.), 2 vols., Cambridge, 1863

Tuveson, Earnest Lee, *Redeemer Nation*, Chicago & London: University of Chicago Press, 1974

Vaughan, Alden T., *American Genesis: Captain John Smith and the Founding of Virginia*, Boston: Little, Brown & Co., 1975

Vaughan, Alden T. (Ed.), *The Puritan Tradition in America 1620–1730*, Columbia, S.C.: University of South Carolina Press, 1972

Washington, George, "The Invisible Hand," *Decision* magazine, February, 1976

Weigle, Luther A., *The Pageant of America*, New Haven: Yale University Press, 1928

Wendell, Barrett, *Cotton Mather,* New York: Dodd, Mead & Co., 1891

Wesley, John, *Journal* (Percy Livingstone Parker, Ed.), Moody Press, Chicago, 1974

Wheeler, Richard, *Voices of 1776,* Greenwich: Fawcett Premier Book, 1972

Whitefield, George, *The Two First Parts of His Life, With His Journals,* London: W. Strahan, 1756

Whittelsey, Chauncey, to the General Assembly of the State of Connecticut, May 14, 1778

Williams, George H., "Christian Attitudes toward Nature," *Christian Scholar's Review,* Vol. II, No. 1, Fall 1971, Gordon-Conwell Theological Seminary

Williams, George H., *Wilderness and Paradise in Christian Thought,* New York: Harper & Bros., 1962

Williams, Roger, *Complete Writings of Roger Williams,* New York: Russell & Russell, Inc.
  Vol. 1, Ed. by Guild, Reuben Aldridge, 1963
  Vol. 2, Ed. By Diman, Rev. J. Lewis and Guild, Reuben
    Aldridge, 1963
  Vol. 3, Ed. by Caldwell, Samuel L., 1963
  Vol. 6, Ed. by Bartlett, John Russell, 1963
  Vol. 7, Ed. by Miller, Perry, 1963

Willison, George F., *Behold Virginia,* New York: Harcourt, Brace & Co., 1952

Willison, George F., *Saints and Strangers,* New York: Reynal & Hitchcock, 1945

Winslow, Ola Elizabeth, *Meetinghouse Hill 1630–1783,* New York: The Macmillan Co., 1952

Winthrop, John (James Savage, Ed.), *The History of New England from 1630 to 1649,* Boston: Little, Brown & Co., 1853

The Winthrop Papers, Boston: Massachusetts Historical Society:
  Vol. I, 1598–1628; 1929
  Vol. II, 1623–1630; 1931
  Vol. III, 1631–1637; 1943
  Vol. IV, 1638–1644; 1944
  Vol. V, 1645–1649; 1947

Witherspoon, John, *Sermon Preached at Princeton on May 17, 1776,* Philadelphia: R. Aitken

Woolman, John, *The Journal of John Woolman,* Cambridge: Riverside Press (Houghton Mifflin Co.), 1871

Wright, Esmond, *Causes and Consequences of the American Revolution,* New York: Quadrangle Books, 1966

Wright, Louis B., *The Atlantic Frontier: Colonial American Civilization (1607–1763),* New York: Alfred A. Knopf, Inc., 1947

Wright, Louis B., *The Colonial Civilization of North America 1607–1763,* London: Eyre & Spottiswoode, 1949

Wright, Louis B., *Religion and Empire,* Chapel Hill: University of North Carolina Press, 1943

Young, Alexander, *Chronicles of the Pilgrim Fathers,* Boston: Charles C. Little and James Brown, 1841

Zintl, Terry, "Love Didn't Make the World Go Round 200 Years Ago," *Miami Herald,* Feb. 7, 1976

General Index